XENIX®

A T W O R K

XENIX®

AT WORK

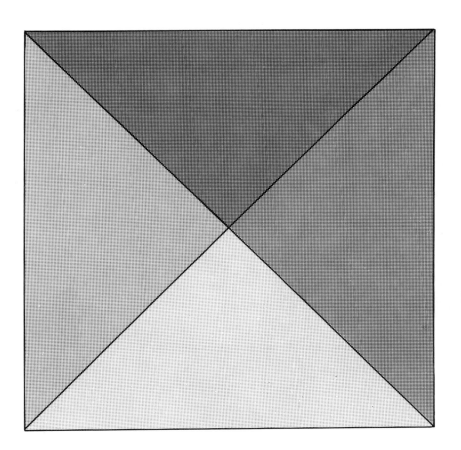

MICROSOFT®
PRESS

EDITED BY JOANNE WOODCOCK AND MICHAEL HALVORSON

PUBLISHED BY
Microsoft Press
A Division of Microsoft Corporation
16011 N.E. 38th Way, Box 97017
Redmond, Washington 98073-9717

Library of Congress Cataloging in Publication Data
Xenix at work.
Includes index.
1. XENIX (Computer operating system)
I. Woodcock, JoAnne. II. Halvorson, Michael.
QA76.76.063X47   1986   005.4'46   86-8500
ISBN 0-914845-55-1

Printed and bound in the United States of America.

   3 4 5 6 7 8 9   FGFG   8 9 0 9 8

Distributed to the book trade in the United States by Harper & Row.

Distributed to the book trade in Canada by General Publishing Company, Ltd.

Distributed to the book trade outside the United States and Canada by Penguin Books Ltd.

Penguin Books Ltd., Harmondsworth, Middlesex, England
Penguin Books Australia Ltd., Ringwood, Victoria, Australia
Penguin Books N.Z. Ltd., 182-190 Wairau Road, Auckland 10, New Zealand

British Cataloging in Publication Data available

C O N T E N T S

ACKNOWLEDGMENTS

No book is ever created in a vacuum, any more than it exists in one. The minds and talents of many people are reflected in this book, from the creators of the original UNIX, to the XENIX group at Microsoft, to the word processors, proof-readers, artists, and typographers who produced the printed pages. Our special thanks go to IBM Corporation and Santa Cruz Operations, for their support and encouragement. Thanks, too, to Bill O'Brien and to the following members of Microsoft Press: Claudette Moore, Salley Oberlin, Debbie Kem, Dale Callison, Marianne Moon, Darcie Furlan, Bonnie Dunham, Karen Todaro, Becky Johnson, Nick Gregoric, Lia Matteson, and David Laraway. Without them, this book could not have come to be.

JoAnne Woodcock
Michael Halvorson
May 1986

I N T R O D U C T I O N

INTRODUCTION   Welcome to XENIX. If you are not very familiar with computers, you may be wondering just what XENIX happens to be. It is an operating system, and it has a rather futuristic-sounding name, but what is it, and what does it do? The answers to those questions are to be found in the following 16 chapters, but for now....

As you'll learn in Chapter 1, any operating system is nothing more—or less—than a set of programs that work closely with your computer, enabling it to perform all manner of tasks—from displaying characters on the screen, to storing and tracking your data, to managing its own internal "house-keeping" chores.

XENIX does all these things, efficiently and, from your point of view, for the most part invisibly. But it does much more besides, because it is designed to perform work for many users, not just one, and it is designed to perform many tasks at the same time.

Very few of us work totally on our own, autonomous and independent of others. At one time or another, we must communicate with our colleagues: share information with them, ask their advice, work with them on projects, collaborate on budgets, reports, and proposals. The ability to function within this type of environment is XENIX' great strength. This is the home for which XENIX was designed, and the result is an operating system that enables you and others to share files, send messages, print one letter while working on another, add and contribute to a single document or information base...all without leaving the keyboard and screen on your desktop.

Of course, neither this book nor XENIX assumes that everyone works as part of a group *all the time*. We all need privacy, too, just as we all create documents that are not meant for general access. Even in XENIX' multiple-user environment you can always protect those documents you wish to keep private. In addition, XENIX functions equally well as a dedicated, single-user system (or as a programmer's environment, though that is not covered in this book).

Altogether, XENIX is not only multiuser and multitasking, it is multifaceted, too. And all it asks of you is a microcomputer to run on, a hard disk to be stored on, a terminal or two if more than one person are to use it at the same time, a printer...and a little concentration on your part, as you learn to find your way around the many features it has to offer.

THE TWO SIDES OF XENIX

In this book, you will learn what XENIX can do for you, and some of the many ways in which you can use it to make your work easier and more productive.

Depending on the role XENIX will play in your day-to-day work with it, you will approach it in one of two ways. You will either use it as a tool to "get things done," or you will take responsibility for ensuring that your XENIX system runs smoothly not only for yourself, but for the other users on your system. In the former case, you will primarily be interested in learning how XENIX can help you accomplish your work. In the latter, you will also be interested in knowing when and how to install XENIX on a computer, how to make XENIX aware of new users, how to manage files and disks, and so on.

Because these two approaches to XENIX are based on different goals and different priorities, we've divided this book into two sections. The first, Chapters 1 through 12, concentrates on what you can do with XENIX. These chapters are dedicated to everyone who uses XENIX, but they concentrate on the needs of those of you who are not computer professionals and simply want to make the best use you can of a most flexible tool for data management.

The second section, Chapters 13 through 16, deals primarily with the needs of the system administrator—the person responsible for maintaining the XENIX system and keeping it running. But these chapters are not for the system administrator alone, they are for anyone interested in learning some of the "behind-the-scenes" details of your system.

WHAT YOU WILL FIND

As you read this book, you will find many examples that illustrate the details and concepts outlined in each chapter. By all means practice these examples if you wish. But we did not intend this book to be simply a workbook or an extended practice session. Assuming that you will not always have a computer or terminal handy, we have provided graphics to show you what you should or would see on your own screen as the examples progress.

In addition, we have presented topics in the order in which we feel you will be most comfortable learning about XENIX. But no one way is the only right way. Read or re-read these chapters as you will. You may, for example, wish to jump right into the XENIX *mail* system, which is covered in Chapter 8. There's no reason not to try. If you stumble over a concept you don't understand, just back up a bit to the chapter in which it is covered. Here is a brief summary of the book's contents:

■ Chapter 1: an introduction to XENIX.

■ Chapter 2: logging in (making XENIX aware of your presence) and a quick look at some interesting features.

■ Chapter 3: creating, using, and removing XENIX directories.

■ Chapter 4: managing data files and using XENIX' line editor, *ed.*

■ Chapters 5, 6, and 7: using XENIX' visual text editor and text-formatting system.

■ Chapter 8: using the XENIX *mail* system.

■ Chapter 9: using advanced file-handling commands and techniques.

■ Chapters 10, 11, and 12: using the XENIX shells (the command interpreters that translate your commands into a form that XENIX can understand).

■ Chapter 13: installing XENIX (the first of the chapters on system administration).

■ Chapter 14: managing the system—adding user accounts and terminals.

■ Chapter 15: managing disks and disk drives.

■ Chapter 16: networking XENIX systems with Micnet.

Finally, for your later use and reference, Appendix A briefly lists and describes the XENIX commands discussed in this book, and Appendix B lists the most commonly used XENIX directories and files.

TYPOGRAPHICAL CONVENTIONS

Since many XENIX features in this book are presented in an "if you do this, then you see that" format, we've adopted certain conventions to help you recognize XENIX commands.

When we are describing a command that you can type as it is shown, you'll see it on a separate line in boldfaced type, like this:

mail johnd

If you are to press a certain letter key, it is shown either in text, like this: "press *a* to append text." Or it is shown on a separate line, like this:

Press the Enter key

Finally, if you are being shown the format in which to use a command, it is shown like this:

copy [file1] [file2]

The items in square brackets indicate entries that you provide, according to your own needs and situation.

A WORD ABOUT SPECIFICS

XENIX is available in a number of different versions. Some come from different manufacturers or are for different brands of microcomputer. For example, XENIX is available from such companies as Santa Cruz Operations, Altos, COMPAQ, Tandy, and IBM. In addition, different "forms" of XENIX are also available. There is, for example, one IBM release of XENIX known as Version 1, which is based on a form of XENIX called System III. There is another, newer, IBM release of XENIX known as Version 2.0, based on the form of XENIX called System V.

This book is based on IBM's release Version 2.0 of XENIX, as it would be installed on an IBM PC AT computer or compatible with a 20-megabyte or larger hard disk. The graphics were generated on an Apple Macintosh computer running as a XENIX terminal, and then printed on an Apple LaserWriter printer. Not all XENIX systems are exactly the same, however, so bear in mind that your system's responses and displays may differ somewhat from those shown in this book. Aside from possible differences in installation, the differences will not be substantial.

AND NOW...

We invite you to join us in exploring the intriguing world of XENIX. In the remaining pages of this book you will encounter an operating system with enormous potential for helping you with the work you do. The journey will be worth your while.

1

For the System User

1

THE FLEXIBILITY OF XENIX   XENIX is an electronic file cabinet, a text processor, a calculator, a calendar, a messenger, a programming environment, and much more besides. How much more, you will discover as you learn to use XENIX for such tasks as building and organizing a file system, creating and printing documents, sharing information, sending and receiving electronic mail, and safeguarding valuable data. Important as these capabilities are, however, each is but one feature among many others. In order to appreciate just how much you can do with XENIX, it's also important to see XENIX as a whole: to know what it is and why you're using it. Knowing what you are dealing with will enable you to use XENIX appropriately and well, just as having a vocabulary enables you to write a letter to suit a particular situation.

With that in mind, let's begin with the question: What is XENIX?

XENIX IS AN OPERATING SYSTEM

From the lap-sized portables you can tuck under your arm to the giant main-frames that can put a rocket on the moon, all computers need an operating system. The operating system coordinates the multitude of activities going on within the machine itself—activities that take place at electronic speeds and, at times, almost simultaneously. At all times, something must ensure that characters are correctly displayed on-screen, that data are saved and retrieved without error, that instruc-tions are processed in an orderly way...that you are informed if a problem occurs. That something is the operating system.

Think of an operating system as a housekeeper, traffic cop, administrator—any type of coordinator—and you have defined its basic function: to keep all parts of the system functioning smoothly and in harmony.

On a more elemental level, an operating system is a set of computer programs (software) designed to work with a particular type of computer or computer sys-tem (hardware). On your computer, the operating system is XENIX.

THE XENIX ENVIRONMENT

All operating systems manage data for you, as well as coordinate the various pieces of equipment that make up a computer system. Why, then, use XENIX instead of another—especially if you are already familiar with another microcom-puter operating system, such as MS-DOS or Apple DOS, or a minicomputer operat-ing system like VAX/VMS?

To answer this question, we'll approach it from two sides: the computer(s) on which you run XENIX, and XENIX itself.

THE COMPUTER SYSTEM

Part of the answer to "Why XENIX?" lies with the type of computer you have. As mentioned earlier, the operating system is the software that runs a computer's hardware. While it's easy to move software from one computer to another, the wires, chips, and boards that comprise the hardware are usually not movable at all.

Each hardware setup, or configuration, can only recognize and function with software specifically designed for it. Thus, an Apple IIe computer cannot use an operating system intended for an IBM Personal Computer, nor can the IBM use the operating system intended for the Apple. The hardware and software are incompatible—they can't work together. XENIX System V is designed to run on computers, such as the IBM PC-AT or the Tandy 3000, that use the Intel 80286 processor (some XENIX machines also use the Motorola 68000 processor).

While the details may vary, a typical XENIX computer system is put together in one of the following three forms:

■ Somewhere in your office building or buildings there is one main computer, which we'll call the host computer. It is the computer on which XENIX itself is installed, and quite likely there is at least one powerful printer attached to it. You are one of several to many other XENIX users who gain access to the host computer through a dumb terminal—a computer-like device with a keyboard and a monitor, but no built-in computing ability—or through a microcomputer, such as an IBM PC or an Apple Macintosh, and some communication software.

5

■ Alternatively, you might be using XENIX by yourself, on a microcomputer of your own. In this case, your machine is the host computer and you are, effectively, the only XENIX user in your system.

■ Finally, you may have XENIX installed on your own computer, just as in the preceding instance, but be linked by a network with other XENIX users, all of whom may also have XENIX installed on their computers. Here, each person in your network can communicate with the others. Essentially, you belong to one of several host computers that are joined by the network.

(There are variations on these three setups. You might, for example, be using a call-in device—a modem—to dial in to the XENIX computer from your home or from another office. We won't be concerned with such variations, unless they affect your use of XENIX. In that case, you'll be given special instructions.)

XENIX ITSELF

The computer installation is only one reason you need XENIX. Another, with far more impact on the work you do, is how the operating system itself does its job. Unlike many others, XENIX is a multiuser, multitasking operating system. That means it is designed to handle the needs of more than one person and, when need be, to work on more than one task at a time. And these are two enormous benefits wherever a number of people need to share resources and data.

For example, in a multiuser environment, several people can share a printer. Several people can use the same set of data. Several people can respond to a single message. And each can do so without jumping up to carry a floppy disk or a bundle of papers from one place to another. In addition, people can interact from across the country as easily as they can from across the hall. For managing, distributing, updating—even creating—customer reports, memos, messages, inventories, phone lists, or any other type of shared information, XENIX is ideal.

Then, too, there is XENIX' multitasking capability. Here, whether you are one user among many or the only user on a XENIX system, you have the ability to tell XENIX to handle a task either in the foreground (while you wait, so to speak) or in the background (while you do something else). Suppose, for example, you have a lengthy list of prospective customers and you want XENIX to sort them for you—alphabetically, perhaps, or by ZIP code. You'd like to distribute copies of the sorted list at a meeting later in the day, but you also have a variety of memos to compose and send through XENIX to others in the office. You can do it all by sending the sorting and printing job into the background while you get right to work on your memos. And XENIX does this with all the requests from all the devices that require its attention—at the same time. More importantly, you get all this and more at microcomputer prices.

6

THE EVOLUTION OF XENIX

In many ways, XENIX' capabilities resemble those you would expect to find on a much larger computer system. The resemblance is not accidental. XENIX is an operating system with an intriguing history—one in which the mainframe world, in the form of an operating system called UNIX, and the microcomputer world, through the efforts of Microsoft Corporation, were joined. The result is XENIX, and the advantage is all yours.

As for the story, it all started a long time ago....

UNIX

Toward the close of the 1960s, a programmer named Ken Thompson was working at Bell Laboratories, a research institution known in the computer world as a source of innovation and new technology. In keeping with this futuristic environment, Thompson had a program named Space Travel that worked out the motions of the planets in our solar system. To run this program, Thompson used a timesharing system, renting time on a large mainframe computer belonging to General Electric. Like renting a car, timesharing works quite well until the amount of time you use begins to increase. Ken Thompson had that problem: Space Travel required a lot of computer time.

His solution was the PDP-7, a minicomputer manufactured by Digital Equipment Corporation (DEC). One step down from a mainframe, a minicomputer is quite a bit less expensive, but loses relatively little computing power. The PDP-7 became Thompson's in-house system for running Space Travel and, not incidentally, the machine on which he developed his own operating system—UNIX.

During the following year or two, UNIX caught the attention of other programmers at Bell Labs, and became a functional entity there in 1971.

THE TRANSLATION TO B

Ken Thompson's original UNIX was written in a programming code known as assembly language. Not too long after developing UNIX, however, Thompson also developed a new language for writing programs. He called this language B and soon rewrote UNIX in the new language, along the way incorporating some new program routines written in B.

FROM B TO C

Now, we meet Dennis Ritchie, another Bell programmer. Ritchie refined Thompson's B, added a few routines of his own, and called it C. On the surface, the development of C may seem unrelated to our story, but it wasn't: Today, UNIX is almost entirely written in C, and with good reason.

To understand the connection, you need to know a little about how programs (and these include operating systems) work. To begin with, programs like Thompson's original UNIX are not generated in a single-step process. The programmer originally codes the program in a form that he or she can read. This form of the program is called source code, and it's written in a programming language, such as assembly language. It is not, at this stage, usable by the computer. Only later, in an entirely separate step, is the source code transformed into executable, or machine-readable, form. This transformation is performed by a program known as a compiler.

The limitation of assembly-language programs, though, is that each type of computer can use a different assembly-language dialect. And to move an assembly-language program from one computer to another that used a different dialect, you would first need to modify the assembly-language source code.

C programs are generated in the same two-step process, but there is one important difference: C is universal. The instructions you write to perform the function you want accomplished are the same, no matter what computer you're using. With C, it's the compiler that is machine-specific, so it's the compiler that is responsible for translating C's universal code into the dialect required by a particular computer. Thus, if a C compiler exists for any given computer and the hardware is compatible, a C program—like UNIX—can be moved (or ported) over to it.

Being rewritten in C, then, meant that UNIX became accessible to a great variety of computers.

7

REFINEMENT

Over the years, UNIX has achieved great popularity in the mainframe-and-minicomputer world. At the University of California at Berkeley, new UNIX utilities (tools) were developed. Programmers there created a better text editor, *vi,* than the one originally built into UNIX, and they enhanced UNIX' file-management capabilities. On a more technically oriented front, they created a better environment for C programmers, which is called the C shell.

PROLIFERATION

UNIX proliferated, and in the process a certain amount of nonstandard features crept into the various versions. *The* version was still the one licensed from AT&T, but manufacturers were free to add new features to it as and when they thought such features would benefit the computer that a particular version was designed for.

Eventually, UNIX existed in several versions. The first licensed version was Version 6, aimed at the education market. Then came Version 7, for commercial consumption. That was followed by PWB/UNIX (standing for programmer's workbench), with a concentration on programming tools. Then came System III, to be superseded, but not necessarily replaced, by System V. And there's still Berkeley's UNIX, which has achieved popularity in engineering fields.

All this is not to mention third-party licensed versions of UNIX, none of which is permitted to use the AT&T name. Thus, if you look, you can also find UNIX called CPIX, HP-UX, PC/IX, UNX/VS, Ultrix, Zeus, and a host of other names.

But if an operating system is to become truly popular, especially when it's meant for use on a variety of different computers, it must possess a high degree of standardization. In other words, people who use the system must be free to wander from machine to machine without needing to learn new commands and procedures for each.

To tie up UNIX' loose ends, a group of users and vendors called */usr/group* met in 1981 and began work on defining a standard version of UNIX. More recently, in January 1985, AT&T announced the System V Interface Definition, which helps to define a standard UNIX version. With the approval of the UNIX community, this System V has become the version of choice today.

And that's the history of UNIX, if in a very small nutshell. Now, how does all this tie in with XENIX and with you?

ENTER MICROCOMPUTERS

The obvious place to begin is with the advent of the microcomputer—the machine in your system on which XENIX is or will be installed, and quite possibly the machine from which you gain access to XENIX.

Chronologically, UNIX and microcomputers developed more or less in tandem. The first microcomputers appeared in the early 1970s, but were too low on the technological ladder to use UNIX. They were much slower than their larger cousins, and had a very limited amount of memory—nothing like the microcomputers so prevalent today, and even less like those that will appear in the near future.

Like any other computers, however, microcomputers need an operating system. If not UNIX, then what?

Through about 1980, the dominant microcomputer operating system was CP/M (Control Program for Microprocessors) from Digital Research Incorporated. The bulk of the microcomputers available at that time were based on processors that handled information eight bits at a time. Eight pieces of information (roughly equivalent to one character) could be passed from the central processing unit, into the rest of the computer, and back again. Although that may not sound like much, since the processor worked at electronic speeds, the overall performance really wasn't poor at all.

CP/M addressed this 8-bit world very well. It was relatively inexpensive (if the computer manufacturer did not actually supply it outright with the machine), and because of its availability, programs, such as word processors and spreadsheets, were written to run in its environment. With a large number of available programs, the operating system became even more popular.

In 1978, Onyx Systems licensed UNIX for a 16-bit microcomputer designed for multiple users, but all in all, UNIX seemed to enter a dormant phase as far as microcomputers were concerned.

ENTER MICROSOFT

Now we come to the second part of our XENIX equation: Microsoft Corporation. Best known at that time for its implementation of the BASIC programming language, Microsoft announced, in 1980, a faster, smoother, trimmer version of UNIX based on UNIX Version 7. This enhanced version was called XENIX, and it was designed especially for a microcomputer environment.

This announcement came at a very hectic time, because microcomputers were in the throes of evolving from 8-bit machines to 8/16-bit computers that offered the double advantage of being able to use 8-bit programs while processing information at increased (16-bit) speed.

XENIX began to generate interest within the microcomputer world, but as yet this was a very small world. Then in August 1981 came the IBM PC, supported by Microsoft's MS-DOS operating system. Within a year, the PC and the MS-DOS single-user operating environment had captured a large share of the market. XENIX, which was aimed primarily at the multiuser, multitasking environment, was momentarily forgotten.

But that was then, and this is now. In the interim, Microsoft followed AT&T's move and revised XENIX from Version 7 to System III and then to System V, the current and accepted version. System V incorporates enhancements of the *vi* editor, the C shell for programming ease, and Microsoft's own invention, the Visual shell, which provides a very simple, easy-to-use system of menu choices for the beginner.

Today, Microsoft licenses XENIX to various manufacturers who release it on their own. Thus, your particular version of XENIX may come from a manufacturer such as The Santa Cruz Operation, Altos, Tandy, COMPAQ, or IBM—on whose System V release this book is based (IBM PC XENIX Version 2.0).

And now, knowing what XENIX is and where it came from, let's take one more look at XENIX as a whole. But this time, we'll approach it from the "Who needs to use it?" angle.

WORKING

There they sit: computer, screen, printer, maybe a few other accessories. All told, you see perhaps $4000 to $7000 worth of hardware. But what happens when the workload increases? Or more than one person needs to use it? You add another computer, and another after that, and another still. There is, literally, no end to the amount of money you can spend. In addition, you may need to duplicate printer costs or add extra dollars for hard disks with each new system.

Or you may have to do all this, if you don't have XENIX.

In a multiuser environment like XENIX, several terminals share the processor time of the host computer. Any computing that is done is originated and controlled from that computer.

This situation is as cost-effective as it sounds. Terminals cost $400 to $500 each, and a four-user system can be bought for as little as $8000. So where's the catch? There isn't any—just a warning: In a multiuser system, both the hardware and the software need to be fully integrated to produce the best results. And both must be proven performers.

In terms of equipment, microcomputers today are running at speeds that are four to six times faster than those of the late 1970s, when these machines were far too limited to handle an operating system as sophisticated as XENIX. Now, too, memory and storage capacity can both be measured in millions of characters—far removed from the mere thousands available only a few years ago.

The hardware stage is set.

As far as the software goes, UNIX is a recognized success in the minicomputer and mainframe markets. In the past 16 years, it has been tempered into a very precise tool. And Microsoft has done an excellent job of maintaining the UNIX environment, while making it compatible with a variety of microcomputers. What do you get? A precise, flexible, proven multiuser operating system.

And you get multitasking, too. Multitasking normally happens in a multiuser system, because each person using the system is, in effect, a "task" being performed at the same time as all the others. Beyond this, in XENIX each person using the system also has the ability to make things happen in the foreground (where computers normally process information) or to send them into the background, where they can be completed on their own while some other task is being handled in the foreground. It's like moving from a world of two dimensions into a world of three.

IN SHORT

As other operating systems evolve, they will begin to emulate more of the UNIX features than they do now. As in any commercial environment, it's the nature of the beast to turn toward whatever is working best. But XENIX—your XENIX—is already a faithful implementation of UNIX, in form, format, and command. For the multiuser, multitasking environment, tomorrow is here today. XENIX is now what most other operating systems will become.

And now has always been better than later.

2

LOOKING AROUND Now that you have been introduced to XENIX, it's time to put it to work. You'll begin by logging in, then try a few commands, and end the session by logging out. If you're not familiar with the terms *log in* and *log out,* the former is the way you begin a session with XENIX, and the latter is how you end it. Whether your system is operational for a few hours a day or around the clock, and whether you are the only user on your system or one of many, you must still log in and log out whenever you use XENIX.

A LOOK AT YOUR SYSTEM

The commands and procedures described in the remaining chapters of Section 1 apply to anyone who uses XENIX, but let's pause for a moment and look at the setup of the computer system you are using. Recall that a XENIX installation can be put together in one of several ways. It can be:

■ A host computer with one to many terminals (and/or computers acting as terminals) connected to it.

■ A single computer operated as an independent XENIX system.

■ A series of independent XENIX computers networked together so their users can communicate with one another.

14

Of these three setups, the first is most typical of the type of computer system XENIX runs on and, for that reason, it is the type assumed in this book. We also assume that you gain access to the XENIX computer from a terminal or from another microcomputer, because in most multiuser environments the job of running and maintaining the XENIX computer itself is the responsibility of one person, the system administrator.

Although XENIX is designed for the type of setup just described, it can be used as easily and effectively by one person. If you are the only user on your system, however, you gain access to XENIX from the host computer, and that means you play the dual roles of system user and administrator. Refer to Section 2 of this book before continuing, if:

■ XENIX is or must be installed on your computer (this applies to either of the last two setups in the preceding list).

■ You are the system administrator.

For either of these situations, the chapters in Section 2 are written to help you, and contain information on the necessary procedures for starting and maintaining XENIX on your computer.

STARTING WITH THE HARDWARE

Assuming, then, that you are one of a group of people who gain access to XENIX through a terminal or a microcomputer, let's begin your work with XENIX by looking at the equipment you use. It's your window into the XENIX world.

If you use a terminal, it consists of a keyboard and a monitor, and actually looks like a microcomputer. It does not, however, have any innate computing ability. If you use a microcomputer, the only real difference between it and a regular terminal is that it can compute, and in order to use your computer with XENIX you need communication software that makes it act like a terminal. (Even though two computers running XENIX can communicate with one another, the current version of XENIX does not recognize your computer itself as a device with its own disk drives and operating system. Hence, the need for communication software.)

Throughout this book, in fact, the XENIX screen images you'll see have been captured on an Apple Macintosh running as a XENIX terminal with MacTerminal communication software.

No matter which device you're using, throughout the course of this book it will be called a terminal for the sake of simplicity.

Elsewhere, perhaps in sight, perhaps in another room or even another building, is the computer that runs XENIX. Typically, the XENIX computer is accompanied by a printer that can be shared by all the XENIX users.

Somewhere along the way, your terminal and the computer are connected, so that they can communicate. There are two ways in which your terminal might be connected to your XENIX system: through *local* or through *remote* access.

If your terminal (or equivalent) is hardwired to the system—that is, the terminal is connected directly to the system by a cable—you have local access. In an office environment, this is the most typical means of accessing the system.

On the other hand, you could be dialing into the system. The dial-up method is called remote access. In this case, your terminal may be at some other location, perhaps your home, and you use a communications device—a modem—to contact the computer through the phone lines. If you use remote access, the XENIX computer must also be equipped with a modem so it can answer your call and understand your transmissions.

15

YOUR TERMINAL

As with all operating systems, when you use XENIX you interact with it. You type a command, and XENIX either responds or requests further information.

THE ENTER KEY

Answering any XENIX questions or prompts requires that you type a reply, so you must have a way of telling XENIX to recognize and accept your reply. That way is the Enter key on your terminal's keyboard. Throughout all your XENIX sessions you must remember to press Enter when appropriate.

However, not all terminals (or computers used as terminals) have a key with the exact label *Enter*. On a few devices, this key is labeled *RETURN*. On some IBM products, the Enter key bears a right-angled, left-pointing arrow. Then again, some devices have *both* an Enter and a Return key. If your terminal is in this group, you can press either as the Enter key; XENIX makes no distinction between the two without special instructions to do so.

THE IMPORTANCE OF CASE

Many things you type will contain a mixture of upper- and lowercase letters. XENIX distinguishes between them, so it's important that you enter commands and other information *exactly* as they are described.

If your terminal has a Shift Lock key (also called Caps Lock or Alpha Lock), which, once pressed, causes all letters to appear in uppercase, make sure that it's not engaged when you begin your work with XENIX. On some terminals, the Shift Lock key lights up when it's active. On others, it may be physically locked in a down position. No matter which, pressing the key is usually all you need do to deactivate it.

16

CHANGING YOUR TERMINAL

In most local-access situations, the terminal to which you're assigned will have been correctly configured (set up) by your system administrator to work with XENIX, and XENIX itself will have been configured to know what type of terminal you have. If you're dialing into XENIX, notify your system administrator so that he or she can modify the XENIX files that contain information about the type of terminal you're using. If at any time your XENIX terminal behaves improperly, notify your system administrator.

YOUR KEYS TO XENIX

In identifying you to XENIX, your system administrator should already have supplied you with two vital pieces of information: your login name and your private password. If, for any reason, you haven't been told what these are, find out. You can't log into XENIX without them.

LOGGING IN

Now it's time to combine theory and practice. Let's log in.

If you're connected to the system via a terminal, switch it on. From a remote location, dial your system's access telephone number and wait for a "connect" message from your modem. If you're using a computer and communication software, begin the software using the communication parameters supplied by your system administrator.

From either starting point, you'll soon see a message like this:

```
AT Login:
```

appear on your display.

If the *AT Login:* message does not appear immediately, press the Enter key a few times. If you still see nothing, check the schedule of your XENIX system or contact your system administrator. If you are a dial-up user, you may need to verify the transmission speed and other telecommunication settings.

Once you see the login prompt, type your login name (remember the importance of upper- and lowercase) and press the Enter key:

```
AT Login: danh_
```

Now, you'll see the following prompt:

```
AT Login: danh
Password:_
```

17

This is where you enter the secret password that allows you to access the system. Type your password carefully. Although XENIX displays the characters you type for your login name, to protect your privacy it does not show those you enter for your password.

If you make a mistake in typing either your login name or your password, no harm is done. XENIX will print a message on the screen, telling you something like *Login incorrect,* and will prompt you to start over again by redisplaying the *login:* message.

GREETINGS FROM XENIX

Depending upon the type of terminal you have, once you have successfully logged in the screen will either clear or advance a few lines. You'll see something like the following:

```
             The IBM Personal Computer XENIX

You have mail.
```

◼ NOTE: *Throughout this book, don't worry if your XENIX system does not display a letter-for-letter match with what is shown. Certain details, such as terminal type, messages from the system administrator, and login name, can and will vary from person to person and system to system.*

Right now, although this is an extreme example of variability, you may see a different opening line and XENIX may even be telling you that you have no mail.

Neither difference is cause for concern, though either or both may be disconcert-
ing if this is your first login attempt. Just remember: Your XENIX reflects your environment and is under the control of your system administrator. What you see here
is a "generic" display.

The opening line, for instance, is often referred to as "the message of the day."
The system administrator can change it, so this line is often used as a type of bul-
letin board, to pass along information that is bound to be seen by everyone who
logs in. Likewise, the mail XENIX is referring to is a message that is automatically
generated when a new user is added to the system. Your system administrator may
already have deleted the message as an unnecessary use of storage space.

Either way, don't become preoccupied with screen variations or with the concept of having mail in your account. You'll be told of possible differences, and mail
will be covered in detail in Chapter 8.

Right now, let's look at what you see after you log in. It's one of three things
that tell you something intrinsic to your use of XENIX.

It's possible that your screen might scroll up a few lines and show you something like this:

```
Terminal type is vt100
$ _
```

Or, your screen might clear and display something like the following:

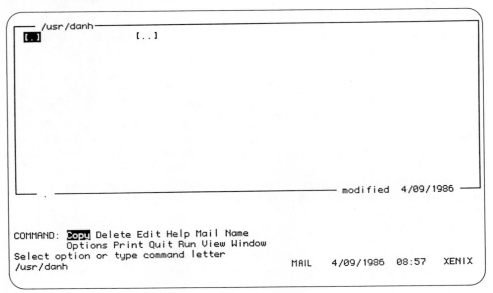

Then again, the message displayed might be similar to this:

```
Terminal type is vt100
1% _
```

In these three examples, the dollar sign ($) in the first illustration, the entire screen in the second, and the percent symbol (%) in the third are important because they indicate the *shell* in which you're operating:

■ The dollar sign prompt tells you that you are in the *Bourne shell.*

■ The screen elements and structured menu of commands at the bottom of the second illustration represent the *Visual shell.*

19

■ The percent symbol indicates that you are in the *C shell* (the number that appears in front of the percent symbol is a line number).

Like *mail*, all three XENIX shells are discussed later, but your involvement with one of those shells has become immediate, so some discussion is in order.

UNDERSTANDING THE XENIX ENVIRONMENT

When using XENIX, any typing you do at your terminal quite likely will fall into one of two categories:

■ A request to initiate some action.

■ A response to a query or situation.

You saw the second possibility when you logged in: Your responses to the queries *AT Login:* and *Password:* provided XENIX with the information it needed to permit you to access the system.

The problem faced by any operating system, however, is one of interpretation. The operating system must understand what you're typing and how the entry applies to present conditions. If it didn't, the text you enter while word processing could very well be mistaken for operating system commands, random mental notes…anything. XENIX accomplishes this interpreting by using a somewhat modular approach incorporating three main components:

■ The kernel.

■ Built-in utilities.

■ The shell.

Each performs a specific function.

THE KERNEL

The kernel is a series of XENIX software instructions that control and monitor all devices connected to the system. The kernel acts as a link between you and that hardware. Among its functions, the kernel:

■ Makes sure all terminals have equal access to the system.

■ Organizes the flow of information to the printer and all other attached devices. (In a multiuser system, two or more people may try to print different documents at the same time. XENIX' kernel acts as a traffic cop, preventing head-on collisions.)

■ Oversees operations, so information is always retrieved from and returned to its proper place on the disk no matter how many people are attempting to use information stored on the system's hard disk.

The kernel also manages the memory in your system, judging how to allocate it effectively so that each user receives the most benefit. And it even controls the flow of error messages and the system's reactions to them if something goes wrong.

BUILT-IN UTILITIES

XENIX' built-in utilities can be anything from *vi,* the visual text editor, to separate sets of information that describe the system, the equipment attached to it, and the people who have access to it. Your login name and password, for instance, are excellent examples of this latter type of utility; they're kept with other information that forms your own profile, as XENIX has been given it.

THE SHELL

And now, we return to the shell. No matter which of the three shells we're talking about, this XENIX component is what's called a *command interpreter.* Its function is to examine everything you type and route it appropriately, calling on or responding to the kernel and the utility programs as required.

The shell you are using may be the result of discussions between you and your system administrator, or you may simply have been assigned the one that is best for you. In any case, you're not locked into the shell to which you've been assigned. XENIX is structured to permit you to travel among them all.

The Bourne shell is the one most frequently assigned. In it, you type your commands after the $ prompt and XENIX responds as needed. The Bourne shell lets you interact quickly and efficiently with XENIX, so it is suitable if you rely frequently on XENIX and use it for more than one or two main tasks.

The C shell, too, is quick and efficient. It was originally designed with programmers in mind (specifically, those who have used the C programming language). The line numbers preceding each occurrence of the % prompt make it easy to specify lines containing commands that you want to reuse in repetitive tasks.

The Visual shell is one of Microsoft's unique contributions to XENIX. Unlike the Bourne and C shells, the Visual shell presents users with a structured arrangement of information and command menus. It was developed for two reasons:

■ It's not likely that someone who first starts using XENIX will know many XENIX commands. The Visual shell's command-menu format makes the most frequently used XENIX commands available just by pressing the first letter of an everyday word associated with a command name. The Visual shell is thus an excellent introduction to the operating system and permits newcomers to work within XENIX while becoming more familiar with its uses.

21

■ Second, some XENIX users log into the system for only a few specific purposes, such as sending and receiving mail. These people have no pressing need to learn all of the XENIX commands, and the Visual shell permits them to function within its environment without that knowledge.

MOVING FROM ONE SHELL TO ANOTHER

Earlier, we mentioned that you can move from one shell to another. Here's your chance to try it out. The commands are very similar, and your ability to travel will be limited only if you have a dumb or tty terminal—neither of which can support the Visual shell.

To enter the Visual shell from the Bourne or C shell, first check the type of terminal you have. Since you have just logged in, XENIX' message line identifying your terminal type should still be on the screen.

If your terminal is ANSI (some others also work), type the following at the $ or the % prompt:

vsh

This is the XENIX command to activate the Visual shell, and a display much like the one illustrated earlier will appear in a few seconds.

(If you happen to try this command with a dumb, tty, or other terminal that doesn't work, you won't hurt anything; you will either be returned to your normal shell prompt or you'll see some random characters appear on the screen.)

When you want to return to your original shell, select the Quit command by pressing the letter Q.

XENIX will prompt you to confirm the request by displaying the message *Enter Y to confirm*. Press Y and you will return to the shell from which you invoked the Visual shell.

If you're in the Visual shell, you use a slightly different procedure to travel to another shell. To move to the Bourne shell, for example:

Press the letter R

to select the Run command at the bottom of your screen. After the *file:* prompt, type the letters:

sh

to specify the Bourne shell.

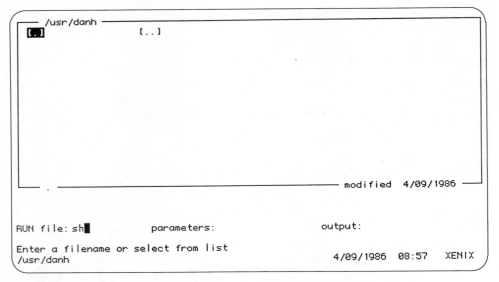

Press Enter, and the Visual shell will be replaced by the $ prompt.

To enter the C shell, use the same procedure, but type *csh* after the Run command's *file:* prompt.

When you want to return to the Visual shell, press the Control (Ctrl) key and the lowercase letter *d* at the $ or % prompt. This key combination, usually printed as Ctrl-D, tells XENIX you'd like to exit the environment you're currently working in and return to the one you came from. Since you were originally in the Visual shell, your terminal will have no problems returning you to it.

If you are a Visual or C shell user, you may want to make use of this ability to move in and out of your normal shell environment. The examples in this book are based on the Bourne shell, and they will be much easier for you to step through if you can see and respond to the same prompts and messages that are illustrated in the examples.

WORKING TOGETHER

The shell, the kernel, and the XENIX utilities are not independent of each other. They interact to provide you with a cohesive system that responds to your requests. They also give XENIX something a little less obvious, at least at first: universality. Regardless of the brand of computer on which you use XENIX, the commands and procedures usually run the same. The only place you are likely to find differences is in the kernel, because it is customized to make optimum use of the particular computer system and its related hardware.

But you never become directly involved with the kernel. The XENIX commands you use are passed through the shell, and it's the shell—the command interpreter—that handles their translation.

Now that you've been introduced to XENIX' components, let's put them to work and see a little of what XENIX can do. Right now, you'll just try out a few commands to develop a feel for the system. Don't worry about understanding everything you do. That understanding will come later.

To begin, enter the Bourne shell if you are in the Visual or C shell (from the C shell, simply type *sh* after the % prompt).

23

WHO'S THERE?

First, you might be interested in seeing how XENIX "sees" you as one user among others. How will it know who you are and what messages and information belong to you? One easy way to find out is with the *pwd* (print working directory) command. Type:

pwd

at the $ prompt and press Enter. XENIX will reply with a line something like this:

```
$ pwd
/usr/danh
$
```

You'll learn the details in the next two chapters, but right now, in that brief response, you've seen two important features of XENIX' method of managing information. First, XENIX keeps track of you and your work by name—specifically, the name by which you identify yourself when you log in. Second, as you can tell from the command you used, you have a directory. If this concept is new to you, think of a directory as a card file or a table of contents. XENIX uses directories to find the storage locations of all the lists, memos, letters, and other information you and everyone else send and receive through the system.

Now, try another command. Again, at the $ prompt, type:

who

and press Enter. XENIX will respond with a display like this:

```
$ who
root          console     Apr  9 08:57
danh          tty00       Apr  9 09:09
stanb         tty01       Apr  9 09:02
$_
```

24

Here, XENIX is telling you who else is currently logged into the system (*root* is the superuser). Note that it identifies other users by their login names. In addition, XENIX is telling you which terminal (tty00 and so on) each person is using, as well as the date and time of login.

A FEW USEFUL COMMANDS

The first paragraph of this book mentioned that XENIX is many things— among them, a calendar and a calculator. Let's stop and take a quick look at these two features now.

XENIX automatically keeps track of the date and time. As you'll see in Chapter 8, you can use its timekeeping ability to create a "tickler" file as a reminder of upcoming events. But you can also check on the day, date, and time whenever you want. At the $ prompt, type:

date

and press Enter. XENIX responds with a display like this:

```
$ date
Wed Apr  9 09:09:53 PDT 1986
$
```

telling you: the day of the week, the month and day, the time (to the second) for the time zone you are in, and the year. It's a handy command. (If you are the system administrator, you may also use the *date* command to modify the existing settings. To do this, consult the appropriate section in Appendix A.)

Then, too, there are XENIX' talents as a desktop calculator. When you want XENIX to perform some math calculations, you can call on a special utility program called *bc*. To try it, type:

bc

at the $ prompt and press Enter. This time, notice that XENIX' only response is a flashing underline. That underline is telling you that *bc* is waiting for you to type something. So, try typing:

1234 + 6789

and press Enter. XENIX responds:

```
$ bc
1234+6789
8023
_
```

Bc can do much more sophisticated calculations, of course, but right now you can try it out on some more arithmetic. Feel free to use this as it's convenient for you. All you need remember is that, to divide, you must use the / symbol (as in 4/2), and to multiply, you must use the * symbol (as in 2*2). When you are finished with *bc,* tell XENIX to return you to the shell by typing:

quit

and pressing the Enter key. The $ prompt will quickly reappear. If you are not in your home shell, you can return to it by pressing Ctrl-D. For a more in-depth discussion of *bc,* see the related sections in the Command Reference portion of your documentation.

READING YOUR MAIL

Now that you've stepped through a few exercises with XENIX, let's go back to where we began: the mail message you received when you first logged in. If you don't have the message, you should read this section anyway. It will introduce the topics of our next two chapters.

From the $ or % prompt, type:

mail

and press the Enter key.

From the Visual shell, press M to select the Mail command and then press R to select *Read.*

You'll soon see something like the following appear on your screen:

```
$ mail
mail version 3.0 August 10, 1984.  Type ? for help.
1 message:
    1 root       Tue Apr 15 12:23  6/125
_
```

As mentioned earlier, we'll cover mail in a later chapter. Right now, all we're concerned with is XENIX' indication that you have one message. To see it, press the Enter key and XENIX' mail system will respond:

```
Message  1:
From root Tue Apr 15 12:23:55 1986
To: danh
Date: Tue Apr 15 12:23:54 1986

        Welcome to IBM Personal Computer XENIX!

_
```

This is the message that was automatically generated by XENIX when the system administrator created your account on the system. Notice the underline character at the bottom left of your display. This character is a prompt from XENIX' mail system, which is now waiting for you to issue another command. Issue the Quit command by typing:

q

and on your screen you'll see something similar to this:

```
q
Held 1 message in /usr/spool/mail/danh
$ _
```

Since you didn't delete the letter, XENIX has stored it away for you. The question is where? There are quite a few slashes (/) distributed between an equal number of words (the last is probably your own login name).

Recall XENIX' response when you used the command *pwd*. There, too, you saw words interspersed with slashes. At that time, you were looking at the name of your working directory—the "table of contents" XENIX uses to locate stored information. Here, those words and slashes indicate the storage place XENIX has used for your mail. Taken as a whole, both collections of words and slashes describe a *path* leading to a location on the hard disk where XENIX keeps information. That path also points to the topic of the next two chapters: the XENIX file system.

CHANGING YOUR PASSWORD

Whether you use XENIX intensively or only on occasion, whether you are a programmer, a standard user, or the system administrator, your key to XENIX is your password. Without your password, XENIX is, and will remain, closed to you.

Passwords themselves originated as a means of maintaining system security. They are XENIX' way of keeping unauthorized users out of the system. That is the reason you have been instructed to keep your password private, and it is also the reason XENIX never echoes on-screen the password characters you type in. Other than the system administrator, no one should know your password.

One of the best methods of maintaining system security is to have users change their passwords periodically. In fact, your system administrator may, on occasion, display a message asking you to do so. Also, if your password should somehow become known to an unauthorized user, you would be well advised to notify your system administrator and change your password as soon as possible. The procedure itself is simple. From the shell prompt, type:

passwd

and press Enter. XENIX will respond with a message telling you it is changing the password for your user name and will prompt for your old password (the root user won't be prompted for this). Type the old one in, and XENIX will next prompt for the new password. As with your old password, make the new one easy for you to remember, but difficult for others to guess.

Once you have entered the new password, XENIX will prompt you to confirm by retyping it. If you make a mistake at this point, XENIX will respond *They don't match; try again.* If this happens, type and verify your new password again. If you forget your password, notify your system administrator so you can get a new one.

LOGGING OUT

When you won't be using XENIX for awhile—when you go home at night, for example, or when you want to disconnect from the system—you tell XENIX you're through by logging out.

If you'd like to log out now, the procedure is simple, though different for each of the three shells.

From the Bourne shell:

Press Ctrl-D.

27

Recall from earlier in this chapter that Ctrl-D is the key combination you use to exit the environment you're working in. If your home shell is the Bourne shell and that's where you are now, pressing a Ctrl-D will log you out of XENIX.

From the Visual shell:

Press the Q key

and when XENIX asks you to confirm:

Press the Y key

to confirm.

If the C shell is your home shell, type:

logout

at the % prompt, to exit XENIX.

In all cases, a login prompt such as *AT login:* will appear on the screen, and you'll be back where you were at the start of this chapter. If you use XENIX from a terminal, you can safely turn it off when you see the *login:* message. If, for some reason, you are using XENIX from the host computer (console) itself, do *not* turn the computer off, because....

A WORD OF WARNING

Logging out is *not* the same as turning off the XENIX computer. When you log out, you tell XENIX that you—and you alone—are through for awhile. XENIX, however, keeps on running. In contrast, turning the system off turns XENIX off, too. No one remains on XENIX—even if they had unfinished work in progress. If, for whatever reason, you are using XENIX from the host computer itself, *never* turn the computer off just because you have finished. There is a special shutdown procedure that must be followed before the XENIX computer can safely be turned off. If the system is not shut down properly, any unsaved work will be lost beyond recall. The results could be disastrous. Leave the shutdown procedure to your system administrator.

DIRECTORY FILES In our everyday lives, we depend on files for organizing all sorts of information—letters, bills, budgets, and so on. Files are central to XENIX or any other operating system also. On a computer, as in a desk drawer, a file is a repository of information. It exists on a disk in one of three varieties: as a data file, a program file, or a directory file. These elements provide the framework for everything you do in XENIX. Understanding their differences is essential. Let's begin with the one most likely to be familiar to you.

DATA FILES

Data files are conceptually the most obvious and the easiest to envision. They contain information that can be saved, recalled, and manipulated according to your needs. For example, mail messages on your XENIX system are stored in a data file.

PROGRAM FILES

Program files (which are usually just called programs or applications) contain the instructions that enable a computer to perform a task. Depending on the task involved, such a file can range from one or two lines up to many thousands of lines. Thus, a program file can be anything from a simple C program that prints HELLO on your screen, all the way up to a word processor or a database-management application, or XENIX' *mail* system.

No matter what it is, however, a program file's function is to do something whenever you tell it to. If you think of a data file as being passive, then a program file is its active counterpart. Usually, programs manipulate data.

DIRECTORY FILES

While programs do and data files are done to, directory files keep information about all the files on a disk. Directory files track the whereabouts of data files and program files, note how big they are and what they're called, and, in general, make sure that people can always find and use these other types of files whenever they're wanted. You can have a multitude of program and data files on a disk, but each disk has only *one* directory file.

Since the XENIX system's hard disk will be responsible for keeping track of your data files (and everyone else's), let's use this chapter to see what it does and how you can use it to your advantage.

LINEAR VERSUS HIERARCHICAL

Before your account was installed on XENIX—indeed, before XENIX itself was installed—your system's hard disk started life as a vast, vacant expanse of available storage area. Microcomputers and their operating systems condition (format) that space and, as it's used, place file after file into it.

LINEAR DIRECTORIES

Early microcomputer directory systems kept track of files simply by keeping a list of them. Perhaps that list was in alphabetic order, and perhaps it was just in the

30

order in which the files were stored. No matter the arrangement, the file names were listed one after the other like the items on your grocery list. Quite appropriately, this scheme is called a *linear* directory system.

A linear directory system is not inherently bad, and when microcomputers relied on floppy diskettes, linear systems were adequate. Floppy diskettes store a limited number of files, so a linear list is relatively short. It was easy to spot a particular file in such a group.

But today, a microcomputer's hard-disk storage system is hundreds of times larger than a floppy diskette, and the list of file names that can be stored on such a disk can be enormous. Searching through 500 or 1000 entries for a single file name can become confusing.

Also, with more available storage space, it's become quite common for more than one person to work from the same hard disk. That can be accomplished through a multiuser environment like XENIX, or simply by allowing different people to use the same computer. Whatever the method, in a linear directory system your files, the next person's files, and files created by everyone else using the equipment are all lumped together on the disk. But when you want to use the system, it's *your* work and *your* files that are important, not everyone else's.

And perhaps more important than lack of organization is the fact that anyone using the system can access your files. They're all right there in the open, so a linear directory scheme also limits the privacy and security available to you.

HIERARCHICAL DIRECTORIES

Given these reasons not to use a linear directory system with a hard disk and in a multiuser environment, it's hardly to be expected that XENIX would use one. And, in fact, it doesn't. XENIX supports a *hierarchical* directory structure. This consists of a series—a hierarchy—of directory "levels" that allow you to be quite specific in locating or placing a data file. Let's rely on a familiar analogy to trace our way through a hierarchical system.

At the front of this book you can find a table of contents. In effect, this table, in its entirety, is a directory to the contents of the pages that follow, providing references to the places in the book you wish to find. And on its simplest level, that's just the way a disk's directory system works—whether it's linear or hierarchical. Within the table of contents, you also find subdivisions—chapter titles—that point out separate sections of the book. And often, in a table of contents, you find under each chapter heading a description of what that chapter contains. These three components, the table of contents itself, the chapter titles, and the descriptions of each chapter, constitute a three-level, hierarchical system that provides you with a reference for finding "data files" in a book.

XENIX manages the files on your system's hard disk in much the same way that information is grouped in our analogy. There is one "table of contents" for your entire disk, the directory file, that XENIX uses to keep track of where everything is.

Within that directory are other descriptions that refine XENIX' ability to find information on the disk. These are called subdirectories. To keep within the book analogy, "underneath" this first subdirectory level there can also be other subdirectories that further describe the contents of the disk.

DEFINING A PATH

A table of contents is an independent section of a book. It does not include the contents of the chapters it describes, only their descriptions and locations. The chapters themselves are separate parts of the book. In addition, convention places the table of contents at the front of a book, but its function would be the same no matter where it was positioned.

Under XENIX, the directory file on the system's hard disk works just like a table of contents. It provides a path that XENIX can follow to get to other places on the hard disk that contain the files you want. The contents of those files do not exist within any directory. Like the chapters in a book, they have their own locations on the disk.

Also, like the table of contents, the directory file itself occupies its own space on the disk. And, to carry through our analogy, both the table of contents and the directory file are data files of a sort, because they contain information. That information, however, tells you (or XENIX) the path to follow to locate the actual data that you seek.

You can visualize such a path easily enough. We'll cover the details shortly, but here's a quick reference point if you'd like one. In our table of contents analogy, you can think of the path to a section of a chapter as something like this:

/Table of Contents/Chapter 3/Using Directories

Start at the Table of Contents, then find Chapter 3, and then find the section Using Directories. In XENIX, think of the path to a file in the same way:

/Directory File/Subdirectory/Data File

(If either of these paths looks familiar, recall that, in Chapter 2, XENIX informed you that it had saved a mail message by displaying something like *Held 1 message in /usr/spool/mail/danh.*) Now, let's take a look at some real-life directories.

USING DIRECTORIES

If you logged out after the last chapter, log in again. As you saw in Chapter 2, you're in the Bourne shell if there's a $ prompt at the left side of your screen, in the C shell if that prompt is % symbol (usually prefixed by a number), or in the Visual shell if XENIX displays a command menu at the bottom of the screen.

◼ NOTE: *Even though the majority of the examples in this book are based on the Bourne shell, directory structures are so important for organizing information that we will begin by stepping through the commands for Visual shell users, too. Instructions for the Visual shell will, however, be phased out at the end of this chapter. At that point, if you are a Visual shell user, you may wish to refer to Chapter 12 for additional information.*

FINDING YOUR WORKING DIRECTORY

The first command we'll use is called *pwd,* short for print working directory. Your working directory is whatever directory you happen to be in at the time you use the *pwd* command.

When the system administrator created your user account, your personal subdirectory was added to the system. That subdirectory was probably given your login name. It's also called your home directory, and you're automatically deposited there whenever you log in.

33

Since you've just logged in, your working directory and your home directory are one and the same. Keep in mind, though, that XENIX uses a hierarchical directory system that allows you to create directories on different levels. As you grow more experienced with XENIX and, presumably, create more directories to organize your information, you may sometimes want to check on the directory in which you're currently working. Hence, the command print working directory.

To check on your working directory, type (in lowercase letters):

pwd

and press the Enter key. In response, XENIX will print a line like the following on your screen:

```
$ pwd
/usr/danh
$ _
```

In actuality, *pwd* is giving you more information than just the name of your working directory. It's actually telling you the complete name of the path it follows to reach your working directory. That name is the *path name.*

◪ NOTE: *If you're in the Visual shell, you don't need the* pwd *command. XENIX always displays your working directory in the upper and lower lefthand portions of your screen. You should see the same general format as the one shown in the preceding example.*

DEFINING A PATH

Let's go back to our table of contents analogy for a moment. Recall that the path to a section of this chapter could be written out as:

/Table of Contents/Chapter 3/Using Directories

How does that relate to your working-directory description? Look again at how XENIX responded to *pwd*.

When XENIX is installed on any system's hard disk, part of that installation involves physically putting all of the XENIX programs on the disk. All the space that XENIX, in its entirety, occupies is referenced by the *root* directory, so-called because it is the main or source directory for the operating system as a whole.

In our example (and probably on your system as well) a subdirectory called *usr* was created within the XENIX root directory. Whenever a new user is added to XENIX, that person's subdirectory is created within the *usr* directory.

Taken in that light, you can see that */usr/danh* is really:

/(root)
↓
usr
↓
danh

and that it reveals the path from the root (which is never stated, though always assumed, because it is the start of things) to *usr* and then to *danh*.

In this illustration, we've displayed XENIX' reply to *pwd* on separate lines for purposes of clarity. But as you saw in the actual response, XENIX uses the forward slash character (/). Within the context of XENIX' directory structure, this slash indicates movement in a (relative) downward direction through the hierarchy. Root being the highest level of directory, the working directory */usr/danh* can be interpreted as "down (from root) to *usr* and then down from *usr* to *danh*."

CREATING DIRECTORIES

Now, let's create a few subdirectories, to develop a feel for the system. To put this session in a "real-world" framework, let's assume that....

It's your first day on the job. You work for a management agency, and you've been assigned three clients. One is in California, one is in Boston, and the third is in New York. You've been assigned the Bourne shell, and you'll be using XENIX to monitor your clients' accounts and generate correspondence to them. For each client, you'll also want to keep any memos of your own that discuss topics you feel concern that client.

You have your whole home directory in which to do all this, but let's use XENIX' directory capabilities to create separate areas for each type of information. You sit down and log into the system. XENIX places you in your home directory. To begin, you decide to create a subdirectory for your California client. You type:

mkdir California

and press Enter.

Mkdir is the XENIX command to make a directory, and you've just created one called *California.* The name you gave it is as simple and descriptive as possible, and it is well within the 14-character name limit that XENIX allows.

◼ NOTE: *Remember this 14-character allowance. In naming either directories or document files, if you try to use a name longer than the legal limit, XENIX will refuse to accept the extra characters. XENIX also won't take a blank space in the name, or any of the following characters:* #, $, %, *, |, ;, ', /, [,], *or* ".

Within XENIX' environment, the directory you just created is one level below the directory from which you're working (your home directory, in this example). You don't need to use a slash in the *mkdir* command, because XENIX assumes that any directory you create is subordinate to the one from which you create it.   35

FROM THE VISUAL SHELL

If you're assigned the Visual shell, here is the procedure you follow to create a directory:

Press the letter O

to select Options from the command menu. The menu will change to this:

    OPTIONS: Directory Filesystem Output Permissions

Now:

Press the letter D

to select Directory, which changes the menu line to read:

    OPTIONS DIRECTORY: Make Usage

which offers you the choice of making a directory or of checking the disk usage of a directory.

Press the letter M

for *Make,* and XENIX will present you with one more choice:

    OPTIONS DIRECTORY MAKE directory: ▮

At this point, type:

California

and press Enter. XENIX will make the directory *California* for you and return you to the original command menu. Your screen will now look similar to the one on the following page.

```
 ┌─ /usr/danh ─────────────────────────────────────────────────╮
 │  [.]              [..]                  [California]          │
 │                                                              │
 │                                                              │
 │                                                              │
 │                                                              │
 │                                                              │
 │                                                              │
 │                                                              │
 │                                                              │
 │ .  ──────────────────────────────────── modified  4/09/1986 │
 │                                                              │
 │                                                              │
 │ COMMAND: Copy Delete Edit Help Mail Name                     │
 │          Options Print Quit Run View Window                  │
 │ Select option or type command letter                         │
 │ /usr/danh                          4/09/1986  08:57   XENIX  │
 ╰──────────────────────────────────────────────────────────────╯
```

     As long as you're starting to use the Visual shell commands, keep in mind that you can escape from any command procedure by pressing the Control and C keys simultaneously. Ctrl-C is a "bail-out" sequence that cancels whatever action you've initiated and moves you back to the top level of the command menu.

ADDING MORE DIRECTORIES

     Let's make two more subdirectories to cover the other clients. From the Bourne or C shell, type:

mkdir Boston New_York

     Here, you've taken advantage of XENIX' ability to deal with more than one element on a command line. Using a space as a delimiter (a character used to separate items in a list), you've made the directories *Boston* and *New_York* with just a single command.

     Now, you can also see why you cannot use a blank space in the name of a directory or a file. Because a space is recognized as a delimiter, typing *mkdir Boston New York* would have told XENIX to create three directories, *Boston, New,* and *York*. However, because XENIX will accept the underline character as part of a name, you were able to substitute an underline between the words *New* and *York* to create a valid directory name. You could also have used a period, to create a subdirectory named *New.York*.

     And finally, while we're on the subject, notice that each directory name begins with an uppercase letter. In Chapter 4, you'll see how this can help you distinguish between directory files and data or program files within the same subdirectory. For now, it's a handy tip to keep in mind.

FROM THE VISUAL SHELL

Because the Visual shell was designed as an easy-to-use interface between you and XENIX, it does not allow multiple entries on a single command line. If you're using this shell, step through the Options Directory Make procedure twice, once to create the subdirectory *Boston* and once to create the subdirectory *New_York*.

LISTING DIRECTORIES

If you're in the Visual shell, XENIX has displayed the results of each make-directory procedure as soon as you completed it. If you're in the Bourne or C shell, other than seeing the system prompt reappear twice, you've been given no hard evidence that anything at all has happened. Perhaps you're skeptical, or you're wondering whether you did everything correctly. If so, try another command:

   ls

to which XENIX will respond:

```
$ ls
Boston
California
New_York
$ _
```

That's the least you'll see. If there are any other files in your working directory, they'll be listed as well, because the *ls* command is XENIX' instruction to alphabetically list all files in the current directory. The results are your proof that you really did create the three subdirectories.

CHANGING DIRECTORIES

But creating and listing subdirectories is just the beginning. In our scenario, you're dealing with three types of information for each of your clients. To help you keep track of which is which, you'll again refine a directory, but this time you'll refine each of the client subdirectories you just created. From the Bourne or the C shell, type:

   cd California

which is the command to change directories.

The *cd* command, used with just the name of your directory and no other symbols, presumes that you want to move in a downward direction. It looks "below" the current directory for the one to which you've specified the change.

FROM THE VISUAL SHELL

Changing directories from within the Visual shell is very simple:

Press the letter V

to select the command menu's View option. The menu will change to reveal:

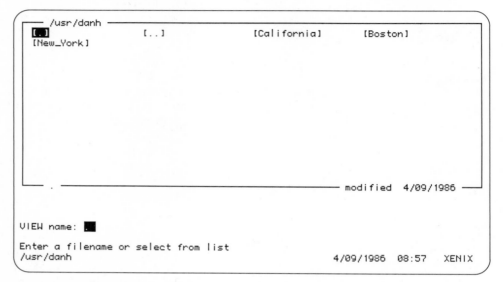

```
 ┌─── /usr/danh ────────────────────────────────────────────────────┐
 │  [.]              [..]            [California]      [Boston]       │
 │ [New_York]                                                        │
 │                                                                   │
 │                                                                   │
 │                                                                   │
 │                                                                   │
 │                                                                   │
 │                                                                   │
 │                                                                   │
 │    .  ─────────────────────────────────── modified  4/09/1986 ────│
 │                                                                   │
 │ VIEW name: ▊                                                      │
 │                                                                   │
 │ Enter a filename or select from list                              │
 │ /usr/danh                              4/09/1986  08:57   XENIX   │
 └───────────────────────────────────────────────────────────────────┘
```

Notice that XENIX displays a single period immediately after the colon. This period is XENIX' proposed (default) response to your View command, and corresponds to the period in brackets ([.]) at the top of your screen. The single period is XENIX' shorthand way of indicating your current (working) directory, and XENIX makes this proposal because:

■ You use the View command to look at data files as well as directories, and XENIX assumes that, in most cases, the file that you want to view is located in your working directory.

■ Proposing the working directory means that, if XENIX is correct, you need only press the Enter key to accept the choice—instead of having to type the name of the directory.

Right now, however, you don't want your working directory. Your immediate concern is to enter the name of the directory to which you want to change. You can do that in either of two ways. You can type:

California

and press the Enter key.

Or, you can select the directory name from the list at the top of your screen. On an IBM PC or compatible terminal:

Press the right arrow key twice to move the highlight to *California*.

If you have a non-IBM terminal, or you find that the arrow key does not work:

Hold down Ctrl and press the letter D twice to move the highlight.

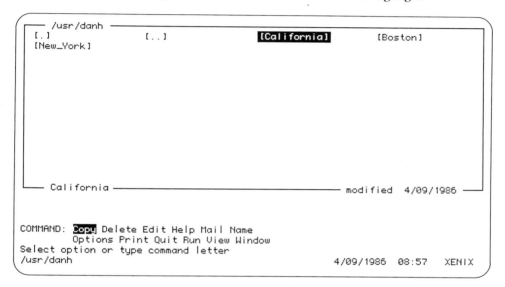

```
┌──── /usr/danh ─────────────────────────────────────────────────────┐
│  [.]                    [..]            [California]      [Boston]   │
│  [New_York]                                                         │
│                                                                     │
│                                                                     │
│                                                                     │
│                                                                     │
│                                                                     │
│                                                                     │
│  ──── California ──────────────────────────── modified  4/09/1986 ──│
│                                                                     │
│  COMMAND: Copy Delete Edit Help Mail Name                           │
│          Options Print Quit Run View Window                         │
│  Select option or type command letter                               │
│  /usr/danh                              4/09/1986  08:57   XENIX    │
└─────────────────────────────────────────────────────────────────────┘
```

39

After you type or select *California,* press Enter. The screen will clear, then reappear with your new working directory, such as */usr/danh/California,* displayed in the upper and lower lefthand corners.

MOVING THE HIGHLIGHT

As you just saw, if you have an IBM PC-compatible terminal, you can make selections by moving the highlight with the arrow keys. When you first enter the Visual shell, your working directory [.] is highlighted. When you choose a command like View from the menu line, XENIX assumes that you want the command to act upon whichever name is currently highlighted on your screen.

Press the right arrow key, and XENIX will move the highlight to the name immediately to the right. Press the left arrow key and XENIX will move the highlight left one name, while the up and down arrow keys will move the highlight to the row of names above and below the current row.

When you reach the end of a row, the right and left arrow keys also advance the highlight to, respectively, tɦe next or the preceding row. If you try to move the highlight beyond the top left or bottom rightmost name on the screen (for example, if you attempted to move the highlight to the left of [.]), XENIX would print the error message *Already at top* at the bottom of your screen and refuse the action.

If XENIX does not recognize the arrow keys on your terminal, you can use Control-key sequences instead, as described in our example. Hold the Control key down and press D to move right, S to move left, E to move up, and X to move down. These letter keys form what is called a diamond pattern:

40

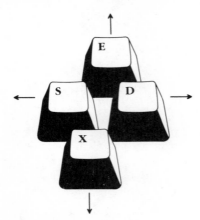

The relationship of each key to the others represents the direction in which it moves the highlight. In all other respects, using the Ctrl-letter key combinations is just like using the IBM PC arrow keys.

MAKING ADDITIONAL SUBDIRECTORIES

From any of XENIX' three shells, you're now ready to add some subdirectories to *California.* If you're in either the Bourne or the C shell, you can accomplish the additions from the *California* directory in one bold stroke by entering:

mkdir Memos Letters Accounts

Just as you created the *Boston* and *New_York* subdirectories at the same time, you've now created three new subdirectories, *Memos, Letters,* and *Accounts,* under *California.*

FROM THE VISUAL SHELL

From the Visual shell, create each subdirectory individually, using the method you did to create the *Boston* and *New_York* subdirectories.

A LOOK AT YOUR DIRECTORY STRUCTURE

Altogether now, you've created six subdirectories. If you consider what your directory system now looks like structurally, you can diagram it like this:

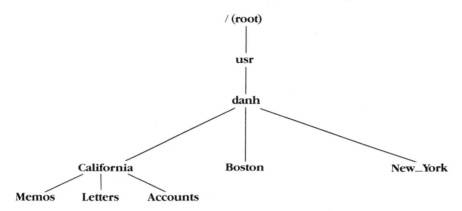

41

The full path name to *Memos,* for example, is: */usr/danh/California/Memos.*

MOVING ON THE SAME DIRECTORY LEVEL

Now, since you also have clients in Boston and New York, you need to move to *Boston* and then *New_York* and create for those clients the same subdirectories you just created under *California.* The command to change directories is *cd,* but neither *Boston* nor *New_York* is below *California.* They were both created on the same directory level as *California.* From where you are in your directory structure, you need to move sideways to enter either of them.

Although XENIX has no "sideways" directional indicator, it does have one that indicates upward movement through a directory system: the double dot (..), which stands for the directory directly above the current directory (often called the parent directory). If you combine the up (..) and down (/) movement indicators, you can reach your goal. To move to the *Boston* directory from the California directory in the Bourne or C shell, type:

cd ../Boston

Effectively, you've moved up one directory level (to *danh* in this example) and then down one level to *Boston.* The net effect has been to move sideways—your original intent.

You could, if you wanted, include a series of double dots and slashes to indicate a more extensive move. XENIX is very intuitive about your instructions, as long as you don't try to send it along an incomplete or incorrect path. But even in that case, an invalid directory path name would only produce the message *No such file or directory.*

FROM THE VISUAL SHELL

If you're in the Visual shell, you can change directories as follows:

Press the letter V

to select the View option. Then, type the same path name:

../Boston

as in the Bourne and C shells. The double-dot and slash commands have the same meanings in the Visual shell as they do in the others.

ABSOLUTE PATH NAMES

42

Even if you didn't know about the slash and double-dot "elevator operators," there is another way to make the same sideways move you just did, while still using a single command. It's:

cd /usr/danh/Boston

(Remember to substitute your equivalent of */usr/danh* in the path name. If you do this from the Visual shell, remember that you select the View option, then type the path name.)

In this instance, you've instructed XENIX to take you to the top of the directory structure and then follow the path name you've supplied to deposit you in the specified directory. With this method, you make an *absolute* reference to the path name, as opposed to a *relative* reference with the directional indicators.

Why use relative references when absolute references are available? Simplicity is the best answer. You're currently not very deep within your directory system (*Boston* is only one level below your home directory), so an absolute reference may not seem too imposing. But as you create more levels, or even if you start to use the full 14 characters available for each of the names you assign, typing the absolute reference, from the root directory through the destination directory, can become tedious.

VARYING THE PATH NAME

If you're in the Bourne or C shell, there's another way to lighten your work when you need to specify the entire path name for a XENIX command. XENIX stores the path name to your home directory (*not* necessarily your working directory) under a special name called $HOME. (The dollar sign is a part of the name, not a prompt symbol, and the name must be typed in uppercase letters.) $HOME exists for everyone who is on the system, but even though everyone can type *$HOME,* in each instance XENIX interprets $HOME to refer uniquely to that user's home directory.

Thus, whenever you need to use an absolute path name that includes a reference to your home directory, you can substitute *$HOME* for the name of your home directory. The path name */usr/danb/California,* for example, can also be typed as *$HOME/California.*

GOING HOME

While we're on the subject, from the Bourne or C shell you can also go straight to your home directory from anywhere in the XENIX directory system simply by typing the command:

cd

When *cd* is used by itself on a command line, XENIX presumes that what you actually mean is *cd $HOME.*)

COPYING DIRECTORY FILES

If you've been following along on your terminal, you're now in the *Boston* subdirectory. You can make new directories here for your three subtopics and then move on to *New_York* and do the same thing. But now that you've learned a few shortcuts, perhaps you're wondering if there's a quicker way. There is. If you're in the Bourne or the C shell (we'll cover the Visual shell in a moment), try something else. Type:

copy -r ../California .

(note the dot after *California*) and:

copy -r ../California ../New_York

These two commands, issued from within the *Boston* subdirectory, have actually done all of the work you wanted by copying the three *California* subdirectories to *Boston* and *New_York.* Let's see how it happened.

To begin with, XENIX gives you quite a few ways to copy files, among them the *copy* command, which can be used to copy groups of files from one directory to another, and to copy more than one directory at a time when it is typed in the following format:

copy -r [source] [destination]

The *-r* option tells XENIX to take all the directories in the source you specify and duplicate them in the destination you specify. The *r* stands for *recursive,* which, in this command, simply means, "repeat the copy procedure again and again until all directories have been copied."

The hyphen (-) is a lead-in character that is used with XENIX options. You can sometimes include more than one option in a single command. In those instances, the hyphen precedes only the first option in the series.

Notice that, since you were in the *Boston* subdirectory when you issued the commands, the path name you used (*../California*) for the source of the first procedure directed *copy* to go up one directory level (..) to your home directory and then down one level (/) to *California* to find what it was to copy. The single dot (.) at the end of the command line indicated the destination—your working directory (*/usr/danb/Boston*). And that's where *copy* duplicated what it found in *California*.

The second copy command duplicated the first until it reached the destination path name. Here, you sent *copy* to a different destination by telling it to go up one level (again, to your home directory), and then down one level into *New_York*.

FROM THE VISUAL SHELL

Copying directories is easier to do from the Visual shell than it is from either of the other two. To begin:

Press the letter C

to select the Copy command. When XENIX asks whether you wish to copy files or directories:

Press the letter D

for *Directory*. XENIX will respond with the following:

```
COPY DIRECTORY from:█                    to:
                    recursive:   Yes(No)
Enter new path
```

Since you're in the *Boston* subdirectory, XENIX will not be displaying the contents of your other directories, so you will not be able to use the arrow keys to select your *from:* choice. Type:

../California

to indicate the path Copy must follow to reach the source directory. Next:

Press the Tab key

to move into the *to:* field. Type a period there to indicate the current directory as the destination. Then:

Press Tab once more.

You'll find yourself on the next line, where you are asked to specify *Yes* or *No* to a *recursive:* prompt. XENIX has highlighted *No,* guessing that you will want its default choice. You don't. You want to copy all the *California* subdirectories, so:

Press the letter Y (or the Spacebar)

signifying *Yes* for *recursive:*. This is the same as adding the *copy* command's *-r* option under the Bourne or C shell. Now:

Press the Enter key.

In a few seconds, the normal command menu will reappear and you'll see the directories *Memos, Letters,* and *Accounts* listed at the top of your screen.

You can use the same procedure to copy those directories into *New_York* while you're still in *Boston.* The only difference will occur when you reach the *to:* field. Be sure to type the path name *../New_York* to indicate the desired destination directory.

CREATING A DIRECTORY WHILE COPYING

Suppose you had not already created the subdirectories *Boston* and *New_York* before you used the copy procedure. Suppose you had only created *California* and its three subdirectories. Because you wanted to duplicate the contents of *California* exactly, you wouldn't have needed to create the other directories before you began the copy. Instead, from your home directory, you could have used the command forms:

copy -r California Boston

and

copy -r California New_York

which would first create the subdirectories *Boston* and *New_York* and then copy the contents of the *California* subdirectory into them. (The same technique will work with the Copy command in the Visual shell, as long as you remember to respond *Yes* to the recursion prompt.)

USING WILD CARDS

You've already used the *ls* command to list the contents of a single directory. You can also use *ls* to display the contents of several directories without having to retype the command for each new directory name—if you can find something that all the names have in common.

Look at the subdirectories that you've created so far: *California, Boston,* and *New_York.* They all contain the letter *o.* If you were in your home directory, you could type:

ls *o*

and XENIX would respond with:

```
$ ls *o*

Boston:
Accounts
Letters
Memos

California:
Accounts
Letters
Memos

New_York:
Accounts
Letters
Memos
$ _
```

Each of the asterisks in this example is a *wildcard* character. If you're a poker player you already know that a wild card is a particular card that can be used to represent any other in the deck. In XENIX, a wildcard character is much the same thing: a special character that you can use to represent all other characters. A wildcard character thus offers you a way to make relative references to file names. It's a way of specifying a range of file names (or only one if just a single file matches the criteria) even if you don't know the actual names. As such, it permits relative references on the *file name* level. XENIX supports two wildcard characters: the asterisk and the question mark. You may also see them referred to as *metacharacters,* which is derived from the Greek word *meta* meaning among, with, after, or (most appropriately in this instance) change.

THE ASTERISK

In our preceding example, we used the asterisk. Within the context of what we did, we told XENIX to list the contents of any directory it found that had an *o* in its name, *no matter what or how many* characters preceded or followed that *o.*

Literally, any directory name that met the criterion was acceptable. When XENIX looked at the directories beneath /usr/danb, it found that *Boston, California,* and *New_York* matched our criterion, and so it listed their contents.

XENIX would not, however, have performed in the same manner if we had used either:

ls *o

or:

ls o*

For the former condition (ls *o), only those directories *ending* in *o* would satisfy the criterion. For the latter (ls o*), XENIX would consider only those directory names *beginning* with an *o*. And none of our directories meet either of those two conditions.

THE QUESTION MARK

Unlike the asterisk, which can be used to represent more than one character, the question mark is the substitute for any *single* character within a file's name. Because it can take the place of only one character, there is no way to use the question mark to produce the same results we got with the asterisk. If, for example, you told XENIX:

ls Cal?fornia

it would list the contents of the *California* subdirectory and no others. (Although, if you happened to have additional directories named *Calofornia, Calafornia,* and *CalLfornia,* their contents would be listed by this command, because they do conform to your criterion, which says that the fourth letter of the file name can be any character.) Likewise, *???_York* would match *New_York, Old_York,* or any other directory name beginning with any three letters, whether upper- or lowercase, as long as the name ended in *_York*.

Wild cards will play an important role in file handling. Like a book of matches, they can be both very helpful and very dangerous if not used with the proper care. Sometimes you might find (too late) that a file matching your wildcard criteria wasn't quite the one you wanted to move, copy, or delete. When we look at them again in the next chapter, you'll see more of both the asterisk and the question mark, as well as some enhancements and safeguards you can use to refine their search capabilities.

47

LOOKING AT DIRECTORIES

The *ls* command is very versatile. Like several other XENIX commands, it has a group of options that can be included when you use it. For instance, typing:

ls -l California

would again produce a complete listing of the files in your *California* directory. The same subdirectories would be listed, but this time the list would look a little different:

```
$ ls -l California
total 6
drwxr-xr-x   2 danh       group        32 Apr 13 21:21 Accounts
drwxr-xr-x   2 danh       group        32 Apr 13 21:21 Letters
drwxr-xr-x   2 danh       group        32 Apr 13 21:21 Memos
$ _
```

The *-l* (for long) option produces an expanded list containing additional information about your files. Though the list may look cryptic at first glance, it's easily deciphered. Each line actually contains seven fields of information, and those fields tell almost everything you need to know about each file.

The first field, *drwxr-xr-x* in our example, is the one most likely to seem "difficult," so let's go over it in detail. This field is composed of a group of ten characters—one initial character, and three groups of three characters each. (Even though, in our example, the hyphens between characters may look as though they break the field into three groups, *drwxr, xr,* and *x,* in actuality the groups are *d, rwx, r-x,* and *r-x.* The hyphens here are not dividers; they have other meanings of their own.)

The first of the ten characters indicates the type of file you have. In this case, the character is a *d,* denoting a directory file. If the file were a data file, the initial character would be a hyphen. If the file were what XENIX refers to as a device-type file, the initial character in this group would be a *b* or a *c.*

The remaining nine characters in this field define the *access permissions* to the file. Each group of three tells you what can be done with the file, and by whom. There are three possible permission indicators for each of the groups. In order, they are: *r,* for read, *w,* for write, and *x,* for execute. If any of these privileges is denied, the position the letter would otherwise occupy is held by a hyphen, as in our example.

These are the people indicated by each group of three:

■ The first three characters refer to the owner of the file: you, if you're the person who created it.

■ The next three characters refer to the group: a predefined selection of individuals who have been identified as a group to XENIX. Perhaps the group would consist of people working on the same projects you are, and who have access to your directory. You were assigned a group by the system administrator when your user account was added to the system.

■ The final three characters refer to the public: any other people who are also on the system but who haven't been specifically granted access to your directory area.

Thus, as you can see in the following diagram, the file's owner can read, write, or execute it (*rwx*). But both the group to which that person has been assigned and the public in general can only read and execute (*r-x*) the file. The hyphens you see in both the group and public access fields indicate that these users can't write to (change) those directories.

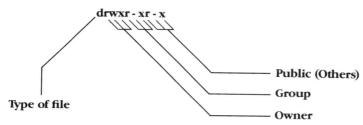

The second field in our long listing, the number *2*, indicates the number of links there are to this file. Linking is an incredible XENIX feature that deserves more than one paragraph of explanation, so it has its own section in the next chapter. For now suffice it to say that links are connections between and among files; all files have at least one link, while all directory files have at least two. The line *total 6* in the example tells you how many links there are in all to the current directory.

Field three, *danh* in the example, is the owner's name. That's followed by field four, the name of the group to which the person belongs; field five, the size of the file in bytes (roughly, characters); field six, the date and time the file was created or last modified; and finally, field seven, the file's name.

XENIX stores even more information than you just saw. We can also combine list options to realign or expand what we see. For example, try typing:

ls -lr California

to which XENIX replies:

```
$ ls -lr California
total 6
drwxr-xr-x   2 danh       group        32 Apr 13 21:21 Memos
drwxr-xr-x   2 danh       group        32 Apr 13 21:21 Letters
drwxr-xr-x   2 danh       group        32 Apr 13 21:21 Accounts
$ _
```

50

Here we have joined the *l* (long) and *r* (reverse) options to produce a new response. This time the contents of the *California* directory are completely listed in reverse alphabetic order. Note that a single hyphen precedes the two options, and that they are *not* separated by a space or any other character.

RENAMING AND DELETING DIRECTORIES

Often, you'll find you have files that are no longer current. For instance, suppose your Boston client was replaced by one from Cleveland. The *Boston* directory (and any files it might contain) would no longer be active. You might need it at some future time for reference, but right now *Boston* would only serve to clutter the directory system. Then again, even if you maintain the same client base, data files themselves can become outdated—inactive, yet still needed.

The ideal solution is to save these files somewhere out of the way, perhaps with others of their kind. In the paper-and-file-folder world, such storage is called archiving. In the XENIX world, you have the same capability. To that end, even though you've already created quite a directory system for your first exercise in using XENIX commands, let's add one more directory to it.

If you're not already in it, return to your home directory (from the Bourne or C shell, type *cd*; from the Visual shell, select the View command and then type ..). Now, create the new directory, deliberately typing *Archeve*, rather than *Archive*.

From the Bourne or C shell, type:

mkdir Archeve

From the Visual shell, choose the Options Directory Make command and type:

Archeve

Now, change directories to *Archeve*. From the Bourne or C shell, type:

cd Archeve

From the Visual shell, choose View and type:

Archeve

Now, under *Archeve,* create three additional directories. From the Bourne or the C shell, type:

mkdir California Boston New_York

From the Visual shell, choose Options Directory Make, and create each of the new directories separately.

These new directories will hold the archived material from the individual clients. You're done, so return to your home directory as you did earlier. But wait. You've made an error and misspelled *Archive.* Let's remove it and start again.

From your home directory use the XENIX command *rmdir* (remove directory) in the Bourne or C shell by typing:

rmdir Archeve

Surprisingly, XENIX replies with:

51

```
$ rmdir Archeve
rmdir: Archeve not empty
$ _
```

Archeve, mistake though it is, is not an empty directory and XENIX therefore will not remove it (although it will be removed in the Visual shell). We complicated the situation by creating *California, Boston,* and *New_York* under *Archeve.* It doesn't matter that they, like *Archeve,* contain no information. As soon as XENIX finds any files or subdirectories in a directory, it puts a stop to an *rmdir* operation. This automatic braking is a valuable fail-safe device, though, as you can see now, it can be somewhat frustrating.

You could erase the three individual directories and then go back and remove *Archeve.* But that's a roundabout approach. Instead, depending on the shell you are in, try one of the following two approaches (the command names are different, because the Visual shell is not directly equivalent to the other two, but the result will be the same).

THE *mv* COMMAND

From the Bourne or C shell, use the XENIX move command. Type:

mv Archeve Archive

You've already seen *copy.* This is its complement. Ordinarily, you use *mv* to relocate a file, putting it in some other portion of the directory (or in another directory entirely), but in this case, we are applying the command to an entire directory, including all the directories under it. Moving does *not* create a new copy of the file; rather, it transfers what already exists, leaving nothing behind. Like *copy, mv* must be balanced: It needs both a source and a destination.

If you look at our example, you can see that you indicated a brand-new directory name as the destination. Since you did not move *Archeve* to an already existing directory, you did not alter the file's location in your directory structure, and the net effect of the *mv* command was simply to change the directory's name. Unlike *rmdir, mv* can be used whether or not a directory is empty.

THE Name COMMAND

If you are using the Visual shell and have read the preceding instructions on using the *mv* command, you may be thinking that your command menu does not offer a choice named Move, Transfer, Shift, or anything similar. Well, actually it does, but the connection is not immediately apparent. Your means of renaming *Archeve* in the Visual shell is the Name command.

Like the Bourne and C shells' *mv* command, Name:

■ Can be used on either data files or directories.

■ Can be used with a directory, whether or not the directory is empty.

■ Requires a source (which XENIX requests with the prompt *from:*) and a destination (which XENIX requests with *to:*).

You can use this command to give a new name to an existing file (or directory) or, by specifying a different path name, you can use the Name command to "move" a file to another directory (remember, files are not physically located in directories, so by changing the path to a file you effectively change the directory it is located in).

To try it out, choose Name from the command menu. When XENIX prompts *from:* and *to:,* type:

Archeve

as the source and:

Archive

as the destination.

That's all there is to it. You've corrected your typographical error by renaming *Archeve* and, as in the case of using *mv,* you've removed the problem with a single command.

ORCHESTRATING DIRECTORIES

You may or may not have created the directories outlined in this chapter. Except for the purpose of following along and gaining experience using XENIX, that's relatively unimportant (although we'll be using the file structure we've created in the next chapter too). What is important is that you can now see through the exercises to the concepts underlying what we have done.

On the theoretical level, you've taken your first steps toward understanding XENIX—not only what it does, but why. Rather than simply creating subdirectories and guessing at how they are related, you've been able to follow XENIX into and among subdirectories that reflect the logic of your own needs. Perhaps you are beginning to appreciate XENIX' directory system as a flexible tool that, once you are comfortable with it, will enable you to keep a file system as accessible and as orderly as any you've kept in drawers or cabinets.

On a more practical level, notice that the names we've used have been chosen with one goal in mind: simplicity. We've kept names as short as possible, while making them as descriptive as need be. There's no glory in being the grand architect of a directory path whose name requires more time to remember than you would otherwise spend just picking through a long list in a linear system. Don't overextend yourself by creating subdirectories when none are really needed. And when they are required, make each one a logical branch from the one above it.

53

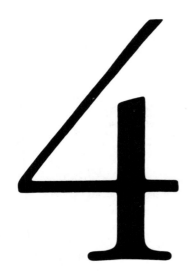

DATA FILES   You've created a directory system, but it's still empty. At the moment, it is much like a file drawer neatly divided into categories. Now, you can begin to add to your directories, filing information wherever it's most useful to you. So, it's time to move on to another file type, the data file. Before you can store a data file in a directory or anywhere else, however, you must have one to store. You'll create your own in this chapter with the XENIX line editor, *ed,* and learn some powerful commands that you can use with all data files.

A SHORT DETOUR

If you're unfamiliar with editors, or have never used one, let's take a quick look at *ed* and some of its relatives, to set the stage for your work in this chapter.

Almost every operating system has a text editor similar to *ed.* MS-DOS has Edlin; the CP/M operating system also has one called Ed. All of them let you enter text from the keyboard, but they have no inherent formatting ability for setting margins, page length, and the like—as compared with a word processor, which does all that and more.

Typically, these editors are designed to give programmers a quick and dirty means of entering and correcting program lines. As such, they work. But they're not meant for prolonged typing activity. XENIX' Visual Editor, *vi,* is better at that, and we'll be looking at it in the next chapter. But for some quick work of our own, of the kind we'll be doing in this chapter, *ed* is just fine.

Actually, two line editors are included with your XENIX system. One is *ex,* the other is a subset of *ex, ed.* For the few things that you'll be doing with either of them in this book, you won't find any major differences between the two.

CREATING TEXT WITH *ed*

◪ NOTE: *This chapter assumes that you have the subdirectory structure we created in Chapter 3. If this is not so, and you wish to try the following exercises, first create the directories* Boston, California, *and* New_York *from your home directory and in each one create the subdirectories* Memos, Letters, *and* Accounts.

If you haven't already done so, log into the system, move to your home directory, and make sure the Bourne shell prompt ($) is displayed on your screen. Type:

ed

After *ed* is loaded into the computer's memory, you can begin using *ed* commands.

You want to enter text, so type:

a

and press the Enter key. The *a* is the *ed* command to enter insert mode and append new text to whatever you've already typed. As you haven't yet typed anything, it becomes your way of starting out fresh.

The only immediate reaction at this point is that your terminal's cursor advances to the next line on the screen. The line is blank, but everything you type from this point on will be entered into *ed*.

Now, type the following line:

This is the first data file I've created with ed.

and press the Enter key. The cursor moves to the next line. On this line, type a period and press Enter again. The period is a special symbol to *ed*. When you type it as the first character on a line of its own, *ed* understands that you are through inserting and now want to stop. You've now returned to *ed*'s command mode, so the characters you enter next will be interpreted as instructions concerning the text that you have inserted.

A data file need not be large. If you wish, it can be as small as a single character. This particular data file will contain only that one line you typed. Now, you want to save the file, so type:

w California/Memos/memo1

This command tells *ed* to write the text to disk, using the path *California/ Memos,* and to place the text in a data file called *memo1,* which *ed* will automatically create for the occasion. *Ed* responds by printing the number *50* on your screen (it's telling you the number of characters it has written to disk) and then returns to its command prompt.

Notice that you didn't begin the path name with a slash. Omitting the slash is a cue to XENIX to look for the *California* subdirectory immediately below the one in which you're working. (The opening slash is only needed when it precedes an absolute path name.)

Also, notice that you began the file's name with a lowercase character, rather than a capital letter as you did in naming your subdirectories. We'll cover the rationale behind that decision very shortly. First, however, let's see how to go about making alterations to a data file.

EDITING YOUR FILE

Editing with *ed* can be done by means of text substitution. Let's change some of the text in our document. You haven't left *ed* yet, so type:

s/first/second

and press Enter. The *s* portion of this command instructs *ed* to make a substitution within the text.

57

Ordinarily, if your document contained more than one line, you'd also need to specify the line number in which you wanted the change to occur. You would do that by typing the number of the line just before the *s*. Thus, *1s* would indicate the first line, *5s* the fifth line, and so on. Used without a line number, *s* tells *ed* to make the substitution in the current line (usually the last one you worked on). You can omit the line number here because the document contains only one line.

Within the context of *ed*'s editing features, the slashes you typed are delimiters separating the two command parameters. The first parameter tells *ed* what to change (*first* in our example). The second parameter (*second* in our example) is the word that is to be substituted. *Ed* responds by redisplaying the line, with the substitution it has made:

```
$ ed
a
This is the first data file I've created with ed.
.
w California/Memos/memo1
50
s/first/second
This is the second data file I've created with ed.
_
```

Save this new version to disk by typing:

w California/Memos/memo2

Now, create a third data file. Change your document's contents again with:

s/second/third

and save it once more:

w California/Memos/memo3

Next, make a data file that's a combination of the three you've just completed. Type the following two commands:

r California/Memos/memo2

r California/Memos/memo1

You've told *ed* to read in the contents of *memo1* and *memo2* and append them to the end of the document on which you're working (the append is automatic when you have existing text and tell *ed* to read in the contents of another file).

Finally, use the append command again to add one more line to the document. Type the following (note the period on the third line):

a
These are the data files I've created with ed.
.

DISPLAYING YOUR FILE

You can look at this new document by typing:

1,$p

The *p* tells *ed* to print text to the screen. When you use this command, you also need to tell it which lines of your document you want it to print. Your document is still short, with only four lines you want to print. You could also use the command *1,4p* to print this document because you know how many lines it contains. But there may come a time when you're working with a long file of unknown length. There are two ways to deal with that.

One way is to take the shortcut you used in the example. Here, you included an *ed* wild card, the dollar sign (*$*), which tells *ed* to print all lines of the file, from first (*1,*) to last (*$*). This is what you see:

```
1,$p
This is the third data file I've created with ed.
This is the second data file I've created with ed.
This is the first data file I've created with ed.
These are the data files I've created with ed.
-
```

These are the only four data files you'll be using for awhile, so you can save this last one under the name *final* by typing:

w California/Memos/final

We're finished for now, so exit *ed* by typing *q* (for quit). Your shell prompt will soon reappear.

COPYING DATA FILES

Now that you have created and saved your data files, you can reassure yourself that everything has worked correctly by listing the contents of your *Memos* subdirectory. Type:

ls California/Memos

XENIX will respond with:

```
$ ls California/Memos
final
memo1
memo2
memo3
$ _
```

Once you've assured yourself that everything's where it belongs, you can now copy those files into any other directory. As you saw in the last chapter, you can do that with XENIX' *copy* command. For example, you could type the command *copy California/Memos Boston/Memos,* which would cause all four files to be duplicated in the *Boston/Memos* directory.

But what if you wanted to copy only *memo1*? Since the *copy* command affects all files in a directory, you can use an alternative command, *cp,* to duplicate selected files. Thus, you would type *cp California/Memos/memo1 Boston/Memos* to copy *memo1* into the *Boston/Memos* directory.

Cp AND WILD CARDS

And what if you wanted to copy the three files with *memo* in their names? Rather than typing the command three times to duplicate each of the three memo files, you could use wild cards, as you did with directory names in the last chapter.

For example, you could use the asterisk, in which case your command might look like this: *cp California/Memos/memo* Boston/Memos.* This instruction tells XENIX to look in the *California/Memos* subdirectory, select all files that begin with the word *memo,* and copy them into the *Boston/Memos* subdirectory.

You could also specify the same files as *California/Memos/m*.* In either case, because you have a limited number of files, your memo files would be the only ones that matched your criteria. In a directory containing more files, however, either *memo*∗* or *m*∗* might cause problems:

■ Since *memo*∗* would specify all files beginning with *memo,* using that designation in an extensive collection of files might include files with such names as *memory_info* or *memo123,* as well as those you actually wanted to copy.

■ Since *m*∗* would specify all files beginning with the lowercase letter *m,* using that designation in a large collection of files would apply to any file beginning with *m* in that subdirectory.

As you can see, the wide-ranging coverage afforded by the asterisk wild card can be more than you need. To limit the scope of your command, you can use the question mark (?) wild card, just as you can with directories. Copying only the files that begin with *memo* and have one additional character in their names becomes a matter of using the command *cp California/Memos/memo? Boston/Memos.*

Unlike the asterisk, the question mark is the wildcard symbol for a single character, so keep in mind that the file specification *memo?* will work only with file names that are five characters long, and in which the fifth character is unspecified (the question mark is holding that fifth position). Thus, if your file names were *memo00, memo01,* and *memo03,* you would need to use *memo??* or (if you had less than ten *memo* files) *memo0?* as the specification.

61

SPECIFYING RANGES

But what if you wanted to copy two of the files, *memo1* and *memo2?* By themselves, the wild cards will handle any name that matches the criteria you use them to specify. But in this instance, you now want to copy only two out of three files that match any combination of characters and wild cards you could use.

XENIX gives you a way to refine wildcard usage. You can specify a range of wildcard values to which XENIX will respond. Thus, to copy just the files *memo1* and *memo2,* you can type:

cp California/Memos/memo[1-2] Boston/Memos

The values enclosed in the brackets ([ ]) comprise a literal wild card that tells XENIX to consider files only if their names begin with the word *memo* and their fifth character falls in the range of numbers between 1 and 2, inclusive. The hyphen indicates the range; in our example, it is the same as if you had typed *[12].*

That range tells you something else that's important: XENIX examines each character within the brackets individually, rather than as part of a group of characters. If you had wanted to copy just *memo1* and *memo3,* the correct command syntax would have been *cp California/Memos/memo[13] Boston/Memos,* to match any five-character file name beginning with *memo* and having either a 1 or a 3 as the fifth file-name character.

It's also possible to specify a range of letters, rather than numbers. For example, suppose you file employee salary records alphabetically by the first letter of the individual's last name. If your files all begin with *salary_,* you can refer to the files for employees A through M with the file specification *salary_[A-M].* Or, you can call the files for employees A through D with the file specification *salary_[ABCD].*

PREFERENTIAL TREATMENT

When you specify ranges, however, you must also remember that there's an order of preference to them. Recall that XENIX differentiates between upper- and lowercase. Thus, although you might consider *A* and *a* to be equivalent, XENIX does not. The reason for this is that XENIX translates characters into code numbers that follow a standardized system known as ASCII. In ASCII, the digits 0 through 9, certain punctuation marks, and the upper- and lowercase letters of the alphabet are assigned the code numbers 48 through 122. Zero through 9 are at the low end of this range, capital A through Z come next, and lowercase a through z are at the high end of the range.

It is not necessary for you to become familiar with ASCII—these code numbers remain invisible to you. If you are going to specify ranges, however, you do need to bear in mind that, for example, the character range 0-Z includes all numbers and uppercase letters, but no lowercase letters. Similarly, the range A-z includes all upper- and lowercase letters, but no numbers. And 0-z includes all numbers, all uppercase letters, and all lowercase ones, too.

USING WILD CARDS TO DISTINGUISH FILES

In Chapter 3 we used the convention of beginning directory-file names with uppercase characters. In this chapter, we've used lowercase characters to begin data-file names. Now that you've had a chance to see how you can use ranges, you're in a position to take advantage of that distinction.

Let's look at what you've created so far. You have three subdirectories, *Memos, Letters,* and *Accounts,* in your *California* directory. As time goes on, you will probably have more subdirectories of your own, and related data files as well. What if you want a listing of only the data files in *California*? The *ls* command ordinarily lists directories and data files both—or it does if you don't take advantage of XENIX' range specifications and sensitivity to case. If you've begun all directory names with uppercase letters and all data files with lowercase letters, you can type:

    ls [a-z]*

and XENIX will interpret your command as an instruction to list all file names that begin with lowercase letters (the [a-z] portion). Likewise, if you wanted to see just the names of the directories, you could enter the command:

    ls [A-Z]*

which would be interpreted as "list all file names that begin with uppercase letters." And since you organized your system so that only directory names begin with uppercase letters, those are the only names XENIX would list.

PREVIEWING A COMMAND WITH *echo*

If you're not quite sure what a specific wild card might do when you use it, or if you'd just like to know what the results of a command will be *before* you actually try it, you can use the XENIX *echo* command. If, for example, you wanted to copy all data files from your *California/Memos* directory to the *California/Accounts* directory, you could preview the results of that command by typing *echo cp California/Memos/m* California/Accounts*. XENIX would print (echo) to the screen all of the file names that match your criteria, but without really copying them.

```
$ echo cp California/Memos/m* California/Accounts
cp California/Memos/memo1 California/Memos/memo2 California/Memos/memo3 Californ
ia/Accounts
$ _
```

Reading through that screen list would let you determine whether your wild-card criteria will do the job, or whether you need to broaden or narrow their scope to achieve the results you want. (Specifying *m* would work well for copying the examples in this book, but you may find that using such a wide-ranging wild-card specification might very well remind you of a few forgotten *m* files—perhaps *my_notes*, or *meetings, miscellany, musings,* and *museums.* If you think this might happen, it's a good idea to use *echo* first.)

COPYING A FILE TO ITSELF

For users of all shells, one procedural note is in order here: XENIX does not allow two identically named files to exist in the same directory, nor does it allow you to copy an existing file onto itself. This means you cannot copy a file from and to its source directory unless the source and destination file names are different. For example, typing:

cp California/Memos/memo1 California/Memos/memo1

will not work because you are trying to copy the file onto itself. Similarly, typing:

cp California/Memos/memo1 California/Memos

will not work. But:

cp California/Memos/memo1 California/Memos/memo4

will work, because the destination file name differs from the source file name. In this case, however, if you specify a destination file name that already exists in the directory, XENIX will overwrite (destroy and replace) the contents of the existing file with the incoming data.

MOVING DATA FILES

If you've followed along with the practice session in this chapter, your *California* directory currently contains four data files:

■ *memo1*

■ *memo2*

■ *memo3*

■ *final*

and your *Boston* subdirectory contains two data files:

■ *memo1*

■ *memo2*

In the last chapter you saw how you can use XENIX' *mv* command to change a file name (in that example, it was a directory file, *Archeve*). Now, we'll use the same command to move files between two directories. To do that, type:

mv California/Memos/final Boston/Memos

Here, you can see the other way *mv* functions. Using the command as you've just done preserves the file name, *final,* but moves the file you specify from one directory, *California/Memos,* to another, *Boston/Memos.*

To see the result for yourself, take advantage of your ability to give XENIX more than one command parameter on a single command line. Enter:

lc California/Memos Boston/Memos

XENIX replies with:

```
$ lc California/Memos Boston/Memos

Boston/Memos:
final   memo1   memo2

California/Memos:
memo1   memo2   memo3
$ _
```

As we planned, *final* has, indeed, been placed in *Boston/Memos.* (Note that this time we used *lc,* a variation of *ls,* to list the contents of the directories in column format. Using wild cards, we could also have typed one of the following variations:

lc Cal*/M* Bos*/M*

lc [BC]*/Memos

lc [BC]*/M*

Which you choose depends on the amount of control you want over the arguments to the command).

CREATING DATA FILES AT THE KEYBOARD

You've used *ed* to create your practice files, but there are times when using a text editor to create just a small data file is impractical. You might, perhaps, just want to leave yourself a note or a reminder about something. The simplest way to create such a file is with XENIX' *cat* command. The word *cat* is short for concatenate, meaning join, but that definition covers a wider range of activities than you might at first suspect.

To see how *cat* works, create a note to yourself. Type:

cat ⟩ itinerary

Literally, this command tells XENIX to join "something" to the file that you named *itinerary* (the file name could be one of your own choosing, of course). The greater-than symbol (⟩) instructs XENIX to either create a new file named *itinerary* or, if it already exists, to erase and re-create it.

But with regard to this particular form of the *cat* command, what you've left out of the command line is as important as what you've included: You haven't specified the "something" you want joined. Because you haven't, XENIX will now consider "something" to be whatever you type at the keyboard, and will join that input to *itinerary*. Notice also that your shell prompt did not reappear. The line with the cursor on it remains blank, as XENIX and *cat* wait for you to do your typing. Try typing the following text, pressing the Enter key at the end of each line, just as if you were using the carriage return on a typewriter:

June 2
United Airlines Flight #2622
Leave Seattle/Tacoma 7:00am
Arrive Sun Valley 10:45am

After you press Enter at the end of the last line, press the Ctrl-D key combination. Ctrl-D ends the command sequence and returns you to your normal shell prompt. If your system doesn't respond immediately, wait. As you know, Ctrl-D is also the key combination XENIX understands as your request to log out. The *cat* command will trap the first occurrence of Ctrl-D as its own signal to end, but a second occurrence will log you out of the system (if you're in your home shell) and you might need to log in again.

65

DISPLAYING DATA FILES

In addition to creating data files with *cat,* you can also use this command to view them. For example, view the file you just created by entering the command:

cat itinerary

That prints on your screen:

```
$ cat itinerary
June 2
United Airlines Flight #2622
Leave Seattle/Tacoma 7:00am
Arrive Sun Valley 10:45am
$ _
```

which is exactly what you entered.

Another good way to view the contents of a file, especially a long one, is to use the *more* command. *More* displays the contents of a file one full screen (24 lines) at a time. To use the *more* command to view the itinerary file you just created, enter:

more itinerary

The result is identical to the output of the *cat* command.

If your file is longer than one complete screen, you can press the Enter key to advance the screen line by line and press the Spacebar to advance one screen of text at a time. To escape from the *more* command, press the Delete key.

BINARY FILES

Regardless of which shell you use, you should know in advance that not all files can be displayed on your screen. The examples we've used are data files that have been stored in "text" format: The information is placed on disk exactly as you entered it.

There is another form of data file called a "binary" file in which information is stored in a special format. Rather than keeping each word or character as it's entered, XENIX translates them into special symbols, some of which indicate a single character, others an entire word.

Usually these binary files are program files. If you were to try to display a binary file, most likely all you would see would be a peculiar-looking, scattered assortment of random characters—whichever ones your terminal is capable of displaying—often accompanied by insistent bell tones.

66

Aside from being somewhat unnerving, there's usually no harm done by trying to display a binary file. Some terminals may act strange afterward, however, displaying characters in reverse video or perhaps changing the size or line length of the display. At worst, a terminal may lock up, preventing anyone from using it. If that should happen to you, consult your system administrator. Simply turning the device off and then back on again will usually clear the condition, but check with the administrator, just to be sure.

ADDING TO A DATA FILE

Now, suppose you suddenly realize your *itinerary* file is incomplete. You forgot to include some necessary information in your reminder. The remedy is simple; try this. Enter the command:

cat ⟩⟩ itinerary

followed by:

Don't forget the sales projections.

and press Ctrl-D to return to the shell prompt.

There is one difference between this form of the *cat* command and the way you used it to create your original *itinerary* file: This time, you used two greater-than symbols.

Rather than creating a new data file named *itinerary* (overwriting the one that already exists), the double greater-than symbols instructed XENIX to append text to the end of the existing file. You can verify that XENIX has done so by typing:

cat itinerary

JOINING TWO DATA FILES

Just as you can add to an existing file, you can use a similar technique to join two data files. Type:

cat Boston/Memos/final ⟩⟩ itinerary

This command tells XENIX to add a copy of the file named *final* to the end of *itinerary* (the "original" remains in your *Boston/Memos* subdirectory).

If you had used a single greater-than symbol in this command, XENIX would have erased the original *itinerary* file and replaced it with a new *itinerary* that was identical to *final*. As when you added a line to *itinerary*, if you told XENIX to add the contents of *final* to a file named *itinerary* that didn't actually exist yet, XENIX would create the file and then copy the contents of *final* into it.

JOINING SEVERAL DATA FILES

The *cat* command doesn't limit you to joining only two files. Suppose you have a number of files you want to join—perhaps all the memos relating to a particular contract or a particular client. Let's use your *memo* files to see how you can join them with one command.

First, type:

cd California/Memos

to move down to the *Memos* subdirectory. Then, type:

cat memo1 memo2 memo3 ⟩ big_file

to create a file called *big_file* in *California/Memos* and fill it with the contents of *memo1, memo2,* and *memo3*. As in all other cases, the source files are not disturbed. Their contents are read and added to the file you've specified.

Note that, for purposes of illustration, you typed the name of each *memo* file. You could also have used wild cards in the command, by typing the command in the form *cat memo? ⟩ big_file* or *cat m* ⟩ big_file*. Likewise, instead of changing directories, you could have used both path names and wild cards, typing something like *cat California/Memos/memo? ⟩ California/Memos/big_file* while still in your home directory. In any instance in which you decide to use wild cards, be certain that you know which files you are concatenating. If you are uncertain, always use the *echo* command first.

VIEWING LONG FILES

In using *cat* to join several data files, we've arrived at an ideal place to consider a situation that may have occurred to you. So far, all the data files you've been working with have been short. But what if they weren't? What if you had a text file that, alone or after it was joined with others, was 40 or 50 lines long, or even longer? How would you go about viewing it all? Your terminal can probably display at most 25 lines at a time.

One way we've already mentioned is the *more* command, which allows you to view one full screen at a time. XENIX, however, offers two additional commands, *head* and *tail,* to help you view long files. Suppose you want to see only the first three lines of your *big_file* file. Type:

head -3 big_file

and XENIX displays only the lines you want displayed. In contrast, type:

tail -2 big_file

and XENIX will show you the last two lines of the file.

You can use any number with either *head* or *tail*. With either command, if you don't specify a number, XENIX displays 10 lines. Conversely, if you specify a number greater than the number of lines in the file, XENIX will simply print the entire file. It is important to remember, however, that in both *head* and *tail,* the number you specify is considered a command option. As with all of the XENIX command options you've seen so far, the number must be preceded by a hyphen.

REMOVING FILES

Unless you like owning large quantities of redundant data, knowing how to create and duplicate files makes it quite important to know how to remove them as well. When we worked with directories in the last chapter, you tried to use the *rmdir* command to remove your purposely misspelled *Archeve* directory file. The complementary command for data files is *rm*. You can apply this command directly to a file, as in *rm California/Memos/memo1,* or you can apply it indirectly by using wild cards to establish criteria for the files you want to remove—for example, *rm California/Memos/memo?* (as we've mentioned before, you must take special care when doing this).

For example, to use the *rm* command to remove the *memo1* file from your *California/Memos* subdirectory, type:

rm California/Memos/memo1

One very important point to remember is that, once removed, a file cannot be recovered. It is gone forever. Thus, *rm* is not a command you should use lightly. And this is especially true if you use wild cards, because there is always a chance that the criteria you specify might result in unexpected matches that remove files you actually wanted to retain.

If you must use a wild card, however, XENIX does give you a way to protect your files from your good intentions. It's an *i* (for interactive) option you can include in your *rm* command. Before XENIX deletes a file that matches your criteria, it will ask you to confirm the delete by displaying the file's name on the screen and waiting for a *y* (for yes) or an *n* (for no).

For example, if you were to type *rm -i California/Memos/m*,* XENIX would print to screen the name of each file that matched *m** and wait for your response before deleting or retaining that file.

```
$ rm -i California/Memos/m*
California/Memos/memo1: ? n
California/Memos/memo2: ? n
California/Memos/memo3: ? _
```

Alternatively, as you saw in the earlier discussion of the *cp* command, you could preview the results of a deletion by using the *echo* command. For our example here, you would type *echo rm California/Memos/m**, and XENIX would print to screen a list of all the files that matched your wildcard criteria. Reading through that list, you could then determine whether it was safe to use the wildcard specification to achieve the results you want.

Both the *echo* command and the *i* option of the *rm* command are your faithful allies, especially in situations that might cause inadvertent deletion of valuable files.

SHARING INFORMATION

70

Up to this point, we've been looking at XENIX as it applies to you and your own files. But remember, XENIX is a multiuser operating system, and one of its key features is the ability to make information accessible to more than a single individual. It's time now for you to leave your own back yard and begin to look around the neighborhood.

To start off, let's obtain a detailed listing of the data files and directory files just below your home directory. If you've been entering the practice examples so far, you are in your home directory. If you're not there, return to your home directory by typing:

cd

Now to request a long directory listing, type:

ls -l

XENIX replies with:

```
$ ls -l
total 10
drwxr-xr-x   5 danh      group        80 Apr 29 18:31 Archive
drwxr-xr-x   5 danh      group        80 Apr 29 18:15 Boston
drwxr-xr-x   5 danh      group        80 Apr 29 18:15 California
drwxr-xr-x   5 danh      group        80 Apr 29 18:15 New_York
-rw-r--r--   1 danh      group       126 Apr 29 18:18 itinerary
$ _
```

(One final reminder: As with all of the illustrations in this book, the displays you see on your terminal will reflect the status of your own files and directories. Even if they differ from what you see here, don't be concerned. The principles behind the actions will still apply.)

Remember, from Chapter 3, that there are seven fields represented in this display, and that the second field tells you the number of links that are associated with the file. Now we'll see why those links are so important, but to do that, we'll need to backtrack a moment.

In describing the XENIX directory system, we compared it to the table of contents in a book. Just as the chapters listed in a table of contents are not physically contained within it, your XENIX files are not physically located within your directory. It simply provides information about, and points to, the actual locations of those files on the system's hard disk.

Remember, however, that not only your files are kept on the hard disk. Everyone else's are too—in whatever space XENIX finds available. So why don't these files get all mixed up? Why is it that you can request a list of your files, and that's exactly what XENIX shows you: your files, and not anyone else's?

It's because XENIX recognizes the individuality of the subdirectory associated with your user account.

But that brings us to a different situation. Very few of us operate totally on our own. In the paper world, for example, copies of memos must often be distributed to several people for approval or just for information. When you move the paper environment into a computer, that requirement doesn't disappear. Information must still be made accessible to more than one individual. And since the operating system files that information, the operating system must help us share it.

Whether we distribute memos to one person or to several, the principles remain the same. So, for the sake of simplicity, let's imagine that there is only one person to whom those memos must be passed and that the user name of that person is *boss* (therefore, boss' home directory is */usr/boss*).

CHECKING FILE PERMISSIONS

Your overall concern now becomes how to transfer your memos from whichever directory they are in to the *boss* account. There is more than one method, but before we cover any of them we must consider one potential stumbling block that is common to all: access permissions.

If you check the file permissions fields in the long file listing of your home directory, you'll notice that, in all cases, people in the same group you are in, and those who are classified as "public," cannot write to any of your files or directories. The access permissions for both groups are listed as *r-x*, read and execute. The *w* parameter, indicating the ability to modify those files, is missing.

Those settings are XENIX' default permission levels for everyone on the system. No one but you can write anything into any of your directories, and the same condition applies to the directories of everyone else, unless the permissions have been intentionally changed. (The means of changing access permissions is a topic covered in Chapter 9. At this point, it is important for you to know that they exist, and that they determine whether or not you can modify information in another person's directory. How they can be changed, however, is not really relevant to our discussion here.)

Because you need permission to write to another directory, the following practice session assumes the following condition:

■ An account named /usr/boss, in which there is a special subdirectory to receive your memos. In the examples, this directory is called *Tom,* so the absolute path name to that directory is /usr/boss/Tom.

Unless your system administrator has created a "teaching directory" named /usr/boss and has modified the access permissions so you can write into that directory, you cannot follow along with the instructions without a little preliminary work in which you create your own local subdirectory system.

First, create a subdirectory named *boss* from your home directory (type *mkdir boss*). Then, create your equivalent of *Tom* under it (type *mkdir boss/[your name]*). Now, you will be able to step through the following examples. Remember, though, that you are not actually writing to another person's directory, so don't include the /usr/ portion of the destination path names that you see here. Save /usr/ for later work.

MAKING SUBDIRECTORIES IN ANOTHER USER ACCOUNT

Even though you can place copies of your memos in /usr/boss/Tom, suppose you prefer to keep those that relate to your California, Boston, and New York accounts in their own separate subdirectories within /usr/boss/Tom. That way, they will be easy to distinguish from one another. To do so, you can use the *mkdir* command and specify the absolute path name to each directory:

```
mkdir  /usr/boss/Tom/California
mkdir  /usr/boss/Tom/Boston
mkdir /usr/boss/Tom/New_York
```

Now, with the destination set up, you have several options for passing your memo files to /usr/boss.

The most obvious, of course, is to use either *cp* or *copy* to copy files singly or in groups (with wild cards) into the directory of your choice. You could also use the *cat* command to copy your memos into one large file in the appropriate directory. Before you choose either approach, however, there is one consideration you should think about.

Hard disks provide large areas for file storage. But they are finite, and in actuality can be filled more easily than you might anticipate. In terms of storage space, then, you can see that, while creating additional copies of your data files may be the simplest way to share information, it is not necessarily the best. And that brings us to a subject mentioned all too briefly in Chapter 3—linking. It's one of XENIX' most impressive features, and once you understand the concepts behind linking, you will have gone a long way toward fully appreciating XENIX' strength and flexibility as a multiuser, multitasking operating system.

MAKING A LINK

To avoid duplication of files, XENIX gives you an *ln* (link) command. With linking, you can connect files instead of copying them. The files will be available to whichever directory they are linked to, just as if you had copied them there, but they will take storage space only in the directory from which they originate.

73

To see how XENIX makes these connections, try linking the files in your *California/Memos* directory to the new directory */usr/boss/Tom/California.* Type:

ln California/Memos/∗ /usr/boss/Tom/California

That was easy. But what have you really done? To see, we'll request a listing of both your source and destination directories, in each case using an *ls* command option called *i* (for inode, as you'll see in a moment) to make the results of your linking visible on-screen. First, type the command:

ls -i California/Memos

and you'll see:

```
$ ls -i California/Memos
   636 memo1
   640 memo2
   641 memo3
$ _
```

The numbers on the left are known as inode numbers. (As you probably won't see the same numbers that are shown here, don't be concerned—it's the similarity between them and the files you just linked that's important.) Whenever you create a file in XENIX, that file is automatically assigned a unique inode number. You need not worry about remembering the inode numbers of your files, nor is it necessary for you to keep track of them—XENIX does it for you. But to see the significance of those numbers, request the same type of listing for your destination directory:

ls -i /usr/boss/Tom/California

XENIX prints the results to your screen as:

```
$ ls -i /usr/boss/Tom/California
   636 memo1
   640 memo2
   641 memo3
$ _
```

Notice that the inode numbers for the files in your home directory and those in the destination directory are identical. While XENIX has not created exact duplicates of your source files and placed them in */usr/boss/Tom/California*, what it has done is to create a path, linking the files to the directory you specified in your *ln* command. The result, as far as you are concerned, is the same as if *memo1, memo2,* and *memo3* actually existed in */usr/boss/Tom/California*—and this means you save disk space. In fact, although this is a restricted definition of inode numbers, you might find it helpful to think of them as "link numbers" in a chain that connects file with file, and directory with directory.

USING LINKS TO SAVE TIME

Now that you've linked your memo files, another advantage of linking should become evident. Suppose you were to make changes to any of those three memos. There is no need to copy those changes into the *boss* directory in order to make certain that user has the most recent version. When "boss" accesses those files from his or her own account, the changes will be evident: The files that person will see are the actual files you changed, not some outdated duplicates.

Similarly, whenever you create a new memo, you can link it to the *boss* directory by typing *ln California/Memos/new_memo /usr/boss/Tom/California*. Or, of course, you can use any other source directory, file name, and destination directory you choose, as long as you have been given access permission enabling you to place files in the destination directory. In sum, links can help you save both time and disk space.

5

THE *vi* EDITOR   In the last chapter, you saw how useful *ed* can be if you need to create a quick, short note or memo. Now, you'll meet a more powerful text editor, *vi. Vi* does everything *ed* can do, and more, because it is interactive. Unlike *ed,* it displays changes to your document as you make them (hence the name *visual* editor). Using *vi,* not only can you create a document, you can immediately see the result of changing wording, inserting or appending text, searching for and replacing characters, deleting text, and so on.

All told, *vi* is a powerful text-editing utility. As long as you can see a line of text on-screen, you can move to and fiddle with it as much as you want. In addition, you can display a screenful of any part of your document at any time. When you're through with that section, you simply go back to the line you were originally working on and continue from there.

Despite its capabilities, however, you should not think of *vi* as a word processor. It is not, nor was it intended to be, the equivalent of a dedicated word-processing program, such as Microsoft Word or Santa Cruz Operation's Lyrix, both of which also run under XENIX. *Vi*, for example, does not offer a word-wrapping feature that automatically moves words to a new line whenever the line you're typing grows too long. Nor does *vi* rearrange the lines of a paragraph for you as you insert and delete text.

76

◼ NOTE: *XENIX provides these features and more with the text formatting utilities* nroff *and* troff *(supplied with the XENIX Text Processing system). These utilities (covered briefly in Chapter 7) can format documents created in a text editor by evaluating codes appropriately placed in the body of the document.*

Once you grow accustomed to working with *vi*, however, and you are comfortable with its commands and capabilities, you may well find yourself turning to it whenever you want to create, display, or make changes to a relatively short or simple letter or memo. Furthermore, you are not restricted to working with files created within *vi*. You can use *vi* with any data file that has been saved in ASCII format, a storage option which is offered by many, if not most, of the sophisticated word-processing programs.

Vi AND YOUR TERMINAL

Because *vi* works intensively with your screen, letting you wander up and down and back and forth with the cursor across any visible portion of text, it demands a considerable amount of control over your terminal's display. It's most likely that you can use *vi* with no trouble at all, but occasionally users encounter difficulties because their terminals lack the screen-control capabilities required by *vi*. Without the ability to control the screen, *vi* cannot function. Should such a problem occur, mention it to your system administrator, who may not be aware that a problem exists with your terminal. If, for whatever reason, the matter can't be corrected, you'll still be able to use *ed*.

But in all probability the *vi* editor and your terminal will cooperate perfectly. The easiest way to find out whether they will is to try, so let's get started. In this chapter, we'll cover the basic cursor-movement and text-handling commands you need. For your future reference, they're summarized, with brief descriptions, in Appendix A.

HOW IT WORKS

Vi is a single program, but there are two different ways in which it works. They're called insert mode and command mode, and if you think about the way you use *vi*, the reason for these modes becomes obvious. Sometimes, all you want to do is enter text, just as if you were typing a document on a typewriter. When you're doing this, you want *vi* to interpret all your keystrokes as text. This is insert mode. At other times, however, you want *vi* to do something with the characters you've typed. You want it to interpret your keystrokes as commands to be carried out. This is command mode.

To change from insert mode to command mode, press the Escape key. Conversely, to return to insert mode, use one of *vi*'s "enter text" commands, such as *insert* (they're described shortly). Most likely, when you become familiar with *vi*, you will switch back and forth between modes without giving your actions more than a passing thought. If you forget whether you are in insert mode or command mode, press the Escape key. If you are already in command mode, your terminal will beep, and you will remain in command mode. If you were in insert mode, you now will be in command mode.

STARTING *vi*

Just as *vi* can operate in either of two modes, you can start it in either of two ways: with or without the name of the file you want to work on. For example, at your shell prompt (or after you've selected the Run command in the Visual shell), you can type:

```
vi
```

and press the Enter key. That command begins *vi*. Since you have not supplied the name of a data file to work on, this is the equivalent of beginning a typewritten document with a blank sheet of paper.

The alternative way to start *vi* is to use the format:

```
vi [file name]
```

and press the Enter key. In this method, you're telling *vi* to begin and also to look for a file with the name you've supplied. If the file exists, *vi* loads a copy of it into memory, displays as many lines as the screen will show, and waits in command mode for your next instruction. If the file does not exist, *vi* leaves the screen blank and holds the file name in reserve, as the default name for a new document you're about to create. (You'll need the path name only if the file is or will be in a directory other than your current working directory.)

In either case, whether or not you named a file, and whether or not it actually exists on disk, you are working with the file *in temporary memory only.* None of your changes, corrections, or new text are stored on disk for future use until you specifically tell *vi* to save a document. As with any other computer application, save your work to disk periodically to avoid losing it if, for some reason, the system becomes inoperative.

USING *vi*

In Appendix A, you can see that *vi* offers you an assortment of basic commands for moving the cursor and editing a document. Since trying out a command is the most effective way of learning it, let's begin an editing session. We'll start by entering a short document on which you can practice.

From the Bourne shell, type:

vi flyer

at the $ prompt. (If you're in the Visual shell, select the Run command, then type *vi flyer.*) From either shell, you will soon see the following screen:

```
π
~
~
~
~
~
~
~
~
~
~
~
~
~
~
~
~
~
~
~
~
~
~
~
~
"flyer" [New file]
```

From top to bottom, this is what you see:

■ The cursor (_) is at the top line of the display. Unless you specify the line of text at which you want *vi* to start, this is the beginning position of the cursor.

■ The tildes you see down the left side of your display mark the positions of lines on your screen. They are indicators only, and are not part of the file. They never appear on your printed documents.

■ The line at the bottom of your display is *vi*'s status line. This is where *vi* displays errors you encounter, strings you are searching for, simple file information (press Ctrl-G for additional statistics), and commands that you type. At the moment, the line is displaying the file name you specified and is telling you that it is a new file. Had you started *vi* without including a file name, the status line on the bottom of the screen would be blank.

Right now, *vi* is in command mode waiting for you to enter a command. You have no document, so tell *vi* you are ready to create one. There are three basic commands you could use:

■ *i,* meaning insert text beginning before the current cursor position. You can also use this command to insert words (or any other combination of characters) within an existing line of text.

■ *a,* meaning append text. With a new file, *a* has the same effect as *i.* If you use this command with existing text, the cursor moves one space to the right before the text is added. Small though it may now seem, the distinction between *i* and *a* will become both apparent and useful when you begin editing a document.

■ *o,* meaning open a new, blank line immediately below the one that contains the cursor. If you begin a document with this command, *vi* will start the text one line below the top of the screen (in other words, leaving a blank line as the first line of your document).

Right now, let's use the *i* command. Press the lowercase letter *i,* and type the following lines, pressing Enter where indicated. If you make a mistake, either backspace to the incorrect character and retype the line or leave it alone for a few minutes. You'll soon learn how to move to and correct an error. Here are the lines to type:

It's that long, hot summer again. Time for ball [Enter]
games and lemonade, picnics, the Fourth of July. [Enter]
Time to keep that lawn watered, too, and check for [Enter]
all those pests that kill your carnations and ruin [Enter]
your rutabagas. [Enter]
     Need help? Call 555-BULB. Rhodie's Nursery--for [Enter]
everything your garden needs.

When you are finished, your screen should look like this:

```
    It's that long, hot summer again.  Time for ball
games and lemonade, picnics, the Fourth of July.
Time to keep that lawn watered, too, and check for
all those pests that kill your carnations and ruin
your rutabagas.
    Need help?  Call 555-BULB.  Rhodie's Nursery--for
everything your garden needs._
~
~
~
~
~
~
~
~
~
~
~
~
~
~
~
~
"flyer" [New file]
```

You're through entering text, so press the Escape key to return to command mode. The cursor will move back one space, to highlight the last character (.) in the last line of text that you typed.

ENDING LINES WITH ENTER

As you've seen, *vi* is much like a typewriter in one respect: You must tell it where and when to end a line. Although it *will* wrap letters around to the next line (instead of piling them on top of each other at the right margin as a typewriter would), *vi* does not wrap by word. If *vi* finds that the next character would extend the current line beyond the right edge of the display, it will carry that character down to the next screen line, without regard for either its position within the word you're typing or the appearance of the resulting word fragment. Thus, if you were typing the word *XENIX* at the end of a line, *vi* might very well break it into *X-ENIX*, *XE-NIX*, or *XENI-X*, depending on the point where you went beyond the limit of the screen display.

Realizing this, it's always a good idea to keep your lines under the 80 character limit allowed by the screen width of most monitors. Although many XENIX utilities like *nroff* don't mind working with lines that have wrapped around several times, text entered in this manner usually doesn't look very good.

Also, despite its on-screen appearance, if you didn't use the Enter key to end each line, your document would consist of one large line of text occupying about four screen lines, rather than a tidy document composed of seven individual lines. Although the difference may seem immaterial, bear in mind that when you edit a *vi* document you can specify the line to be edited. Thus, you won't be able to do much with a four-line "line." *Vi* also has a line-length limit of 512 characters (about 6½ lines). If you exceed this line length, you'll have some problems with *vi* until you restart the program.

MOVING ON

Now that you've created a document, you have several courses of action available. Right now, since your document resides only in temporary memory or RAM (Random Access Memory), you can:

■ Save it to disk under the file name that you used when you started, and continue working with *vi.*

■ Save it to disk under a new file name.

■ Abandon it.

Let's look at each of these options.

SAVING UNDER THE SAME NAME

Of the four options, the following is the one you should actually take to follow along with the examples in this chapter. The other courses of action are alternatives that you will find useful in other situations, with data files of your own.

You should be in command mode (if you are not, or are not certain, press the Escape key). Now to save the document using the default name (*flyer*) you supplied, type a colon, immediately followed by *vi*'s *write* command, as follows:

   :w

(Remember that when you requested the *i* command, *vi* gave no visual indication to acknowledge that command. Here, notice that as soon as you press the Shift-Colon sequence to produce the colon, the bottom line of the screen clears and then the colon appears as the first character on that line.)

```
    It's that long, hot summer again.  Time for ball
games and lemonade, picnics, the Fourth of July.
Time to keep that lawn watered, too, and check for
all those pests that kill your carnations and ruin
your rutabagas.
    Need help?  Call 555-BULB.  Rhodie's Nursery--for
everything your garden needs.
~
~
~
~
~
~
~
~
~
~
~
~
~
~
~
~
~
~
~
:
```

82

Press the Enter key after typing *:w,* and *vi* saves the document to disk with the name you gave it (or the name you last used if you had saved the document before). When the document has been saved, *vi* prints some information about the file on the status line and places you back in command mode:

```
    It's that long, hot summer again.  Time for ball
games and lemonade, picnics, the Fourth of July.
Time to keep that lawn watered, too, and check for
all those pests that kill your carnations and ruin
your rutabagas.
    Need help?  Call 555-BULB.  Rhodie's Nursery--for
everything your garden needs_
~
~
~
~
~
~
~
~
~
~
~
~
~
~
~
~
~
~
"flyer" [New file] 7 lines, 302 characters
```

As an alternative, if you had finished your session with *vi* but wanted to save your document to disk and, at the same time, quit the editor, you could do so by typing the command:

> **:x**

Note that a colon precedes this command as well. When you use *:x*, *vi* saves your document to disk under the default name you gave it at startup, then displays a message telling you the document has been saved and returns you to the shell from which you started. (If you had not yet specified a file name, *vi* would print the message *No current filename* on the status line at the bottom of the screen.) In situations like this you can use the *:x* command with an argument to specify a new file name, save your document to disk under that file name, and also exit *vi,* by using the form:

> :x [file name]

83

THE COLON

The colon you type in front of *w, x,* and certain other commands is a necessary part of their format. These commands are known as *vi*'s *editor* commands. The colon tells *vi* that these commands must be evaluated and acted upon outside of the normal text-handling environment, which includes *vi*'s *screen* commands, such as the *a* and *i* commands you've already been introduced to.

Even though you must type the colon, however, you needn't worry about having to remember which are editor commands and which are screen commands: If you try to type an editor command without the colon (or if you enter any other combination of keystrokes that *vi* doesn't recognize) , *vi* will remind you by causing your terminal to beep—and no harm will have been done.

SAVING UNDER A NEW NAME

You could also save your document to a file with a different name by using the form:

> :w [file name]

Should *vi* find that there is already a file with that same name on your disk, it will tell you so. If that happens, you must decide whether you want to overwrite (and thus destroy) the existing file with the contents of this document. If you are sure that's what you want, you can modify the *write* command like this:

> :w! [file name]

The exclamation point, which can be used after other commands as well, tells *vi* that the command is *absolute.* Whenever it receives an absolute command, *vi* carries it out despite the consequences. For this reason, be certain you know what will happen whenever you include an exclamation point in a command.

ABANDONING THE DOCUMENT

Finally, you could decide that your document simply isn't what you wanted. You really need to start over, and you want to abandon what you've done so far. To do that, you would type:

    :q

When you use this command, *vi* checks your document before it responds, and will let you quit only if you haven't made any unsaved changes to the document. If the document is new or contains changes you haven't saved to disk, *vi* tells you so with the message *No write since last change (:quit! overrides),* thus somewhat tersely noting that you must type the absolute form of the command, *:quit!,* to abandon the document. (You needn't, by the way, type the whole word; the form *:q!* will work just as well.)

84

CHANGING THE DOCUMENT

There is, of course, one other course of action you might want to take: You might want to make some editorial changes before you save your document. From the standpoint of safeguarding your work, though, it's not a particularly good idea. Suppose you change your document too radically? If you haven't saved the original, you have no prior version to fall back on. *Vi* makes it so easy to change names and overwrite outdated files, you should always save the current version of a document before you make any changes to it. That way, you can always retrieve an earlier copy and start over again.

But making changes to a document is a major element of using any editing program, and now that you've saved this document, we'll look at how you can make some changes to it.

MOVING THE CURSOR

Generally, before you can change any part of your document, you need to move the cursor to the word or character you want to change. The following sections will show you how to attain this mobility. As long as you've saved your practice document, you can try out the cursor movements described here. Remember, there's no need to memorize or master each of these commands. They're summarized in Appendix A. In addition, as you work with *vi,* you'll probably find that your own work habits and preferences lead you to rely extensively on some commands, but not at all on others.

To start out, press the Escape key to be sure you're still in command mode.

MOVING BY LINE OR BY CHARACTER

If your terminal is an IBM PC or compatible, you can move the cursor one character or one line at a time by pressing the left, right, up, and down arrow keys on your keyboard.

If your terminal is not IBM PC–compatible, the arrow keys may not work, for hardware-related reasons, even if you have them on your keyboard. But you can still rely on four keyboard characters: the lowercase *h, j, k,* and *l.* The cursor movement associated with each is shown in the following table. (The command option [number] means that you can specify the number of characters or lines you want to move the cursor. The only restriction on using this option is that you cannot specify more than the number of characters remaining in a line or more than the number of lines above or below the current cursor location.)

85

[number]h	Moves the cursor left.
[number]l	Moves the cursor right.
[number]j	Moves the cursor down.
[number]k	Moves the cursor up.

From command mode, you can also use the Spacebar to move the cursor to the right, and the Enter key to move the cursor down the left margin. As with the direction keys and the four keyboard characters, you can also precede these with the number of characters or lines you'd like to move. Use these if you prefer, but be certain you are in command mode when you do; in insert mode, using the Spacebar and Enter key will add extra spaces or lines to your document.

OTHER KEYS FOR UP AND DOWN

Picture your display screen as a grid, like a piece of graph paper, on which blank spaces are neatly arranged in rows and columns. Each space can contain one character, and as you move the cursor, it travels from one space to another.

When you use *j* to move the cursor down, you are telling *vi* to move the cursor down one or more lines, but also to keep the cursor in the same place within the line—within the same column of spaces on your graph paper. And with *k,* you move the cursor up but maintain its relative position in the line it moves to.

But there is another way to move up and down in a document. You can use the plus (+) key to move both down and to the first character in a line, or the minus (−) key to move up and to the first character of your destination line. Like *j* and *k,* both + and − can be preceded by a number specifying how many lines you wish to move up or down.

And to give you yet another option, there's the Enter key. Just as it moves the cursor to the start of a new line when you are in insert mode, it moves the cursor to the first character of a line when you are in command mode. The difference here is that, in command mode, *vi* interprets each press of the Enter key as a cursor-movement command, rather than the command to end one line and begin another.

MOVING TO A SPECIFIED CHARACTER

As varied and flexible as the preceding commands may be, you also need faster ways to move around in a document. Again, *vi* gives you many options.

One quick way to move around in a line is to move the cursor to a specific character. Suppose, for example, you've typed the line:

The quick brown fox jumps over the lazy dog.

In command mode, you could place the cursor on the line and move to a specific character within that line by using the commands in the following table:

f[char]	Moves the cursor to the right, stopping at the first occurrence of the character specified by [char].
F[char]	Moves the cursor to the left, stopping at the first occurrence (moving right to left) of the character specified by [char].
t[char]	Moves the cursor to the right, stopping at the character immediately to the left of the first occurrence of [char].
T[char]	Moves the cursor to the left, stopping at the character immediately to the right of the first occurrence (moving right to left) of [char].

If the cursor were at the beginning of our sample line, you could easily move it to the *d* in *dog* with the command *fd*. To move it back to the *b* in *brown*, you could use the command *Fb*.

When you use these commands, remember that XENIX (and *vi*) distinguish between upper- and lowercase characters. Thus, to move the cursor right, to the first occurrence of the letter *Q* in a sentence, you would need to specify *fQ*, not *fq*.

Whether you use *f* or *F*, *t*, or *T* to move the cursor will really depend upon what you intend to do next. For instance, if you want to insert characters within a word, you will use *f* or *F* to move the cursor to the character that will immediately follow the new letters. Then, you will select the *i* command, type the characters, and continue on your way.

If you want to add a new word, use *t* or *T* to place the cursor on the space between words, then use either *a* or *i* to add the text.

In either case, if you've practiced adding characters or words to your sample document, press the Escape key to return to command mode. We'll stop mentioning this shortly, but don't forget. If you do, you'll inadvertently add unwanted characters to your document.

EXPANDED CURSOR CONTROLS

Now you know the basic cursor movements. There are others that expand your control over cursor movement within the document. The easiest of these are uppercase *H* and *L*, which enable you to move directly to the first or last line on the screen:

H	Moves the cursor to the top left corner of the screen.
L	Moves the cursor to the bottom left corner of the screen (or to the bottom left corner of the document if it's less than a full screen in length).

Here, you have an easy aid to memory: *H* is High and *L* is Low.

MOVING BY THE WORD

Vi will also let you move across a line by the word, as well as to and from the beginning and end of the line. If you specify more words than are on the current line, *vi* will continue to look in the direction you're searching. From command mode, the following are valid movement instructions:

[number]w	Moves the cursor [number] words forward to the right; counts punctuation marks as words. As with all word movements, using the command with no number specified moves the cursor one word.
[number]W	Moves the cursor [number] words forward to the right; does not count punctuation marks as words.
[number]b	Moves the cursor [number] words backward to the left; counts punctuation marks as words.
[number]B	Moves the cursor [number] words backward to the left; does not count punctuation marks as words.
0 (zero)	Moves the cursor to the beginning of the line.
$	Moves the cursor to the end of the line.

Note that whether you use *w* or *W, b* or *B* depends on whether you want *vi* to take punctuation marks into account. For example, suppose the cursor is under the first character of the word *lemonade,* as it appears in your practice document, *flyer*:

```
     It's that long, hot summer again.  Time for ball
games and lemonade, picnics, the Fourth of July.
Time to keep that lawn watered, too, and check for
all those pests that kill your carnations and ruin
your rutabagas.
     Need help?  Call 555-BULB.  Rhodie's Nursery--for
everything your garden needs.
~
~
```

If you use *w*, the cursor will move right, to the position beneath the comma. If you use *W, vi* will ignore the comma and move the cursor to the position beneath the first character of the word *picnics.*

And, as shown in the preceding table of commands, *vi* lets you begin either the *w/W* or the *b/B* command with a number, to indicate how many words you want to move the cursor. Typing:

6w

for example, would move the cursor six words forward (including punctuation) from the first character of the word *lemonade* to the first character of the word *of.*

MOVING TO A SPECIFIC LINE

88

You can move directly to a specific line on the screen by using:

[line number]G

where [line number] is the number of the line at which you want *vi* to stop. When *vi* executes the command, it will place the cursor on the first character of the line you specified.

You can also use *G* by itself to tell *vi* to go to the last line in the document. (This is not necessarily the last line on the screen—remember, a document can very easily grow to contain many screenfuls of text.)

DISPLAYING LINE NUMBERS

For a short document of one screenful or less, it's relatively simple to determine line numbers. In a longer document that extends beyond the limits of a single screenful, it's not that easy. Fortunately, like *ed, vi* associates a line number with each line of text you enter. It doesn't display those numbers until you ask for them, but there are several ways to make them appear.

While in command mode, you can type:

:set number

to display your file with its associated line numbers. When you use this command, the line numbers remain on-screen until you tell *vi* to turn them off again. To do that, you type:

:set nonumber

There are also variations that allow you to display line numbers temporarily. If you type:

:nu

this tells *vi* to temporarily display the current line and its line number, and:

:[number],[number]nu

tells *vi* to temporarily display a numbered range of lines. For example, *:1,5nu* would display lines 1 through 5 of your document, with line numbers added. You can also use the $ character, meaning "the last line of the document," and display a temporarily numbered version of your entire document by typing:

:1,$nu

In some instances, you might find *:1,$nu* preferable to using *:set number,* followed by *:set nonumber.*

If you use either of *nu*'s temporary-display forms, *vi* prompts you to press the Enter key to continue. When you press Enter, your text display reverts to its original unnumbered format.

◼ NOTE: *When you use either* setnumber *or* nu, *don't be surprised to see your lines of text shift eight characters to the right. This is normal, and even if some characters disappear from the right edge of the screen, there's no cause for concern. Your text remains undisturbed. Also, when you use the* nu *command, you'll notice that* vi *displays the numbered line at the bottom of the screen, just above a message telling you to press Return to revert to unnumbered lines.*

MOVING THE CONTENTS OF THE SCREEN

Finally, there are the *vi* commands that scroll full or partial screens of text:

Ctrl-U   Scrolls up half a screen.
Ctrl-D   Scrolls down half a screen.
Ctrl-F   Scrolls forward one screen (toward the end of the document).
Ctrl-B   Scrolls backward one screen (toward the beginning of the document).

CHANGING LINE LENGTHS

Suppose you're typing in a new document. You want to concentrate on what you're writing, not on what it looks like. In order to get all your thoughts into the document, you decide to just keep typing, pressing Enter whenever a line looks as though it's about to overflow the screen. Now that you've been introduced to *vi*'s cursor commands, you have all the tools you need to break and rebreak lines of text wherever you wish.

Adjusting the length of each line is the simplest type of change you can make to a document, and *vi* has two commands that can help you do it: *J* and *r.*

If a line is too long, move the cursor to the space just to the left of the character at which you want to break the line. Press *r,* then press Enter; *vi* will make the
remainder of the line a new line, and all succeeding lines in your document will be
shifted down accordingly. For example, suppose you had the lines:

Vi can take a very long line and break it into two new lines.

To which you can join a third.

You could place the cursor on the space between the words *into* and *two,* press *r,*
then press Enter, and the result would be:

Vi can take a very long line and break it into

two new lines.

To which you can join a third.

But that would leave you with a very short new line that you would now like
to lengthen. Move the cursor to the end of this new line, and press *J.* The line
below will shift up and attach itself to the end of the short line. Notice that spaces
have been added to maintain the document's integrity. In the preceding example,
you could use this command to join the second and third lines:

Vi can take a very long line and break it into

two new lines. To which you can join a third.

You can keep using *r* and *J* in this way to adjust the lengths of as many lines as
you want.

EDITING YOUR DOCUMENT

So far, you've entered a document, learned to move the cursor and, perhaps,
used the Backspace key to back up in a line and correct a typing error. Right now,
this is what your *flyer* document should look like:

```
    1     It's that long, hot summer again.  Time for ball
    2 games and lemonade, picnics, the Fourth of July.
    3 Time to keep that lawn watered, too, and check for
    4 all those pests that kill your carnations and ruin
    5 your rutabagas.
    5    Need help?  Call 555-BULB.  Rhodie's Nursery--for
    6 everything your garden needs.
  ~
  ~
```

(The line numbers are for your reference. You'll see them like this only if you've used the *:set number* command.) We'll use this example in the next chapter too, so for the rest of the chapter refrain from saving your edits to disk.

If the cursor is at any location other than the first character of the first line, make certain you are in command mode, then:

Press H

to move the cursor to our starting point.

DELETING CHARACTERS

To begin, let's change the word *Time* in the first line to read *Ripe.* Move the cursor to the first occurrence of the letter *T* in line 1 by entering:

fT

Now with the cursor in position, the easiest way to make the change is to delete the characters *Tim* and replace them with *Rip.* To do that, enter:

3x

The lowercase *x* is a delete-character command. By prefacing it with the number 3, you've told *vi* to delete three characters, beginning at the current cursor location and moving to the right. You could, if you wished, accomplish the same task by pressing the lowercase *x* three times—once for each character. If you did this, you would see the other characters on the line move left to fill in the void left by each deleted character.

You can also delete characters to the left with the uppercase version of this command, *X.* Suppose, for example, that you had moved the cursor to the *e* in *Time.* You could enter *3X* or you could press uppercase X three times to delete, in order, *m, i,* and *T.*

(Note that there is a subtle difference in the characters deleted by *x* and *X*: The lowercase command includes the character at the cursor position in the deletion; the uppercase command does not include this character.)

IN WITH THE NEW

To complete the change from *Time* to *Ripe,* you now need to insert some new letters. You should still be in command mode, so:

Press *i*

to begin inserting. Next, type:

Rip

As you do, each letter appears and the remainder of the line is moved to the right to accommodate the addition.

When you've finished typing:

Press the Escape key

to exit from insert mode and your substitution is complete.

DELETING LINES AND UNDOING COMMANDS

We've already saved what we want to of the *flyer* file, so let's play with a few of the lines on-screen (remember, any changes you make will be in temporary memory only).

First, try deleting an entire line of text. Move the cursor to anywhere in a line and, from command mode:

Press the *d* key twice.

The line containing the cursor disappears.

But suppose you have quite a few lines to delete? Eliminating them one at a time could become tedious. There are several versions of the *delete* command to help you here. For example, if you wanted to remove all of the lines in your file, you could enter (from command mode):

:1,$d

and press Enter. Remember your brief experience with *ed.* The general format:

[number],[number]

specifies a range of line numbers.

You could have indicated any starting and ending line numbers in the document, but just as you found earlier with the command *1, $nu*, *vi* applies 1,$ to the first through the last lines of the file.

Now, if you've deleted every line you typed, don't press any of the cursor keys: Even though your entire document remains safe on disk, none of the file remains for you display or work with in memory.

But there's still more to do with it. So you want it back. Ordinarily, you would read a document into *vi* with:

:r [file name]

And in a case like this, where you're reverting to the original version of the file you were just working on, you could just type *:r* (or *:r!* if *vi* insists that you use the absolute form), because *vi* remembers the name of the current file until you supply a new one.

But there's no need to do even that much. Instead, from command mode:

Press the letter *u*.

That's *vi*'s *undo* command, which tells *vi* to retract the last command you issued. Your deleted lines reappear in their entirety. Press *u* again and your lines disappear once more, because you undid the undo command. A third press of the *u* key will bring the lines back yet again. (Alternatively, press *U* and *vi* restores the current line to its original state—no matter how many edits have occurred.)

And that command brings us to another important point: How did *vi* know what to put back on the screen when you told it to undo your delete command?

BUFFERING TEXT 93

Whenever you delete characters from a document, *vi* places the deleted text in a *buffer*, a segment of memory that's used to store text that's in transition. Altogether, *vi* has nine buffers for deleted material, and it manages these in rotation, with the first buffer containing the last (newest) deletion. When *vi* is told to undo a delete command, it can thus go to the first buffer, retrieve whatever text it finds there, and place the text back on the screen. When you undo an undo, *vi* re-deletes the text and places it back into the first delete buffer. Since there are nine buffers, *vi* can handle up to nine separate deletions. It's unlikely that you'll need to keep track of which deletion is in which buffer—at least under ordinary circumstances. If necessary, however, bear in mind that a tenth deletion will cause the first (oldest) deletion to be discarded. The following illustration may help you visualize the way in which *vi* manages its delete buffers.

Deleted Characters: A B C D E F G H I J

Delete Buffers

(newest deletion) ... (oldest deletion)

1   2   3   4   5   6   7   8   9

We'll cover buffers in more detail in the next chapter—this explanation is simply to help you understand how *vi* can find deleted text. As long as we're on the subject, though, we may as well take a quick look at inserting—it's the opposite of deleting, so does *vi* allow you to undo inserts too? As a matter of fact, it does. *Vi* handles its delete buffers automatically, allocating them as needed and discarding text whenever they become too crowded, but you can manage up to 26 additional buffers (labeled *a* through *z*), into which you can place text and from which you can retrieve it. These insert buffers are independent of the delete buffers but, like the latter, they can hold as much text as was affected by a single command. Since *vi* considers all your keystrokes, from the time you press the *i* key until you press Esc, as being part of *one* command, that means you can use *u* to remove all the text you insert with any one command.

94

DELETING A RELATIVE RANGE OF LINES

More often than not you'll probably find that you want to remove only a portion of your document, as opposed to either one line or all of the lines. You can delete selectively by indicating a range of line numbers:

:[start],[end]d

But if you're composing your document as you type, you may decide you want to delete only the current line and the line above it. In a four-line file, it's easy to tell what the line numbers are without resorting to the *set number* command. But in a longer document, it might not be that easy.

Rather than going through the trouble of turning on the line numbers, try the following. If necessary, move the cursor so there is at least one line of text above the line it is in. Press the Escape key to enter command mode and then type:

:-1,.d

As when you deleted all the lines in your document, you've used a range of line numbers here, too. This range is just a bit different from any you've used before.

The period is a shorthand method of indicating the current line (the line containing the cursor). The comma, of course, separates the two values in the range (as it did when you used 1,$). And the -1 is a *relative* line number indicating that this range extends from the line *above* to the current line, inclusive. *Vi* responds by deleting these two lines.

You could have used a positive range, as well. A $+1$ would have deleted the current line and one line below it. Nor are you limited to specifying only one line above or below the current line. If this document were long enough (which it is not), you could just as easily have specified -13 or $+9$. The limit to relative line numbers is the number of lines in the document itself. *Vi* will not erase more lines than exist.

The only thing to remember about the use of these ranges is the order in which you specify them. The line you specify first should always be the line closest to the top. For example *:2,5d* would be acceptable, but *:5,2d* would cause the error message *First address exceeds second* to be generated.

DELETING WORDS

Finally, there's the matter of deleting words. Start by moving the cursor to the beginning of a word you want to delete (remember, your file is safe on disk, so you can play with the version now on-screen). While in command mode, enter:

dw

and press Enter. *Vi* deletes the word and then rearranges the line to fill the gap.

Had you used:

3dw

vi would have deleted three words (recall this includes punctuation marks) immediately to the right of the cursor. Again, any number is valid within the command, up to the actual number of words remaining beyond the cursor's position.

REPEATING COMMANDS

Any of the screen commands you've seen (those that are not preceded by a colon and are not echoed on *vi*'s status line at the bottom of the display) can be repeated as many times as you wish. To repeat the last command you used, just press the period (.) key, while in command mode, after you've issued the screen command you want repeated.

Cursor-movement commands do not affect your ability to repeat a screen command. If you've just deleted a line, you can move the cursor up or down to the next candidate and press the period key. The line will be deleted in the same way as the one before. Pressing the period key to repeat a command works with *any* of the screen commands.

Vi, PART 2

The commands you've learned in this chapter give you the foundation you'll need to start working with *vi*. In the following chapter you'll see how to use the text you create to its best advantage. If you have not saved the original version of the file *flyer,* do so. You'll be using it again when we cover cutting and pasting and using boilerplate text.

95

EXPANDING YOUR USE OF *vi*

The basic cursor movements and editing commands that you learned in Chapter 5 are all you need to create short, simple memos and other documents. But there is much more to *vi*. As you'll see in this chapter, you can also use *vi* for such sophisticated tasks as cutting and pasting, creating boilerplate text, and searching for and replacing letters, words, even whole lines of text.

First, we'll take a look at alternative ways you can start *vi*—ways that not only allow you to begin with the cursor at a particular location in a file, but also enable you to queue up a group of files you want to work on. As before, don't feel you must memorize these and other commands you're introduced to; they're summarized for you in Appendix A.

OTHER WAYS TO START *vi*

Sometimes, when you call up a data file, you want to begin at the beginning and start editing. At those times, starting *vi* with the command *vi [file name]* is all you need do.

At other times, though, you may not want to start at the first line of the file. Perhaps you want to continue writing a partially completed document. Or you may want to verify that the file you requested is, indeed, the one you wanted. Then, too, you may want to recycle an existing document after making a few appropriate changes to specific sections. With *vi,* it's easy to begin editing a file at a location other than the first line of text.

To start *vi* at a particular line, the command form is:

    vi +[line number] [file name]

For example, the command *vi +3 flyer* starts *vi* with the cursor on line 3 of the file named *flyer.* You can also use this startup method as a quick and easy way to continue writing a document at another time. The next time you call up the file, use the command *vi + $ [file name],* and *vi* will start up with the cursor on the last line of the file. All you need do is press *o,* to both open a new line at the end of the document and enter insert mode at the same time.

You can also start *vi* at the first occurrence of a particular word. To do this, the command form is:

    vi +/[word] [file name]

Thus, *vi +/VCR sales_rept* would begin *vi* with the cursor on the first occurrence of *VCR* in the file named *sales_rept.* This startup method offers you another way to return to your prior position in a document. Suppose, for example, you must end your session with *vi* before you complete *sales_rept.* To be able to pick up where you left off, insert a unique word—StarTrek, Scheherazade, anything you want—in the document before you save it to disk. Later, start a new session with the command *vi +/StarTrek sales_rept* to return to your prior location in the document.

USING *vedit*

You also have the option of starting the visual editor with the command *vedit* rather than *vi.* For all intents and purposes, the *vedit* editor is identical to *vi* (the Visual shell uses *vedit* when you begin editing a file with the Edit command). Its only real variation is a helpful one: *Vedit* displays an *INPUT MODE* message on the right portion of the status line while you're in insert mode. Use *vedit* anytime you like simply by typing it instead of *vi.*

QUEUING FILES

Have you ever been in the middle of a thought and found that you needed to refer to another document in order to complete it or to verify your facts and figures? *Vi* lets you jump from one document to another. All it takes is a little forethought on your part in deciding which documents you might need.

Going back to our *sales_rept* example, suppose you know that in composing this document you will want to refer to the files named *budget* and *sales_1-86* through *sales_6-86*. You can start *vi* with all of these files on tap by putting them into a queue, and you can do so with a single command in the form:

vi [file name(s)]

99

If the files you want to see share enough common characters in their names, you can also use wild cards (* and ?) in requesting a queue. So, for example, you could queue the files in our example with the command:

vi budget sales *

Recall that the * wild card can represent any number of characters. Here, it will cause *vi* to queue all files beginning with *sales*. If you would like to specify a more limited list of your sales files, such as *sales_1-86, sales_2-86,* and *sales_3-86,* specify a range instead:

vi budget sales_rept sales_[1-3]-86

Note that here you would have to request *sales_rept* separately, because it would not be included in the range you specified.

If, during a session with *vi,* you happen to forget which files you've queued, you can find out quickly by typing:

:args

from command mode. *Vi* will show you the list of all files you began the queue with on the status line at the bottom of the screen, with the name of the current file enclosed in square brackets.

MOVING ABOUT IN THE QUEUE

When you queue files with wild cards, *vi* places those affected by the wild cards into the queue in numeric and/or alphabetic order following the ASCII coding system. Otherwise, it uses the sequence in which you entered file names to establish each document's position within the queue. In our example, *vi* would thus begin by displaying the file named *budget.*

Assuming that you want to work on *sales_3-86,* how would you tell *vi*? The sequence of your files in the queue would be: *budget, sales_rept,* then *sales_1-86* through *sales_3-86.* You want to jump from the beginning of the queue to the end, and *vi* gives you two ways to do so.

You could use the *next* command over and over to move sequentially through the queue, or you could use *vi*'s *edit* command, which moves you to the file you specify—if necessary, loading the file if it is not in a queue.

To use the *next* command, you would enter:

   :n

and *vi* would display *sales_rept* for you. When you entered *:n* again, *vi* would move to *sales_1-86,* and so on. An easier way, however, would be to enter:

   :e sales_3-86

and move directly to the file you want. Note, however, that although you're editing another file, your position in the queue has not changed.

To move back to the beginning of the queue, you would use the command:

   :rew

That's short for *rewind,* and it is a holdover from the days of tape storage. Functionally, this command closes the current document and moves back to the first file in the queue.

During your session with *vi,* you could also use the *:n, :rew,* and *:e* commands to skip about between files. If you do, you can use the command:

   :e#

to return to the file you edited just prior to the current file (the # symbol tells *vi* you want the previous file).

If you use *:n* to move to the next file, bear in mind that *vi* takes you to the file that *it* considers to be next in the queue. Thus, if you begin at file number 1, then you use the *:e* command to edit file number 6, and then you use the *:n* command to move to the next file, what *vi* will display will be file number 2—the next in the queue—rather than file number 7 as you might expect.

When working with queued files, you should also keep in mind that *vi* does not maintain them all in memory. Each time you move from one file to another, *vi* abandons the current file and reads in the new one. If you have made any changes to the current file and try to move to another without saving first, *vi* will remind you that you haven't saved the new version. As in other situations, you can add an exclamation point to the command (for example, *:rew!*) to confirm your intent, but doing so could cost you any revisions you have made. Whenever you want to keep the editing you've done, be certain to use the *:w* command to save changes before you rewind or move on to the next file.

COPYING AND MOVING TEXT

As convenient as it is to be able to start *vi* with a particular file or at a specific location within that file, there's still more to editing a document than inserting and deleting text. Perhaps you've had the experience of writing a letter, memo, or report and later thinking to yourself:

■ This document needs reorganizing.... Or,

■ This section would fit right into another document I'm working on.... Or,

■ If I changed a few words here and there, I could borrow whole sections from document xyz.

Vi lets you do all of this type of cutting and pasting without scissors, tape, or glue. You use *vi*'s memory instead—specifically, its delete and insert buffers.

USING *vi*'S BUFFERS

Recall that *vi* has nine delete buffers, numbered 1 through 9, in which it holds information that is in transition. You can use these buffers for text that you cut out of one document, and you can reinsert that text in either the same or a different document by calling for the contents of the appropriate buffer.

Likewise, for text that you want to duplicate, rather than delete, *vi* has 26 insert buffers that you can use as holding areas. These insert buffers are labeled *a* through *z*.

To move information, you refer to the buffers by number (for deletions) or letter (for insertions), so it's always necessary to remember which segment of text has gone to which buffer. But bear in mind that sequence is important in working with deletions: They don't stay put—they are moved successively through the buffers, with the latest one occupying buffer number 1.

The commands you use with *vi*'s buffers are:

■ The *d* (*delete*) command to move text to a delete buffer.

■ The *y* (*yank*) command to move text to an insert buffer.

■ The *p* (*put*) command to move text from a delete or an insert buffer.

You were introduced to the *delete* command in Chapter 5, so here we'll concentrate on *yank* and *put.* First we'll look at how they're used, then we'll move on to a practice document where you can try out these and other commands.

YANKING TO AN INSERT BUFFER

Whenever you yank text, you must specify an insert buffer. The general format of the command is:

    "[buffer][number of lines]yy

So, for example, the command:

    "a3yy

tells *vi* to yank three lines, beginning with the current line, to buffer *a.*

Normally, the letter *a* refers to *vi*'s command to append text. By preceding the *a* in this command with a double quotation mark, you have told *vi* to accept the character literally; it's your signal telling *vi* to open the *a* insert buffer.

When you use a lowercase buffer letter, the text you move replaces any text currently in the buffer you name. But there's also an uppercase variation of this command that you may find useful. If you use the form:

    "[BUFFER][number of lines]yy

but capitalize the letter of the buffer you'd like to append, *vi* will append the text to the current contents of the buffer, rather than overwrite the existing material.

As you use these commands, don't be concerned if you get no response from *vi.* Just as, when you use the insert commands, your keystrokes are not echoed on the screen, with the *yank* command neither your typing nor the loading of buffers (in most cases) will provoke any visible response from *vi.*

MARKING LINES FOR YANKING

Yanking a specified number of lines to an insert buffer works well with a relatively short range of lines. There's also another method you can use—one that does not involve knowing or even counting the number of lines you're yanking. In this method, you move the cursor to the first line of text you want to duplicate, and then type:

mk

with no colon or quotation mark. This command marks the current line with the letter *k* (you may use a different letter if you wish).

Now, you can jump the cursor to the last line you want to copy (use any of the cursor-movement commands). Once there, you can yank all lines from the one containing the cursor up to, and including, the one you marked by using the command form:

"[buffer name]y'k

Note that you again use the double quotation mark to tell *vi* to interpret the buffer name literally. The 'k part of the command tells *vi* to copy everything from the current line to the line containing the *k* marker.

PUTTING TEXT INTO A DOCUMENT

You use the *put* command to move lines of text from either an insert or a delete buffer (recall that delete buffers are numbered 1 through 9). The *put* command takes the form:

"[buffer]p

and puts the entire contents of the buffer on the line(s) immediately below the current line. For example, if buffer *a* contained the phrase *This is a complete line,* then the command:

"ap

would move *This is a complete line* from insert buffer *a* to the line below the current line in your document.

And finally, there is an uppercase form of the *put* command. Using an uppercase *P* places text in your document either above the current line or just before the current cursor location.

103

CUTTING AND PASTING IN THE SAME DOCUMENT

To see how to use the delete and insert buffers, let's suppose you've written the letter in the following illustration. (The letter is based on the file *flyer,* which you created and saved to disk in the last chapter. If you want to try cutting and pasting on your own document, start *vi* with *flyer* and insert the additional text shown here.)

When you're finished, your letter should look like this:

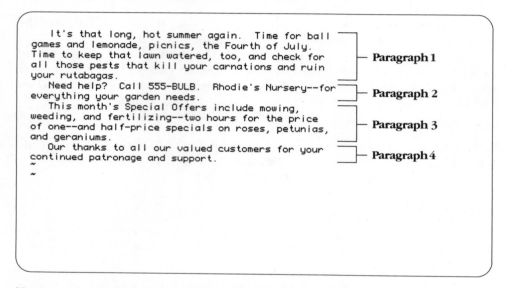

```
    It's that long, hot summer again.  Time for ball
games and lemonade, picnics, the Fourth of July.
Time to keep that lawn watered, too, and check for
all those pests that kill your carnations and ruin
your rutabagas.
    Need help?  Call 555-BULB.  Rhodie's Nursery--for
everything your garden needs.
    This month's Special Offers include mowing,
weeding, and fertilizing--two hours for the price
of one--and half-price specials on roses, petunias,
and geraniums.
    Our thanks to all our valued customers for your
continued patronage and support.
~
~
```

— **Paragraph 1**

— **Paragraph 2**

— **Paragraph 3**

— **Paragraph 4**

Now you think a bit of reorganizing might be in order. As long as you've saved this or any other document on disk, you can reorganize it as many times as you want; you can chop and change a copy of it to your heart's content, because you always have the prior version to fall back on if your editing is less than successful.

COPYING TEXT WITHIN A DOCUMENT

Sometimes, when you're revising a document, you may wonder whether a block of text should remain where it is or be moved and inserted somewhere else. *Vi* makes it easy to "try out" such potential relocations. There are actually two approaches you could use. One involves using the insert buffers, the other relies on *vi*'s *copy* command.

Suppose you're wondering whether paragraph 4 might not be better as the opening paragraph. Duplicate it at the beginning of the document, and see where you prefer it. If you're not already there, press Esc to enter command mode, place the cursor on the line that begins *Our thanks,* then type:

"a2yy

to yank the two-line paragraph to buffer *a.* Now, move the cursor to the first line of the document and type:

"aP

and *vi* duplicates the paragraph at the top of your letter.

(If the paragraph had been longer—especially if it had been more than one screenful of text—you could have marked the lines to yank, as described earlier, with the commands *mk* and *"ay'k.* The means you choose for specifying the lines to yank will vary according to your own preferences and the length of the text you are working with.)

An alternative method, using the *copy* command to duplicate the text, would involve either knowing or displaying the line numbers of your document. The format of the *copy* command is:

:[first,last] co [destination]

In this example, the lines you want to move are lines 12 and 13, so the copy command would be:

:12,13 co 0

Using line number 0 tells *vi* to put the copied text at the beginning of the document. If you specify a destination line other than 0, *vi* will place the copied text immediately below the line you specify. If you wish to copy only the line you are on, the [first,last] range is not needed. If necessary, display some or all line numbers with the *:nu* or the *:setnumber* command.

Let's assume that paragraph 4 is, in fact, better as your opening paragraph. You've moved it to the top of your document, so to delete it from its original location, all you have to do is move the cursor to the first line of the two-line paragraph you want to delete, then type:

2dd

to remove the current line and the one immediately following it (you could have also used relative notation and typed *:. , +1d*).

MOVING TEXT WITHIN A DOCUMENT

Now, suppose you decide to transpose the third and fourth paragraphs in the revised letter. You have three choices: using *vi*'s delete buffers, using the *copy* command, or using the *move* command.

If you want to use the delete buffer, move the cursor to the beginning of the line that starts *Need help?* and, from command mode, enter:

2dd

to delete the paragraph. Since this is your most recent deletion, the text is placed in buffer number 1. To reinsert it, at its new location, move the cursor to the line beginning *and geraniums* and enter:

106

"1p

to finish transposing the paragraphs.

Like the *copy* command, *vi*'s *move* command requires that you either know or display line numbers. The command's format is:

:[start,end]m[destination]

In the preceding example, you would want to move lines 8 and 9 to just below line 13, so the command would be:

:8,9m13

Whether you had used *vi*'s buffers or the *copy* and *move* commands, the result of your reorganizing would now look like this:

```
    Our thanks to all our valued customers for your
continued patronage and support.
    It's that long, hot summer again.  Time for ball
games and lemonade, picnics, the Fourth of July.
Time to keep that lawn watered, too, and check for
all those pests that kill your carnations and ruin
your rutabagas.
    This month's Special Offers include mowing,
weeding, and fertilizing--two hours for the price
of one--and half-price specials on roses, petunias,
and geraniums.
    Need help?  Call 555-BULB.  Rhodie's Nursery--for
everything your garden needs.
~
~
```

CUTTING AND PASTING BETWEEN DOCUMENTS

Moving text between documents combines two techniques presented so far in this chapter: queuing files and using *vi*'s delete and insert buffers. To see how they work, let's assume that you've completed the letter in our preceding example. You have saved it to disk with the *:w* command, and are about to begin a new letter you'll call *prospect*. For purposes of cutting and pasting, we'll use one of the paragraphs in *flyer*. Here's how it works.

If you are not currently in *vi*, you can begin by queuing the two file names you're interested in:

vi prospect flyer

Note that you've queued a file that does not yet exist. But that's all right. *Vi* accepts the name you gave as the default name for the file you will soon create. Since you listed *prospect* first, *vi* begins with a blank screen and a message telling you that *prospect* is the new file.

Insert a few lines of text (with an indentation of three spaces in the first line):

Thank you for your recent inquiry regarding [Enter]
our landscape installation and maintenance service.

Now you're ready to try cutting and pasting between documents. Save your new file to disk with the *:w* command. Then, call up the next file in your queue:

:n

When *vi* displays *flyer*, move the cursor to the paragraph beginning *This month's Special Offers* and copy the paragraph to an insert buffer using either of the following methods.

Specify the lines to copy with the command:

″b4yy

Or mark the first line:

mk

then move the cursor to the last line of the paragraph and yank all text between the current line and the marked line with the command:

″by′k

Now, return to *prospect* by entering:

:e#

or

:rew

Finally, when *prospect* reappears on-screen, move the cursor to the last line of text and enter:

"bp

to *put* the contents of buffer *b* into the document, below the current line.

In a real-life situation, you could now add to or edit the letter, save it, abandon it...whatever you wanted. Before we move on and discover more about *vi,* let's look quickly at one other approach you could have taken to cutting and pasting between documents.

BEGINNING FROM *vi*

If you had already begun a session with *vi* when you decided to begin your new file, your procedure would have been a little different. After saving (or abandoning) the current document, you would start the new file with the command:

:e prospect

As in other situations, *vi* would tell you this was a new file, and you could then enter text just as described in the preceding section. When you wanted to call up *flyer,* you could not use the *:rew* command, because you have no queue. You could, however, enter:

:e#

if *flyer* was the file you had just worked with. If it were not, you would then type:

:e flyer

to specify the correct file.

From that point on, you could cut and paste between documents as was described earlier.

BOILERPLATING

Cutting and pasting within or between documents is closely related to another timesaving technique—boilerplating. Using boilerplate text, you can compose different "templates" containing information that can be mixed, matched, and individualized to cover a variety of situations. Boilerplate documents don't have to be simple form letters, either. Using *vi*'s buffers, queues, insert modes, and powerful text-handling abilities, you can transform a basic, all-purpose document into one that is both personal and special.

As an example, we'll use the two files *flyer* and *prospect* as two elements of a form-letter system.

CREATING A TEMPLATE

If you want to practice on your system, you can begin from *vi* by using the command:

:e form_letter

If you're starting from the shell, enter the command:

vi form_letter

From either starting point, press *i* for insert mode, and type the following lines, including the arrowheads and the identifying words within them (as before, press Enter where indicated):

<date>[Enter]
[Enter]
[Enter]
Dear <name>[Enter]
[Enter]
<news>[Enter]
   In keeping with our policy of maintaining close[Enter]
contact with all of our valued customers, I am happy[Enter]
to enclose a copy of our new booklet, "Dusty's Guide[Enter]
to Growing Roses."[Enter]
<comment>[Enter]
   Remember Rhodie's, and see how your garden grows![Enter]
[Enter]
Sincerely,[Enter]
[Enter]
[Enter]
Dusty Miller[Enter]
Rhodie's Landscaping and Nursery

109

When you're finished, return to command mode and use *:w* to save the document to disk.

The words enclosed in <> symbols indicate places in the document where specific text will be inserted or changed as you customize your form letter. The words, as well as the symbols, are unimportant beyond the scope of our example. (The symbols themselves are actually unnecessary, and have been used here only to make those items stand out.) You can use other "flags" in your own documents. The idea is simply to include reminders so that you don't forget what you intended to add, and where.

For the sake of our example, let's assume you have a mailing list that includes three groups of people: one group who will be sent *flyer,* another who will get *prospect,* and a third who will get just the basic letter. With the three segments of your mailing system in place, sending these letters becomes less a challenge in creativity than a matter of assembling the components. Let's compose a letter for a customer named Mr. Wright.

SUBSTITUTING TEXT

You will want to begin at the top of the letter, so move the cursor to the top with the command:

1G

This first line of text contains a reminder. You want to substitute the actual date for <date>, so enter:

:s/<date>/June 25, 1986

and press Enter. The *:s* you typed is *vi*'s *substitute* command. Essentially, you've told *vi* to substitute the text *June 25, 1986* for the text *<date>* that it will find in the first line of your document. You'll learn more about replacing text later in this chapter. For now, it's enough to know that the existing text must always precede the substitution text in the command. The slashes (/) separate the two.

Right now, you want to make another substitution. Move the cursor to the line containing <name> and type:

:s/<name>/Mr. Wright

to replace <name> with Mr. Wright in the salutation. And now for the <news>.

Move the cursor to the first character in <news> and press D. You just used the uppercase version of the *delete* command, which removes all text from the cursor position to the end of the line without disturbing the position held by that line.

INSERTING ANOTHER FILE

With the cursor still at the first position of the now vacant line, type:

:r prospect

The *:r* command is *vi's* *read* command. When you use it, *vi* reads the contents of the file you specify and inserts the document at the current cursor position. Thus, in response to your command here, *vi* reads *prospect* and inserts that text at the line containing the cursor. The rest of your document moves down to accommodate the new material:

```
June 25, 1986

Dear Mr. Wright:

    Thank you for your recent inquiry regarding
our landscape installation and maintenance service.
    In keeping with our policy of maintaining close
contact with all of our valued customers, I am happy
to enclose a copy of our new booklet, "Dusty's Guide
to Growing Roses."
<comment>
    Remember Rhodie's, and see how your garden grows!

Sincerely,


Dusty Miller
Rhodie's Landscaping and Nursery
~
~
```

That leaves only your <comment> line to account for. Given *vi's* capabilities, you could probably maintain a set of appropriate one-line comments, but let's use an editing command instead.

REPLACING LINES OF TEXT

Move the cursor to the <comment> line and, once there, type cc. This command deletes the entire line containing the cursor and retains the line's position within your document. While it may seem much like the uppercase *D* command, it differs in two important respects. First, it deletes the entire line, whereas *D* deletes only from the cursor location to the end of the line. Second, *cc* not only deletes, but puts you into insert mode at the beginning of the line; the *D* command does not activate insert mode.

Now you can insert your comment. Type:

Please call if you would like a free estimate.[Enter]

Press Escape, and you're done. Your letter is finished, with only a minimal amount of effort on your part.

SEARCHING A DOCUMENT

One short example cannot possibly show you all the ways you can use *vi*. You might, for instance, want to replace one or more words a number of times within a long document. Or, you might simply want to search for a particular word or set of words. It's not difficult to scroll through a short document to find what you're looking for, but in a long document the line-by-line approach is hardly practical.

By design, *vi* gives you several ways around such issues.

SEARCHING FOR WORDS

Recall that one of the ways you can start *vi* is by specifying a particular word at which you want to begin. From within *vi* you have a similar option.

Suppose, for example, you wanted to find the specific place in your document where you used the words *alternatives are* and, at that point, insert additional text. You can enter:

/alternatives are

and *vi* will search forward from the position of the cursor (toward the end of the document), stopping on the line containing the first occurrence of *alternatives are*. If you start the search in the middle of the document, *vi* will not stop when it reaches the end—it will go back to the top of the document and continue the search until it either finds the text you specified or returns to the starting point.

The slash character (/) preceding the search words tells *vi* to search forward through the document. You can also tell *vi* to search backward by prefacing the search text with a question mark (*?alternatives are*).

In either type of search, if you want *vi* to stop when it reaches the end (or the beginning) of the document, you can tell it so with the command:

:set nowrapscan

(In less concise English, this command changes *vi*'s mode to one in which it will not continue scanning the document by wrapping around the end of the file.) To return *vi* to its normal mode, the command is:

:set wrapscan

And, if the first occurrence of your text that *vi* finds is not the one you are looking for, continue the search by pressing the lowercase letter *n*.

112

IGNORING CASE

Of course, there's always the possibility that the search phrase you're looking for could appear as *Alternatives are,* as at the beginning of a sentence. Or, it might appear in both upper- and lowercase forms within your document.

If you want *vi* to ignore such variations in case, use the command:

:set ignorecase

before beginning the search. The command:

:set noignorecase

restores *vi*'s case sensitivity.

113

SEARCHING WITH WILD CARDS

You've already seen wild cards and ranges used with file names to broaden XENIX' flexibility in matching patterns of characters. It should come as no surprise that wild cards and ranges can also be used in searching for words with *vi*.

To find all uppercase characters, you can use:

/[A-Z]

The same search for lowercase characters would be:

/[a-z]

And the variations that you saw in Chapter 4 for numbers and upper- and lowercase mixtures are all valid here as well.

You can also exclude certain characters from your search by including a caret (^) within the range brackets. If you wanted to find the first word beginning with a capital letter followed by the letters *at,* you would use:

/[^a-z]at

to tell *vi* you are interested in every ASCII character *except* lowercase letters. *Vi* would thus stop at *Bat, Cat, Fat,* or *Hat,* but not at *bat, cat, fat,* or *hat.*

The first and last characters or words in a line are also viable candidates for search criteria. The command:

/^in /

would find the first line, including the current line, that started with the word *in.* Note that the caret symbol has an entirely different meaning here, when used without brackets—it now restricts the search to the first word of each line (provided that word is not a space or a Tab character). Note, too, that a space is included in this example to ensure that only whole words are considered, rather than any words that begin with *in.* The trailing slash tells *vi* where the characters you wish to search for cease. It is usually optional, but in this case it's needed to tell *vi* that the space character is to be included in the search.

Alternatively, you can enter:

/ing$

to search for the first line in which the last word ends in *ing.*

And for matching single characters within a word, there is the period:

/ Pi. /

Used as in this example, this command would cause *vi* to find any combination of characters beginning with *Pi—Pit, Pin, Pip,* and so on. Again, note the use of blank spaces to limit the search to whole words.

INCLUDING SPECIAL CHARACTERS

As you've just seen, there are some search characters that *vi* considers special. The complete list is:

. * \ [ ] ~ $ ^

It's quite possible that one of more of these characters could be part of the text you're searching for (an obvious example would be a dollar amount, such as $1000.00). In a case like that, you need to make *vi* understand that it must accept the character or characters literally.

You saw a similar situation in using the *yank* and *put* commands to move text to and from an insert buffer. There, you used a double quotation mark (") to tell *vi* to interpret the letter *a* as a name, rather than as a command. In searches, you precede any special characters with a backslash (\ ). For example, to find the figure $1000.00, you would use the command:

/\$1000\.00

Of course, if much of the text you're searching for contains special characters, the command line might begin to look rather ungainly with all of the backslashes (imagine searching for a mathematical formula). *Vi,* as usual, offers relief.

The feature within *vi* that enables the editor to recognize the special characters we've been looking at is called *magic.* To turn off *vi*'s ability to recognize these characters, you can type:

:set nomagic

The backslashes will no longer be needed. To restore recognition of special characters, type:

:set magic

SEARCHING AND REPLACING

Quite often when you search for a particular word in a document, you want to replace it with another. You did that earlier when you substituted words in the form-letter example. Then, however, replacements were made on a case-by-case basis: You selected the word and the replacement each time a change was made.

For a document in which you want to replace words that appear only once, the *substitute* command works well. But for a document in which you want to find and replace the same word several times, it's far easier to be able to tell *vi* to make the change globally (throughout the entire document).

Vi's global search-and-replace command follows the format:

:g/[search for]/s//[replace with]/[options]

For example, suppose you had a document in which you wanted to change all occurrences of the word *we* to *I*. To make this change everywhere, including the beginnings of sentences such as *We strongly recommend...*, you would first tell *vi* to ignore all upper- and lowercase differences with the command *:set ignorecase*. Then, you could enter the replacement command:

:g/ we /s// I /g

which tells *vi*:

:g	Look at every line of the file.
/ we /	Search for *we*, preceded and followed by a blank space.
s/	Substitute for *we*.
/ I /	The word *I*, preceded and followed by a blank space.
g	Do this for each occurrence on each line of text.

Note the blank spaces preceding and following both *we* and *I* in the command. They ensure that the command works as you want it to, and that the proper spacing between words is maintained. Without the spaces, *welfare* could become *Ilfare, stewed* could become *steId*.

Also, even though this search-and-replace command both begins and ends with the letter *g*, the final *g* is not redundant. It is the command option that tells *vi* to make the substitution more than once per line, if need be.

There are two other options you can use in combination with the *g* option. They are *p*, which tells *vi* to print (on the screen) a copy of every line it changes, and *c*, which allows you to confirm each replacement before it is made. To use the *p* option with the preceding example, your command would take the form:

:g/ we /s// I /gp

Vi would show you every line it changed, and you could check them for errors. When you finished, pressing Enter would eliminate the display of changed lines.

Likewise, to use the *c* option in our example, your command would be:

`:g/ we /s// | /gc`

This time, *vi* would show you each occurrence of *we* before the substitution was made. To accept the change, you would press *y*; to reject the change, you would press the Enter key.

Both *p* and *c* are valuable aids in verifying the accuracy of a global search-and-replace command. The *c* option, in particular, is a good one to get in the habit of using even though it adds a little time to the substitution process.

ENTERING THE SHELL WITHOUT EXITING *vi*

Suppose you tried to save a document and *vi* told you that a file of the same name already existed in the same directory. You would have to either choose a different name or overwrite the existing file. But what if you couldn't remember what that file contained?

You could save the document under an alternate name, exit *vi*, and then use XENIX' *cat* command to look at the contents of the file that obstructed your original intention. But that's not necessary.

At any point in your work with *vi*, as long as you are in command mode, you can type:

`:!sh`

to enter the Bourne shell. (To enter the C shell, the command would be *:!csh.* For the Visual shell, the command would be *:!vsh.*)

In each of these instances, the exclamation point at the beginning of the command line becomes an escape command that lets you temporarily slip out of *vi* and use any valid shell command, including the command to enter the shell itself. If this concept seems elusive, try thinking of it this way: When you invoke *vi*, you do so from one of the shells. *Vi* is active within that shell. When you use the exclamation point, you are opening a temporary doorway into the shell you request.

(In actuality, you can use the exclamation point to temporarily leave other parts of XENIX, too—the *mail* facility, for example—so the subject will crop up again, in other parts of this book.)

Right now, however, what you want to do is look at the contents of a file. You can shorten the procedure even further by using the *cat* command (or any other command) directly from *vi*. Thus *:!cat [file name]* will take you directly to the file, because *cat* is a valid shell command and hence is as effective when used this way as it is when you enter it at the shell prompt.

If you haven't saved your document before you use the exclamation point and a shell command, XENIX will tell you as much. But your text and *vi* are not disturbed when the command you request is carried out, so the message is more of a friendly reminder than anything else. It's a good practice to save your document before you invoke the shell, though. As long as your document resides only in temporary memory, the second or two it takes to type *:w* is well worth the effort.

RETURNING TO *vi*

If you use the exclamation point to enter either the Bourne or C XENIX shell, press Ctrl-D to return to *vi*. If you enter the Visual shell, use the Quit command.

Ordinarily, Ctrl-D is the logout command for users of the Bourne shell. In a sense, it is the same here, but instead of taking you off the system completely, it returns you to the shell level from which you arrived—the one containing *vi* and the work you were doing. Using Ctrl-D is thus somewhat like backing up and closing the door you just opened.

In all cases, whether you've entered the shell or just used a shell command (such as *cat*), once the command has run its course, you'll be prompted to press the Enter key to continue with *vi*.

SIZING UP YOUR DOCUMENT

Before we leave *vi*, we should look at one more thing: the size of a *vi* document. Because your document is carried in XENIX' user memory, its size is limited by the amount of memory *vi* has available. This amount can vary from one installation to another, but should remain relatively constant within any one system, so the document that fits in memory today will still fit tomorrow. As a general guideline, we recommend you never edit a file larger than 250K in size.

It is possible, however, for a document to become so large that you can no longer edit it. It is also possible that your system administrator might need to change the system for some reason, and in the process reduce the amount of memory available. If either of these situations occurs, you have an aid in the form of *split,* a XENIX utility that lets you break one long file into two shorter ones. The command format looks like this:

split -[lines per file] [file name] [new name]

For example, suppose you had a 3000-line file named *xenix_book*. You could use *split* to break it into two 1500-line files identified by the new name *xenix_files* with the command (entered at the shell prompt):

split -1500 xenix_book xenix_files

Here, the − symbol is the usual lead character for XENIX command options; 1500 is the number of lines per file (if you don't supply a number, *split* will use 1000 lines as the default); *xenix_book* is the original file; and *xenix_files* is the name you specify for the new files.

When XENIX carries out your command, it will add a two-character suffix to the new name. The suffixes begin with *aa* and proceed through the alphabet, so the resulting two files will be:

    xenix_filesaa

    xenix_filesab

Split also allows you to divide the file into more than two pieces if you wish. To do so, specify a size that is a smaller multiple of the file's total line length. For example, if *xenix_book* were 110 lines long and you wanted it broken into six files (five 20-line files and one 10-line file), one way to accomplish it would be to type:

split -20 xenix_book xenix_files_

Note the underline character added to the end of the file name (*xenix_files_*). This will make the name more readable after *aa* is added (*xenix_files_aa*).

7

POLISHING YOUR TEXT *Romeo and Juliet* would be a great play whether scrawled on a child's notepad or beautifully typeset on the finest paper. Likewise, it would remain great whether it contained one, two, or twenty typographical errors. But very few of us can claim Shakespeare's genius with words, and in the world in which we function, appearances do count. An attractively presented document has much more impact than one that is unappealing or difficult to read. Spelling errors in the letters you write home are no problem; the same errors in your business letters can make you look foolish or sloppy. There are other considerations, too. Are your sentences long and unwieldy? Are your phrases out of date? Do you tend to repeat yourself? These are all elements of style with which writers must contend. And writers aren't only the people whose names appear in books and magazines. Writers are all the people who care about how they present ideas in written form.

XENIX' Text Processing System is an impressive package of programs and utilities that help you with these things and more. Here, we'll cover the basics of making your documents look good—from formatting to sentence structure to printing. But there is a wealth of information concerning this system, so use the Text Processing guide you received with the XENIX system as a complement to the following introduction.

120

■ NOTE: *The Text Processing System is installed separately from the rest of XENIX, so before you try to use the commands and programs described here, ask your system administrator whether the Text Processing System is available to you.*

We'll look at spelling first.

SPELLING CHECKERS

A spelling checker is a utility that matches patterns of characters and words. You performed a similar task yourself when you searched for words to replace in the *form_letter* document in Chapter 6. But a spelling checker matches patterns on a vaster scale. It compares literally every word in your document against the contents of a dictionary data file that may contain upwards of 20,000 words. All words from your document that have no match in the dictionary are reported as errors, including legitimate words, such as your name, that are not physically included in the program's dictionary. So, spelling checkers are not intelligent.

Also, spelling checkers do not verify context. No error would be found in the sentence *That is fare,* if all the words in that sentence are written as they appear in the program's dictionary. Yet, you probably meant *fair,* not *fare.* So, spelling checkers are not infallible, either.

But they are very good for checking for typographical errors. And XENIX' *spell* program can even perform extra functions that you would not typically find in a spelling checker. The easiest way to see how *spell* works is to use it.

CHECKING YOUR SPELLING

Let's check a document named *sample,* into which we've deliberately introduced a number of errors. Try *spell* for yourself by entering the lines shown in the following illustration with the *vi* editor and saving the file to disk (the quotation is from Thoreau):

```
    Here is a test for the XENIX spelling checker.  All errors
will be flagged.  What could be easier?
    "Why shoudl we be in such desperate haste
to suceed, and in such desperate enterprises?
If a man does not keep pace with his companions,
perhaps it is because he heers a different
drummer.  Let him step to teh music which he
hears, however measured or far awey."
~
~
```

Check the file you've created with the *spell* command by typing:

spell sample

You may or may not have visually picked out the errors, but *spell* certainly finds them all. In just a few seconds, it produces the list:

```
$ spell sample
XENIX
awey
heers
shoudl
suceed
teh
$ _
```

Although *XENIX* is spelled correctly, it's listed as a misspelled word. *Spell* could not find it in the dictionary and thus assumes it's incorrect.

Spell makes other assumptions, too, and some are not only beneficial, they're also impressive. For example, not all of the words in *sample* are actually in the dictionary. *Spell* made certain value judgments about word construction, based on the rules it knows. You can see these assumptions by using *spell's v* option:

spell -v sample

Applied to the same file, *spell* produces the same list of misspelled words. But it also displays another list of words, along with the rules it used to determine whether they are correctly spelled:

```
$ spell -v sample
XENIX
awey
heers
shoudl
suceed
teh
+er       checker
+s        companions
+s        does
+m+er     drummer
-y+ier    easier
+s        enterprises
+s        errors
+g+ed     flagged
+s        hears
+d        measured
+ing      spelling
$ _
```

122

In the left column, you see *spell*'s assumptions. With *checker,* for example, it found both the word *check* and the valid suffix *er.* Putting the two together, *spell* assumed that *checker* was a valid word.

Furthermore, you see two other examples of just how far *spell* can go. When it found the word *flag,* it doubled the *g* before adding the suffix *ed.* In the same way, when it found the word *easy* and the suffix *er,* it knew that the *y* should be dropped in favor of an *i* in the correct spelling.

Spell has other options, too, among them a *b* option that checks for British spellings, such as *colour, civilise, centre,* and *travelled.*

⊠ NOTE: *We'll be using* sample *for other examples in this chapter. You may want to take a minute or two now to call up* vi *and correct the errors. They will not appear in any following illustrations.*

A WORD ON REDIRECTING

If you use the *v* option, as in the preceding demonstration, *spell*'s list of errors and its assumptions may turn out to be longer than your screen can display at one time. Of necessity, part of the list will scroll off out of sight. But when you are checking for mistakes, you don't want that to happen. Then, too, you might prefer a paper printout of the list, so you can use it as the basis for a search-and-replace cleanup operation with *vi.*

The solution is simple. You can tell *spell* to send its output somewhere other than the screen—to a data file on disk, for example. This technique is called redirecting output, and uses the greater-than symbol (⟩) to "point to" the new destination. Thus, the command:

    spell sample ⟩ sample_errors

would perform the spelling check you request but, instead of printing the results on your screen, it would save them in a data file called *sample_errors.*

This technique is identical to the one you used with *ed* when you created a memo file in Chapter 3. The output file you specify can have any name you prefer and can be located in any valid directory, but if a file with the same name already exists in the same directory, the existing file will be overwritten by the new version. As you did with *ed,* however, you can add the new text to an existing file by using double greater-than symbols, as in the command:

    spell sample ⟩⟩ sample_errors

(You can redirect both input and output to perform many tasks. Because redirection is such a valuable tool, we will also cover it in Chapter 9, "Advanced File Techniques.")

CHECKING MORE THAN ONE DOCUMENT

Just as you can handle multiple documents with *vi,* you can use *spell* to check more than one document at a time. For example, if you had four files named *doc1, doc2, doc3,* and *doc4,* the command:

    spell doc[1-4] ⟩ doc_errors

would instruct *spell* to check the four documents named and place any errors it found in a file called *doc_errors.* The resulting file would contain an alphabetized list of the errors found in all documents. (It would not, however, identify the file in which a particular misspelling occurred.)

REFINING *spell*

As you can see, *spell* can be a valuable aid in helping you find inadvertent spelling errors. Most documents, however, include a number of proper names, acronyms, and other valid words that *spell*'s dictionary does not contain. If you rely on *spell* fairly often, you may wish to "educate" it, so that these words are not reported as misspellings time after time. To do so, create a file that contains these words (one word to a line). Then, when you run *spell,* include that file name as an option. For example, if you create a file named *my_dict* containing words like George, Halifax, or RAM, you can use the command form:

    spell +my_dict letter

to have *spell* include these words as valid spellings.

123

CHECKING YOUR STYLE

Evaluating a person's writing style is largely a matter of opinion, interpretation, and judgment. Such subjective criteria are difficult to measure, but there are some standards that can be applied to all documents. XENIX' *style* program can check your text against those standards. As with *spell,* you can specify several file names at once and redirect the output to a disk file instead of the screen.

The command:

style sample

produces five types of information about our sample document:

124

```
$ style sample
-- sample
readability grades:
        (Kincaid)  4.6  (auto)  4.1  (Coleman-Liau)  6.6  (Flesch) 6.8 (81.6)
sentence info:
        no. sent 6 no. wds 65
        av sent leng 10.8 av word leng 4.28
        no. questions 2 no. imperatives 0
        no. nonfunc wds 34  52.3%  av leng 5.65
        short sent (<6) 33% (2) long sent (<21)  0% (0)
        longest sent 19 wds at sent 5; shortest sent 4 wds at sent 3
sentence types:
        simple  67% (4) complex  33% (2)
        compound    0% (0) compound-complex  0% (0)
word usage:
        verb types as % of total verbs
        tobe  45% (5) aux  27% (3) inf   18% (2)
        passives as % of non-inf verbs  11% (1)
        types as % of total
        prep 6.2% (4) conj 3.1% (2) adv 4.6% (3)
        noun 21.5% (14) adj 15.4% (10) pron 9.2% (6)
        nominalizations  0 % (0)
sentence beginnings:
        subject opener: noun (2) pron (1) pos (0) adj (1) art (0) tot  67%
        prep  0% (0) adv   17% (1)
        verb  0% (0)  sub_conj   17% (1) conj   0% (0)
        expletives   0% (0)
$ _
```

The first item, *readability grades,* measures *sample* against four standardized tests called Kincaid, Automated Readability Index (auto), Coleman-Liau, and Flesch. According to the premises on which these systems are based, documents with high ratings require more sophisticated reading skills than do documents with low ratings. William Faulkner and James Joyce would have very high ratings on these tests—probably at or about 17, the maximum the program reports.

The second and third groupings give information about sentence structure. In general, these reports can help you evaluate the effectiveness of your writing style. By checking *style*'s report on the average sentence and word lengths in your document, and the number of sentence types you used, you can determine whether you've overused one element or another.

Style also reports on your *word usage* and *sentence beginnings.* Under *word usage,* you might want to pay particular attention to the percentage of passive verbs in your document. Too many passive verbs can lessen the impact of your writing. In most instances, *Your dog bit me* is a much more effective sentence than *I was bitten by your dog.*

The last section of the *style* report, *sentence beginnings,* is less important for the individual statistics it provides than it is as an indication of the ways in which you begin your sentences.

CHECKING YOUR DICTION

XENIX' *diction* program is another writing aid that is subjective in approach. *Diction* uses a library of phrases, much as *spell* uses a dictionary of words, but this library is a collection of words and phrases generally considered either awkward or verbose. If any of the words in your document match any of the phrases in its library, *diction* prints the sentence to the screen with the phrase enclosed in brackets. The program also tells you the number of sentences it examined and the number of "hits" (matches) it found.

If you were to run *diction* on the sample document with the command:

diction sample

you'd see the following report:

```
$ diction sample
-- sample
  let him step to the music[ which ]he hears  however measured or far away.

number of sentences 6 number of hits 1
$ _
```

Perhaps you have a personal list of words and phrases you tend to misuse or overwork. If so, you can have *diction* check your list in addition to its own with the command form:

diction -f [your phrase file] [file name]

Or, you can have it ignore its list and use yours alone:

diction -n -f [your phrase file] [file name]

Diction is a good, impartial reviewer if your writing tends to be wordy or too reliant on trite expressions, slang, or jargon. As with *spell* and *style,* you can include several file names and redirect *diction*'s output to a disk file.

125

WORKING IN THE BACKGROUND

If you tried any of the preceding examples, you found that checking your spelling, style, or diction is not quick. It can't be. Even if your document were only ten words long, each word would have to be checked or otherwise accounted for.

If you chain several documents for any of the programs, you extend the time even more. And, if your documents contain thousands of words, rather than the 66 in our small sample file, you can sit at your terminal for a long time waiting for the task to be completed.

But remember: XENIX is a multiuser, multitasking operating system. While you are doing your work, other people may be logged into the system doing theirs. Their use of the system—the tasks XENIX is performing for them—is transparent, running somewhere in the background. To you, their work is out of sight and mind, because it has little or no effect on what you're doing in the foreground.

Since XENIX can perform other people's tasks in the background, it's logical to expect little or no impediment to relegating a task of your own into the background. In fact, there's none at all. You can tell XENIX to execute a task in the background, and thus leave your terminal free for other work, simply by ending a command line with an ampersand (&). For example, you could check the spelling of all files beginning with *doc* and redirect the output to a file named *doc_errors* with the command:

spell doc ∗ ⟩ doc_errors &

XENIX responds to a request for background processing by placing a number on the line just below the command line. This number is the *process number* for the task. Your shell prompt then appears on the line just below the process number, and at that point you can move on to any foreground task you want, including another request for a background task.

Here's a different example. Suppose you are using *vi* and have just finished creating a long document, *doc1.* It will be sent to an important client, so you want to check your spelling, but you have more documents to create. You want to continue your session with *vi* and cannot afford to wait while *spell* performs its check.

This is an ideal situation for illustrating a real touch of XENIX magic. One command, and a short one at that, lets you drop into the shell, request the spelling check, redirect the output to a file on disk, and send the whole process into the background:

:!spell doc1 ⟩ errors &

That's all you have to do. *Vi* will prompt you to press Enter to continue. When you do, you'll be back in *vi,* able to continue your work while *spell* checks your document and puts any misspelled words in a file named *errors.*

126

When you use foreground and background processes as in this example, remember to redirect your output to a disk file, rather than let it appear on the screen. Redirection is useful in its own right, and it can become very important in situations like this one.

If you did *not* redirect the output in this example, the list of misspelled words would still be printed on your screen. Just because you assign the *spell* process to the background does not mean you automatically reassign its output to any location other than where it normally appears.

With no redirection, *spell* will print its output on your screen, despite any foreground process you are working on. *Spell* doesn't care what you're doing. It knows only that it must present the results of its check to you. Needless to say, if you happen to be in the middle of another document, the appearance of a list of spelling errors on your screen will create a lot of visual confusion. (If this happens when you're in *vi,* don't be concerned. No changes have been made to your document, and pressing Ctrl-L will redraw your screen.)

There is, despite their many advantages, one respect in which redirecting and background processing are less efficient than working in the foreground, and that involves error messages. If, for some reason, the process you initiate encounters any errors, those errors will be reported in your disk file, not on the screen. You won't know about them until you look at the contents of the file. On the other hand, though, you can rest assured that any errors will be reported, and you will be able to try and resolve any problems later.

USING BACKGROUND PROCESSING EFFECTIVELY

You can send quite a few different types of tasks to the background. Spelling checks and printing (which you'll see later in this chapter) are just two possibilities. Sorting lists numerically or alphabetically is another. But should you push everything you possibly can into the background?

For your convenience, that answer may be yes. But when you consider everyone else who might be on the system at a given time, then the answer must be no.

As you push more processes into the background, you start to burden the entire system—not only the portion you're sharing, but *all* of the system and *all* of the people who are using it. Eventually, the delays caused by background work can boomerang and begin to slow the foreground processes you're attempting.

There is no way to stop that delay, but you can lessen its effect. All it takes is a chat with your system administrator and some scheduling on your part. Find out when the peak use of your system occurs. Background processes slow the system most when the most people are logged in. If you can limit your background work to the times when the fewest users are on the system, you will help minimize delays. In effect, your background tasks will only be taking time that would normally be assigned to other users.

127

LOGGING OUT WHILE RUNNING A BACKGROUND PROCESS

Unless you're calling in on a dial-up line, a background process you've initiated on IBM Version 2.0 of XENIX will continue, even if you log out. On other versions of XENIX, this may or may not always be the case. If XENIX does terminate a background process when you log out, no damage will be done to your source files, but your output file will be incomplete, and you will have to restart the process when you next log in.

It's thus wise to protect your background work, just as you protect unsaved editing changes while working with *vi*. For a background process, begin the command line with the word *nohup*, an abbreviated form of *no hangup*. For example, to protect a background spelling check of the documents *sample* and *proposal*, with the results stored in a file named *errors*, you would type the command:

nohup spell sample proposal ⟩ errors &

After you take this precaution, whether you log out or not, XENIX will continue the spelling check to completion.

FORMATTING A DOCUMENT

Spell, style, and *diction,* used in the foreground or the background, care for the basic needs of every document. But there's still the matter of what some call "pretty printing." Even before electronic typewriters were commonplace, printers attached to computers were churning out documents containing boldfaced and underlined words. Margins and spacing could be set, and the tops and bottoms of pages could automatically be printed with headers and footers.

Like your terminal's display, printers require control-character sequences that initiate such enhancements. Certain control codes are unique to each printer make or model, but many simple ones, for features such as boldfacing and underlining, can be applied to most printers.

None of those enhancements originate within the printer, however. They begin as special instructions contained in the body of the text—instructions that are inserted and processed by the formatting program and then converted into the appropriate control codes needed by the printer.

XENIX has two formatting programs for such instructions, *nroff* and *troff* (pronounced en-roff and tee-roff). Both have many commands in common, but the latter is used principally in preparing text for a typesetting machine and, as such, is a more sophisticated program than you need for many of the functions you require from your system's letter-quality or dot-matrix printer. For this reason, we'll concentrate principally on *nroff* here.

To begin, let's do something simple with *nroff* and our *sample* document.

CENTERING A LINE OF TEXT

Call *sample* into *vi* from your shell prompt with the command:

vi sample

If the cursor does not appear at the first character of the first line of text, move it there by pressing *H.* Then press uppercase O to open a new line above the current line and, at the same time, place you into insert mode. Now, type the following three lines of text:

.ce[Enter]
Document Fragment[Enter]
.sp3

Press Escape to exit insert mode. Save the document with the *:w* command.

The *.ce* you typed is an *nroff* command that will center the following line of text (*Document Fragment*). Note that the command appears on a line by itself and is preceded by a period. The period is always the first character of a line containing an *nroff* command. When *nroff* scans your documents, it looks for such lead-in characters to differentiate between commands and the ordinary portions of your text. (The formatting commands are called *dot commands* because of that lead-in character.)

Because you want some empty space between the title and the body of your text, you used another dot command, *.sp3,* to place three blank lines after the title. You could also insert those lines by pressing the Enter key three times. But why not save time and space? The command *.sp3* occupies one line, while three physically entered blank lines would occupy three.

Now that you've tried some formatting commands, use *nroff* to do the actual formatting. You could exit *vi* and run *nroff* at the shell prompt, but to save time let's activate *nroff* from within *vi.* Type:

:!nroff sample ⟩ sample2

to scan *sample* for formatting commands, modify it according to those commands, and store the new document in a file called *sample2.* (Note that *nroff,* though closely related to *vi* in function, must still be called as a separate program—from *vi,* with the ! shell escape symbol or at the shell prompt itself.)

129

When *nroff* is finished, you'll be prompted to press the Enter key to continue. Do so, and then enter the command:

:e sample2

to tell *vi* you now want to work with *sample2.* The result should look like this:

```
                    Document Fragment


   Here is a test for the XENIX  spelling  checker.   All   errors
will be flagged.  What could be easier?
   "Why should we be in such desperate haste to succeed,  and  in
such desperate enterprises?  If a man does not keep pace with his
companions, perhaps it is because he hears a  different   drummer.
Let him step to the music which he hears, however measured or far
away."
```

For comparison, here is your original sample (spelling corrected):

```
   Here is a test for the XENIX spelling checker.  All errors
will be flagged.  What could be easier?
   "Why should we be in such desperate haste
to succeed, and in such desperate enterprises?
If a man does not keep pace with his companions,
perhaps it is because he hears a different
drummer.  Let him step to the music which he
hears, however measured or far away."
```

Two changes are immediately noticeable. First, *nroff* has carried out the *.ce* and *.sp3* commands by centering the heading three lines above the body of the document. You've accomplished your first formatting instructions.

Less obviously, *nroff* has also formatted the body of your text according to one of its built-in defaults: The lines of your document are now justified, with the first and last characters of each full line aligned vertically.

ADJUSTING YOUR TEXT

The justification you see is handled by an *nroff* formatting adjustment called *fill.* To make each line start and end at the same position, the line is padded, or filled, with spaces wherever needed. As mentioned, *fill* is *nroff*'s default. There are actually four ways you can align your lines of text:

| fill | *.ad b* | Aligns your document along both the left and the right edges. |
| right | *.ad r* | Aligns your text along the right edge, leaving the left side ragged. |

| left | *.ad l* | Aligns your text along the left edge, leaving the right side ragged. |
| center | *.ad c* | Centers each line of text with equal left and right margins. This produces a ragged edge on both the right and the left sides. |

You can use these commands to adjust the edges of different sections of text in your document simply by entering the appropriate command above the text you want to format. If at any time you wish to change the way you're aligning the text, also include *.fi* between the *fill* commands. For example, if you wanted the first paragraph of *sample* to be aligned right, but the second to be fill-justified, your file would appear as:

131

```
.ce
Document Fragment
.sp3
.ad r
   Here is a test for the XENIX spelling checker.  All errors
will be flagged.  What could be easier?
.fi
.ad b
   "Why should we be in such desperate haste
to succeed, and in such desperate enterprises?
If a man does not keep pace with his companions,
perhaps it is because he hears a different
drummer.  Let him step to the music which he
hears, however measured or far away."
```

The resulting document would look like this:

```
                    Document Fragment



        Here is a test for the XENIX spelling checker.  All errors
                     will be flagged.  What could be easier?
   "Why should we be in such desperate haste to succeed,  and  in
such desperate enterprises?  If a man does not keep pace with his
companions, perhaps it is because he hears a  different  drummer.
Let him step to the music which he hears, however measured or far
away."
```

Of course, at any point in your document you can include the command *.nf* (*no fill*) to turn the formatting adjustments off. This causes the text to appear exactly as you typed it. To turn formatting back on, use *.fi* (fill).

INSIDE *nroff* DOT COMMANDS

There is no magic to dot commands. Just as two characters, *vi,* represent a sophisticated program composed of a great many instructions, *nroff*'s dot commands, such as *.ad,* represent sets of instructions two, three, four, or more lines long. The complete set of instructions, not the dot command, contains the *exact* information *nroff* needs to perform the function indicated by the dot command.

If, however, you had to enter several lines of instructions each time you wanted to change the appearance of some portion of your document, you might quickly tire of the process and simply accept your text "as is."

Enter *macroinstructions* (*macros,* for short), a type of shorthand that makes commands easier for you to type and remember. Macros typically are one- or two-character commands. Within the program or operating system in which it is designed to be used, a macro represents a (long) list of instructions. Rather than entering the list, you enter the macro command associated with it, and the program or operating system carries out the involved set of instructions. Of course, this means the program or operating system must know what commands each macro represents. These definitions are built into *nroff.*

SETTING PAGE DIMENSIONS

In addition to the more obvious changes in your document, there has been another, subtle transformation. In the original document, you ended each line of text with a carriage return. In adjusting the lines of your document, *nroff* has ignored the distinctions you made among separate lines. Where the third line of text originally ended with the word *haste,* it now ends with the word *in.* In carrying out your formatting instructions, *nroff* disregarded the end-of-line carriage return and moved the words *to succeed, and in* from the beginning of the fourth line to the end of the third. You'll also notice that there is a lot of blank space at the end of your document. This is because *nroff* has prepared the document for a standard 8½- x 11-inch piece of paper and padded the bottom of the page with an appropriate amount of blank space.

Actually, *nroff* bases all of its decisions about line width, page length, line spacing, and page offset (width of the lefthand margin) upon certain default settings that it's been programmed to use, unless told otherwise. The defaults for these parameters are:

```
Page offset   =  0
Page length   =  11 inches
Line length   =  6.5 inches
Line spacing  =  Single
```

SETTING THE PAGE OFFSET

One of the most visible settings you can make is the page offset. Cryptic as the name may seem, it's simply the adjustment for the left-hand margin. When you print your document, the initial page offset of 0 causes your text to be printed as close to the left edge of the page as your printer can reach.

That setting may be fine for rough drafts or wide documents, but margins for printed pages usually allow for a one-inch border all around. To create such a border, you need to offset the body of your text, moving it in one inch from the left edge of the paper. The command form for this is:

    .po [number]i

where you replace *[number]* with a number. The *i* appended to the number indicates that your selection is in *inches*. Without the *i, nroff* will assume that the measurement represents number of characters, in which case the equivalent command to move in one inch would be either *.po 10* or *.po 12,* for reasons we'll cover next.

CHARACTERS AND INCHES

Let's examine a "standard" $8\frac{1}{2}$- x 11-inch page and your printer.

In the world of computer-driven printers, the majority of printers are given a default setting of 10 characters per inch (10 cpi) across the page. On a page $8\frac{1}{2}$ inches wide, 10 cpi gives you a theoretical line length of 85 characters. (It's theoretical because very few printers can actually begin and end printing at the exact left and right edges of the paper.)

If you look at the preceding table of *nroff*'s default settings, however, you can see that the actual line length is $6\frac{1}{2}$ inches. On a 10-cpi printer, that translates to 65 characters per line. The remaining 2 inches, or 20 characters, form the margins.

With a page offset of 0, however, the printer will begin each line as close to the left edge of the paper as it can. That means you have a right margin somewhere in the neighborhood of 2 inches, or 20 characters.

When you adjust the page offset to provide a 1-inch left margin, you use 10 of those "extra" character positions. After you add 65 characters for the printed line, that leaves 10 characters (or 1 inch) as the default right margin.

The most frequently used alternate character pitch is 12 cpi. On a page $8\frac{1}{2}$ inches wide, that's a theoretical line length of 102 characters. Your 1-inch left and right margins still leave $6\frac{1}{2}$ inches for the line length. But at 12 pitch, that line will now contain 78 characters.

133

SETTING FULL-PAGE PARAMETERS

As you can see, the dimension of the right margin is dependent on the page offset and the line length. The general formula for determining the right margin is:

right margin = (page width) − (line length) − (page offset)

Now, here are the other dot commands you need for setting up full pages:

.pl [number]i   To set page length
.ll [number]i   To set line length
.ls [number]   To set line spacing

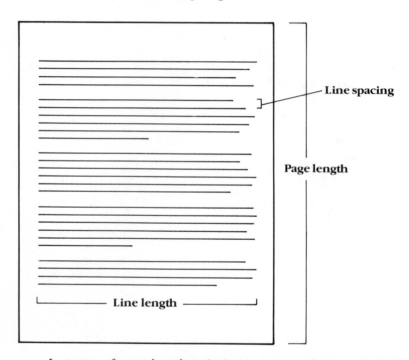

In terms of page length, printing is more or less standardized at 6 lines per inch (lpi). On an 11-inch page, you could print 66 lines, not allowing for top or bottom margins (84 lines on a page 14 inches long). The most common alternate is 8 lpi, producing 88 lines on an 11-inch page, or 112 lines on a sheet 14 inches long.

Let's look briefly at some ways you might use these commands.

If you were working with an 11- x 14-inch sheet and you wanted to set up a 1½-inch left margin and a 1-inch right margin, you'd do so with the following *nroff* commands at the beginning of your document:

```
.po 1.5i
.pl 14i
.ll 8.5i
```

If you wanted the document to be double-spaced, you'd add this command to that list:

```
.ls 2
```

If you knew that the printer operated at 10 cpi and 6 lpi, then you could write that same series of commands, using character positions (and line counts for the page length), as:

135

```
.po 15 (10 cpi x 1.5 inches)
.pl 84 (6 lpi x 14 inches)
.ll 85 (10 cpi x 8.5 inches)
.ls 2
```

You still have two other sections of your paper to account for—the top and bottom margins. If you leave *nroff* with its default values of 0 for these two dimensions, your document will begin at the very top of the first page, and a new page will not be started until the printer reaches the very bottom of the paper.

Since *nroff* has no simple dot commands to accommodate changes to the top and bottom margins, you need to create a new dot-command macro. You could start from scratch, given a knowledge of relevant, pre-existing *nroff* dot-command macros and an understanding of the correct format for defining a macro.

But someone's already done most of the work for you.

THE MEMORANDUM MACROS

There is a collection of *nroff*-compatible macros contained in a file called *mm* (short for *memorandum macros*). Most of the commands you need can be found there—including the macro you need to set top and bottom margins with *nroff.*

The dot command itself is .VM (for vertical margins) and takes the form:

```
.VM [top] [bottom]
```

The command must be typed in uppercase letters. You replace *[top]* and *[bottom]* with the appropriate number of lines—not inches—for each vertical margin.

When the .VM command is carried out, the instructions in the macro itself add the two values you've supplied to *nroff*'s default top and bottom margin settings. Since *nroff*'s values are zero, the process works quite well—as long as you tell *nroff* that you've used a memorandum macro. Remember: The memorandum macros exist in a separate file, so *nroff* must be told to use it. To do that, you include *mm* as an option in your *nroff* command line. For example:

```
nroff -mm sample ) sample2
```

tells *nroff* you've used *mm* macros in the text file *sample* and also tells *nroff* to send the formatted output to the text file *sample2*.

After *nroff* begins, it calls in *mm,* which goes through the file, interpreting the dot commands and macros (*mm* understands the dot commands you've already seen, even though they are *nroff,* rather than *mm,* macros). Formatting with the *nroff* dot commands is straightforward, but when *mm* reaches the vertical-margins command, the situation changes. Now, you are combining *nroff*'s defaults with your instructions to *mm*. While *nroff* assumes a zero value for top and bottom margins, *mm* does not. In fact, it assumes quite a bit more:

```
                              - 1 -



                        Document Fragment



         Here is a test for the XENIX spelling checker.  All
     errors will be flagged.  What could be easier?
         "Why should we be in such desperate haste to succeed, and
     in such desperate enterprises?  If a man does not keep pace
     with his companions, perhaps it is because he hears a
     different drummer.  Let him step to the music which he
     hears, however measured or far away."
```

Here, you see *mm*'s default vertical margins: three blank lines at the top of the document, a page number on the fourth line, and below it three more blank lines before the text begins. Altogether, that gives you a seven-line top margin. (You can't see it here, but the default bottom margin is eight lines.) If you do adjust the vertical margins, you will need to take these existing values into account, because your own values will be added to the defaults. For example, the command *.VM 6 6* would add six blank lines to the existing defaults for the top and bottom of the page.

You may, however, find that the default spacing is fine for your purposes. Seven lines at the top and eight lines at the bottom are reasonable margin settings. But the page number may or may not be part of your plans.

The page number is a default header—one or more lines that are printed at the top of each page of your document—and in this case, it causes the page number to be printed. (The complement of a header is a footer, which is printed at the bottom of the page.)

While page numbering is appropriate in long documents, one- or two-page letters can suffer from such numbering—especially when it is centered at the top of the page. The default page numbering here is easy to change, however.

To find our way around this situation, we'll look—relatively briefly—at how macros are used, constructed, and modified. In this discussion, however, bear in mind that the examples are "artificial" to some degree. They work because the page number and the header are one and the same—the page number *is* the header, and the header *is* the page number. They are not necessarily directly transferable to other situations. Our purpose here is to look at the nature and purpose of macros, not necessarily at their best use. You'll see the simplest way to remove the page header when we discuss headers and footers a little later in the chapter. For now, it's best to view the following examples simply as a means of illustrating several alternatives before we reach the optimum.

ALTERING *mm* VALUES

Each value contained in the actual commands that are applied when you invoke a macro must be stored somewhere. In XENIX' text-formatting system, the storage locations are called number registers. Each register has a name, and that name identifies the parameter (value) stored in it.

The actual registers, and the values they can contain, are described in your text-processing manual. Here, we'll look at just one of them. It's named N, and it holds a number that controls *mm*'s page-numbering style. Number register N can contain one of six possible values:

0   All pages receive the current header (this is the default).

1   A header replaces a footer on the first page of the document.

2   No header is placed on page 1.

3   Page numbering is done by section (1-1, 1-2, 1-3) instead of consecutively throughout the document.

4   Default page headers are not printed, but any headers you supply will be printed.

5   Page and figure numbering are by section.

138

Obviously, if you could place the value 4 into the N register, the default page numbering would vanish. It's simple to do. You would use the command:

.nr N 4

in your text. The dot-command macro *nr* indicates that you're about to change the value in a number register. The name of the register is N, and 4 is the value you want to place in it.

If you applied this command to your sample text, along with double-spacing and a left margin of 1 inch as already discussed, the formatted document would now look like this:

```
                         Document Fragment


     Here is a test for the XENIX spelling checker.  All

errors will be flagged.  What could be easier?

     "Why should we be in such desperate haste to succeed, and

in such desperate enterprises?  If a man does not keep pace

with his companions, perhaps it is because he hears a

different drummer.  Let him step to the music which he

hears, however measured or far away."
```

As with the other dot-command macros, you could change the value of register N at any other place in your text to produce headers in other parts of your document.

DEFINING A MACRO

Using a number-register command is an adequate solution to the page-number problem, but you still might not be happy with the spacing of the top margin. To change it, you would need to redefine the macro that controls the way the top of your page is handled. This macro is called TP (for top of page), and you redefine its contents with the command *.de*.

For example, suppose you wanted a 1-inch top margin with no header. You could redefine the macro like this:

```
.de TP
.sp 1i
..
```

In the first of these three lines, the *.de* dot command calls in a macro that will accept a definition from you. *TP* is the macro you want to redefine. It already exists as part of *mm*, but its contents can be modified, and that is what you do in the second command line, simply by giving the command to print a one-inch space. The double dot on the third line ends the definition.

Inserted at the beginning of the sample text, your new *TP* parameters would produce a document very much like the preceding illustration, but with a one-inch top margin (there, you suppressed the header, so the top margin is slightly larger than it would be here). It is important to include this at the beginning of the text, as it takes effect on the *next* page.

Easy as it is to define this macro, adding a few subtleties to it should prove no problem. Try this (substitute your own name inside the brackets):

```
.de TP
.sp 1
[your name]'s  test—
.sp 4
..
```

Again, you've begun by redefining the macro *TP*. This time, the first entry into the definition is a command to skip only 1 line. That's followed by a simple line of printed text. It's part of the new *TP* definition, because it is between the beginning (*.de*) and ending (*..*) markers of the macro. The last command in the macro skips 4 lines of text, and the double dot ends the definition.

139

In the sample, your newly modified macro produces a formatted document that looks like this:

```
    Mike's test-



                    Document Fragment


    Here is a test for the XENIX spelling checker.  All
errors will be flagged.  What could be easier?
    "Why should we be in such desperate haste to succeed, and
in such desperate enterprises?  If a man does not keep pace
with his companions, perhaps it is because he hears a
different drummer.  Let him step to the music which he
hears, however measured or far away."
```

with a header positioned one line below the top of the page and the body of the text beginning four lines below the header.

When redefining *TP,* you can even include formatting instructions. If you wanted the header to be right-justified, you could modify the definition as:

```
.de TP
.sp 1
.ad r
[your name]'s test—
.sp 4
..
```

Since that adjust command is used within the macro, it will affect only the text within the macro, not the body of your document.

While this technique has solved the top-margin problem (there is no equivalent for bottom margins), using the *TP* macro to also set up a header is a backhanded approach to headers in general. It's very much like starting your car every morning by rolling it down a hill and popping the clutch. It works, but why not just turn the key?

CREATING HEADERS AND FOOTERS

Six *mm* dot commands control variations in both headers and footers:

.PH   The standard header command, prints the header you supply at the top of every page of your document.

.EH   Prints your header at the tops of even-numbered pages only.

.OH   Prints your header at the tops of the odd-numbered pages only.

.PF   The standard footer command, prints the footer you supply at the bottom of every page of your document.

.EF   Prints your footer at the bottoms of even-numbered pages only.

.OF   Prints your footer at the bottoms of odd-numbered pages only.

The format for any text placed after the header or footer commands is:

    "'flush left'center'flush right'"

That is, the entire header or footer text is enclosed in quotation marks. Within those quotes, you can specify any or all of three possible positions for that text by using apostrophes. And if you're not certain which apostrophes signify left, center, and right, here's a diagram to help you out:

"|This is left' | This is center' | This is right'|"

Figure 7-1. Left, center, and right justification in headers and footers.

So, for example:

    "'Title''Author'"

would place the text *Title* at the left edge of the sheet and *Author* at the right.

If, as you'll see in a later example, an apostrophe occurs as part of the header or footer text, you can either precede the apostrophe with a backslash or you can signify left, center, and right justification with a character (of your choice) other than an apostrophe. For example, if your header contained *The Emperor Jones* and *Eugene O'Neill,* you could enter it as either:

    "'The Emperor Jones''Eugene O\'Neill'"

or as something like:

    "*The Emperor Jones**Eugene O'Neill*"

Also, even though we haven't included any text to be centered, note that the apostrophes (or other separators) must still be included, to hold the relative centering position in the line.

For text that you want flush left on the page, you can just use:

```
"'Title'"
```

without the trailing apostrophes. But if you want the text to be flush right, you must include them, as in:

```
"'''Title'"
```

Let's go back to the sample text and set up a header and footer.

SELECTING HEADER AND FOOTER OPTIONS

Assuming that you have a document several pages long, let's set up headers on both the odd and even pages with .OH and .EH. The equivalent result could be achieved by using the standard .PH dot command, but this way, you'll have greater control, with very little extra work. (For this example we won't use the TP macro we just created.)

From *vi*, insert the even-page-header macros:

```
.EH  "'Title'"
.OH  "'''Title'"
```

into the sample document. Pay close attention to the placement of the apostrophes in the second line. There are three of them following the quotation mark. This format sets the odd-page header at the right of the page.

Had you used the standard .PH command instead of the odd and even header designations, you would have been able to specify a left, right, or center justification—but not a combination, as you have here.

Write the file with the changes back to disk with *vi*'s :w command and then slip into the shell temporarily to run *nroff*:

```
!nroff -mm sample > sample2
```

(You could have added an ampersand to the end of that command line and pushed it into the background for processing. But since the next file you'll be looking at is *sample2*, the output file, and it won't be ready for access until *nroff* is finished, it's just as easy to stay in the foreground and wait.)

After the file *sample* has been formatted, and the results placed in *sample2,* load in *sample2* with *vi*'s *:e* command. It should look like this:

```
                          - 1 -
                                                    Title


          Document Fragment


     Here  is  a  test  for  the  XENIX  spelling  checker.   All

errors  will  be  flagged.   What  could  be  easier?

     "Why  should  we  be  in  such  desperate  haste  to  succeed,  and

in  such  desperate  enterprises?   If  a  man  does  not  keep  pace

with  his  companions,  perhaps  it  is  because  he  hears  a

different  drummer.   Let  him  step  to  the  music  which  he

hears,  however  measured  or  far  away."
"sample" 66 lines, 629 characters
```

143

Aside from the odd and even header commands, you've used *mm*'s default values for all other formatting parameters. And a strange thing has happened. Despite your header instructions (which have been faithfully followed), the document still contains a page number, centered at the top of each page.

You've accepted *mm*'s default values for *all* other formatting instructions— including the .PH main header, which, as you've seen, includes standard page numbering.

This is an important point. The odd and even header parameters are used *in conjunction with, not exclusive of,* the main header. If there is a main header, whether it is the default value or one you've included with a .PH command, the odd or even header you asked for is printed in addition on the line below it.

To remove the default header, you can either change it to some value of your own (using the same format that you did for the odd and even variety) or you can just include a blank main header at the top of your text with:

.PH

The .PH line substitutes your main header for *mm*'s default. Since you haven't specified any text for the header, you've effectively blanked the default value. As with all header and footer commands, this will be in effect for all subsequent pages of the document until you change it with another .PH macro.

ADDING A FOOTER

You create a footer with the same text parameters you use in a header. One thing you might use a footer for is to include the author's name at the bottom of each page. Such a footer might look like this:

```
.PF  "'O\'Hara'"
```

Note the backslash in the name. Without it, the additional apostrophe would force *O* to be aligned on the left margin and *Hara* to be centered.

ADDING PAGE NUMBERING

144

Although *mm*'s default settings will number the pages of a document, you might prefer to incorporate page numbers within the text of your header or footer, rather than have them printed on a separate line. You can do so by adding:

```
nP
```

to the text of your header or footer command line. But because the page number is controlled by the number register (P), you cannot simply type those two characters in the command line. When you include a number register within a header or footer instruction, *nroff* actually evaluates the request three times.

To make *nroff* and *mm* take the request literally, as a page-numbering macro, you precede the command with four backslashes: one each for the three examinations, and one more to ensure that the page numbering is carried out.

USING WHAT YOU KNOW

As a final example, let's suppose you wanted to create a set of headers and footers for your company's annual report. You could incorporate most of what you've learned and create the headers and footers in several ways. If the pages were to be printed back to back (as in a book), your commands might look like this:

```
.PH
.PF
.OH "'''Annual Report for Fiscal Year 1986'"
.EH "'Annual Report for Fiscal Year 1986'"
.OF "'C\'est la Vie Card Company''Page \\\\nP'"
.EF "'Page \\\\nP''C\'est la Vie Card Company'"
```

You begin by supplying blank lines for both the main header and main footer to remove any default values. You're setting even and odd headers and footers because the pages are printed back to back, and you're reversing their format for the same reason. On all odd-numbered pages, the header will be aligned on the upper-right margin of the sheet. In the footer, the company name will be flush left, and the word *Page,* followed by the page number itself, will be flush right. On even-numbered pages, the header and footer elements will be reversed. Notice the back-slash (\ ) in the word *C'est.* As already mentioned it must be included because an apostrophe is part of the name and not a positional instruction.

As the first page of a document is normally printed without a header, you'll want to add the odd header (OH) line somewhere within the *body* of the first or second page of text. That way it won't be read by *nroff* in time to place it on the first page, but it will be read before it's needed on the third page. Likewise, the first page usually is printed without a number. That's easy to accomplish. When you looked at the function of the N register earlier, you saw a list of values you could use to produce a variety of results. If you use the dot command:

.nr N 2

as the first line of your document, you place the value 2 in the N register, and *nroff* will omit the numeric header on the first page of text. (Notice that the number-register command precedes the other macro commands. In order for it to work from the beginning, the value in the register must be set before *nroff* begins processing the other commands.)

ENHANCING YOUR TEXT

Dot-command macros work well when you want to format your entire document or a range of lines. But what about formatting a single word or a group of words? To do that, you would need to insert the dot command in your text at the appropriate place. But you can't do that. The period lead-in character must be the first character on the line. Enhancements can be made on the word level, though.

The most commonly used text enhancements in document preparation are boldfacing and underlining, neither of which is likely to be used throughout an entire document. To begin either of them within the body of your text, you must inform *nroff* that it's about to encounter a format command. That requires the two characters:

\f

For boldfaced text, you would follow the format command with a *B*. For underlining, you would type an *I*.

BOLDFACING

Although you can place an enhancement instruction anywhere in your text, let's direct *nroff* to boldface the words *Document Fragment* in our sample text.

First move the cursor under the *D* in *Document*, then press *i* to enter insert mode. Type:

\fB

to begin boldfacing at that character. Press the Escape key to exit the insert mode, move the cursor under the *t* in *Fragment*, press *a* to append text, and type:

\fR

This instructs *nroff* to end the effects of the preceding formatting command.

To see the results, write the file to disk and use *nroff* to format the text as you have before:

:!nroff -mm sample ⟩ sample2

When *nroff* is finished and you return to *vi*, read in the contents of *sample2*. The document should appear on your screen looking like this:

```
_



                              D^HD^HD^HDo^Ho^Ho^Hoc^Hc^Hc^Hcu^Hu^Hu^Hum^Hm^Hm^H
me^He^He^Hen^Hn^Hn^Hnt^Ht^Ht F^HF^HF^HFr^Hr^Hr^Hra^Ha^Ha^Hag^Hg^Hg^Hgm^Hm^Hm^
Hme^He^He^Hen^Hn^Hn^Hnt^Ht^Ht^Ht



        Here is a test for the XENIX spelling checker.  All

    errors will be flagged.  What could be easier?

        "Why should we be in such desperate haste to succeed, and

    in such desperate enterprises?  If a man does not keep pace

    with his companions, perhaps it is because he hears a

    different drummer.  Let him step to the music which he
```

An odd transformation has taken place. The title is almost incomprehensible, given the mixture of ^H's and other apparently duplicate characters you now see. Despite appearances, though, all is well.

Different printers use different methods of producing boldfaced type. Not knowing which method a particular printer might use, *nroff* has opted for the easiest, and the one most likely to work on the largest variety of printers. It's called double-striking. Each character is printed once, after which the printing element advances one character position to the right. To create the darker print, a backspace instruction returns the printing element to the character, and the character is reprinted over the original. And so it proceeds for the entire phrase.

What you see on your screen, then, is the entire sequence of events that occur in double-striking the words *Document Fragment*. (Pressing the backspace key produces a Control character, $^\wedge$H, that is an instruction to move the cursor one space to the left. That same control character produces identical results on your printer—thus, the repeated occurrences of the characters $^\wedge$H on your screen.)

By the way, don't be alarmed because your two-word phrase now stretches onto more than one screen line. *Vi* still considers the whole string to be one line of text, even though it visually appears to be more like three.

147

UNDERLINING

As you might expect, underlining works on the same general principle as boldfacing. If you want to underline the title in your sample text, the formatting commands would be:

\fIDocument Fragment\fR

While typing an *I* may not seem appropriate for underlining, it is. In typesetting, a single underline is used to indicate *italic* type. The *I* instruction is primarily used with XENIX' phototypesetting formatter, *troff;* there, it indicates that the marked word or words are to be italicized. When it's used with *nroff,* the *I* is interpreted as an underline.

If you try underlining the words *Document Fragment* in your sample document, you'll see that underlining is accomplished in the same manner as boldfacing. First an underline character (available on most printers) is printed, then the printing element is backspaced and the text character is printed at the same position. (The space between two words, however, is *not* underlined.)

As with boldfacing, this approach may not be the most elegant way to handle underlining. But given the variety of methods that can be used on an equally wide variety of printers, *nroff*'s method has the great advantage of working correctly most of the time.

PRINTING

All of which does, finally, bring us to the last phase in processing a document, printing. There are two ways you can print a document: locally, directly from your terminal, or through the system, via the XENIX computer.

PRINTING LOCALLY

Many computer terminals on the market today have local printing facilities. You can attach a printer to the back of the terminal. When you press a particular key, anything that appears on your display is sent to that local printer, as well as to your screen. With these terminals, timing is important because the key to printing successfully is to activate the printer at just the right time.

Some terminals, however, have their own memory. These devices can capture several "pages" of information, so printing is easier. When you activate a local printer connected to such a terminal, you usually have the option of printing either whatever is on the screen or what is in the terminal's memory. Timing, on these terminals, is not particularly critical.

148

Other terminals, like the IBM 3101, are supplied with special instructions—usually a keyboard sequence—that tell them to retain incoming text in a special buffer until the key sequence is given again. Then, you can tell the terminal to print the contents of the buffer. If you're using this or a similar type of terminal with a local printer, consult the terminal manual for specific instructions.

Finally, if you're using a microcomputer with telecommunications software that places it in terminal-emulation mode, you can probably capture all text that's printed to the screen in a text file and then send it to your printer.

PRINTING THROUGH THE SYSTEM

If you don't happen to have a local printer, no matter. Nothing could be easier than using a printer that is connected to the XENIX computer. The key to doing that is the command format:

```
lp [file name]
```

which prints the document named [*file name*] to the line printer attached to the system. But, like driving, there's more to printing than just starting the engine. Just as yours may be one of many cars currently on the road, you may be one of many users currently on the system.

SPOOLING PRINTED TEXT

If you've used a single-user operating system, such as MS-DOS, you know that unless the printer is shut off or configured improperly, when you send a document to the printer either it is printed immediately or it waits its turn in a queue.

With XENIX, the opposite situation generally holds true. The reason is that XENIX *spools* your printing, and the reason for spooling is that there may be other users on the system who also want something printed. In fact, the printer might even be in use when you issue your print command.

To handle multiple printing requests, there is a directory on the hard disk called */usr/spool.*

(You've seen this name before, in Chapter 2 when you logged in. After you read the mail that was left by *root* and quit the *mail* program, that message was saved in */usr/spool/mail,* in another subdirectory with your login name.)

Also in */usr/spool* is a subdirectory called *lp.* It's into this subdirectory that XENIX places a copy of the file you want printed. The actual printing of the document thus occurs from */usr/spool/lp.*

Printing your file from the *lp* subdirectory serves two purposes. First, it keeps you from waiting while your document is being printed. Second, your document is in a First Come First Served queue while it's in *lp.* If the printer is busy or otherwise unavailable, your printing isn't canceled, as it would be in some other operating systems. Rather, XENIX holds onto your document until it reaches its turn in the queue and can be printed.

KEEPING INFORMED ABOUT YOUR PRINTING

Your system printer may not be within sight, so you may not know when your document has been printed. But you can use the XENIX *mail* system, which you'll meet in the next chapter, to keep yourself informed. Simply by including an *m* option in your print command:

```
lp -m [file name]
```

you can send your document to the printer and rest assured that you will be told when it is printed: XENIX will send you mail telling you so.

LOOKING TO THE FUTURE

This chapter has illustrated the basic commands available with *nroff* and the memorandum macros, because most documents require little more than header, footer, margin, and line-spacing formats and, perhaps, boldfacing and underlining for word enhancements.

There are many, many more *nroff* and *mm* commands. Along with the features you've seen for simple word handling, these utilities contain commands that whittle away at the tasks of formatting complex tables, technical reports, and mathematical formulas.

These features are specialized, so they haven't been covered. But if you need them, or feel that they will make your work easier, consult your XENIX Text Processing Guide. All of the commands you'll find in the manual follow the same general principles as the command macros you've just learned about.

You have the foundation now. From this point on, the manual can serve as your dictionary and your guide.

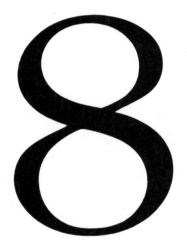

COMMUNICATING WITH OTHERS

One of the most important features of a multiuser system is communication. You've seen the ways and means available for you to communicate with XENIX. Now, it's time to see how you can communicate with the other people on your system. You can do so in a variety of ways.

You can try the commands described in this chapter, but before you do, be certain to enlist the aid of the person who will be receiving your messages. Until now, your activities with XENIX have all been strictly between you and the system. Now, you are about to learn the XENIX commands that affect other people working on the system.

TALKING USER TO USER

One of the fastest and simplest ways of communicating is to have a message that is sent from one terminal appear immediately on another. In concept, doing this is very much like making a phone call. But unlike dialing someone's telephone number and hoping that person is home, with XENIX you can first determine whether the person you want to reach is currently using the system.

From your shell prompt, enter:

who

This is the same command you saw briefly in Chapter 2. Again, XENIX responds with a list like the following, showing the users who are currently logged in and information about them:

```
$ who
root        console     May 11 14:04
kates       tty00       May 11 13:47
danh        tty01       May 11 13:08
$ _
```

The login name of each user, the address of that person's terminal, and the date and time of login are displayed in XENIX' reply.

Note that you're included in that list as well. You're not likely to forget your own login name, but if you should happen to need the address of the terminal you're using or the time you logged in, you don't have to ask for a list of everyone on the system. You can type:

who am i

and XENIX will let you know.

WRITING TO ANOTHER TERMINAL

If the person with whom you want to communicate is on the system, you can send a message directly to his or her terminal screen. Suppose you wanted to pass along some information to *danh*. Use the command:

write danh

After you press Enter, your cursor will advance to the next line on your screen but the shell prompt will not reappear. Instead, every time you type a line and press Enter, the line you typed will be sent to the destination you specified, until you signal XENIX that you are through by entering a Ctrl-D at the beginning of a new line.

USING A WRITE ADDRESS

Although the preceding example specified the recipient of your message by name, there are actually two possible forms of the *write* command. The other includes the recipient's terminal name.

This latter option is available because more than one person can log in under the same name and the same password, and do so at the same time. In fact, when a portion of the hard disk is dedicated to such tasks as accounting or word processing, the system administrator very often assigns a single user name and password to several people.

It is not possible, however, for two people to log in from the same terminal at the same time. Thus, once you know a person's terminal name (easy enough to find out if he or she types *who am i* and passes the information along), you can use the terminal name as an additional parameter of the write command, in the form:

write [user name] [terminal name]

For example, if *danb* is one of several people who are sharing the login name *accounts,* and you know that his terminal name is *tty01,* you can send a message directly to him with the command:

write accounts tty01

No matter how many people may be logged in under the same name, only the one using the terminal with the address you supply will receive your message.

(To do this same thing from the Visual shell, press R to select its Run option. When that command line appears, type the word *write* at the *RUN file:* prompt. Then press the Tab key to advance to the next option field, labeled *parameters:.* Enter the user name and/or terminal address of the person you want to contact and then press Enter.)

Once you've used the *write* command, an alert similar to:

`Message from root (console) [ Mon May 12 20:12:06 ] ...`

(with your user name, terminal name, and the date and time in the appropriate places) appears on the destination user's terminal to notify him or her that you want to make contact.

Now, before you actually write anything, let's cover some points of protocol.

153

SENDING MESSAGES FROM THE KEYBOARD

While the users of most established XENIX systems have evolved their own protocols for writing messages between terminals, you might want to consider the following hints if you and your system are new at this.

The *write* command's alert message will appear on your recipient's screen, no matter what else that person might be doing. If you just start typing away while he or she is in the middle of composing or editing a document, the arrival of your message will cause all manner of disruption (although the document itself will be unharmed).

Rather than jump to the conclusion that the other party is ready and willing to receive your message, wait. Wait for that person to *write* back, saying "OK to send." When that occurs, you can begin your message with confidence.

Even better, if your group or company is establishing protocols to follow, either limit *write* messages to certain times of the day, or agree that such messages should be sent only in emergencies, with the bulk of user-to-user communications being handled by XENIX' *mail* facility.

Once you begin sending the body of your message, you and the person you are sending to will have to remember that XENIX does not send each character as soon as it's typed. Rather, it waits until you press Enter, and then sends the entire line to the other terminal. Whoever is on the receiving end may find it a little awkward to watch a line appear and then, after a short delay (while you type), see another line appear.

That delay might also cause a slight problem. You or the person to whom you're "talking" may mistake the pause between lines as a signal that it's time to respond. To prevent such a misunderstanding, it's traditional to send some type of signal indicating that your part of the dialogue is complete, and you're now waiting for a response.

On a XENIX system, it's best to simply follow the accepted practice. If you're in the process of setting protocols, you can use almost any signal you can think of:

■ The manual suggests using the lowercase letter *o* (for *over*) between messages, and *oo* (for *over and out*) to terminate a *write* session, but any other convention will do nicely.

■ Pressing the Enter key twice produces a blank line below the last line you've sent, and that's a possibility.

■ You might also use a special character or series of characters, such as three hyphens or the letters *OK*.

Just make certain your signal is one that everyone knows about and agrees upon.

SENDING A FILE

The *write* command is useful for more than emergency messages, last-minute reminders, and idle chatter. Suppose you have a message that must be delivered immediately to more than one person. Rather than retype it each time, it's much more convenient to create a single text file containing that message, and then *write* the file to the terminal of each person concerned.

To send the contents of a text file called *activities* to the user named *danh*, you would use the command:

write danh 〈 activities

Note that the format here is similar to the redirection symbol you've been using periodically throughout the book, but with one major exception: The character preceding the file name is the less-than symbol (〈). Just as the greater-than symbol indicates a transfer *to* a file or device, the less-than symbol signifies movement *from* the named file.

There is one disadvantage to using the *write* command in this way, however. The recipient cannot capture the contents of that file. He or she must read it as it appears on the screen, so if nothing else, try to keep such files short enough that none of your message will scroll off the top of the screen.

ENDING THE MESSAGE

When your "conversation" is over, and you want to terminate the *write* session, press Ctrl-D on a new line to exit message mode. On the other terminal, *(end of message)* will appear on the screen, and your shell prompt will reappear on your own display.

Pressing Ctrl-D does *not* disconnect the other person as well. Recipients who are also using *write* will also need to press Ctrl-D to disconnect. If they've simply been receiving messages, a press of the Enter key will return the shell prompt. Remember, however, that Ctrl-D is also the logout command from the Bourne shell. When you disconnect after a *write* session, the message system will trap the first Ctrl-D it receives. But if you are in the Bourne shell and press these keys more than once, you'll probably log yourself out and will have to log back in.

DENYING ACCESS

Because the *write* command has the potential to disrupt (though not destroy) work in progress, XENIX offers you and other users a measure of privacy while you're working if you request it. If you enter the command:

mesg n

anyone who tries to write to you at your terminal address will receive the message *Permission denied.* Denying access in this manner does not affect the terminal of anyone else logged in under the same user name, so this is an excellent alternative to use whenever you don't want to be disturbed or you don't want your concentration broken.

To check on your message permission status, type:

mesg

XENIX will reply with *is n* or *is y,* according to the current status of your terminal. If you have denied access and want to restore the message ability, use:

mesg y

USING MAIL

If an environment (such as an operating system) instead of an application (such as a word processor) can be said to have a salient feature, then one of the strongest features in XENIX is its *mail* system. You saw some mail briefly when you first logged in. It's time for a closer look. Why not send a message to yourself?

SENDING MAIL

Just as with your mailbox, you use XENIX' *mail* system either because you already have mail and want to read it, or because you want to send mail to someone. To send a message to yourself, you simply enter the following command at the shell prompt:

m [user name]

Substitute your own user name for *[user name].* After a few moments, XENIX' *mail* system responds:

Subject:

You don't have to include a subject with your message, but it's helpful to identify the content in some way. Adding a subject helps *mail* users keep track of messages and, as you'll see later, can also help your recipient decide which correspondence should be read first.

For your message to yourself, type the phrase:

Trying out the mail

and press Enter.

Visually, all that happens is that the cursor advances to the next screen line. But you can now enter the text of the mail you want to send. Type the following (pressing Enter at the end of each line):

Although none of the mail sent through
XENIX is ever processed by hand, it is not
delivered instantaneously. There is a
short delay between the time that it is
sent and the time it is received.

Press Ctrl-D on a new line to tell the *mail* system you're finished and that you want to send the message.

Although you just typed a sample message, the text itself also represents something you need to know. There is a delay between the time you send a message and the time it's received, and that delay varies according to what else is happening on the system. Generally, when many background processes are running, documents are printing, or several users are online, mail delivery is slower than when the system is quiet.

For example, suppose you're the only person online as you try the preceding example. As soon as you press Ctrl-D, the words *you have mail* and the shell prompt will appear so quickly that you're liable to miss the event if you blink. On the other hand, if your system is very busy when you try this example, your mail may not be delivered for a few minutes.

157

■ NOTE: *As a courtesy, XENIX will only send you new-mail messages after you've pressed the Enter key. If you want to know whether new mail has arrived, press Enter to check.*

If people you've sent mail to are not currently logged in, their messages will be saved in their mailboxes and they will be notified that they have mail the next time they log into the system.

CANCELING A MESSAGE

If you start a message and then decide not to send it, type:

~q

to quit *mail*'s compose mode (you can also press the Delete key). Your message isn't totally discarded. *Mail* saves it in a file called *dead.letter* that it creates in your home directory. If your *dead.letter* file already exists, each message you cancel is appended to it.

RECEIVING MAIL

When you pressed Ctrl-D to send the message you just composed, you were removed from *mail* and returned to your shell. Now, return to *mail* and read the message you sent yourself. At the shell prompt, type:

mail

Assuming that the original welcome message XENIX sent you is still in your mailbox, you'll see something like this:

```
$ mail
mail version 3.0 August 10, 1984.   Type ? for help.
2 messages:
    2 danh      Mon May 12 21:59  11/300 "Trying out the mail"
    1 root      Tue Apr 15 12:23  6/125

_
```

The second line of this display identifies your *mail* system and tells you that you can type a question mark if you need help using the *mail* facility. Next is the first item of information about your own mailbox: the number of messages currently in it. That line is followed by a list of your mail in chronological order, with the newest message at the top of the list.

Note that all of your mail is numbered for you. That number is the first entry in each line. It's followed by the user name of the person who originated the message; the day, date, and time the message was received; the number of lines and words (lines/words) in the message; and the subject of the message.

READING YOUR MAIL

There are four basic methods you can use to read your mail once the *mail* system's introductory message is on your screen. The simplest is just to press the Enter key. Your messages will be printed on your display, one at a time, in the order they were received—in other words, with the oldest message first.

That's fine if all your messages are new ones. But many times you'll also have mail that you've read but left in your mailbox for later reference. If you press Enter to read your mail, you'll see all these messages, too, as the *mail* system goes through the list.

SKIPPING WITH + AND −

One way to skip messages you don't want to read is to use the + key, to jump forward toward the newest message in the list, or the − key, to jump backward toward the oldest message in the list. If you also specify a number, the command skips over as many intervening messages as you indicate. (If you need to find out which message is currently displayed, press =.)

By itself, + is equivalent to pressing Enter. It causes *mail* to display the next message in the list. Used with a number, the command causes *mail* to display the message *x* places closer to the top of the list. For example, if message number 11 is currently displayed and you type +6, the next message that *mail* displays will be number 17 (assuming messages 12–16 exist in the list).

Conversely, the minus symbol, by itself, causes *mail* to display the preceding (earlier) message in the list. Used with a number, the command causes *mail* to display the message *x* places closer to the bottom of the list. In the preceding example, −6 would cause *mail* to display message number 5.

You can also jump directly to the first or last message in the list. To go to the first (oldest) message, press:

∧

and to go to the last (newest) message, press:

$

ACCESSING A MESSAGE DIRECTLY

A third method of reading your mail allows you to access any message directly by typing its number before you press Enter. We'll use this method to retrieve the message you sent yourself. First, however, look at its summary header. In particular, notice that *mail* tells us our sample message contains 11 lines and 300 characters (11/300). (Depending on the date, and your user name, your sample may have a slightly different number of characters.) You typed only 5 lines of text, so where did the 11 come from? Type the message number and press Enter:

```
2
Message  2:
From danh Mon May 12 21:59:05 1986
To: danh
Subject: Trying out the mail
Date: Mon May 12 21:59:04 1986

Although none of the mail sent through
XENIX is ever processed by hand, it is not
delivered instantaneously. There is a
short delay between the time that it is
sent and the time it is received.


-
```

Now you can see where the difference in the line count arises. *Mail* has added four header lines and a blank line to the top of the text and another blank line at the end.

The four header lines are just a detailed listing of the information you saw in the summary. The top header line tells you who sent the message and when it was received. The meanings of *To:* and *Subject:* are obvious. The bottom header line shows you when the message was sent. (Note that there was a one-second delay between sending and receiving.)

DISPLAYING RANGES OF MAIL

The fourth method of reading your mail is much like the third, but it adds a new dimension to the way that your messages can be displayed. You can use the command:

160

    p [start]-[end]

to display the contents of the messages in the range that you've specified by *[start]-[end]*. Thus, the command:

p 1-5

would print the contents of messages 1 through 5. (If you've specified more than a full screen of messages, be prepared to press Ctrl-S to pause the scrolling—the messages will march by without stopping.)

Alternatively, if the messages you want to see are not sequential in a range of numbers, you can use:

    p [message number(s)]

to display the messages identified by the numbers you supply. For example:

p 1 4 6 10

would show you the contents of messages 1, 4, 6, and 10 while bypassing all in between. (These messages, too, would scroll by without stopping.)

You can also specify the name of a specific user if you like with the form:

    p [user name]

If you do this, *mail* will display only the messages you've received from the person you named.

In addition, you can quickly scan specified messages to find one you are seeking by telling *mail* to display only the first (top) few lines of each. The command:

    t [start]-[end]

or:

    t [message number(s)]

causes *mail* to display the first six lines of each message.

As you can see, there are quite a few options. Select and use the ones you find most helpful.

READING NEW MAIL

Whenever you press Enter in *mail,* the *mail* utility checks to see if any additional messages have arrived. If one has, you'll see this message:

```
New mail has arrived -- type `restart' to read.
```

Type either *restart* or *rest* and press the Enter key to see the message.

By itself, the new-mail message does nothing more than notify you of the arrival of another message. It is only when you type *restart* (or *rest*) that *mail* will actually add the new message to the list of those it already knows about. At that time, *mail* will include the new message's header summary in the list it displays, and assign the message a number so you can select it. Without the *restart* command, you will not be able to access the new mail.

161

REPLYING TO A MESSAGE

If you've been following our examples, your cursor is now two lines below the practice message you just sent yourself. Because you just displayed the contents of this message, XENIX views it as the current *mail* message. Just as the XENIX line editor, *ed,* uses each command you enter to manipulate the line you just specified, *mail* uses each command you enter (if you don't include a range) to manipulate the current message.

The cursor itself gives us another piece of information. When you're not composing mail and the cursor is on a line by itself, you're in *mail*'s command mode. From here, you can do anything with the mail in your mailbox: read it, remove it, print it, or reply to it. Let's assume you want to compose a reply.

If the reply is directed to the person who sent the message you just read, the easiest way to answer is to type an *r* on the line containing the cursor and then press Enter. The *mail* system will respond with two header lines:

```
Message  2:
From danh Mon May 12 21:59:05 1986
To: danh
Subject: Trying out the mail
Date: Mon May 12 21:59:04 1986

Although none of the mail sent through
XENIX is ever processed by hand, it is not
delivered instantaneously. There is a
short delay between the time that it is
sent and the time it is received.

r
To: danh
Subject: Trying out the mail

_
```

The first header line indicates the user to whom your reply is being sent (in this case, yourself). *Mail* has taken this name from the original message's *From:* field. The second line duplicates the *Subject:* field, if one exists, of the original.

Once you see these header lines, you can type the reply as you would normally when sending someone mail.

The *r* command can also be used with a range or list of messages and specified user names. For example, to reply to messages from users named *kenh* and *lindaz,* you would type:

r kenh lindaz

The *mail* system would then add a subject heading from the earliest recorded message from either user. After you had composed a reply and pressed Ctrl-D, your message would be sent to both users. (If you have more than one message from a user you reply to in this way, and you see that user listed more than once in the *To:* section of the message you're sending, don't be concerned. Each user will receive only one copy of the message.)

If, in addition, the message(s) you're replying to included more than your name in the *To:* field, or if the originator sent "carbon copies" to other users (by a means you'll see shortly), you can send your reply to one and all by typing an uppercase *R* instead of a lowercase *r* before beginning your message. The uppercase version of the *reply* command ensures that everyone who was sent the original message receives a copy of your response.

COMPOSING MAIL

Of course, you can also respond to any message at any time or you can compose an entirely new message while you're in *mail.* While the cursor is on a blank line waiting for a command, use the form:

m [user name]

to begin composing a new message to the person you've specified. That person need not be anyone who has already sent you mail. You can send a message to anyone on the system, as long as you know his or her user name. To send one message to a group of people, you can use the format:

m [user name] [user name] ... [user name]

(This ability to address multiple users also applies when you use *mail* at the shell prompt without entering the *mail* system first.)

Recall that, when we used *ed* in Chapter 4, we could leave insert mode by pressing Ctrl-D at the beginning of a new line, and leave the editor itself by pressing Ctrl-D again (although this wouldn't save any editing changes). Ctrl-D is used similarly in *mail.* Once you've finished composing a message, send it by pressing Ctrl-D on a new line. If you have at least one message in your mailbox, you'll remain in the *mail* environment. To leave *mail,* press Ctrl-D or use the *quit* command.

FORWARDING MAIL

On occasion, you might need to forward a copy of a message to another user. Simply enter the command in the form:

    f [user name]

to have that done. The original of the message remains in your mailbox, and the recipient receives both the forwarded message and a heading showing that you are the person who sent it:

```
Message  2:
From danh Tue May 13 10:29:28 1986
To: joannew
Subject: Trying out the mail
Date: Tue May 13 10:29:27 1986

        From danh Mon May 12 21:59:05 1986
        To: danh
        Subject: Trying out the mail
        Date: Mon May 12 21:59:04 1986

        Although none of the mail sent through
        XENIX is ever processed by hand, it is not
        delivered instantaneously. There is a
        short delay between the time that it is
        sent and the time it is received.


-
```

Note that the message you forward is indented one tab stop inside the new message. At times, you may not want this to happen—perhaps because the indent would cause the text of the message to go beyond the right border of the screen. You can omit the indentation by using an uppercase *F*. For example, if *danh* were to forward the preceding message to *joannew* in this way, the result would be this:

```
Message  3:
From danh Tue May 13 11:26:18 1986
To: joannew
Subject: Trying out the mail
Date: Tue May 13 11:26:17 1986

>From danh Mon May 12 21:59:05 1986
To: danh
Subject: Trying out the mail
Date: Mon May 12 21:59:04 1986

Although none of the mail sent through
XENIX is ever processed by hand, it is not
delivered instantaneously. There is a
short delay between the time that it is
sent and the time it is received.


-
```

You can also include a *mail* message in a message you are sending by using the command format:

~m [message number]

on a new line in your *mail* message. This is useful if you want to comment on the message you are including. The receiving user will soon see a message like this:

164

```
Message  5:
From danh Tue May 13 11:43:41 1986
To: joannew
Subject: of interest
Date: Tue May 13 11:43:40 1986

Below is a message I sent to myself that may be of interest to you:

        From danh Mon May 12 21:59:05 1986
        To: danh
        Subject: Trying out the mail
        Date: Mon May 12 21:59:04 1986

        Although none of the mail sent through
        XENIX is ever processed by hand, it is not
        delivered instantaneously. There is a
        short delay between the time that it is
        sent and the time it is received.

Let me know what you think!

Dan

-
```

Note that the included message is indented one tab stop to set it apart from the rest of the message. Using an uppercase M will avoid the indent.

As with other commands, ranges, lists, and user names can be used to forward or include a message.

DISPOSING OF YOUR MAIL

There's always the question of what to do with your mail once you've read it. You can leave it in the mailbox by doing nothing at all. But in a typical system, mail tends to build up at an alarming rate, so collecting all your messages is not the best of choices.

Since XENIX' data-handling ability centers on files and directories, it is no surprise that you have many options for storing and renaming the messages you've received. Let's look at some techniques for collecting and moving your mail to places where you can make the best use of it.

TRANSFERRING YOUR MAIL

XENIX maintains a separate area for mail storage in your home directory. It's called *mbox,* and you can transfer specific messages to it. From *mail*'s command mode, use the command format:

    mb [message number]

to store the message indicated by *[message number].* If this is the first message you're placing in *mbox,* the file is created to accommodate it. If *mbox* exists, any messages you send there are appended to those already in it.

The *mb* command doesn't immediately remove the message from your mailbox. Until you quit the *mail* session, the message stays there for you to look at. Only when you leave *mail* are the messages you've marked for transfer sent to *mbox* and deleted from your mailbox.

As elsewhere, lists and ranges of messages, as well as messages from specified users, can be transferred.

MOVING YOUR MAIL

It could be, however, that you want to save one or more messages to a file other than *mbox.* You can do so from outside *mail,* at the shell prompt but, as already mentioned, that type of transfer moves every message in your mailbox to the file you name.

To select just the messages you want to save, use the *mail* command format:

    s [message number] [file name]

(or use a list or range). The *s* (*save*) command copies the entire message, including all five header lines, into the file you've named.

An alternative is:

    w [message number] [file name]

(or a list or range of messages), which *writes* just the body of the message, without the headers, into the file you've named.

In either case, if the text file you've specified does not exist, *mail* creates it. If the file does exist, the messages you've selected are appended to the end of it. Here, too, the messages remain in the mailbox until you exit the *mail* session.

165

PRINTING YOUR MAIL

You may want a printed copy of some or all of your mail. To send the mail to the line printer attached to your system, use the command format:

lp [start]-[end]

to print the range of messages indicated by the numbers you supply. You can also use a list of numbers for non-continuous messages, and specify a user name if you want only the messages from a particular person from within that list or range.

If your system has more than one printer attached to it, or if you need more specific information about when and where printouts are distributed, check with your system administrator.

DELETING YOUR MAIL

If you decide that you don't want to save a message or leave it in your mailbox, then you can delete it. If the message is the current message, press *d* and the Enter key. That deletes the current message. If you want to delete some other messages in the list, press:

d [message number(s)]

You can use a range of messages or indicate only those originated by a specific user. The summary lines for deleted messages will not be displayed again during the current session, so you will have no way to access them. The messages themselves, however, will not be eliminated until you actually exit the *mail* system.

A timesaving alternative, particularly when you are clearing out the contents of an overfull mailbox, is the *dp* command, which not only deletes the current message or the one whose number you've included, but also prints the next message that is in the list.

UNDELETING MAIL

If you haven't yet left the *mail* system and decide that one or more of the messages you deleted really should not be thrown away after all, press:

u [message number]

(or use a range or list of messages that have been deleted). This is the *undelete* command, and it will recover any messages you specify that have been marked for deletion during the current session. Keep in mind, however, that the *undelete* command works only if you have not ended the current *mail* session. Once you exit *mail,* deleted messages are irretrievably lost.

RECOVERING REMOVED MAIL

At any time during the current *mail* session, you can redisplay a list of the summary lines for your mail by pressing *h* and the Enter key. That's *mail's header* command, and it will redisplay the headers for all of the messages in your mailbox, other than the summary lines for deleted messages.

If you've marked mail for transfer, there will also be one additional field on each line:

```
h
M  7 root     Tue May 13 14:33  7/113  "new printer use"
   6 carriel  Tue May 13 14:32  7/104  "Hello"
*  4 jonv     Tue May 13 14:30  7/122  "contract deadlines"
*  3 susang   Tue May 13 13:40  7/126  "New offices"
   2 danh     Mon May 12 21:59  11/300 "Trying out the mail"
   1 root     Mon May 12 21:22  6/118
_
```

If you've transferred messages to *mbox,* the leading character on the summary header will be an *M.* If you've used either the *s* or *w* option to transfer the message to another file, the first character in the summary will be an asterisk (*).

In any case, when you exit the *mail* system, all of the marked messages will be removed from your mailbox. If you decide you really want to keep some or all of them in the mailbox, use the command format:

ho [message number]

(or list, or range) to have *mail* hold the specified messages and not remove them.

EXITING THE MAIL SYSTEM

When you've finished with the *mail* system, you can leave it in one of three ways. If you're a user of the Bourne shell and you're through using XENIX altogether, press Ctrl-D twice on the line containing the cursor—once to signal *mail* that you've finished, and the second time to log out.

If you want to return to your shell, press a single Ctrl-D, a *q* (for *quit*), or an *x* (for *exit*) on the line containing the cursor, and then press the Enter key.

With the *q* command or a Ctrl-D, you'll be told which (if any) messages you've stored in *mbox,* and how many remain in the mailbox. The messages you've marked will be removed from your mailbox and you'll be returned to the shell.

The *x* version of the command ignores any changes you may have specified for your mailbox and leaves all files intact. It's actually an abort request that immediately returns you to the shell, leaving the contents of your mailbox unchanged.

167

EDITING YOUR MESSAGES

If we were all exceptional writers, the first draft of every document we typed would be totally correct. We would have no need for the editing functions in *vi* and *ed.* Unfortunately, such is usually not the case.

In *mail,* as in either of XENIX' text processors, we are prone to make mistakes. There are no inherent editing features in *mail,* but you do have alternatives other than continually deleting not-quite-right messages.

VIEWING THE MESSAGE

168

If you're comfortable with the text of your message, but would like to review its contents before you send it, use the command:

~p

This will display the *To:* and *Subject:* fields, followed by the text of the message.

The tilde (~) you type here is the *mail* system's escape command. Similar in function to the backslash in *nroff,* the tilde is a signal to *mail* that the next character you type is to be interpreted as a command, not as part of your text. The *mail* system includes a number of such *tilde escapes,* or *compose escapes.* Their purpose is to allow you to move out of compose mode temporarily, and they increase *mail's* flexibility enormously. They are recognized only at the beginnings of lines. You can request a summary of them all by typing ~? on a new line while you're composing a message. You'll see the following help screen:

```
~?
HELP:  Mail Compose Escapes

EDITING HEADING FIELDS               OTHER COMPOSE ESCAPES
 ~s subject      Set Subject field    ~!cmd            Execute shell command
 ~t users        Add users to To list ~:mail-cmd       Execute mail command
 ~c users        Add users to Cc list ~~               Begin line with tilde
 ~b users        Add users to Bcc list ~A [name...]    Print global aliases
 ~R users        Add to Return-receipt ~a name <users> Set/print aliases
 ~h              Edit all fields       ~p or ~P        Print message so far
                                       ~q              Abort message
READING IN MESSAGES                    ~w file         Write message to file
 ~r file         read file
 ~d              read dead.letter
 ~m <list>       read messages         EDITING MESSAGE BODY
 ~M <list>       same; doesn't tab     ~e or ~v        Use ed or vi
                                       ~!cmd           Pipe message thru cmd


Typing two interrupts is the same as ~q.

(continue)
_
```

INCLUDING TEXT FILES IN YOUR MESSAGE

Among other possibilities, *mail* lets you use either *ed* or *vi* to help you with your message writing. And you can use these editors either before or while you are composing your message. Even though the *mail* system does not allow you to jump from line to line, you can create all or part of the message in *vi* (or *ed*), save it, and then send it as all or part of your message.

For example, suppose you create a text file named *activities* and you want to send it to user *danh* for review. You could create the file in *vi* and, from the shell prompt, enter the command:

mail danh ⟨ activities

Alternately, to include a text file as part of a message, enter the *mail* system as usual and start typing. When you reach the line on which you want the insert to appear, use the command form:

~r [file name]

The text contained in the file you specify will appear in the message and you can go on from there.

EDITING THE BODY OF YOUR MESSAGE

On the other hand, at any point after you begin the body of your message (that is, after you've filled in whatever header information you want included), you can use the command:

~v

In this case, the *~v* loads *vi*, which reads in any text you've typed so far and assigns a temporary file name to it. (If you prefer *ed*, use *~e.*)

While you're in the text editor, you can use all of its features. When you've finished, exit the editor and save the document with the *:x* command, and you'll be deposited back into the *mail* system's compose mode. You'll see the message *(continue)*. Any text you've typed or changes you've made while in the editor will be included in your message, and you can go on as if you had never left *mail*.

EDITING THE *Subject:* FIELD

Perhaps when you began your message you decided there was no need to fill in the *Subject:* field. If you later change your mind or want to alter the text you did include, the command format:

~s [subject]

will do that for you. The text you supply as *[subject]* will replace any contents of an existing *Subject:* field.

EDITING THE *To:* FIELD

After entering the name of your message's recipient in the *To:* field, you may decide that the message should be sent to other people as well. The command format:

~t [user name(s)]

adds recipients without replacing the name you originally entered.

SENDING COPIES

Of course, along with other ways to send mail to several people, there is the carbon-copy approach. While you're in the body of your message, the tilde-escape command format:

~c [user name(s)]

sends a copy of your message to the people you've indicated. When you use this command, *mail* adds a sixth field, *Cc:*, to the message's header. The field includes the names of all people to whom copies have been sent.

Alternatively, you can use the variation:

~b [user name(s)]

to send blind carbon-copies of the message. Here, the blind-copy recipients' names will not be listed in the *To:* or *Cc:* fields.

REQUESTING A RECEIPT

Suppose you're organizing a conference or drafting a long report. Your deadline is not far off, and as last-minute details occur to you, you dash off quick messages asking for information from other users. We've mentioned that there may be delays in transmission if your system is busy. While those delays are usually only a matter of seconds, they could stretch out to minutes or more. How can you confirm that your message has been received?

If you want a return receipt to indicate successful delivery, just use the command format:

~R [user name]

before you end the message, to specify that a receipt should be issued and to whom it should be sent. The receipt is a message placed in the user's mailbox.

Note that this command uses an uppercase *R* to distinguish it from the *~r* file-read command.

On the message itself, a *Return-receipt-to:* field is added to the header so the recipient knows that the arrival of the message has been acknowledged.

EDITING HEADER LINES

Any of the header lines in your message, whether you've supplied entries for them or not, can be edited with the general-purpose command:

~h

entered at the beginning of a new line while you're composing your message. *Mail* will print each field (*To:, Subject:, Cc:, Bcc:,* and *Return-receipt-to:*) with its current contents, or leave the field blank if nothing has been entered. You can then change the fields as you see fit.

171

CREATING A MAILING LIST

So far, we've looked at sending mail to multiple recipients in terms of stringing together a list of user names in the *To:, Cc:,* and *Bcc:* fields. Effective as that method is, what if you send mail to the same group of people on a regular basis? Typing the same names each time can become a chore. In those circumstances, it's much better to create a mailing list.

Creating such a list is not a difficult task in *mail.* You have no addresses to worry about. The user names are all you need to supply. And all you need to know is the correct technique for creating the mailing list:

alias [alias name] [user names]

In this command, *[alias name]* is the name you wish to assign to the group as a whole. That name is followed by the names of the people you want to include. To be more specific, suppose you send regular mailings to a group of users named *barryp, jeffh, chrisk,* and *daver.* Rather than type their names each time, you can gather them all into a mailing list under an alias called *teched* with the command:

alias teched barryp jeffh chrisk daver

Then, when you want to send messages to this group, you can simply type:

mail teched

to reach all four of your correspondents.

If, however, you define an alias during a *mail* session, the *alias* list is temporary. It disappears as soon as you leave *mail.* There's a way to make that list permanent, but in order to do so, you need to know something about the options that are available with *mail.*

CREATING A MAIL-OPTIONS FILE

Like the rest of XENIX, the *mail* system is very flexible and can be molded to suit your own needs. *Mail* starts out with certain defaults, but you can change them. From within the *mail* system, type:

set ?

and press Enter. When you do, you'll see a screen full of information like the following:

```
HELP:  Mail Options

askcc            Prompt for carbon copies after composing
asksubject       Prompt for subject before composing
autombox         Automatically save messages in mbox
autoprint        Print next message after deleting
chron            List messages in chronological order
dot              Allow dot (.) to terminate messages
EDITOR=          Use editor set by string
escape=          Character for compose escapes (default=~)
ignore           Ignore interrupts
mchron           display messages in chronological order but
                           list them in numerical order
metoo            Send to self when self is in an alias list
nosave           Don't save aborted messages in dead.letter
page=            Set page size.   "set page" uses page size of 23
quiet            Don't print sign-on header and message numbers
record=          Copy outgoing messages to file set by string
SHELL=           Use shell set by string for shell escapes
toplines=        Number of lines typed by "top" command
VISUAL=          Use visual editor set by string
verify           Verify mail recipients

Use "set" with no argument to print current option settings.
```

172

In one way or another, all these options affect your *mail* session. They are either in effect or not available, depending on the contents of two files.

When you enter *mail,* the program looks at a file called */usr/lib/mail/.mailrc,* the general options file for everyone on the system. It also checks for another file, called *.mailrc,* which is located in your home directory. This latter file contains specific *mail* options. The options are either *mail*'s default settings or those that you've requested. Your personal *.mailrc* file is the place to include all the options, such as system-wide aliases, that you would like to enjoy.

By the way, if you haven't used it, don't bother looking for *.mailrc* in your home directory. The dot in front of its name means that it's an *invisible* file—not one for casual observation. You can look at invisible files with the command *ls -a* from the shell, but the fact is, if you don't already know about that file it probably doesn't exist for you. And because it doesn't exist, you're using the default options in the general *mail*-system file.

You can always check on the options that are in effect, though. Just type the command:

set

Used alone on a line, *set* displays the options settings in both the general and personal *.mailrc* files.

If you prefer other settings, you can create your own *.mailrc* file. The command to turn on an option is *set,* and the command to turn off an option is *unset.* You can set or unset several options on a single command line, and to make the change(s) to *.mailrc* you can use *vi* to edit the file.

If you're in the *mail* system, precede the command to edit the *.mailrc* file with an exclamation point (the ! symbol enables you to escape to the shell temporarily). From the shell, just type:

vi .mailrc

Once in the editor, you can set your own options. For example, you might include a *set* command and an *alias* command to create a *.mailrc* file like this one (note that the alias doesn't require a leading *set* command):

alias teched barryp jeffh chrisk daver

set askcc nosave

Use :*x* to write the file to disk and quit *vi,* and then enter *mail.* (If you've used *vi* from within *mail,* you'll return to *mail* automatically after :*x.* If you are already in *mail* when you create or make changes to *.mailrc,* however, you'll need to exit and then re-enter *mail* for the *.mailrc* options to take effect.)

In the preceding example, the first line you entered created an *alias* list (you can create as many as you like, provided that each list has a unique name and is entered on a separate line).

The second line sets two *mail* options. The first option, *askcc,* tells *mail* to prompt for the names of any people you want included in the *Cc:* field. Once that option is set, whenever you press Ctrl-D to send a message, you'll see a *Cc:* prompt asking for the names of people to whom you want to send copies of your message. You have to respond to this prompt before *mail* will send your message. Simply press Enter to leave the *Cc:* field blank. (To eliminate the prompt, you would remove the *askcc* statement from your *.mailrc* file.)

The second option in our example, *nosave,* can be a major convenience. As already mentioned, whenever you abort a message, *mail* saves it in a file called *dead.letter.* Just as, in the real world, you would crumple up an aborted message and throw it away, the *nosave* option ensures that aborted messages are discarded, rather than saved in *dead.letter* for possible future reference.

ALTERING OTHER OPTIONS

As you saw in the Mail Options list, there are quite a few other options you can set in *mail*. For example, the *top* command is a default that shows the first five lines of the messages you specify. If you prefer that fewer lines be shown, you could use a command such as:

set toplines = 3

in your *.mailrc* file to specify the number of lines you want displayed. Your new setting would cancel the default value.

Here's another example. If the thought of using Ctrl-D both to send messages and log out makes you uncomfortable, you might include the option:

set dot

after which, instead of Ctrl-D, you could press a period (.) and the Enter key at the beginning of a new line in order to send a message.

Then, too, you could keep copies of all outgoing mail in a file of your choice, with a command like:

set record = my_mail

As we noted earlier, you can also *set* or *unset* any option for just the duration of your *mail* session by using the command while you're in *mail's* command mode.

COMMUNICATING WITH YOURSELF

As you've seen, you can send mail to yourself. That's a good way to use the *mail* system as a reminder of things you need to do. But there's a better way— especially if you have a tendency to forget to remind yourself to remember. XENIX has an excellent calendar system that can help you keep track of days, weeks, months, and years. And short of a system breakdown, XENIX rarely, if ever, forgets.

But before you see how to tie XENIX into your time-critical responsibilities through *mail*, let's look at the calendar system itself.

ACCESSING THE CALENDAR

The simplest way to become acquainted with XENIX' calendar is to type the command *cal*, with the month and (optionally) year of your choice:

cal [month] [year]

You can specify the month either by number (1-12) or by typing enough letters to identify the month uniquely (*Jun* or *Jul*, for example, instead of *Ju*, which would be ambiguous). If the year you want is the current year, there is no need to specify it. If the year is other than the current year, however, specify it as a four-digit number; *cal 87*, for example, would refer to the year 87, not the year 1987.

To see a calendar for the entire current year, type *cal* and the year. If you don't specify either a month or a year, XENIX will show you a calendar for this month, last month, and next month. Here are a few interesting examples.

If you type:

cal may

in 1987, you'll see:

```
$ cal may
   May 1987
 S  M Tu  W Th  F  S
                 1  2
 3  4  5  6  7  8  9
10 11 12 13 14 15 16
17 18 19 20 21 22 23
24 25 26 27 28 29 30
31
$ _
```

If you type:

cal 7 1776

you'll find that the Fourth of July fell on a Thursday.

If you type:

cal 9 1752

you'll find 11 days missing from the month of September. (XENIX' calendar is based on English chronology, and September 1752 is the year England changed from the Julian calendar to the Gregorian.)

Finally, if you type:

cal Jan 2000

you'll see that the next century will begin on a Saturday.

(All of the responses to the different varieties of the *cal* command are based on information XENIX obtains from your computer's clock, which actually records the current day and date. If you find that the displays are not accurate, check with your system administrator. The system clock may need to be reset, or, if the XENIX computer does not have a clock, the time and date may have been entered incorrectly when the computer was last booted.)

CREATING A CALENDAR FILE

Now that you know XENIX has a calendar to help you organize your reminders, you can create some reminders to be organized. You'll place them in a special text file named *calendar.* (The name of the file cannot be varied. *Calendar* it is, and must be, even if you would prefer to call it *my_diary.*) You can create *calendar* with *vi* or *ed,* or just by redirecting output with the *cat* command, as we'll do here. At your shell prompt, type:

cat ⟩⟩ calendar

If you remember from Chapter 4, that command will take all further input from the keyboard and, in this case, direct it to the file called *calendar.* By using the double greater-than symbols, you are ensuring that if such a file already exists, the input will be appended to the file rather than overwrite the information already in it. Of course, if the file doesn't exist, it will be opened to hold your input.

Assuming that today is Thursday, October 9, 1986, type the following:

176

10/9 Call Salley to confirm scheduling meeting at 10:00 a.m.

October 9 Final Cost Analysis due

10/11 Pick up Sun Valley tickets

10/10 Lunch with Support Group at 12:00 p.m.

Press Ctrl-D on a new line when you're finished to close the *calendar* file.

Notice the format suggested for the file. Each reminder is on its own line, and each begins with the appropriate date. The reminders themselves need not be in chronological order, and the format for the date is flexible. As you can see, it can be in *mm/dd* or *mmm d* format.

REMINDING YOURSELF

With the calendar available and the *calendar* file in place, type the command:

calendar

Even though you have a data file named *calendar,* this command tells XENIX to look for a program file with that name.

The *calendar* program is one of XENIX' utilities. It refers to your *calendar* data file and, based on the information it finds there, shows you a list of all your reminders for today and tomorrow:

```
$ calendar
10/9 Call Salley to confirm scheduling meeting at 10:00 a.m.
October 9 Final Cost Analysis due
10/10 Lunch with Support Group at 12:00 p.m.
$ _
```

Note that the reminder for 10/11 is excluded here. It will, however, be included as of 12:00 a.m. on October 10. (XENIX is also considerate of a five-day work week—on weekends, "tomorrow" extends to the following Monday.)

MAILING A REMINDER

You can, as mentioned earlier, also use the *mail* system to jog your memory about upcoming events. All you need are the *calendar* data file and the discipline to update it faithfully.

Once each day, XENIX scans the home directory of each user, looking for a *calendar* data file. If it finds one, it searches through the file for entries dated for that day or the following day (XENIX' search is actually an automatic version of the *calendar* command).

If it finds entries for today or tomorrow (or Saturday through Monday if it's Friday), XENIX sends you a message containing the information it found. In your mailbox, you'll find that the message has been sent by *root*.

There is only one initial stumbling block to this automatic reminder service, and it's a small one: On the day you establish your *calendar* file, you might not receive any reminders, even if you've generated some for that and the following day. The reason is that there is no way to tell whether you've created the file before or after XENIX has made its daily rounds looking for *calendar* files. If XENIX has already checked your home directory, reminders for today and tomorrow will not be mailed to you.

If this happens to you, be patient. XENIX will begin to catch up on the following day, and on the day after you can count on its being reliable and up-to-date. After that, your auto-reminder should work flawlessly.

177

9

ADVANCED FILE TECHNIQUES To manipulate files, you ordinarily need an application program that has been designed to perform the operations you need. A word processor, for example, is a program that controls the functions that let you enter, format, and rearrange text in a document. From there, it's easy to assume that a function such as data management would also require a program designed specifically for that purpose. But data, all data, are really nothing more than patterns of characters separated by some sort of delimiters—usually blank spaces. Put together, those patterns, whether they are words or numbers, convey information. Separately, however, especially to a computer program, they are just patterns of characters.

You've seen that XENIX, through *vi* and *nroff,* can give you tremendous flexibility in editing and formatting documents. And XENIX has even more. Among its many utilities are programs that enable you to handle character patterns in more ways than most operating systems can hope to offer.

Let's start with something easy.

CREATING A PHONE BOOK

We all need to use the phone. Sometimes that means we must stop what we're doing, hunt down a phone book, and find the number before we can make the call. With XENIX, your terminal, and a little bit of preparation, you could eliminate the need to resort to paper when you need a phone number.

This example will show how you can create a sample phone book. Once you've stepped through the exercise, you'll be able to start one of your own. To begin, use the *cat* command:

```
cat >> phonebook
```

(Recall that the double greater-than sign either appends information to the end of an existing file or creates a new file if one doesn't already exist. You can thus use this same command at any time to add entries to your own phone book or any other file.) Now make a few entries:

```
Tom Jugh (413) 555-5422
Fred Disen (808) 555-1233
Wil Ohmsford (617) 555-9866
Ira Figh (743) 555-3476
Zeb Diffle (808) 555-3443
```

When you've finished, press Ctrl-D on a new line to end the file.

◼ NOTE: *Be very careful when you use any form of output redirection in XENIX. Although the double greater-than sign will not overwrite a data file, the single greater-than sign will.*

Now you have some data. How do you manage it?

MATCHING A PATTERN

One of the things you'll do most often is search for a number in that file. You've used *cat* to display the entire contents of a file on the screen, and that might seem a logical choice, but it's not always the best one. With only five entries, it's no problem to scan the file for the number you want. But if you had a hundred entries, the first 76 would quickly scroll off the top of your screen.

What you need is a way to find a particular entry among those in the file, and XENIX has a command that's almost custom-made to do the job. It's the search command *grep,* whose name comes from the search pattern *g/re/p,* which means "globally locate a pattern and print it." In a nutshell, *grep* searches for a particular pattern in every line of a set of files that you specify. The command takes the form:

grep [-(options)] [pattern] [file name(s)]

For example, if you want the phone number for Wil Ohmsford, you can enter the command:

grep Ohmsford phonebook

In a few seconds, *grep* replies *Wil Ohmsford (617) 555-9866.*

Grep is a pattern-matching command. You supply the pattern you want it to search for, in this case the word *Ohmsford,* and it searches through the file you've specified. If it finds a match, *grep* prints the entire line to the screen.

If you want to search for an exact match of the pattern you entered, surround it with single quotation marks and blank spaces where appropriate. For example, if you'd like to search for occurrences of the name *Wil,* but not *Will, William,* or other words that begin with *Wil,* you would type:

grep 'Wil ' phonebook

at the shell prompt (note the initial capital *W* and the extra space included after *l*). *Grep* would search for and display all occurrences of *Wil* followed by a blank space.

Note from the preceding example that *grep* is case-sensitive. If you had typed *wil,* no match would have been found. You can, however, make *grep* less selective by entering the command as:

grep -y wil phonebook

The *y* option causes *grep* to ignore case differences between the pattern and any potential matches contained in the file. With the *y* option included, you can enter the search word in any combination of upper- and lowercase, including *wIl* or *wIL.*

ADDING VARIETY

There are two variations on *grep*, *egrep* and *fgrep*, and they can be used in slightly different situations.

If you want to search for more than one pattern of characters within a file, use *egrep*. For example, suppose you need to call both Fred Disen and Zeb Diffle. You can search for both their numbers with a single command:

```
egrep 'Disen|Diffle' phonebook
```

Notice that the pattern you're searching for is again enclosed in single quotation marks. Although not always necessary, they are used to avoid possible confusion and errors. It's useful to form the habit of putting these marks around the pattern. As well, if the pattern you're searching for consists of more than a single word, as it would if you specified *'Wil Ohmsford'*, the pattern must be enclosed in single quotation marks.

The broken vertical bar (a solid vertical bar on some terminals), when used with *egrep*, represents an either/or function. *Egrep* will print any lines that contain either the pattern *Disen* or the pattern *Diffle* (or both).

Fgrep searches for fixed patterns of text. We'll look at it again in Chapter 10, but one way to use *fgrep* here is to match an entire line of text in our *phonebook* file. *Fgrep* has an *x* option that displays a match only when the entire line it finds matches the character pattern you specified. For example, if you typed:

```
fgrep -x 'Wil Ohmsford' phonebook
```

fgrep would display a match only if *Wil Ohmsford* were on a line by itself in the *phonebook* file.

CHANGING FILE PERMISSIONS

Back in Chapter 3 you were introduced to the concept of file-access permissions. In any multiuser environment, controlling access to files is fundamental to maintaining order and offering privacy to individual users. Data (and program) files need to be protected from unauthorized change, and sensitive or confidential information needs to remain private. File-access permissions are XENIX' method of controlling who can work on which files, and with what degree of freedom.

For example, even though you now can have the convenience of keeping a phone book on the system, you may be concerned about maintaining the privacy of certain numbers.

Recall that there are three types of users (not counting the system administrator) on a XENIX system:

■ There is you, the owner of your files and directories.

■ There are group users (you are a member of at least one group) who share a common set of files and directories. For example, you might be user *johnd* in the user group *accounts*.

■ There are all other users of the system.

When your user account was created, the system administrator most likely left the various components of your account readable, but not writable, by these three types of users. To get a listing of these protections, type:

ls -l

at the shell prompt in the directory you'd like to check. As you may recall from Chapter 3, an *r* in the permissions field means a file is readable, a *w* means a file is writable, and an *x* means a file is executable.

Those permissions are not carved in stone, however. You can alter them for individual files and directories with the *chmod* (change mode) command. Its format is simple:

chmod [who][permission level] [file or directory]

So are its options. *Who* can be:

a	All users.
g	The group.
o	Others, or the public.
u	The user, or creator, of the file or directory.

Permissions can be:

+	This is an operator that adds the specified permission.
−	This is an operator that removes the specified permission.
=	This is an operator that adds the specified permission, but removes any others already in effect.
x	This is the permission to execute a file.
r	This is the permission to read a file.
w	This is the permission to write to a file.

Now, look at the permissions for your *phonebook* file by using the *long* option of the *list* command:

```
ls  -l  phonebook
```

You'll see that the current permissions are *-rw-r--r--,* meaning that you have read and write permission (*rw-*) and both your group and the public have read permission only (*r--*).

To remove the read permission from *phonebook* for both your group and the other users on the system, use the *chmod* command and type:

```
chmod  go-r  phonebook
```

Read permission has now been removed (*-r*) from the group and from the others. Notice the order in which the options are included. First, you specify the group to which the change applies. Next, you include the assignment operator that either adds or removes permissions. Finally, you set the actual permission levels themselves. (Be careful not to include spaces between these three parts.)

Of course, you can set different levels for different people. If you later decide to remove all restricted phone numbers so that persons in your group can read and write to the phone book, and the public can read but not change it, use the command line:

```
chmod  g+rw,o+r  phonebook
```

to add the new levels. Here, notice that you segregate the access permissions for the two sets by separating them with a comma.

CREATING A DATABASE

Many people find that, other than a phone list, they most often refer to lists of names and addresses. Consider a file called *adlist,* which contains 1000 names and addresses. A portion of it might look like this (if you want to try these examples, enter the following lines and name the file *adlist*):

```
Jonn Jonzz, 13 Waverly Pl, NYC NY 10033
Tim Brahms, 132 Amsterdam Ave, NYC NY 10143
Fred Jonzz, 16 Oxford Rd, Buffalo NY 13221
Ed Porter, 1232 Maiden Lane, NYC NY 10101
```

To do any extensive file handling with a data file like this one, you must first give that file some structure based on how you intend to manipulate and use it. Our *adlist* will serve as a sample database. There are generally three elements common to all databases:

The file	Known by a descriptive title that indicates the entire contents of the database.
A record	A segment of the file, a record holds all of the facts associated with a single entry in the database. In *adlist,* each line is a record.
A field	A segment of a record. In a name-and-address file, one field could contain the name, another could contain the street address, another could contain the city, and so on.

These three elements form a natural hierarchy: Fields are contained in records, which are themselves contained in the file.

185

While the distinction between a record and the file itself may be obvious, the exact nature of a field might not be, especially when the fields are stretched out along a single line. Under those conditions, it's the delimiters you include that set off one field from another.

In our example, there are two possibilities. Either the spaces or the commas can be chosen to show where one field of information ends and another begins. From a conceptual point of view, it may not seem to make much difference which you choose. But from a structural point of view, your choice of delimiter does make a difference. If you choose the space character, then each record has eight fields, and the commas are part of the fields. If you declare that the comma is the delimiter, there are only three fields, and the spaces are contained within them.

From an operational point of view, the character you decide upon will depend on how much control you want to exert over the record. Generally speaking, you have more flexibility when you break a record into more, rather than fewer, individual units of information. In our example, that would be the case if you chose the space as your delimiter. Luckily, the space also happens to be XENIX' default delimiter.

RETRIEVING INFORMATION

What if you needed to extract from *adlist* all of the information about everyone who has a 10143 ZIP code? That's a simple *grep* command:

grep 10143 adlist

But remember, the whole of *adlist* is 1000 records long. The matches from your *grep* command, perhaps several hundred in all, could scroll off your screen. It would be better to redirect *grep*'s output to a new file with the command:

grep 10143 adlist ⟩ zip_10143

All of the output will now be sent to a file named *zip_10143* for future reference.

But even though you've got the information you want, there's no reason just to leave the new file, or even the old one, in the same order in which it was created. Wouldn't it be more useful if the file were alphabetized?

SORTING INFORMATION

XENIX' *sort* utility can handle that chore. Perhaps you want to sort the original file by the person's name. If *adlist* were as short as our example, the simple form of the *sort* command would almost do that for you:

sort adlist

After a few seconds, you'd see the results:

```
$ sort adlist
Ed Porter, 1232 Maiden Lane, NYC NY 10101
Fred Jonzz, 16 Oxford Rd, Buffalo NY 13221
Jonn Jonzz, 13 Waverly Pl, NYC NY 10033
Tim Brahms, 132 Amsterdam Ave, NYC NY 10143
$ _
```

Well, that isn't quite what you had in mind. The file is, indeed, sorted, but the records are sorted by *first* name. If you don't include any sorting options, the sort is made on the basis of the entire line, with the order determined by the first and following characters in each line. Let's look at some of the *sort* options that make this utility more flexible:

b	Ignores leading blanks in field comparisons.
d	Sorts in dictionary order. Only letters, digits, and blanks are significant; punctuation marks and special symbols are not.
f₀	Interprets lowercase letters as uppercase.
i	Considers only the ASCII characters in the decimal range 32–126 in non-numeric comparisons. (This includes every visible character on standard English keyboards but excludes various foreign-language, graphic, and control characters.)
n	Sorts numbers according to their arithmetic value, not the ASCII value of each of their components. (This implies the *b* option.)
o	Precedes the name of the output file in which the sorted data are to be stored. This file can have the same name as one of the files being used for input.

r   Reverses the order of the sort (high to low).

t[character]   Recognizes [character] as the new delimiter. (Use this, for example, to change the delimiter from a space to a comma.)

c   Checks to determine if the file is already sorted according to any other options included in the command.

[+ number]   Begin the sort on the field number you specify. Fields are numbered
[− number]   from 0 (at the extreme left edge of the record). If the [− number] option is included, the sort examines only the field between the + and − numbers; if a [− number] is not included, the sort examines the record to the end of the line.

Even though all those *sort* options may look a bit bewildering, you have the tools you need in order to sort a file with the results you want. For example, you can see that you need to specify the field (with the + option) if you want to sort the records by last name.

sort +1 adlist

produces the screen display:

```
$ sort +1 adlist
Tim Brahms, 132 Amsterdam Ave, NYC NY 10143
Jonn Jonzz, 13 Waverly Pl, NYC NY 10033
Fred Jonzz, 16 Oxford Rd, Buffalo NY 13221
Ed Porter, 1232 Maiden Lane, NYC NY 10101
$ _
```

That's better, but it's still not correct. The last names were nicely alphabetized, but *sort* made no attempt to adjust either of the Jonzz brothers in relation to the other.

The first sorting field (the only one you specified) is called the *key* field. But most sorting routines will also permit you to specify at least a *secondary* field to act as a "tie-breaker," and XENIX is no different. You want *sort* to examine first names, to alphabetize the Jonzz brothers correctly, so try the the command:

sort +1 +0 adlist

Notice how the field-selection options work. The specification *+1* is actually the second field, not the first, and *+0* is actually the first field. Remember that in specifying sort fields you must begin counting from 0, not 1. Also, notice that these field numbers are separated by a blank space.

187

This time, you've told *sort* to begin by judging the contents of each line at the first character in field one. When that's done, you've told it to resolve duplicate records by using field zero as the second criterion. The result looks like this:

```
$ sort +1 +0 adlist
Tim Brahms, 132 Amsterdam Ave, NYC NY 10143
Jonn Jonzz, 13 Waverly Pl, NYC NY 10033
Fred Jonzz, 16 Oxford Rd, Buffalo NY 13221
Ed Porter, 1232 Maiden Lane, NYC NY 10101
$ _
```

Even with the addition of the second field criterion, the sort is still incorrect. Why?

When you specified field number one, you gave *sort* the starting position within the record. But you didn't restrict it to just that field, so it used the entire line, beginning at the first character of field one, as the basis for its initial sort. So the sort on field one was done on the line fragments:

Jonzz, 13 Waverly Pl, NYC NY 10033

Jonzz, 16 Oxford Rd, Buffalo NY 13221

Notice that the lines are not identical. When *sort* compared the first *3* in John Jonzz' record and the *6* in Fred Jonzz' record, John Jonzz took precedence. To *sort*, there were no duplicate records, and so the secondary field you specified became immaterial.

To narrow *sort*'s focus, change the line one more time to read:

sort +1 −2 +0 adlist

This time, your addition of − 2 tells *sort* to end its first sort at field two—in other words, you've restricted the first sort only to field one. This time, you'll see the correct display, with the names properly ordered.

```
$ sort +1 −2 +0 adlist
Tim Brahms, 132 Amsterdam Ave, NYC NY 10143
Fred Jonzz, 16 Oxford Rd, Buffalo NY 13221
Jonn Jonzz, 13 Waverly Pl, NYC NY 10033
Ed Porter, 1232 Maiden Lane, NYC NY 10101
$ _
```

Here's one more example. Suppose you wanted to sort on the ZIP code field, with secondary and tertiary sorts on the last names and the first names, respectively. The field numbers are:

Fields

0	1	2	3	4	5	6	7

Tim Brahms, 132 Amsterdam Ave, NYC NY 10143

The command would be:

```
sort  +7n  +1  -2  +0  adlist
```

In more familiar words, this means: Sort on the seventh field, which is numeric (no limiting field is needed, since this is at the end of the line). Then, within identical groups of ZIP codes, sort again on the second field. And, if there is identical field information there as well, sort again starting on the first field and continuing to the end of the line. (Notice that you can tack a letter option onto a field assignment.)

DETAILING SIMILARITIES BETWEEN TWO FILES

One problem with mailing lists is the possibility that entries may be included in more than one file. Consider these two files, called *mlist1* and *mlist2*:

```
Ed Porter, 1236 Maiden Lane, NYC NY 10101
Frank Jeffries, 1717 Third Avenue, NYC NY 10101
Frank Jonzz, 26 Oxford Rd, Buffalo NY 13221
Fred Jonzz, 16 Oxford Rd, Buffalo NY 13221
Jim Jonzz, 13 Waverly Pl, NYC NY 10033
John Jonzz, 18 Waverly Pl, NYC NY 10033
Sam Winters, 1712 Third Avenue, NYC NY 10101
Ted Porter, 1232 Maiden Lane, NYC NY 10101
Tim Brahms, 132 Broadway, Albany NY 12143
Tom Brahms, 152 Broadway, Albany NY 12143
```

Contents of the file mlist1

```
Ed Porter, 1232 Maiden Lane, NYC NY 10101
Frank Jeffries, 1717 Third Avenue, NYC NY 10101
Sam Winters, 1712 Third Avenue, NYC NY 10101
Ted Porter, 1232 Maiden Lane, NYC NY 10101
```

Contents of the file mlist2

(We're using small files as examples, so the similarities are obvious. XENIX sorts large files rapidly too, and you will find that this command is very useful when you work with them.)

To determine the names that are duplicated in these two files, you can use XENIX' *comm* utility, which tells you the lines that are common to both files.

Unless you specify otherwise, *comm* processes two files by printing three columns of information. The first column displays all the lines in the first file, the second column displays all the lines in the second file, and the third column displays all the lines that are common to both files.

The lines in our sample files are long, however, so this three-column output is not very easy to read. *Comm* has three possible options, the numbers *1*, *2*, and *3*. If you include one or two of these numbers as arguments in your command, *comm* will suppress the corresponding column of output. (You wouldn't want to include all three—that would amount to suppressing all lines of output.)

Before you use *comm*, however, there might be some preparatory work to be done. *Comm* can't compare the lines in any files if they aren't sorted (beginning

189

with the first field) in ASCII order, according to the first character in each line. Although *mlist1* and *mlist2* are already arranged in this order, to perform such a sort with another set of files, you would use the commands:

　　sort -o mlist1 mlist1

and

　　sort -o mlist2 mlist2

The *o* option tells *sort* to send its output to the specified file name. Essentially what you are doing is telling *sort* to send its output back to the input file. It's a good way to avoid proliferation of files. (Note, however, that there is a potential danger here. Using this form of the *sort* command will overwrite the original file. Only overwrite your source file if you're sure that what replaces it is correct.)

Once the two files are sorted correctly, enter the command:

　　comm -12 mlist1 mlist2

and you'll see the response:

```
$ comm -12 mlist1 mlist2
Frank Jeffries, 1717 Third Avenue, NYC NY 10101
Sam Winters, 1712 Third Avenue, NYC NY 10101
Ted Porter, 1232 Maiden Lane, NYC NY 10101
$ _
```

The option *-12* suppresses the printing of lines that appear exclusively in either file. Only the lines that are common to both will appear on the screen—or in a disk file, if you were to redirect the output (for example, to a file named *mlistcomm* with the command *comm -12 mlist1 mlist2 > mlistcomm*).

In our example you might wonder at first why the record for Ed Porter was not included in the list of common lines. If you check the lines, however, you'll see that there is a difference in the last digit of the street number. So, having done its job correctly, *comm* has not printed that line.

REMOVING DUPLICATE ENTRIES FROM A FILE

Now that you know which lines are in both files, you probably want to extract the duplicates. If you want to keep both lists separate and simply cull entries from one file or the other as appropriate, you can use the output of the *comm* command as a reference while you edit the two files with *vi.*

Another approach you could take, however, and the one we'll look at now, is to remove all duplicate entries from one of the original two lists. To do this, use a XENIX utility called *uniq.* (Like *comm, uniq* requires a certain amount of pre-processing.)

190

Let's assume the same starting point, the files *mlist1* and *mlist2*. First you create a new file that contains the lines that are common to both:

comm -12 mlist1 mlist2 ⟩ mlistcomm

In order for *uniq* to work, however, duplicate lines must occur in the same file, and they must must be adjacent to each other. To prepare such a file, you'll need to merge *mlistcomm* with one of the source files and sort the result. (Since the contents of the file *mlistcomm* are common to both *mlist1* and *mlist2,* you could use either file for the next step; for illustration, we'll use *mlist1.*)   ♦

To accomplish the merging and sorting (by last name) in one step, use the command:

sort +1 −2 +0 -o mlistmerge mlist1 mlistcomm   191

Here, you've produced the single output file *mlistmerge.* Use the *cat* command to view its contents. You'll see:

```
$ cat mlistmerge
Tim Brahms, 132 Broadway, Albany NY 12143
Tom Brahms, 152 Broadway, Albany NY 12143
Frank Jeffries, 1717 Third Avenue, NYC NY 10101
Frank Jeffries, 1717 Third Avenue, NYC NY 10101
Frank Jonzz, 26 Oxford Rd, Buffalo NY 13221
Fred Jonzz, 16 Oxford Rd, Buffalo NY 13221
Jim Jonzz, 13 Waverly Pl, NYC NY 10033
John Jonzz, 18 Waverly Pl, NYC NY 10033
Ed Porter, 1236 Maiden Lane, NYC NY 10101
Ted Porter, 1232 Maiden Lane, NYC NY 10101
Ted Porter, 1232 Maiden Lane, NYC NY 10101
Sam Winters, 1712 Third Avenue, NYC NY 10101
Sam Winters, 1712 Third Avenue, NYC NY 10101
$ _
```

You're ready to use *uniq* to extract the records that are duplicated.

Uniq has three options. They are:

u   Omits all occurrences of duplicated lines in the output (only the lines that are not repeated are printed).

d   Includes one copy of each duplicated line in the output (disregards all other lines).

c   Includes one copy of each line in the source file, preceding the line with a number showing how many times it is repeated in the file.

Used without any options, *uniq* blends the *u* and *d* options: Its output includes all unique lines in the file, plus one copy of any duplicated lines. The remaining duplicates are discarded.

Applied to *mlistmerge, uniq* without any options would produce results that are identical to the original *mlist1* file. This time, that's not the result you want. Likewise, the *d* option alone would produce output identical to *mlistcomm.* And the *c* option is purely statistical in value.

What you really want is a file that contains only unique lines—no copies of the duplicated lines. For that you need to use the *u* option in the command line:

uniq -u mlistmerge mlistuniq

This command processes the lines in *mlistmerge* and places the results in the file *mlistuniq.* Note that you do not need a greater-than symbol to redirect the output from the screen to the disk file *mlistuniq. Uniq* assumes redirection if you include a file name for the output.

Indeed, if you were to print the contents of *mlistuniq,* you would now see the desired results. Any lines that appeared more than once in the input file would be gone. The only file (other than the temporary files you created to make *mlistuniq*) in which they would now exist is *mlist2.* In other words, you've successfully used the commands *comm* and *uniq* to create the file *mlistuniq* which, with *mlist2,* forms a complete mailing list with no duplicate entries.

TESTING FOR UNIQUE FIELDS

There are two additional options that can be used with *uniq*:

| [−number] | Skips the first [number] fields in each line and begins the comparison at field [number]+1. |
| [+number] | Skips the first [number] characters at the beginning of the line or at the beginning of a field, if one is specified. |

In any of our mailing-list files, these options could be used to exclude more than one person with the same first or last name or from the same street address, city, state, or ZIP code. It also points out one problem that can arise in the absence of careful planning.

Look at the first and last lines of *mlistmerge*:

Tim Brahms, 132 Broadway, Albany NY 12143
Sam Winters, 1712 Third Avenue, NYC NY 10101

If you count the fields in each line, you'll notice that one contains seven, while the other contains eight. In Tim Brahms' entry, the street address occupies only two fields; in Sam Winters', it occupies three.

Because of this inconsistency, you could not make a meaningful comparison of the information on the lines beyond the fourth field position, unless you used the *sort* command with the *t* option to redefine the field separator. In that case, specifying the comma as the separator would let you process the file on the basis of lines containing three fields.

There are two other possible solutions. The first is to plan ahead or edit your file to make certain that all lines have the same number of fields. The second is to combine fields. For example, *Third Avenue* could be rewritten as *Third_Avenue* to standardize the lines at seven fields.

With the latter alternative, of course, you would want to remove the underline when it came time to print mailing labels. Actually, you would want to do more than that, so let's move on to see about readjusting the output file.

EDITING A FILE AUTOMATICALLY

Let's modify our short *adlist* file to appear as:

```
$ cat adlist
:Jonn Jonzz, 13 Waverly Pl, NYC NY 10033::
:Tim Brahms, 132 Amsterdam Ave, NYC NY 10143::
:Fred Jonzz, 16 Oxford Rd, Buffalo NY 13221::
:Ed Porter, 1232 Maiden Lane, NYC NY 10101::
$ _
```

We've added a single colon (:) to the beginning of each line and a double colon (::) to the end. These characters are used to hold three positions open on the line. Other than that, they have no special function. But why do that?

As mentioned earlier, one of the reasons to extract information of this sort is to create a mailing list for printing labels. Unfortunately, mailing addresses, when printed, are vertically oriented, not horizontal like these.

In order to convert the result of a *grep* or *sort* routine, an editing session is necessary to adjust the shape of the resulting file. All of the commas need to be stripped out, and each of the three fields they separate has to be placed on its own line. Furthermore, a standard one-inch-high label takes six printed lines. There are only three fields in the label file, so it must be padded with three additional lines. Those three lines are the reason for the three colons, as you'll soon see. But first, let's look at the editing you'd need to do.

If you assume 100 records to be edited (not to mention the original 1000 we mentioned for *adlist*), you would be faced with a substantial editing session. Each occurrence of a comma and a space, as well as each colon that's been added, would have to be replaced by a carriage return (called a *newline* character in XENIX terminology).

You could choose either *vi* or *ed* to do the job. You might assume that their global find-and-replace commands would do it with relative ease. But inserting a carriage return with *vi* or *ed* is not as easy as replacing *abc* with *xyz*, because both editors interpret a carriage return to mean, "Do what I just typed on this line."

You have another approach, though. It's called *sed,* the XENIX stream editor. Generally, *sed* is used to perform editing functions on data files that are too large to fit into memory with *vi* or *ed.* But it has some excellent features that can be used with a file of any size.

CREATING A SCRIPT

In the next chapter you'll be introduced to a special type of text file called a *shell script,* which contains a series of commands that can be used in place of keyboard input to control various aspects of XENIX' operation. (If you're familiar with macros or batch files, you'll find that scripts are very similar in function.)

Scripts are not confined solely to shell operations, though. At the lowest level, just as in our everyday world, scripts are simply lines of text. Instead of recording dialogue in a play, however, they record actions and responses, and instead of being interpreted by actors, these scripts are interpreted by XENIX.

Let's create one based on the editing commands we need to convert *adlist* into a usable mailing list.

Use the command:

vi label

to start *vi* and have it accept the name *label* for the script file you'll create. Once *vi* is on the screen, you can begin to insert the contents of the script. You know what must be done to adjust *adlist.* Let's examine the procedure one step at a time.

First, for all lines in the file you're processing, you want a carriage return to replace all occurrences of a comma followed by a space. You want that replacement made for every occurrence within every line. That requires a global command. Press *i* to enter insert mode and type, without pressing Enter:

1,$s

Earlier in this book, you learned that 1,$ is a shorthand means of indicating the range of all lines in a file (1 is the starting line, and the wild card $ refers to the last line, no matter what its number). The *s* you typed is the *substitute* command.

Substituting requires two parameters, the text you want to replace and the text you want in its place. The general format is:

[range]s/look for/replace with/global parameter

with the slashes denoting the beginning and end of each parameter. Continue your *vi* line, then, by adding the text you want to replace. The line looks like this:

1,$s/, /

But now, how do you indicate a carriage return? That is a special character, and pressing it would only move the cursor down to the next line in the file.

Recall from Chapter 7 that when you are going to include a special character in a line that *nroff* interprets as a command, you must precede it with an escape character, the backslash (\ ). The same applies here. Add the escape character to your current line and then press Enter. Fill in the new line that you're on, so that both lines look like this:

1,$s/, /

/g

Mystifying though it might look, you've just done what you set out to do. When *sed* reads this script, it will accept the first three characters as a range command. It will also understand that the comma and space between the first and second slashes are the values you want replaced. Then, when *sed* comes to the escape character, the backslash will tell it to accept the next character literally.

Since the next character *sed* encounters is the carriage return, that is the character it will interpret literally. And, because the carriage return is followed by the third slash, *sed* will accept the carriage return as the character to be substituted for the comma and space. The *g* ending the line makes the command global, so it will affect every occurrence on each line, not just the first.

195

Because this is a script that is read by the operating system itself, you have literally, with a one-line command, finessed a change that would be awkward if attempted manually from within the editor.

All that remains now is to replace each colon in every line with a carriage return. The finished script looks like this:

1,$s/, /

/g

1,$s/:/

/g

Press Esc to exit insert mode, and then use *:x* to write the file to disk and quit *vi*.

(For your future reference, note that the script commands used here were taken directly from the commands available with *ed*. While we haven't covered that line editor in much detail, refer to Chapter 4 and your XENIX Command Reference manual for more information.)

And now to produce the play.

EDITING WITH *sed*

The *sed* non-interactive editing utility has three options:

n	Suppresses output. This option can be used to test an editing script without sending the results to the screen or to a file.
e	Precedes script instructions that are written into the command line instead of read from a separate file.
f	Precedes the name of the file from which *sed* should read its script (editing commands).

Now that the entire cast is assembled, you can start the production. Use the command:

```
sed  -f  label  adlist  >  labels
```

to tell *sed* to read the script file called *label,* use it to process the data file called *adlist,* and redirect the output to a file called *labels.* The results you get should be in this form:

```
Jonn Jonzz
13 Waverly Pl
NYC NY 10033

Tim Brahms
132 Amsterdam Ave
NYC NY 10143

Fred Jonzz
16 Oxford Rd
Buffalo NY 13221

Ed Porter
1232 Maiden Lane
NYC NY 10101
```

As your script directed, each group of three lines is preceded by one blank line and followed by two—in place of the colons. All you'd need to do now is have your line printer set up with label stock and you could use the *lp* command to send the file off for printing. (Knowing the procedure, you could now include instructions in your script that would substitute a space for any underline characters you've used to even out the number of fields in your records.)

Finally, one of the nicest features of *sed* is its ability to process several files at the same time. If, for example, you had extracted lists for different ZIP codes (or some other criterion), you could use a command such as:

```
sed  -f  label  [file1]  [file2]  [file3]  >  labels
```

to process all of the files and send the output into the one file called *labels.*

PREVIEWING PRINTED OUTPUT

At the end of Chapter 7, we discussed printing a document locally. This is an ideal solution for printing labels, because there is no need to halt other printing within your XENIX system, change the paper to label forms, and then change back again when your labels are printed.

196

For printing locally, we also pointed out that using a simple *cat* command to examine an *nroff*-formatted document could be sufficient for previewing a document before printing. And it can be. But *cat* doesn't have to be the only way you print a document to the screen. There's also the XENIX *pr* utility, and there are a host of related options that can emulate paper printing on the screen. The *pr* command line format is:

pr [-(options)] [file names]

and its list of options is impressive (we've broken them down in the following table by function):

Page-setup options

w[number]	Sets the line width to [number] characters when the document contains multi-column output (the default is 72).
o[number]	Sets the page offset to [number] character positions (the default is 0).
l[number] (lowercase L)	Sets the page length to [number] lines (the default is 66).

Output-formatting options

+[number]	Starts printing at page [number] (the default is 1).
d	Double-spaces printing.
p	Pauses and rings a bell before displaying the next page and waits for a carriage return before continuing.
f	Pauses for a form-feed instead of a series of line-feeds to advance to next page (this feature is handy if you're using a terminal with paper output instead of a video screen, or if you are printing locally).
h	Uses the next argument as the output page header (the defaults are date, file name, and page number).
n	Prints each line in the file with an accompanying line number (this feature is used to its best advantage when printing programming source code).

Multiple-column printing options

[number]	Formats printing into [number] columns. (See the Command Reference manual's descriptions of options *e* and *i*, as well.)
a	Prints multiple-column output across the page. This option is not the same as −[number]; it prints line 1 to the left, line 2 to the right, line 3 to the left, and so on. It's not suitable for all output.

m	Merges and prints all files, one per column (use of this option negates the effects of the −[*number*] and −*a* options).
t	Suppresses the default five-line header and five-line footer for the top and bottom of each output page.

Applying this information to the *labels* file you created with *sed,* you can preview the output on-screen with the command line:

pr -2 -l24 -tp labels

Pr will print the contents of the file, in two-column format, on a 24-line page (the "page" length of your screen), with no header or footer, and a pause between pages. Since you've included a pause, *pr* will cause your terminal's bell to ring and will wait for you to press Enter before each page, including the first, is printed. The output will look like this:

```
$ pr -2 -l24 -tp labels

Jonn Jonzz              Fred Jonzz
13 Waverly Pl           16 Oxford Rd
NYC NY 10033            Buffalo NY 13221


Tim Brahms              Ed Porter
132 Amsterdam Ave       1232 Maiden Lane
NYC NY 10143            NYC NY 10101


$ _
```

After you've previewed the printing on the screen for accuracy, you can make any changes necessary (in page length, for example) to suit your label paper. If you have a label sheet that is more than two columns wide, you can increase the column value.

Finally, you can use whatever procedures are required to send the file to your local printer.

DEALING WITH DOS FILES

If you are moving to XENIX from an MS-DOS environment, there's a good chance you'll want to move some of your data files with you. It's possible, but will only work with text (unformatted, or ASCII) files. That restriction isn't as great as it might seem, however. Many programs can produce text output. Microsoft Multiplan and Microsoft Word are just two examples.

There are eight commands that can be used to look at, modify, and transfer DOS files to XENIX. But before we discuss them, let's cover three important facts.

ACCESSING DOS DISKS

First and foremost, if you want to handle files on DOS diskettes, you must have a DOS diskette mounted in one of your XENIX computer's floppy disk drives. Some versions of XENIX will also allow you to access the hard disk's DOS partition (if you have one) from XENIX. Both activities *must* be coordinated through the system administrator. Only one person at a time can access a DOS disk. If more try, the results can be unpredictable.

199

ACCESSING DOS DISK DRIVES

During the initial phase of your transition from MS-DOS to XENIX, you'll probably remain more familiar with DOS drive names than their XENIX counterparts. To assist you, XENIX allows you to address a DOS disk with DOS drive names. The drive names may be entered in uppercase or lowercase.

If your system has 360K drives, the drive names are A: and B:, just as they are in versions of MS-DOS higher than 2.0. If you're using IBM PC AT–compatible 1.2-megabyte drives, the drive names are X: and Y:. You can also read 360K diskettes in the 1.2-megabyte drive by naming the drive A: (but the DOS commands *dosmkdir,* *dosrmdir,* and *dosrm* usually won't work if the drive doesn't match the disk type).

If your system has only a single floppy disk drive, its name is either A: or X:. In dual floppy-drive systems, the leftmost or top drive is usually A: or X:, and the rightmost or bottom drive is B: or Y:.

If a DOS partition exists on your hard disk in addition to the three XENIX partitions, you may access it by naming the drive C:. If another disk drive has been added to your XENIX system, you may access the DOS partition on that device by naming it D:. You will find accessing these partitions from XENIX very useful, especially if you are the only user on your XENIX system. For information on installing a DOS partition, see Chapter 13.

CONVERTING DOS FILES

Text files are text files no matter what operating system they were created in. The only actual conversion that occurs happens to a character found at the end of each line of text in DOS and XENIX. Typically, DOS uses a combination of a carriage return and a linefeed as its end-of-line character. XENIX uses just the linefeed. When you use the *doscat* and *doscp* commands (which we'll cover in a moment) to transfer files, this conversion occurs automatically. To suppress the removal of the carriage-return character (or its addition if the conversion is from XENIX to DOS), include the *r* option in the two file-transfer commands.

THE DOS COMMANDS

These are the eight XENIX commands that are used to handle DOS text files:

doscat [-r] [drive name]:[file name]	Prints the contents of a DOS file to the screen. It's similar to the DOS *type* command.
doscp [-r] [drive name]:[file name] [XENIX file name]	Copies the specified file from a DOS disk onto a XENIX disk, giving the file the specified XENIX file name.
doscp [-r] [drive name]:[file name] [XENIX directory]	Copies the specified file from a DOS disk onto a XENIX disk and into the directory that is specified.
dosdir [drive name]:[DOS directory]	Lists the contents of a DOS disk's directory in standard DOS format. The argument can be a specific subdirectory on the disk or just the drive name.
dosls [drive name]:[DOS directory]	Lists the contents of a DOS disk's directory in XENIX format, with just the file names and no detail. The argument can be a specific subdirectory on the DOS disk or it can be just the drive name.
dosmkdir [drive name]:[DOS directory]	Creates a DOS directory on the specified DOS disk.
dosrmdir [drive name]:[DOS directory]	Removes the specified DOS directory from a DOS disk.
dosrm [drive name]:[file name]	Removes the specified DOS file from a DOS disk.

200

For example, if you wanted to copy a file named *dbase10.txt* from a DOS diskette in the first drive of an IBM PC AT or compatible, you would use the command:

doscp x:dbase10.txt dbase10.txt

This command would copy the file into your current working directory with the same name it had on the DOS disk.

You can also redirect the screen output from *doscat, dosdir,* and *dosls* commands into a XENIX disk file just as you could from any XENIX command, but it's preferable to simply copy the text files you want into your XENIX directory and use the DOS disk for as short a time as possible.

The Bourne Shell As we mentioned briefly in Chapter 2, XENIX' shells are command interpreters. They take input, examine this information, and then determine how it should be handled and where it belongs.

Often, the input comes from you, at the keyboard. At other times, it comes from files that define certain aspects of the XENIX environment, or from programs, such as *vi*. And, as you've seen throughout this book, the information handled by the shell can be sent to a file, to another user via the *mail* system, to a program of some sort for further processing, or to a device, such as a printer.

Because the Bourne shell is the role model for both the C and Visual shells, the concepts and descriptions in this chapter are valid for the other shells as well. The chapters on the C and Visual shells won't repeat any of the information here, so regardless of which shell you are assigned, this chapter is the place to begin.

We'll set out by looking at some preliminary information.

COMPOUNDING SIMPLE SHELL COMMANDS

Whenever you sit down at the keyboard and enter a command, you initiate a process. A simple example is using the *who* command to discover which users are currently on the system. When you use this command, XENIX returns a list of users presently logged in. You look through the list and, if the person you want to find is on it, perhaps you use the *write* command to send him or her a message.

Altogether, those actions result in a series of processes:

■ One shell process—*who.*

■ Followed by two user processes—scanning the list of users and then entering the *write* command.

■ Followed by another shell process—*write.*

But what if you could turn some of your actions over to the shell and let it decide whether the person you're looking for is logged in? You could certainly save some time and effort.

USING WHAT YOU KNOW

The knowledge you already have gives you one (long) way to have XENIX look for the person you want to find. Suppose you're looking for the user named *danh.* You could enter two XENIX commands:

```
who ⟩ loglist
grep danh loglist
```

(If you want to try this for yourself, substitute your own user name for *danh.*)

The first command line takes the output of the *who* command and redirects it into a file named *loglist.* Then, the *grep* command takes the value *danh* and scans through the file you specified (*loglist*). If *grep* finds the value for which it's searching, it prints the corresponding line of text from *loglist* on your screen.

While this procedure would relieve you of the need to scan the screen list yourself, there's a shorter way to do the same thing—and without creating an unnecessary disk file that, since you have no more use for it, is a waste of the system's storage space.

LAYING A PIPELINE

The redirection you used in the preceding two commands actually points to a shorter method. In the first command, you redirected the output from one device (the screen) to another (the disk file). In the second command, you told *grep* to scan the redirected output for the value *danb*. The procedure works, but it's a little like walking around the block to go next door. What if you could skip the disk-file stage and redirect the output of the *who* command directly to the *grep* command?

While the word *redirect* describes what happens, there's another XENIX term for rerouting output and input: *piping*. Since you're controlling the flow of a process, the piping you do creates a *pipeline*.

In the preceding example, you piped output to the hard disk by using the greater-than (>) symbol. When you were practicing with the *mail* system in Chapter 8, you used another form of redirection, the less-than symbol (<), to channel output *from* a file.

To pipe the output of one process directly to the input of another, you use either a solid vertical bar (|) or a broken vertical bar (¦). Which you use depends on the terminal you are working from; either version is interpreted by the shell as the piping symbol.

By way of example, let's create a compound command by using a pipeline to send the output of one command (*who*) as input to the other (*grep*). Enter the following command, substituting your own user name:

```
who ¦ grep [user name]
```

Normally, two parameters follow a *grep* command. The first (your user name in this example) is the pattern to be matched. The second, which you've omitted here, is the file where you want XENIX to search for the pattern. This is where the pipeline enters the picture.

Rather than allow the output from *who* to be printed on the screen, the vertical bar in your command pipes the output into *grep*'s missing second parameter. As a result, instead of seeing the list of all users currently logged in, you see only the line from the list that refers to the user you specified (if the person were not currently logged in, you'd see no response at all).

PIPING TO THE PRINTER

If you have the Text Processing System, you can use the same type of procedure to print a newly formatted text file. In Chapter 7, you saw how to format a text file, write the formatted file to disk, and then print it. The command sequence looks like this:

```
nroff -mm sample ⟩ sample2
```

Next, the command:

```
lp sample2
```

sends that formatted file to the printer.

If you don't want to preview the formatted text, you can create a pipeline and condense these two commands:

```
nroff -mm sample ¦ lp
```

With no output file specified, *nroff* would normally print the formatted version of *sample* to the screen. But, with the pipe symbol, that output is supplied as the missing parameter in the *lp* command. Without creating an intermediate file on disk, you've sent the formatted version of *sample* directly to the printer.

Remember, too, that if *sample* were a very long file and you needed to move on immediately to other tasks on the system, you could append an ampersand (&) to the end of that command line and push the entire process, pipeline and all, into the background.

MAKING A PROCESS CONDITIONAL

Compounding the *who* command with *grep* gives you a simple way to determine whether someone is now logged in. But let's return to our original task for a moment. You still need to check the screen to see if *grep* found the person, and then decide whether or not to type the *write* command.

If you could incorporate those responses into the command line, there'd be little left for you to do other than type the actual message. But to make the command work properly, you would need to make the entire response process conditional, based on *grep*'s findings. Otherwise, your *write* command would be sent out, whether or not the recipient was logged in.

Let's take it step by step. If you want to try these commands, it's best to enlist the cooperation of two real users on your system. Notify them in advance and schedule a "learning period" that's convenient for all of you.

First, enter the following line at the shell prompt:

```
if who ¦ grep [user name1]
```

Notice that something odd happens when you press the Enter key. The usual shell prompt symbol does not reappear. In its place is a new character, a greater-than symbol (>).

204

As you've already seen, certain words and symbols have a special meaning to the shell. *If* is one of them. The greater-than symbol notifies you of a change that has occurred because you entered a command line containing *if.*

When the shell encounters any special word or symbol at the beginning of what would otherwise be a command line, it stops processing the line on an immediate, interactive basis. For that line and those that follow it, the shell redirects the keyboard output into a subshell, where the lines are retained for later evaluation.

This redirection continues until the shell encounters another special word or symbol telling it to evaluate and perform the instructions it's been given and then return to immediate processing of every line.

Right now, then, you need another special word that you'll find easy to remember. In XENIX, as in everyday English, *if* is part of a compound clause that is often used in one of two variations. The first is an *if... then* statement, in which you add a command that is executed only if the result of the conditional is true. (This is equivalent to, "If the sun shines, then I'll go to the beach.") The second variation is an *if... then... else* statement, in which you add a second alternative to be executed if the conditional is false. (This is equivalent to, "If the sun shines, then I'll go to the beach, else I'll go to the library.")

Using the line you've already typed, the first form of the *if* statement might be:

205

```
if who | grep [user name1]
    then write [user name1]
fi
```

(The indent is to help you vizualize the structure of your conditional statement. Here and in other conditionals, you can either include or ignore the indents when you type.) The second line, *then write [user name1],* contains the process you want carried out if the user you specified is currently logged in. You *must* include *then* to indicate that this command is a continuation of the *if* statement. *Fi* (*if* spelled backwards) ends the entire conditional statement and causes the shell to begin carrying out the process you've created.

What results might you expect?

■ If the user is logged into the system, you'll see the results of the *grep* command on the line following *fi.* Your terminal's cursor will be on the line below, indicating that the *write* command is now under way.

■ If the user has requested privacy with the *mesg n* command, you'll see the results of the *grep* command and the message *Permission denied.*

■ If the person isn't logged into the system, his or her name will not be in the group of users examined by *grep,* and your *write* command will be passed over. But instead of the typical *[user name1] not logged in* response you would ordinarily receive with the *write* command, your shell prompt will simply return.

If you receive the last response, you could assume that the person you are looking for is not online. But there's an outside chance that something may have interfered with your process and stopped it. How can you tell which is true? You can extend the *if* statement to include an *else* clause. To try it, enter:

```
if who | grep [user name1]
    then write [user name1]
    else echo "not logged in"
fi
```

Echo is the shell's print command. Whatever follows it on a line is printed to your screen. If the user you named is not on the system, you'll see the message *not logged in* as a result of the *else* clause. (The quotation marks used around the *echo* message in this example are optional, but it's a good idea to use them—especially if the text you want to include is more than one line long.)

Else now gives the statement somewhere to branch to. So, rather than having to make an assumption about the conclusion of your process, you've told the shell what else to do if *grep* does not find the user you named. In this case, you set another process in motion if the first is not activated.

POSING A DOUBLE CONDITIONAL

As in many attempts at conversation, you may wish to try someone else if the first person you look for isn't available. Why do so manually? Instead, use:

```
if who | grep [user name1]
    then write [user name1]
    elif who | grep [user name2]
        then write [user name2]
    else echo "neither logged in"
fi
```

The first two command lines come directly from the last *if* example. You must have either a *fi* or an *else* statement on the third line of an *if* statement; in this case you have *elif,* short for *else if.* This line is your second conditional, and executes only if the result of the first conditional is false.

If *grep* finds that *[user name1]* is contained in the list of users generated by the *who* command, your *write* command to that person is executed. The additional lines in the statement are ignored.

However, if *[user name1]* is not logged in, flow moves to the *elif* statement and *grep* determines whether *[user name2]* is on the system. If so, it activates the second *write* command. If neither *[user name1]* nor *[user name2]* is present, then flow proceeds to the final *else* statement and echoes the message *neither logged in* on your screen.

Given this type of conditional, it's also helpful to know with whom you are talking if one or the other of these conditions is met. You can find out with two additional lines and a little juggling of those you've already entered:

```
if who ¦ grep [user name1]
    then echo "talking to [user name1]"
    write [user name1]
    elif who ¦ grep [user name2]
        then echo "talking to [user name2]"
        write [user name2]
    else echo "neither logged in"
fi
```

Adding the *echo* command after *then* in each of the conditionals will tell you who is online. Notice that *write* is now on the following line. Placing the command in that position produces an implied *and*, which makes *write* a second result of *then*.

CREATING A SHELL SCRIPT

Even though you've now given the shell the job of checking for and writing to other users on your system, stop and think a moment. You would still have to re-type those command lines each time you wanted to use them.

As you saw in the preceding chapter, there's a way around this task as well: shell scripts—executable text files that make XENIX even easier to use.

To create a shell script to carry out the commands in our example, type the following at the $ shell prompt:

```
cat ⟩ altwrite
if who ¦ grep [user name1]
    then echo "talking to [user name1]"
    write [user name1]
    elif who ¦ grep [user name2]
        then echo "talking to [user name2]"
        write [user name2]
    else echo "neither logged in"
fi
```

Press Ctrl-D on a new line after you've entered *fi.*

You've created a text file called *altwrite* by redirecting the keyboard output to the disk, and the lines you entered represent the entire conditional statement that you've been experimenting with. Now, you need some way to execute the commands in that file.

Simply typing the file's name, as you would with any of the XENIX utility programs, would produce a somewhat misleading response:

```
$ altwrite
altwrite: cannot execute
$ _
```

208

The shell would be telling you that an *executable* file called *altwrite* could not be found. The shell is correct. Even though you intend *altwrite* to be a shell script—a series of executable commands written in a text file—XENIX doesn't know that's what you intend. At present, *altwrite* is still simply a text file. And text files are not normally executable.

One way to make your intentions clear to XENIX is to invoke a XENIX *subshell* with the command *sh,* followed by the name of the text file:

sh altwrite

When you do this, the shell assumes that you specified a text file containing executable commands, and it responds by spawning another version—a subshell—of itself. This subshell is a *process,* just as *who* and *write* are processes, and its job is to read the lines in the specified file and execute them to their completion. When all the commands (and additional processes) the subshell has created are complete, the subshell itself will terminate.

SETTING SHELL OPTIONS

There are several options available to the shell that alter the way it reacts. For example, to test the shell procedure you just developed without actually executing the shell instructions, you could use the command:

sh -nv altwrite

The *n* option is a *no execute* option. Including it causes the shell to examine each line in the process and check it for syntax errors without actually executing any of the commands. That's possible because the shell normally reads and interprets the entire script before it begins to act on the individual lines.

The *v* option in the command causes each line of your script to be printed on the screen as it's evaluated. Without the *v* option, any error would appear only as a line number and a terse explanation of the mistake. With the *v* option in effect, both the line and the explanation appear on-screen (if the *n* option is selected).

Using the *v* option is valuable in another respect, as well. Remember, the shell examines the lines in your script file for errors that it can recognize. It will not necessarily catch other mistakes. For example, a typographical error in a command line would be accepted if it were part of a text string surrounded by quotation marks, as in a message you want echoed to the screen. To you or other users, however, that typographical error could make other lines confusing or meaningless. With the *v* option, all lines are printed to the screen, so you can double-check yourself as the shell processes the file.

An additional option you might like to use is the *x* option. When this is included, each script command and its arguments will be displayed on the screen, preceded by a + symbol, when they are executed. For example, if the user *danh* were substituted for [user name1] in the *altwrite* script file example, and he were currently logged in, the results would look like this:

```
$ sh -x altwrite
+ who
+ grep danh
danh          console       May 15 00:03
+ echo talking to danh
talking to danh
+ write danh
_
```

You can also insert options *within* the script with the command format:

    set [-(options)]

Place this command on its own line, anywhere in the script that you want it to take effect. When you type the *sh [script name]* command, the script process will be based upon the options you've included, from the point in the file at which you included them. If at some point you'd like an option turned off, use the format:

    set [+ option]

on a new line in the script, and the option will be unset.

CREATING AN EXECUTABLE SHELL SCRIPT

Using the *sh* command is fine for files, like our sample, that will be used sporadically, and it's ideal when you're testing a new script. But if you create shell scripts that you'll be using every day, you can alter the script files themselves to make their execution even simpler than typing the *sh* command.

To make this change, let's first find out what is keeping *altwrite* from being an executable file. Request a long directory listing of *altwrite* with the command:

ls -l altwrite

Unless they've been changed, the file's permissions fields will look like this:

    -rw-r--r--

The permissions indicated are (r)ead and (w)rite for yourself and (r)ead for everyone else. But nowhere do you see the *x* that would indicate that this file is executable. There's your problem and, as you saw in the last chapter, it is one you can easily do something about. Type the command:

chmod +x altwrite

and look at the file's permissions field again. This time, it appears as:

-rwxr-xr-x

As simply as that, you have made a text file executable. When you want it to run, all you need do is type its name (or the appropriate path and the name if you're in a different directory).

210

LOOPING WITH VARIABLES

You've learned to create shell scripts for automatic command execution, but there's still more you can do. So far, your command arguments (such as user names) have been typed into the script itself. Let's loosen things up a little.

Imagine that each day you must format and print a list of text files. (For our example, we'll use *nroff* to complete this task.) The names of the files on that list change each day, but there is always more than one. This type of task is repetitive—not so much because it needs to be done frequently, as because the procedure itself must be repeated in order to complete the task.

If you were a programmer, you might create a routine called a *for… next* loop to accomplish this task. It's no more complicated than an *if… then… else* statement, and its general format is:

>*for* every element in a list

>>*do*

>>>-select the next item

>>>-process the list item as specified

>*done*

To use such a *for… next* loop in terms of your list of files to be printed, the file names must be moved sequentially from the list into the command. These names are the arguments for the command.

In most commands that accept an argument, the argument you specify can be one of two types: literal or variable. A literal argument is the name of something that actually exists. The file name *altwrite,* for example, is a literal argument because it refers to *altwrite* by its literal name. A variable, on the other hand, might be a word like *filename,* which stands for any one of a set of actual file names. A variable represents something real, but of itself is not a real entity. Let's examine how assigning literal values to variables works and take care of the looping situation at the same time.

From the shell prompt, enter the following lines (you'll see in a page or two why we've used the somewhat cryptic *fmt* to stand for *formatted file*):

```
cat ) print_fmt
for filename
    do echo "now processing $filename"
    nroff -mm $filename | lp
done
```

Press Ctrl-D on a new line to close the text file. Now, use the command:

```
chmod +x print_fmt
```

to change *print_fmt* into an executable shell script. As you can see, the shell's version of a *for...next* loop consists of three keywords: *for, do,* and *done.*

For sets up the list of arguments—in this case, represented by the variable *filename. Do* begins the list of commands that you want applied while you're cycling through the loop. In our example, there are two *do* commands:

■ The words *echo "now processing $filename"* echo on-screen the name of the file that's being processed. The $ sign preceding *filename* tells the *echo* command that it is a variable and should not be printed literally. (The *echo* line isn't essential. It's included simply to keep you informed as each file is formatted and then printed.)

■ The command *nroff -mm $filename | lp* tells *nroff* to format the file and pipe the output to the line printer without creating an intermediate file.

Done ends the loop, but not until the last item in your list has been processed by the commands in the *for...next* loop. Between the *nroff* command and *done,* the shell knows it must go back (loop) to the top of the list and look for another item.

And where does the list come from? It comes from you. You enter it as a series of arguments when you run the shell script. Let's assume that you need to process the files *sample1, sample2,* and *sample3.* Once you have created an executable shell script, you can use the command:

```
print_fmt sample1 sample2 sample3
```

211

Although the text of the actual script looks like this:

```
for filename
        do echo "now processing $filename"
        nroff -mm $filename | lp
done
```

the first time through the loop, the shell "sees" it as:

```
for sample1 sample2 sample3
        do echo "now processing sample1"
        nroff -mm sample1 | lp
        (sample2 and sample3 remaining)
done
```

(Changes are italicized for emphasis.) The second time, your script becomes:

```
for sample1 sample2 sample3
        do echo "now processing sample2"
        nroff -mm sample2 | lp
        (sample3 remaining)

done
```

And, finally, on the third pass, it becomes:

```
for sample1 sample2 sample3
        do echo "now processing sample3"
        nroff -mm sample3 | lp
        (no more files remaining)
done
```

after which the process ends.

The shell counted the number of arguments you entered (three file names), and processed the loop an equal number of times, substituting each successive file name in the argument list for the variable.

CREATING FILE NAMES FROM VARIABLES

It's not always the best policy to send formatted text straight off to the printer without first previewing it on the screen.

To format your files and keep them for previewing before they're printed, use the following script:

```
for filename
        do echo "now formatting $filename"
        nroff -mm $filename > $filename.fmt
done
```

If you were to supply the same three arguments you did previously, the output now would be the files *sample1.fmt, sample2.fmt,* and *sample3.fmt.* Notice that the shell lets you append literal text (the extension *.fmt*) to the contents of the variable.

After you had previewed the documents, you could then print them all with the shell command:

```
lp *.fmt
```

Of course, you might have other files, that you don't want to print, stored under names that would fit the wild card. If so, you could create another script to handle the printing:

```
for filename
        do echo "now printing $filename"
        lp $filename
        rm -c $filename
done
```

This script actually performs two tasks at the same time. First, each of the files you designate when you run the script is sent to the line printer. The *c* option puts a copy of the file in the print queue rather than establishing links with the original. Second, immediately after each file is submitted, it's deleted from your directory.

CONTROLLING A SCRIPT

The only reservation you might have about this last script is that you have no control over it. Once you press Enter, the script goes off and does everything it's meant to do, until it's finished or until you press the Delete key to interrupt the process. But rather than have only the ability to terminate a process, it's far better to be able to monitor and direct it. XENIX gives you that type of control with two more conditional clauses and two commands.

213

SPECIFYING THE DURATION OF A CONDITION WITH *while*

The first conditional clause is called *while.* Its general syntax is:

while a specified condition exists

    do a command or command list

        -check to see if the condition has changed

        -if it has not changed, redo the command or command list

        -if it has changed, end

  done

214

As with the *for...next* loop described earlier, only the keywords in italic type should be included in your script literally. The explanatory phrases should be used as conceptual guidelines.

When you use a *while* clause, you specify a condition that exists (for example, while a list contains the names of files to be printed). As long as the condition remains unchanged, your command is repeated. When the condition changes (the list is now empty), the process is complete. You'll do something practical with *while* in a moment.

MATCHING A PATTERN WITH *case*

The second conditional is *case,* which is just a little more involved than *while.* The syntax for *case* is:

case "of this text occurring" *in*

    "this pattern of text") perform this command;;

    "this pattern of text") perform this command;;

    .

    .

    .

    "this pattern of text") perform this command

  esac

Here you tell the shell that, for each case in which the text you specify appears within another pattern of text you specify, the command(s) following the second pattern are to be carried out. If no match is found, the shell continues on to the next command in the script (if there is one).

Since *case* allows you to include more than one command line to be examined, you can match one text pattern against several others and execute different commands for each. Note that double semicolons (;;) must be used to end each line of possible commands except the last.

Note too that you must include a right parenthesis between the pattern you're examining for a match and the command list you want to execute if a match is found. Finally, keep in mind that the shell's cue to exit a *case* clause is *esac* (*case* spelled backwards).

STARTING AND STOPPING A LOOP

While, for...next, and *case* enable you to control the manner in which commands are processed in a script. Two other commands are also essential, and they are actually your means of controlling the process itself. These commands are *break* and *continue,* and they're used inside *while* and *for...next* loops. *Break* terminates execution of the loop level at the point at which the *break* command occurs, and *continue* restarts the loop when the *continue* command occurs. But rather than try to explain these commands abstractly, let's use them.

215

CREATING AN INTERACTIVE SCRIPT

We'll use the same general example we have before: You need to format a number of text files for printing. This time, though, let's assume you want to enter each file name individually and be able to stop the process at any time. In order to create the script, start *vi* with the name of a text file called *interact.*

❌ NOTE: *As we mentioned earlier, the lines in this script were given a structured look by indenting them (here, with the Tab key). The alignment certainly isn't needed to make the script run correctly, but it's useful. When you review this script (or one of your own) at a later date, these "nested" indents can help you see immediately where the different levels begin and end. The shell considers the Tab character a delimiter, so for all practical purposes, such indents are ignored when used as they are here.*

When *vi* opens, enter the series of lines you see in Figure 10-1.

After you type the last line, press Esc to leave insert mode, and use :x to write the text to disk and quit *vi.* Now let's step through the script and see what you've accomplished.

The first line is the key to the whole procedure. The phrase *while true,* with no additional condition specified, is a command to repeat the entire process forever. While forever may seem like a long time, this is really the way you want to construct this script. Bear in mind that you won't always be formatting the same number of files. One day perhaps you'll only work on two or three, the next day

```
while true
do echo "Enter the file's name:"
    read answer
    case "$answer" in
    "end")    break
              ;;
    "")       break
              ;;
    *)        if ls | fgrep -x $answer
                  then nroff -mm $answer > $answer.fmt
                  echo "$answer processed and $answer.fmt created"
                  else echo "No such file..."
              fi
              continue
    esac
done
```

Figure 10-1. An interactive script.

you may have ten or twelve to do. Since your script is ready to go on forever, it's flexible enough to accommodate any number of files. Besides (as you'll see in a moment), you've built in a way to stop whenever you want.

Next, you echo the prompt *Enter the file's name:* on the screen. The shell waits for an answer, then captures your response with the *read* command. It reads every character you type until you press the Enter key, and assigns your reply to the variable *answer.*

Now the *case* comparisons begin. You've told the shell to compare the answer it received to three values: *end, "",* and *.

If you have finished your formatting session and have typed the reply *end,* your reply matches the comparison pattern *end,* and the shell carries out the following command, *break.* As a result, you break out of the process and the session is over. If your reply does not match *end,* the shell moves on to the next comparison.

The double quotation marks here indicate a *null* (empty) string of text, as would be transmitted if you pressed the Enter key without typing any characters. This line, then, tells the shell that, in addition to the word *end,* a press of the Enter key signals the end of the session and the *break* command is to be carried out. If your reply was not a null string, the shell goes on again, to the next comparison.

Here, you see the familiar asterisk (*) wild card. As you know, it matches *any* string of text. Essentially, its use here tells the shell, "No matter what is typed, perform the next command."

The entire *if* statement is that command. You're using *fgrep* to verify that the file name you typed is included among the list of files in your directory. This variation of the *grep* command is the only one that allows the *x* option, which tells *fgrep* to search only for complete lines that exactly match the variable *$answer.*

In essence, the *if* clause causes your file to be formatted if the file is found, or it prints the message *No such file...* if the file name you typed doesn't exist in your working directory. Whichever, you then return to the beginning *while* statement.

You may be wondering why the *if* clause and *fgrep* were included in the script to begin with. After all, there's no real need to use them. If the file name you supplied didn't match one of the files in your directory, the shell would print an error message on the screen. Your script would simply cycle back to the beginning and start over. The error would be handled effectively, so why bother with extra command lines? The answer is that your procedure would not be as precise as it could be. By letting the shell handle the error, you relinquish a small amount of control over the process. And the more control you keep for yourself, the less room you leave for unexpected and potentially frustrating errors to occur.

217

TESTING CONDITIONS

Your script, as it stands, is complete and ready to use. Now, let's broaden our viewpoint a bit. You've stepped through the commands in this script, so you know how it works, and why. But what about the other people on your system who might want or need to use it?

They can if they specify the complete path name to the script and if you've set the protection properly. Actually, though, from their point of view, the result of the *fgrep* command could be a bit distracting. If *fgrep* finds the file name typed in response to the *Enter the file's name:* prompt, it prints that name to the screen. The sudden appearance of the file name on-screen is far from outrageous, but a stray response of that sort might be confusing to someone who doesn't know how the script works. And, as we mentioned, if you're going to take the time to control a process, then do so as completely as you can.

A new command that you can use in place of *fgrep* is called *test.* And, as a side benefit, *test* is actually processed faster than *fgrep. Test* also maintains the conditional nature of the *if* statement. If *test* finds the file you've named, the statement is evaluated as *true.* Otherwise it's *false*—just as in the case of *fgrep.*

So, change the first line of the *if* statement from:

```
  *)        if ls ¦ fgrep -x $answer
```

to:

```
  *)        if test -s $answer
```

The *s* option will cause *test* to return a value of *true* only if it finds the file *and* if that file has a size greater than zero. This is another advantage of *test.* At one time, you might possibly have created a blank (empty) file in your directory and given it the same name you've supplied in response to the script's prompt for a file name.

As far as the shell is concerned, a blank file is just as valid as a non-blank file. Being empty, however, the file contains nothing for *nroff* to format. With *fgrep, nroff* will try anyway, and the net result will be another blank file. With *test* and the *s* option, a blank file will not be processed.

Like most other XENIX commands, *test* has many other options. In the case of *test,* the options provide true/false responses to conditions ranging from single bits of information on the disk itself all the way up to comparing the characters in two variables you supply. You will find details in the XENIX Reference manual and in Appendix A, but three options in particular deserve mention here: =, *eq,* and *!.*

As with the arithmetic you learned in school, the = sign, to the shell, symbolizes equivalence. When used with *test,* however, the = sign is non-numeric. It tells the shell to check two character patterns, rather than two numbers, for equality. For example, the command *test dog = cat* would be true if *dog* and *cat* were variables describing two identical character strings.

For numeric expressions, you would compare variables with the *eq* option, as in the command *test number1 eq number2.*

The functional opposite of = in the *test* command is *!.* Elsewhere in this book, you've seen the exclamation point used as an escape key to temporarily exit the shell. Here, it is used in combination with the = sign to test whether character strings are not identical. For example, the command *test dog ! = cat* yields the true result when *dog* is not identical to *cat.*

SHELL VARIABLES

So far, you've been dealing with variables that *you've* created. But the shell has its own set of variables, too. It uses them to keep and transmit information about you when you log in. In fact, you already saw one of them in Chapter 3. It's HOME, the variable that defines your home directory. (You may recall that as you type it as *$HOME,* indicating that it's a variable.) But there are others:

IFS   With *vi* or any other procedure that lets you access several text files sequentially, you leave a blank space as a delimiter between the names in the list. The other delimiters recognized by the shell are Tab and Enter. IFS (Internal Field Separators) can be used to add new delimiters to that list.

MAIL   Your mailbox is a file that's given the same name as your login name and is kept in the subdirectory */usr/spool/mail.* The MAIL variable can be used to change the names of that directory and file.

PATH | A quick listing of your home directory will show that none of the XENIX utility programs can be found there. Yet, whenever you type a valid command or program name, XENIX accurately finds what you're asking for. These programs are stored in the directory */usr/bin,* while your home directory is */usr/[user name].* How does XENIX know to look in *bin*? It uses the PATH variable, which contains the names of all the valid directories that should be searched, and the order in which they should be searched whenever you issue a command.

TERM | When you see the message *Terminal type is* on your screen, XENIX has used the TERM variable to extract the name of the particular terminal type following that message.

TERMCAP | The actual definition of your terminal type must be found some-where. TERMCAP supplies the path name to the data file that contains that definition.

PS1 | For the Bourne and C shells, this variable contains the characters used as the shell prompt. The default value is either the $ sign (For the Bourne shell) or a % symbol (C shell) and a space character.

PS2 | This variable contains the secondary shell prompt that you see when the shell expects more input than you've currently supplied—for example, when you use shell commands like *if,* as we did earlier in this chapter.

Armed with this information, let's set out to explore how some of those variables are used.

READING YOUR *.profile*

When your user account was created on the system, XENIX generated a file called *.profile.* It's pronounced "dot profile" and it holds some login parameters that XENIX associates with you. (That file has a different name and slightly different parameters in the C shell and is nonexistent in the Visual shell.)

You can look in your directory, but you won't necessarily find your *.profile* file. The period (.) used as the first character in its name makes the file invisible to the normal *ls* or *lc* commands. If you want to see it listed, add *a* as an option to either of those commands. This option will make any invisible files in your directory appear in the listing.

Your *.profile* doesn't incorporate *all* of the shell variables, but it does use quite a few. If you're curious, print its contents to the screen from the shell prompt with the command:

```
cat .profile
```

In response, you'll see:

```
$ cat .profile
# Copyright Microsoft Corporation, 1983
# User $HOME/.profile - commands executed at login time
#
TERMCAP=/etc/termcap; export TERMCAP      # terminal database
tset -r                                   # do terminal initializations
PS1='$ '                                  # set prompt
PATH=/bin:/usr/bin:$HOME/bin:.            # set command search path
MAIL=/usr/spool/mail/$LOGNAME             # mailbox location
umask 022                                 # set file creation mask
export PATH MAIL
$ _
```

220

Here, you can see the actual ways XENIX uses the shell variables. Most of them should be recognizable from the table in the preceding section. The comments at the right side of the illustration should help you interpret what they mean.

Notice that there are also some XENIX commands in the file. *Tset* is one of them. As the comment field indicates, *tset* is used to set the terminal initializations. The *r* parameter causes the terminal type to be printed on the screen during the login opening message.

Umask is another XENIX command. This one is used to set the default permissions level for files you create. The three numbers that follow the *umask* command are octal (base 8) rather than decimal (base 10) numbers. Technically, they comprise what is called a *mask*, whose values XENIX combines with any system-wide default values (using a binary "add" technique, the details of which are really beyond the scope of this book). The result of this operation is three individual masks: for the owner, for the group, and for the public.

In terms of their meaning to you, the current *umask* settings provide read and write permission for you as the file's owner (the 0 mask), read-only permission for the group (the first 2 mask), and read-only permission for the public (the last 2 mask). You could reset this default to include read and write permission for the group and public by changing the mask to 000 (or you could use 020 or 002 for any combination of permissions).

Changing *umask* will set new default permissions for any new files you create, but you might find that the *chmod* command described in Chapter 9 is easier to use. Then, too, since you know how to write a shell script, you could create one that uses *chmod* to change the permissions for several files at once. Combining the *while, case,* and *read* commands, you could even create a script that would prompt for a choice of permissions.

In the last line of the file, there's one more XENIX command, *export*. It's used to send the values contained in the shell variables out to the system, where they are put into effect either until the current session ends or until you change them.

Now, the only question remaining is "how?" How can you modify *.profile* and your login characteristics? As you have done many times, begin by starting *vi.*

CHANGING *.profile* DEFAULTS

At some time in your work with XENIX, you may need to use a terminal of a different type from the one assigned to you. This is especially likely if you're a dial-up user, because such a need could arise from any situation, from equipment failure to simply being at a different site with a different terminal.

Ordinarily, you'd need to ask your system administrator to redefine the terminal type for you. But if the change is only temporary, another redefinition will be needed when you return to your original equipment. In such circumstances, you can redefine the terminal yourself.

CHANGING YOUR TERMINAL TYPE

To change your terminal type, you'll need to place a new definition for the TERM variable in *.profile*. You can find a list of the most common terminal names in the file */etc/termcap* and some additional descriptions in Chapter 14. If you have difficulty finding the correct terminal type in either of these places, check with your system administrator.

For a onetime change, effective only for your current session with XENIX, you can change the TERM variable directly from the keyboard. Immediately after logging in, use the following command format:

TERM = [terminal name];export TERM

For a change that will last longer than one session with XENIX, use *vi* to change the contents of *.profile.* To do this, load the *.profile* file and move the cursor to the line containing the *tset* command. Next, press the uppercase letter O both to open a new line above the current one and to move into insert mode. Now enter the TERM command as described before, and press the Escape key to leave insert mode. Use *:x* to write the new file to disk and exit *vi.*

From now on, the new terminal type you've set will be what is defined for your terminal. When you need to change the terminal type again, just do this again, using the new terminal name.

EXPANDING YOUR DIRECTORY PATH

As your ability to create and use shell scripts increases, you may find them beginning to clutter your home directory. You might store them in a subdirectory called *Scripts,* which you've created just for that purpose. The only drawback to this is in accessing *Scripts* from some other directory. From your home directory, all you need do is type the path name in the form:

Scripts/[script name]

But supposing you want to access one of your script files while you're in a general data directory called *Data,* and it's on the same level as *Scripts*? Then the path name to *Scripts* would take the form:

../Scripts/[script name]

But as directory levels expand and you move among them, keeping track of where you are in relation to *Scripts* and other directories can become more complex. Needless to say, there's a solution.

EXAMINING THE PATH VARIABLE

Recall that XENIX has a shell variable called PATH. When you printed your *.profile* to the screen, you saw a PATH variable that looked something like this: *PATH = /bin:/usr/bin: $HOME/bin:..*

The PATH variable in this particular example describes four paths that XENIX takes to find any program, command, or executable file. They are */bin, /usr/bin, $HOME/bin,* and the current directory (.).

The first three paths are obvious—their names are used. In contrast, the path name of the current directory, which is any directory you happen to be in at the time, is an implicit instruction created by the final colon (a delimiter) and period (:.) in the list. That construction represents a null string of text (in this case, a null directory path), and XENIX interprets this as the current directory.

The order in which XENIX searches for any command contained in a request you initiate is implied in sequence of the path names in the PATH variable. In this case, the search begins in */bin.* If the command is not found there, XENIX searches */usr/bin,* then *$HOME/bin* and, finally, the current directory.

It's a simple matter to modify PATH, either to include one or more additional directory paths or to alter the search order of those that are currently included.

To add a directory path, simply include it at the point you feel is most appropriate. For example, if you often use script files in a directory named *Scripts* and want XENIX to search that directory automatically after it has searched the other paths indicated in the PATH variable, add the path *:$HOME/Scripts* to the end of the current PATH statement. (You may also want to delete some of the space between the PATH statement and the comment, which has now spilled over the right margin.) Your PATH assignment would now look like this:

PATH = /bin:/usr/bin:$HOME/bin:.:$HOME/Scripts

You can also change the order in which the paths are listed. For example, to move the current directory (.) to the beginning of the search on the PATH statement we just created, change the line to read:

PATH = .:/bin:/usr/bin:$HOME/bin:$HOME/Scripts

Once you've made the changes to *.profile,* the most reliable way to implement them is to log out and then log in again. In the short time it takes to do that, you'll have reset the shell variables you've changed.

A FEW USEFUL SUGGESTIONS

Although we haven't stepped through all the procedures, you now have the knowledge to add any of the shell variables, even program names, to your *.profile* file. If you maintain a list of reminders on XENIX, you might, for example, want to add *calendar* to your *.profile.* Doing so will automatically produce a current reminder list each time you log in.

Another helpful use for a script file is including its name as the last line in your *.profile* file. The next time you log in, the script will be run automatically as soon as XENIX' introductory messages have finished. (You'll need to have made the script executable with the *chmod* command and included the appropriate path name in the PATH variable if the script is in a directory other than your home directory.) With some imagination, you'll be able to create scripts that save you both time and trouble, and you will have greater control over your electronic environment.

223

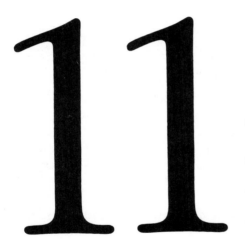

THE C SHELL The C shell (*csh* for short) is a product of the University of California at Berkeley, where it was created as an environment for programming in the C language. Some of the procedures you learned in the last chapter can be executed in *csh,* but the C shell also has its own commands and variables, which we'll cover here. As a general rule, however, a command that works in the Bourne shell will also work in the C shell. Let's take a look at the *csh* environment for a user named *mikeh.*

ENTERING THE C SHELL

There are two ways you can enter the C shell: through logging in directly or by using the *csh* command from another shell. If you log in directly, your prompt appears as a percent (%) symbol preceded by a number. If you enter from another shell, your prompt is a percent symbol without an accompanying number. But even though the prompt is your first look at *csh*, quite a bit happens before it appears on your screen.

Whenever you enter the C shell, *csh* begins by checking your home directory for a file called *.cshrc*. If it finds this file, it carries out the commands contained in the file. Next, if you're logging in rather than entering from another shell, *csh* reads a second file named *.login,* which, unless it has been modified by you or your system administrator, contains just two commands, *tset -r* (which initializes your terminal) and *set ignoreeof* (which forces you to use the word *logout,* rather than Ctrl-D, to log out).

Once the shell prompt appears on your terminal, the C shell is ready to go to work. From this point on, every command you type is handled in a three-step sequence:

■ First, the shell reads your command line and breaks it into units called *words* (usually delimited by blank spaces or Tab characters).

■ Second, these lines of words, or *events,* are saved for future reference in a list called the *history list.*

■ Third, the command line itself is carried out.

BUILT-IN VARIABLES

Like the Bourne shell, the C shell contains a number of built-in variables. To see some, let's take a look at your *.cshrc* file. Type:

```
cat .cshrc
```

at the C shell prompt (%). In response you'll see a display like the one at the top of the next page.

```
6% cat .cshrc
#
# Copyright (C) Microsoft Corporation 1984
#
# Example .cshrc file for demonstration C-Shell account.
# Commands here are executed each time csh starts up.
#
set noclobber                           # don't allow '>' to overwrite
set history=20                          # save last 20 commands
set path=(. $home/bin /bin /usr/bin)    # execution search path
set cdpath=(.)                          # directory search path for cd
set prompt=\!%\                         # set prompt string
alias v vi                              # quick command alias
alias h history                         # quick history alias
alias print 'pr -n \!:* | lpr'          # print command alias
setenv  SHELL   /bin/sh                 # use regular shell for scripts
setenv  TERMCAP /etc/termcap            # terminal data base
set mail=(30 /usr/spool/mail/$LOGNAME)  # mailbox location for csh
setenv MAIL /usr/spool/mail/$LOGNAME    # mailbox location for environment
7% _
```

227

Even though they're used somewhat differently here, some commands, such as *alias,* and some variables, such as *SHELL, TERMCAP,* and *MAIL,* should be familiar from preceding chapters.

SETTING SHELL VARIABLES

You've already seen the *set* command. In fact, you used it with *vi* to turn line numbering on and off with the *number* and *nonumber* options. And that use should give you a clue as to why it's included in *.cshrc.* The variables in *.cshrc* are put into effect when the commands in this file are executed, and it's the *set* command that initializes these variables. The variables themselves are defined as follows:

■ *noclobber* protects files from being overwritten through accidental use of output redirection commands and ensures that the ⟩⟩ redirection symbols are interpreted to mean an existing file.

■ *history,* when assigned a numeric value, sets the number of previously executed shell commands that will be saved in the history list. In the default *.cshrc* file, the last 20 commands are saved.

■ *path,* which is similar to the Bourne shell's PATH variable, is used to set the search path for programs, utilities, and executable scripts. Note that blank spaces must be used to separate path names (in the Bourne shell, the colon is used as a separator).

■ *cdpath* provides a list of directories to be searched in response to a *cd* command to change directories.

■ *prompt* sets the prompt character—in this case, the percent (%) symbol. The exclamation point indicates that the prompt is to be preceded by a number indicating the current event (line).

■ *mail* sets the path name that's checked for mail arrival. If, as in the example, the path name is preceded by a number, the number represents the elapsed time, in seconds, that *csh* waits between checks for new mail. The default is 30 seconds between checks. Recall from the *mail* chapter that certain processes can be instructed to send you mail when they are completed. By specifying a shorter interval between checks, you can be informed more quickly when such a process is complete. Specifying a very short interval, however, can burden the system.

As you can see, the *set* command is used to activate all these variables. To remove the effect of a variable that you've set, you use the command *unset.* (This deactivating is unlike the use of *set* in *vi* where, for example, you turn off line numbering with the command *set nonumber.*)

You can set variables from within *.cshrc* (or *.login*) by loading the file into *vi* and making changes to it there. You can also set variables from the shell prompt.

SETTING YOUR OWN VARIABLES

As mentioned earlier, if you enter the C shell from another shell, your prompt character is the percent symbol only—there is no accompanying event number. The reason is that you have escaped from your home shell into a subshell. As a result, even though *csh* searched your home directory, it found no *.cshrc* file. Therefore, it hasn't been told to set any variables indicating either that a history should be kept or that events should be numbered.

If you want to set features like numbered events, there's a simple solution: Create your own *.cshrc* file. You can use the lines shown in the previous example.

If you already have a variable set (such as PATH in your *.profile* file), and you are satisfied with it, there is no need to add it to the *.cshrc* file. Also, keep in mind that if you include the *set ignoreeof* line, Ctrl-D will no longer allow you to leave the subshell. You will have to use the command *exit* to return to your own shell.

You can also set just those variables you want to set from the keyboard after you enter the subshell. For example, use the commands:

    set history = 20

and

    **set prompt = \ ! % **

to put just those variables into effect until you log out. (This holds true for all of the shell commands and works whether you have a *.cshrc* file or not.)

228

CHANGING YOUR HOME DIRECTORY

As you learned in Chapter 3, your home directory is the place to which XENIX automatically returns you whenever you use the *cd* command without an argument. One of the C shell variables, *home*, sets the path to your home directory. Initially *home* has the same value as the Bourne shell's HOME variable. Thus, for a user named *mikeh*, *home* would be */usr/mikeh*. You can also use the *$home* variable within a path name, just as you can use $HOME from the Bourne shell (note the difference in capitalization). Also note that a $ sign precedes the *home* variable when it should be expanded to the path it *represents*.

In addition, there is a metacharacter in the C shell that can be used in place of the *$home* variable. It's the tilde (~), and it can be incorporated into a directory path. For example, suppose you have a subdirectory called *Temp* just below your home directory. The path names:

229

/usr/mikeh/Temp

$HOME/Temp

$home/Temp

~/Temp

are all functionally equivalent. Likewise, if you generally work from a directory named */usr/mikeh/Scripts,* you can change the value of *$home* to reflect that directory path with the command:

set home = (/usr/mikeh/Scripts)

Now, no matter where you happen to be in your directory system, you can use */usr/mikeh/Scripts* as your home directory. So, for example, you could copy a file directly to it with the command format:

cp [file name] ~

This is now your home directory as far as the C shell is concerned; but bear in mind that using *cd* without an argument will also place you in the *Scripts* directory.

To return to your original home directory, */usr/mikeh,* all you need type is:

cd $HOME

As you'll see later in this chapter, *$HOME* is kept distinct from *$home*.

Also, if you do change these variables around and forget what assignments you've made, use the command:

echo $home $HOME

to print their current values.

SETTING THE ENVIRONMENT

If you refer back to our sample *.cshrc* file, you'll notice that the last several instructions help to set up the environment. But what is the environment? Isn't it the C shell in which you are working, and isn't that environment already set up for use? Yes, it is—for *you*. These instructions, however, refer to the environment relative to the C shell itself. That environment is the Bourne shell, from which the C shell originates. That's why *set* commands use C shell variables and *setenv* commands use Bourne shell variables.

In particular, the *setenv* command is used here to establish:

■ The shell that should be used for scripts that do not begin with the pound symbol (*setenv SHELL /bin/sh*).

230

■ The data base of terminal types and capabilities (*setenv TERMCAP /etc/termcap*).

■ The destination for mail that does not originate from the C shell (*setenv MAIL /usr/spool/mail/$LOGNAME*). In general, it's simpler to keep all your mail together, so both the Bourne shell's MAIL and the C shell's *mail* variables are defined as the same location.

If you find it necessary to modify your terminal type, that too is controlled via *setenv*. The command syntax is:

    setenv TERM [terminal code]

where you substitute the correct terminal code (for a list of terminals and their codes, check the file */etc/termcap* described in Chapter 14).

Also, as you did for the *home* variable, you can use *setenv* to change the value of *HOME* (the directory in which you're placed when you log in). There is, however, no metacharacter that can be substituted for $HOME in the way a tilde can be substituted for *$home*.

GAINING ACCESS TO HISTORY

A little earlier in this chapter, you were introduced to the *history* variable and told that it saves the last 20 commands you used. To produce a list of these command lines and their event numbers, type *h* for history. You'll see a display something like the one at the top of the next page.

```
20% h
     1   mail
     2   lc
     3   cd Scripts
     4   ls -l
     5   vi accounts
     6   cp accounts ..
     7   h
     8   write danh
     9   cd
    10   show /usr Scripts accounts
    11   pwd
    12   mail
    13   who
    14   write susang
    15   cd Scripts
    16   ls -l
    17   cd $HOME
    18   mkdir Pastdue
    19   cd Pastdue
    20   h
21% _
```

Nice as it may be to know that these commands have been saved in a history list, you might still be wondering what good this list does for you. How can you access any of the last 20 commands that you've used, and when would you want to? Try the command *cat [file name]* using a file of your own. When the command has completed, type:

cat !$

The *cat* command is repeated.

As it does in the *prompt* variable, the exclamation point invokes the history mechanism itself. The dollar sign you've included in the command is used to indicate the argument you used for the command in the last line. In effect, *cat !$* tells the C shell to execute the *cat* command with the file on the preceding line as its argument. To simply repeat the last line in the C shell, type *!!* at the % prompt.

You could also use:

!-1

to indicate the *relative* command (or *event* number) that is one less than the current command number.

Or, you could use *absolute* referencing by typing:

![event number]

where *[event number]* is the number preceding the shell prompt (%) of the line the *cat* command is on. Recall that, as the *history* variable in your *.cshrc* file is set to 20, you'll only be able to reference commands as far back as 20 event numbers.

As well, the command:

!c

will cause the last command that began with a *c* to be invoked. In this example, the last and only command was *cat,* so the single letter *c* is enough to specify it. In other situations, you can provide longer partial lines, such as *!ca* or *!cat,* if you need to refine the specification further.

And, if you're unsure of the exact command that will be invoked, you can add *:p* to your request. So, for example:

!c:p

would print the last command that began with a *c,* but it would not execute that command. The *:p* allows you to verify that the command you invoke is actually the one you want to execute, without actually executing it.

EDITING COMMANDS

One good way to use your access to historical events arises from the possibility of typing errors. The command line:

la Marketing/Accounts

is an attempt to list the files contained in the directory *Marketing/Accounts.* But the typographical error caused by hitting the *a* key instead of *s* for an *ls* command results only in the error message *la: Command not found.*

You could retype the entire command, correctly substituting *s* for *a* to produce the desired results. Or, you could simply type:

^la^ls

and press Enter to substitute the letters *ls* for *la.* You've already seen this type of substitution with *vi* and in the *sed* script in Chapter 9. In each case, you used the command format:

s/[find]/[substitute]

to perform the operation. In C shell history substitutions, the caret (^) is used instead of the slash, and the substitution is made to the command line immediately preceding the current one. Note that the exclamation point is unnecessary and the *s,* for *substitute,* is assumed. You could also have simply used:

^a^s

and the first occurrence of the letter *a* would have been changed in the last command line. The degree of substitution that you use depends on the possible variations in the pattern that you're trying to match.

ANALYZING ALIASES

As you learned in Chapter 8, using aliases in the *mail* system can make your work much easier to perform by making commands shorter and easier to remember. In *mail,* you saw how to compress your list of user names into a single alias. In the C shell, an alias actually becomes a miniature shell script.

If you refer back to the *.cshrc* file at the beginning of this chapter, you'll see that it contains three useful aliases that simplify your work: *v, h,* and *print.* The first and second are simple shortcuts: *v* for running *vi* and *h* for the C shell's history buffer. For example, instead of having to type *vi,* you can call up the text editor simply by typing *v.*

The third alias is an exercise in using pipelines:

alias print 'pr -n \!:* ¦ lpr'

Essentially, this alias has compressed two procedures into a single command. Thus, when you enter a *print* command in the form:

print [file name]

the *pr* command first processes the named file for printing to the screen. The *-n* option in the alias causes *pr* to number each printed line sequentially, beginning with 1. Then the output of the *pr* command is piped into the *lp* utility, which sends the file to the printer. The result is a numbered printout of all lines in the file. Furthermore, each page of that listing contains the default header for *pr*: the current date, the file name, and the page number. (This format is widely used for printouts of programming source code and, perhaps, is the reason this alias was devised in the first place.)

CREATING YOUR OWN ALIASES

You are free to design your own aliases in the C shell. In fact, one can help MS-DOS users in the transition to XENIX.

To request a directory listing in MS-DOS, you use the command *dir,* which is roughly equivalent to the XENIX *ls* command with the *l* option. Simply by inserting the following line into *.cshrc*:

alias dir ls -l

you can ensure that, whenever you (or someone else) slip and use *dir* instead of *ls -l,* XENIX doesn't display the error message *dir: Command not found.* Rather, the alias causes an *ls -l* command to be executed either on the current directory or on the directory that was named after the *dir* command.

You can also expand your alias to make the C shell friendlier yet, and eliminate a potential problem at the same time. The command *ls -l* produces a significant amount of information about a list of files, but in a directory containing more than 20-odd files, some of that information can scroll off the top of the screen. You can, of course, use the Ctrl-S sequence to start and stop the scrolling...or, you can use your alias to make the procedure more useful. Try the following line (type *l24* as a lowercase L and the number 24):

```
alias dir '\ls -l \!:* | pr -ptl24'
```

Thereafter, whenever the command *dir* is entered, XENIX will sound a bell tone. When the Enter key is pressed, one screenful (24 lines) of a long listing of the current or named directory will be displayed via *pr,* the print-to-screen command. Another press of the Enter key, and the next 24 lines of the listing will appear, and so on, until all of the files have been displayed. (Note the *t* option we used with the *pr* utility. This suppresses the default five-line header and footer usually included.)

Of course, as with the *history* and *prompt* variables mentioned earlier, you can make the alias temporary by entering the alias only at the shell prompt and not including it in the *.cshrc* file. *Csh* will remember the alias only for the duration of the current session.

CREATING A C SHELL SCRIPT

As we mentioned in Chapter 10, if you are going to control a process, it's best to control it as completely as possible. With that in mind, let's look at the alias you just created.

When you request a directory listing, you'll hear the bell tone. That's fine — it's what you intended to have happen, and since you devised the alias, you know what that signal means. But does everyone know that? Quite conceivably, someone who is unfamiliar with your alias could sit staring at the terminal waiting for something to happen. And, of course, nothing will. The simple solution is to expand the alias into a shell script that also includes a prompt.

If you have tried creating the *dir* alias, you first need to "uncreate" it by using the command:

```
unalias dir
```

(Likewise, if you ever want to remove all of the aliases that are in effect, use the asterisk wild card:

```
unalias *
```

To find out which aliases are in effect, you can print a list of all current aliases by typing *alias* with no arguments.)

Now, to create your script, start by redirecting all keyboard input to a disk file called *dir*:

```
cat > dir
```

234

Then enter the following three lines:

```
#This script file prints the contents of various directory elements.
echo 'Press Enter when you hear the tone...'
ls -l $argv | pr -ptl24
```

and press Ctrl-D to close the file. Next, add execute permission to the file:

```
chmod +x dir
```

which gives you an executable shell script that does several things.

Now, suppose someone types *dir /usr.* First, the script echoes the prompt *Press Enter when you hear the tone...* onto the screen. Then it uses a C-shell variable called *argv,* which can accept multiple arguments from the shell's command line. If, as in this case, you enter only one argument in your command, the first script command line that contains *argv* extracts that single argument. (As you'll see shortly, if you enter more than one argument, *$argv* extracts successive arguments for use in successive script command lines.)

In this script, however, the *$argv* in the third line extracts the only argument you entered (*/usr*) and uses it in an *ls -l* command to produce a long directory listing. Then, the output from this listing is piped into the *pr* utility, which causes a beep to sound, and then prints the listing to the screen (*p*), with a "page" length of 24 lines (*l24*) and no five-line default header and footer (*t*).

You can use this new *dir* script as *dir [directory name], dir [file name],* or just the simple command *dir.* In any case, the script will assign to *argv* the name of either the specified directory or file, or the contents of the current directory. The result will be a long directory list that prints only as many lines of information as will fit on the screen. The script then causes the terminal to beep, pauses until you press Enter, prints another screenful of information, and pauses again. The script will repeat the printing until it runs out of directory entries.

You may be wondering what role the line *#This script file prints the contents of various directory elements* plays in the script file we just created. There's another example of this type of line at the beginning of the *.cshrc* file. Such lines are called C shell comments, and are denoted by the pound sign (#) at their start.

Here, the pound sign means two things to XENIX. First, that it is to interpret the following characters on the line as descriptive commands that should not be executed. Second (because the pound sign is at the beginning of the file), that the C shell should automatically be used as an interpreter when you type the script's file name. If you omit the pound sign, you'll have some problems when you type *dir memo,* because XENIX uses the Bourne shell as the general default.

235

A CLOSER LOOK AT C SHELL SCRIPTS

One nice feature of the *ls* command is the ability to specify more than one file or directory in a command. Knowing this, we could, for example, use the *dir* script file we just created to display the long listing for the subdirectory *Scripts,* for the subdirectory *New_York,* and for the data file *fred,* one after another, by typing:

dir Scripts New_York fred

at the shell prompt.

But wouldn't it be nice if our script told us which of the arguments that we entered were directories and which were ordinary files? And wouldn't it be even better if our script gave us the option to see a directory's long listing, view a file's contents, or move on to the next argument we had entered? Designing such a script is no problem in the C shell. Before we get to the specifics, though, let's take a look at two of the fundamental C shell structures we'll need to carry out the task: the *foreach* loop and the *if…then…else* conditional.

236

LOOPING WITH *foreach*

The basic format for a *foreach* loop is:

foreach variable (variable_list)

  -Carry out the command list

  -Get the next variable from variable_list

  -If no more variables exist in variable_list then end the loop

end

The equivalent of this structure in the Bourne shell is the *for…next* loop. Like *for…next,* the *foreach* loop repeats a series of commands (called the command list) specified between the initial *foreach* statement and the concluding *end* statement. Each time the loop is executed, a new variable is taken from *variable_list* (the old variable is discarded) and is made available for use in the body of the loop. This process ends when all arguments specified in *variable_list* are exhausted.

Given this structure, it's simple enough to change the *dir* script we just created to include a *foreach* loop that takes as its variable list the names of each file or directory we enter on the command line. Such a script would look like this:

```
#This script file lists the contents of various directory elements.
echo 'Press Enter when you hear the tone...'
foreach dirname ($argv)
    ls -l $dirname ¦ -ptl24
end
```

Notice the variable *argv* specified in the variable list section of line three. This is a special C shell parameter that's used to send variable information from the shell to the script (recall that we used this in the first *dir* script). Each time the loop is executed, *argv* brings in another variable, until every argument specified on the command line in the shell has been sent.

Once in the script, the variable information is transferred from the *argv* parameter to the script variable *dirname*. From here, *dirname* is used throughout the body of the *foreach* loop, as needed. As in the first *dir* script file, a $ sign is used to signify that a variable should be transformed from a variable name to the information the variable actually represents. Here, when the script is executed, the variables are transformed into any specified directory names.

Our new *dir* script pauses and produces a beep before displaying the file or directory's long listing. It gives us quite a bit of flexibility with regard to manipulating the information passed into the loop, and we'll be using this flexibility in a moment. But first let's look at another C shell structure, the *if...then...else* conditional.

237

USING *if...then...else*

The format of the C shell's *if* statement differs from the Bourne shell version you saw in the last chapter. Here, the format is:

if ([conditional_1]) *then*
    [command list]
else if ([conditional_2]) *then*
    [command list]

        .

        .

else [command list]
endif

Note that *if* and *else if* must appear on the same line as the *then* statements, and that you can include any number of *else if...then* pairs. Using *else* with only a command list is optional. *Else* used in this way can only be included if it is the last *else* statement in the conditional.

The basic operation of the *if... then... else* conditional is this: If *conditional_1* is true, then the commands following the *then* statement are executed and the loop terminates. If *conditional_1* is not true, then the direction of the loop is guided to the *else* statement, which evaluates *conditional_2*. This process continues until either a command list has been executed or all the conditionals have been evaluated as false.

WRITING A CONDITIONAL SCRIPT

Now let's use the *dir* script file we created earlier to write a script that pulls together the preceding concepts. The *dir* script is fine for listing the contents of directories, but suppose we would also like to view the contents of files and, when appropriate, be notified if one of the arguments does not represent a file or a directory? The C shell gives us access to the specific file information we'll need, and the *if... then... else* conditional gives us a way to compare and evaluate that information.

Start by redirecting your input to a new script file named *show* by typing:

```
cat 〉 show
```

at the shell prompt. Now, type the following lines (you can create the indents by pressing the Spacebar a few times, but don't press Enter until you reach the end of each line):

```
#This script file identifies and displays files and directories.
foreach file ($argv)
    echo ''
    if (-d $file) then
        echo $file 'is a directory.'
        echo 'When you hear the tone, press Enter to list it or Del to continue.'
        ls -l $file ¦ pr -ptl21
    else if (-f $file) then
        echo $file 'is a file.'
        echo 'When you hear the tone, press Enter to view it or Del to continue.'
        cat $file ¦ pr -ptl21
    else echo $file 'is not a file or directory.'
        echo 'When you hear the tone, press Del to continue.'
        cat errormessage ¦ pr -pt
    endif
end
```

Notice the number of lines to be printed at a time by *pr* has been changed from 24 to 21. That is to accommodate three extra lines of text *show* will print.

When you've finished, press Ctrl-D on a new line to close the file, and then make the file executable by typing:

chmod +x show

at the shell prompt. Next, redirect your input to another file named *errormessage* by typing:

cat ⟩ errormessage

239

at the shell prompt. Enter the contents of this one-line text file by typing:

That file or directory does not exist!

then press Ctrl-D on a new line to close the file.

Let's run *show* to see just what it does and, in the process, find out what the C shell variables and structures are doing. (In our example, we'll use the directories */bin* and */usr/mikeh/Scripts,* and the files */usr/mikeh/fred* and */usr/mikeh/accounts.* You should substitute your own directories and files. For clarity, we'll also specify an absolute path to each directory and file. You could use relative referencing if you preferred.)

At the shell prompt, type your equivalent of:

show /bin /usr/mikeh/accounts

XENIX responds with a display like this:

```
37% show /bin /usr/mikeh/accounts

/bin is a directory.
When you hear the tone, press Enter to list it or Del to continue.
—
```

You included two arguments when you invoked the *show* script. The first, the */bin* directory, is being processed now. If you refer to the *show* script itself and compare it with the revised *dir* script we created, you can see that the second line in *show* is essentially the same as the third line of *dir*: *foreach file ($argv).*

This line signifies the beginning of the *foreach* loop, and marks the place at which files and directories are passed from the shell into *show,* through the *argv* parameter. Now, however, the command list of the *foreach* loop is many lines long, rather than just one line, as in the *dir* script.

As you can see on the screen, the first command executed in the *foreach* loop's command list is the *echo* command. Followed by two single quotation marks and no specified text, *echo* will print a blank line on the screen each time the loop is executed. This helps separate *show*'s responses to the arguments and makes the display easier to read.

The next command in the loop is the *if...then...else* conditional. Here, we are taking advantage of some information the C shell can give us about each file's structure. The *if...then...else* conditional allows us to search for the following file attributes:

r	Read access
w	Write access
x	Execute access
e	Existence
o	Ownership
z	Zero size
f	Ordinary file
d	Directory

240

We want to know if the argument passed from the C shell represents a directory or an ordinary file, or neither. The initial *if* conditional on line four checks whether the file is a directory. If the current argument ($file) is a directory, then the directory name is printed with the message *is a directory.*

Next, the line *When you hear the tone, press Enter to list it or Del to continue.* is printed to the screen and the long listing of the directory is piped to the *pr* utility. If you press the Enter key, you'll see the long listing of the directory (*/bin* in our example) printed one screen at a time (remember, with the *p* option, *pr* waits for you to press the Enter key). You can also press the Delete (Del) key, instead of Enter, if you wish to continue on to the next file or directory you entered. The Delete key is XENIX' break key, which lets you escape from the loop you're currently in. In this case, the Delete key terminates the current command list and moves you back up to the top of the *foreach* statement. If there are no more new arguments in the variable list, the shell script is terminated.

But if the file is not a directory, what happens? The flow of the *if...then...else* conditional moves to the first *else* statement, which reads *else if (-f $file) then.*

As did the first conditional, this conditional also checks *$file*'s structure. If the file is an ordinary file, an appropriate message is printed and you can either press Enter to view the file or press the Delete key to continue to the next argument. This time, *$file* is first processed by the *cat* command, which then pipes its output to the *pr* utility.

At the moment, if you've been following along, XENIX is still waiting for you to either list the */bin* directory or continue on. Press the Delete key to continue, and XENIX next displays a prompt like this:

```
/usr/mikeh/accounts is a file.
When you hear the tone, press Enter to view it or Del to continue.
_
```

Recall that our second argument was an ordinary file name. *Show* is telling you so. After the beep, you could press Enter to view the contents of that file. In our example, the results looked like this:

```
/usr/mikeh/accounts is a file.
When you hear the tone, press Enter to view it or Del to continue.

Assets                 June 1984      June 1985      June 1986
-----------------------------------------------------------------

Cash                 $   18,790    $   20,007    $   24,886

Securities               12,503        31,777        46,000

Inventory               234,578       222,687       267,232

Prepaid expenses          4,200         3,799        12,557

Accounts receivable      21,505        29,125        28,430

-----------------------------------------------------------------

Total Assets         $  291,576    $  307,395    $  379,105

38% _
```

We didn't specify any more directory or file names when we ran *show*, so the script has completed its conditionals and loops and has terminated at this point.

Now, let's try one more example. This time, we'll run *show* with the following arguments (note the misspelling of the current directory in the second argument):

show /usr/mikeh/fred /usr/mihek /usr/mikeh/Scripts

As you would expect, the first message tells us that */usr/mikeh/fred* is a file and we can either view it or continue on to the next argument. If we press the Delete key to move on, the next response looks like this:

```
40% show /usr/mikeh/fred /usr/mihek /usr/mikeh/Scripts

/usr/mikeh/fred is a file.
When you hear the tone, press Enter to view it or Del to continue.

/usr/mihek is not a file or directory.
When you hear the tone, press Del to continue.

_
```

Show is telling us that the argument */usr/mihek* is not a file or a directory, and is prompting us to press the Delete key to continue.

To see exactly why the script found this spelling error and told us the word wasn't a file or a directory, let's take another look at the *show* script itself.

If *$file* is neither a directory nor an ordinary file, then the flow of the *if...then...else* conditional moves to the final *else* statement. Recall that these read:

```
else echo $file 'is not a file or directory.'
    echo 'When you hear the tone, press Del to continue.'
    cat errormessage ¦ pr -pt
endif
```

(Notice that there is no conditional here. That means all the remaining commands in the command list will be executed.)

We could simply have used a single *echo* statement to display the appropriate message, but doing so would have made our script inconsistent. As you design scripts, it's important to create an environment, however small, that processes each request in the same manner. Therefore, we've used the *cat* command and the *pr* utility to provide users with a consistent "interface" within the script. Although we have no intention of printing anything to the screen, we've used *pr* to pause and beep for us. Perhaps one of humanity's most predictable traits is curiosity, and for that reason we've created and included the *errormessage* file. Script users aren't advised to press Enter, but if they do, they will see the message *That file or directory does not exist!* and will be moved on to the next file or directory. (It is assumed that the *errormessage* file exists in your current directory. If this is not practical for you, include an absolute path to the *errormessage* file.)

One final item to note is the change in options for the final *pr* command in the script. The *errormessage* file is only one line long, and we don't expect it will ever be more than a few lines long, so we've removed the *-l21* option that prints more than one screenful of text. As a rule, it's always a good idea to clean up loose ends like this right away. You might even want to include a comment or two (preceded by a # sign) to help refresh your memory the next time you work on the script.

You now have a script that lets you view a file or request the long listing of any file or directory you specify. More importantly, you've stepped through the design and implementation of a C shell script. You've begun to develop a new and useful talent.

242

THE VISUAL SHELL   If you think of a XENIX shell as an environment waiting for the structure imposed by commands, then the Visual shell is a prestructured environment waiting to be used. Using the techniques described in Chapter 10, a competent shell programmer could create an environment very much like the Visual shell. But there's no need. It's already been done.

Microsoft's addition to XENIX, the Visual shell is a unique construction within the total XENIX environment because you need little or no knowledge of the operating system in order to use it. And, unless you have a pressing need to learn all about XENIX, there are any number of reasons why you and the Visual shell may suit each other perfectly well.

You may, perhaps, need to become proficient in using *mail* and the basic file-creation and file-storage facilities in as short a time as possible. Or, your use of XENIX may involve simply leaving and picking up mail, working the occasional application, and chatting with other users online. There's nothing wrong with that. The Visual shell then becomes your tool that helps you get your work done with the least amount of effort.

Of course, as with any tool, you still need to know which end is the handle.

⊠   NOTE: *If you are new to XENIX or to computers in general, you may have turned to this chapter first because you are assigned the Visual shell. We would suggest that you read Chapters 1 through 4 before proceeding. While this chapter will introduce you to the Visual shell, it depends on your having a basic understanding of the way XENIX manages files. Chapters 3 and 4 in particular will give you this background.*

DECIPHERING YOUR SCREEN

Your involvement with the Visual shell (*vsh* for short) begins almost at the moment that you first log in (or type *vsh* from one of the other shells). After you see the XENIX login messages, several seconds pass with what seems to be no reaction from the screen.

Finally, however, the Visual shell menu appears. And when it does, it dominates the display, presenting you with some information it has about you, your current directory, and all of the files it has found there. As well, the Visual shell displays its command list at the bottom of your screen. Let's take a look at one such possible display for a user named *nickig* and examine what you find there and how you can use it. The opening display is shown in Figure 12-1.

The outline bordering the top five-eighths of your screen is the frame of the Visual window. Notice that it's broken in places by some text. At the top, in our example, is the path name */usr/nickig*. This represents the current working directory: It's what you would see in response to a *pwd* command.

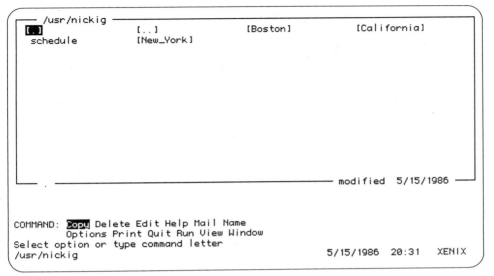

Figure 12-1. The Visual shell display.

At the bottom of the frame, near the lefthand side, you see a period (.). This corresponds to the name of the current directory (*/usr/nickig* in our example) that's also highlighted inside the Visual window. (Whenever you enter the Visual shell, *vsh* chooses the first file name in the upper lefthand corner of the window as its starting point. You'll see how to move around in a moment.)

Continuing around the window border, at the righthand side of the bottom you see the date on which the currently highlighted entry was last modified.

Inside the window display itself, all of the file names enclosed in brackets ([]) refer to directory files. Those without brackets are the names of data files. One additional marker you don't see here is the asterisk (∗). If the names of any executable files are displayed, that character will precede each of them.

The single period (.) currently highlighted is XENIX shorthand for the current directory name. The double periods [..] represent whatever directory level is immediately above the one in which you're currently working.

As you can see here, *vsh* provides its own visible distinction between directory files and data files. If, as suggested in Chapters 3 and 4, you have been using uppercase letters to begin directory file names and lowercase letters to begin data file names, you may be thinking such a custom is unnecessary in the Visual shell.

In the *vsh* screen representations of directory and data file names, that's quite true: You don't need to distinguish between the two. But that's as far as the rationale goes. When you begin to do any work with files and directories, you will still need to keep track of which is which and refer to them correctly. And for wildcard usage, the distinctions between upper- and lowercase make it as easy to handle groups of files here as anywhere else.

MOVING IN THE VISUAL WINDOW

246

The file names displayed in the window are not provided simply for reading. Any file-handling command has at least two parameters: the command itself and the name of the file (or directory) you want the command to act upon. From the command menu at the bottom of your screen you have easy access to a variety of such commands, and the names appearing in the window provide you with a selection from which to choose the argument to many of those commands.

On many terminals, the arrow keys will move the screen highlight, so you can use these keys to make your selections. For example, when you first enter the Visual shell, the [.] directory is highlighted. Press the right arrow key and XENIX moves the highlight one name to the right. In like fashion, the left arrow key moves the highlight one name to the left, while the up and down arrow keys move the highlight to the row of names immediately above or below (respectively) the row it is currently occupying.

If you try to move to a row or a column of names that does not exist (for instance, above or to the left of the current directory, [.], or below or to right of *New_York* in our example), you hear a beep and XENIX prints a reminder at the bottom of your screen and refuses the action.

If your terminal has no arrow keys, or you find that XENIX does not recognize the arrow keys it does have, you can use Control-key sequences instead. Hold the Control (or Ctrl) key down and, as described in Chapter 3, press E to move up, S to move left, D to move right, or X to move down. (If you're emigrating from MS-DOS and have used the word processor WordStar, this key sequence should present no problem to you. It's the same sequence that WordStar uses to permit cursor movement if you're using the keypad for numeric entry.)

During your travels about the Visual window, if your movement from one file name to another lands you on a data file, *vsh* will print the length of that file in bytes (roughly equivalent to characters) at the center of the bottom line of the window frame.

VIEWING FILE LEVELS

The minus (−) and equal (=) keys also play a role when you're moving around your shell display. Although you'll soon learn another way to do the same thing, you can use the cursor-control keys to select and display the contents of any directory or data file.

If you select a directory file name and press the equal sign (also known, in the Visual shell, as the Show key), *vsh* displays the names of the files in that directory. In effect, you're changing your working directory. This will be apparent in the lines, at the top and bottom of the screen, that reference your current working directory.

If you select a data file and press the equal key, you will see the contents of that data file.

To return to your original directory level or screen display, use the minus (or Goaway) key.

You can also use the minus key to view other directory levels. For example, if you're in your home directory, the path name to it is in the form:

/usr/[user name]

There are still two directory levels above your home directory, *usr* and / (the root directory). If you press the minus key, you'll move up one level into the closest one, */usr*. (The minus key moves you up one directory level, no matter which file or directory is highlighted.)

The screen itself will readjust to display the new directories. These will show, among other things, the user names (as directories) of all the people installed on the system. Your own user name should be highlighted. Once you've had a look around, press the equal key to return to your home directory.

FINDING COMMANDS AND INFORMATION

Between the frame of the Visual window and the command menu below it you have some blank screen space. It's not wasted space, though. The Visual shell puts it to use whenever you enter a command. After the command is executed, the command, the parameters, and any resulting output are displayed there.

Below this blank area are the Visual shell commands themselves. The two screen lines of the command menu give you access to the file-handling commands most commonly used in XENIX.

Beneath the command menu is the Visual shell's status line for command procedures. While the shell is waiting for you to make a choice, you will see the prompt *Select option or type command letter*. If you make any mistakes in your command selection or in moving among the file names, this is also where an appropriate message will appear, to prompt you to correct your error.

At the left, on the very bottom line of your screen, you again see the name of your current working directory (you'll find out why it's duplicated here when we look at the commands themselves). On the same line, at the right, *vsh* prints the current date and time (the time is updated automatically) and the name of the operating system (XENIX).

Finally, between the current directory and the date, you may see the word *MAIL*. This word appears as a reminder if you have unread mail in your mailbox. If no new mail or letters are waiting to be read, you won't see *MAIL*.

ACCESSING COMMANDS

Within the command menu, notice that no two command names start with the same first letter. Each is unique, so you can choose any of them by pressing the first letter of the command name. (If the command is already highlighted, you can also press the Enter key to select it.)

This procedure is the same for any command options as well. If you make a mistake and press the wrong key, the bell tone will sound and the message *Not a valid option* will appear directly above the status line. Also, if you begin a command procedure and decide not to continue, press Ctrl-C and you'll be returned to the main menu.

COPYING DATA FILES

Let's try using the Copy command:

Press the letter *C*

for *Copy*. As with all Visual shell commands, you may use either an upper- or a lowercase letter.

Most of the commands in the command menu have their own secondary menu of command options. When you press C for *Copy*, *vsh* responds:

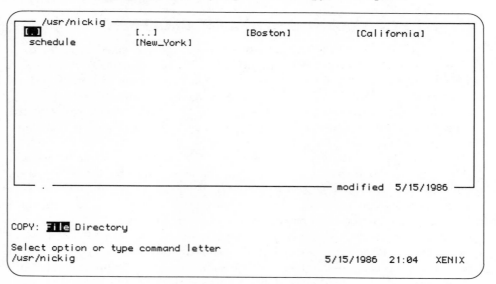

with the word *File* highlighted in the command-menu area. Now press F, and the following submenu appears:

```
COPY FILE from: ▄               to: .
Enter one or more filenames or select from list
```

Note how the command thread has been maintained. The words *COPY* and *FILE* both are in all capitals to indicate the level at which you've arrived.

In the submenu itself, you now have two parameters to supply: the file you want to copy (*from:*) and the name or directory to which you want to copy it (*to:*). After you've supplied one parameter, you press the Tab key to move to the other.

The periods after *from:* and *to:* represent the default values that *vsh* has assumed from the highlighted name in the window. Right now, those references are to the current directory. If you try to accept them by pressing the Enter key, you'll receive an error message in return. Remember: You selected *COPY File,* rather than *COPY Directory,* and the *COPY FILE* thread handles only data files.

At this point, you have two main choices:

■ You can copy a file from one directory to another, keeping the same file name for both copies.

■ You can copy a file from and to the same directory by giving the copy a different file name.

For either choice, you can begin by either typing the correct *from:* value or using the cursor-control keys to assist you in making your selection. As you scroll through the names in the window, they'll appear as the object of *from:.* When you have chosen the name of the file you want to copy, press the Tab key to move to the *to:* parameter.

Here, if you're copying a file from the current directory, you cannot simply accept the period default value. Essentially, you would be attempting to copy a file onto itself and XENIX does not allow you to do that. You can, however, type or select the name of a different directory. Or, if you're copying from and to the same directory, you can type a file name that does not yet exist in that directory. Once you've selected or entered the destination, press the Enter key and the contents of the file will be copied.

You've just used the standard XENIX *cp* command. Its syntax is:

cp [from] [to]

and requires the same parameters as the *vsh* version of the command.

COPYING DIRECTORIES

If you had pressed D, for *Directory,* the Copy submenu would have led you to:

```
COPY DIRECTORY from: █                    to:
                     recursive:   Yes(No)
 Enter new path
```

The *COPY DIRECTORY* command can be used in either of two ways: to make a copy of a directory itself (including all immediate data files), or to make a copy of the complete contents of a directory (including all its files and subdirectories). To copy a directory, you simply select or enter the appropriate directory names for the *from:* and *to:* parameters and use the default *No* value (enclosed in parentheses) for the *recursive:* parameter. If you want to copy all the directory's related files and subdirectories (as outlined in Chapter 3), specify the *from:* and *to:* parameters as before, but change *recursive:* to *Yes* by pressing Y or the Spacebar.

The corresponding XENIX commands are quite similar, having the syntax:

copy [source] [destination]

to copy the directory itself, or:

copy -r [source] [destination]

to make a complete copy of the directory's contents (*r* is the *recursive* option for that command).

DELETING FILES

Like Copy, the Delete command is multifaceted. When you press D, you're prompted for the name of the file you want to delete:

```
DELETE name: █

Enter one or more filenames or select from list
```

Type or select a file name, and press Enter. *Vsh* will determine whether your selection is a directory or a data file.

If you specify a directory, you can delete it, unless it either contains the current directory or is, itself, the current directory. If the file you've selected is a data file or a directory *below* the one you're currently in, you may delete it. But heed this warning: Deleting a subdirectory means everything in it is also deleted. Don't do this unless you're sure you don't want to save any of the additional files or directories associated with that directory.

The Visual shell's Delete command corresponds to two of the standard XENIX commands:

    rm [data file name]

and

    rm -rf [directory file name]

The former is used only with data files, while the latter affects directory files and, if need be, recursively deletes associated data or directory files.

EDITING FILES

251

To create a new file or make changes to an existing file, you choose the Edit command:

    EDIT filename: █

    Enter a filename or select from list

Type the name of a new file or select an existing file, and the Visual shell sends you to the XENIX Visual editor, *vi.* Once in *vi,* you can edit your file with the commands and procedures described in Chapters 5 and 6.

GETTING HELP

Especially when you are new to the Visual shell, you may find yourself in need of help. Aid is available for all topics with the Help command, accessed by pressing H:

```
INTRODUCTION

You may ask for help at any time during your work.  Just press the Help
key or the Help command. You will see the helpful information about
the command you were using when you asked for help.

If you need information on a specific command, highlight the command
name on the proper menu before asking for help. To move the
highlight, press the Tab key or use the Space bar.

When you wish to resume your work, press "R".  Your work will be
exactly as you left it.

Right now you may view information on special topics by choosing
one of the topics listed at the bottom of the screen.  Type the first
letter of the desired word.




HELP: Resume Next Previous Introduction
      Commands Keyboard Filters Menus
Select option or type command letter
/usr/nickig                            5/15/1986  22:14   XENIX
```

If you're involved in a command and have forgotten what to do, press a question mark (?, also called the Help key). Whatever you're doing will vanish from the screen, replaced by topic-specific help instructions. You can go on from there to more general help or resume what you were doing. (As with the command menu, make your choices from the displayed list.) When you return to your work, the screen will reappear exactly as you left it.

Be prepared. The help screens are meant to jog your memory with information that you already know but may have temporarily slipped your mind. The help facility is not meant to be used as a stand-alone tutorial.

SENDING MAIL

The Mail command enables you to send and receive messages:

```
MAIL: Read Send

Select option or type command letter
```

Once you're beyond the choice of sending or reading mail, everything follows the typical *mail* commands described in Chapter 8. Choosing the *Read* submenu is equivalent to entering *mail* by typing *mail* at the shell prompt and pressing Enter. *Send* is equivalent to sending mail to a specific user from the shell prompt without entering *mail.* Check your mailbox when you see *mail* appear on the bottom line of your screen.

CHANGING NAMES

The Name command actually serves two functions. In response to pressing N, you see this submenu:

```
NAME from: ▮            to:

Enter a filename or select from list
```

(Like many other *vsh* commands, Name accepts the currently highlighted file name as its default.)

As the command line implies, on its lowest level, the Name command is used simply to change the name of a data file or a directory. But it can do more than that. As indicated in Chapter 3, the Name command can be used to "move" a file from one directory to another. Remember, a directory contains information about the location of a file, but does not physically contain the file itself. Thus, for all intents and purposes you can remove a file from one directory and put it in another simply by changing its directory path with the Name command.

For example, if you had a data file named *fred* in the subdirectory *Memos,* and you wanted to transfer that file (*not* copy it) to a subdirectory called *Letters,* you could select the Name command and fill in the command line like this:

```
NAME from: Memos/fred      to: Letters/fred█
```

The data file would no longer exist in the original directory, but would now be found in *Letters.* You could change the file's name at the same time if you liked.

CHANGING OPTIONS

The Options command is a collection of file- and disk-management tools. To use it, press O to display the Options submenu:

```
OPTIONS: Directory Filesystem Output Permissions

Select option or type command letter
```

While two of these choices are quite simple, the other two are not. We'll cover each one separately.

WORKING WITH DIRECTORY OPTIONS

To select the *Directory* option, press D. There are two associated choices in the submenu, *Make* and *Usage.*

If you press M you can create (*Make*) a new subdirectory by supplying its name. This command follows the same rules as XENIX' *mkdir* command (described in Chapter 3).

The *Usage* option produces a list of the number of blocks (segments of disk space) used by a specified directory, including any files and directories contained within it. As the report is a running list (not a single item of information), part of it will almost certainly scroll off the top of the screen if the directory contains many files and subdirectories. You can stop the scrolling by pressing the Ctrl-S key combination and restart it again by pressing any key.

The *Usage* option is handy for determining roughly how large your files and directories are (in kilobytes), especially in relation to one another. In your everyday use of XENIX, however, it's unlikely that you'll need to call on it, so don't be overly concerned if you don't understand quite what it's all about.

ACCESSING FILE-SYSTEM OPTIONS

Most of the *Filesystem* options assume that you have a formatted diskette, with or without files on it. If you're operating from a terminal, however, there is no

253

diskette drive available to you personally, and any command you use that tries to access a floppy diskette drive will be routed to the equivalent drive in the XENIX computer itself. *This is very dangerous.* As one of the commands, *Create,* destroys existing data, we *strongly* advise you to coordinate any floppy disk activity with the system administrator.

All of the file-system options, as they are executed from the Bourne shell, are covered in Chapter 15. The comparable commands and parameters in the Visual shell are obvious, so you can read through Chapter 15 and then apply that information as (or if) needed.

CHANGING OUTPUT OPTIONS

254

In terms of comparing Visual shell commands with the standard XENIX commands, the *Output* option can be very helpful. When you select *Options Output,* you are offered two choices: *Vshell* and *XENIX.*

Normally, when you select a command from the Visual shell, it appears in Visual format in the command-output area (the blank space between the window and the command menu). For example, if you create a subdirectory called *Demo,* *vsh* displays that command as *Options Directory Make (1) Demo* to indicate the command thread it followed and the argument you used.

However, if you select *Options Output*'s *XENIX* option, the same command will appear as *Running mkdir Demo,* showing the XENIX command used to per-·form that procedure.

To stop displaying commands in XENIX format and return to Visual format, you reset the option to *Vshell.*

SETTING FILE PERMISSIONS

The reasons and rationale for setting various file-permission levels are found in Chapter 9. The procedures you need to do so from the Visual shell are under the *Options Permissions* option. The command line appears as:

```
OPTIONS PERMISSIONS name: █                          who: (All)Me Group Others
                       read: (Yes)No    write: Yes(No)   execute:  Yes(No)
Enter a filename or select from list
```

Setting permission levels is just a matter of filling in the blanks for the files, directories, and people involved.

PRINTING DATA

The Print command is fairly straightforward. Once you press P, you supply the name of the data file that you want printed. Keep in mind that you can use the cursor-control keys, and the plus and minus signs, to select any file in any directory.

QUITTING

Although it is the last thing you do during a XENIX session, Quit is not at the end of the list because the Visual shell's commands are arranged in alphabetic order. When you select Quit, you are asked to confirm your request by pressing Y. If you do, your Visual shell session will end, and if this is your home shell you will be logged out of the system. If you decide not to quit, you can get back to the main Visual shell command menu by pressing any other key.

RUNNING A PROGRAM

Run is the catch-all command for the Visual shell. You can use it to execute any utility, program, or shell script (discussed in Chapter 10) that's not covered by the other commands in the menu. (If you want, you can also use Run to enter the XENIX equivalents of commands that *are* included in the menu, though that's a rather circuitous way to reach your goal—unless, of course, you're practicing before transferring from the Visual shell to the Bourne shell.)

When you press R, the resulting command line looks like this:

```
RUN file: █          parameters:              output:
Enter a filename or select from list
```

If you wanted to run *nroff,* for example, you'd supply the program name, *nroff,* at the *file:* prompt, press Tab to move to *parameters:,* and enter the name of the data file you want *nroff* to process. At that point, if you wanted *nroff's* output to appear on the screen, you could press Enter to execute the command. If, on the other hand, you wanted the output redirected to a new file, you would press Tab again and enter the output file name after the *output:* prompt.

Although the Run command uses *parameters* and *output* to prompt for your responses, it follows the same general pattern you'd use for any other XENIX shell process:

procedure [arguments]

In this case, the procedure is your response to the *file:* prompt and the arguments are the parameters and output (if any) that you supply.

ENTERING ANOTHER SHELL

Among the commands available from Run are two that give you access to the other XENIX shells. Entering:

sh

at the *file:* prompt places you in the Bourne shell. Alternately, the command:

csh

places you in the C shell. To return to the Visual shell, press Ctrl-D.

CREATING SHELLS WITHIN SHELLS

If you think about running a command that brings you into another shell, and add to that an understanding that a shell is a command interpreter, you might wonder just what you're actually doing when you run the *sh* or *csh* commands.

Are you leaving the Visual shell? No. What you're doing is creating a subshell that interprets your commands from a new level. To get a clearer picture, let's try an example.

Press R to select Run and enter the command *sh.* You'll soon see the dollar sign ($), which is the prompt for the Bourne shell. When it appears, enter the command *vsh.* On the surface, it will seem as though you've returned to the Visual shell. But the important word is *returned.* Actually, the shell you are in now is not the shell you originally left, and the proof is simple.

Press Q for Quit and Y to confirm your intention. If you were in the shell from which you started (and it was your home shell), this act would log you out of the system. But it doesn't. Rather, you're returned to the Bourne shell prompt. Now, press Ctrl-D and you return to your original shell.

While it's not critical to using XENIX, especially in the Visual shell, a basic understanding of subshells may add some insight to your understanding of how XENIX can perform tasks in the foreground and the background without having them collide with each other in the process. You can see movement to and from subshells diagramed in Figure 12-2.

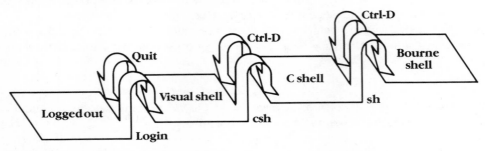

Figure 12-2. Working with XENIX subshells

256

VIEWING DIRECTORIES AND FILES

The View command produces a very simple command line:

```
VIEW name: ▮
```

```
Enter a filename or select from list
```

If you enter (or select with the cursor-control keys) the name of a directory file, you'll see the contents of that directory. If you specify a data file, that file will be printed to the screen. (If the results of either choice extend either above or below the boundaries of the window, you can use the up and down arrow keys to move from line to line.)

After using View for the first time, you may be a little at a loss when the display does not automatically clear and return you to the original file listing. Just press the minus (−) key and you'll move to the previous level. For either a data file or a directory, that should be the directory level from which you originated the View command.

257

CHANGING THE WINDOW CHARACTERISTICS

The last command in the Visual menu is Window. Its command line offers you two options:

```
WINDOW redraw:  Yes No    height in lines: 15
```

```
Select option
```

The exact results of setting these options differ, according to what you are doing.

When you log in, the Window command's default settings cause the Visual shell to create a permanent window that is 15 lines high. The window is considered permanent because it appears prior to, during, and after you've used a command. (Two exceptions to this rule are the Edit and Mail commands.)

If you select the Window command and change the *redraw:* option to *No,* the window will no longer be permanent. It will not reappear when you execute a command, unless the command is one like View, which forces output to the screen. (Other uses of the Visual shell place output on the screen, too. The cursor-control keys, for example, will also make the window reappear.)

Why turn the window off in the first place? We've mentioned that the blank area between the window and the command menu is where the Visual shell keeps track of the commands you've used. But space is limited. With the default window height, the Visual shell has enough room to display, at most, your two most recent commands. As your list of commands grows, the earlier ones disappear "behind" the window.

If you want to keep track of a longer list of commands, one way you can do so is to turn off the window and use the full height of the screen (less the bottom five lines). Or you can use the second option, *height in lines,* to modify the size of the window. The minimum value you can use is 1 (15 is the maximum).

MODIFYING THE COMMAND MENUS

There is one additional command that is not shown in the command menu. It's the @ key (Shift-2), and you can press it to modify any of the menu options, thus molding the Visual shell to suit your particular needs or preferences. To see how it works, let's start with something simple.

The View command, while convenient, doesn't actually perform any task you can't carry out in another way. For example, if you enter a directory name in response to the *View file:* prompt, the responses you receive duplicate what you see when you press the plus and minus keys. Although you can enter a more complete path name with View and, therefore, move among directory levels more quickly than you can with the plus and minus keys, the command itself is not unique. Similarly, if you specify a data file for viewing, you can accomplish the same result and access the *vi* editor in the process with the Edit command. Let's assume, then, that you consider the View command expendable.

DELETING A MENU

If you press Shift-2, the @ symbol, when the command menu is displayed, the shell responds with:

```
MODIFY: Delete Insert Rename

Select option or type command letter
```

Press D for *Delete* and you see:

```
DELETE menu item: Copy

Enter name of menu item or select from list
```

Because Copy is the first item in the command menu, *vsh* has supplied its name here as the default. Ignore it and type *View.* Press the Enter key, and when the command menu reappears, the View command is no longer included.

RENAMING A MENU COMMAND

The Edit command both opens a file for you to view and places you in *vi.* You can change its name to reflect that. Again, you start by pressing @. This time, when the submenu appears, press R to select *Rename.* You see:

```
RENAME menu item from: Copy          to:
        place before item: Copy
Enter name of menu item or select from list
```

Type the word *Edit* to overwrite the default, *Copy.* Use the Tab key to move to the *to:* field and type *Vi.* Press Tab once more and you arrive at the positioning field.

Originally it said *Delete,* but RENAME has re-alphabetized the menu and now suggests that Vi should be placed before Window. That's correct, so you can press Enter to accept the location. When the command menu reappears, your new entry, Vi, will appear with the others.

It functions in the same manner that Edit did, because it *is* Edit. You haven't changed the intrinsic nature of the command, just its name.

Of course, if you had not already deleted View from the command menu, the Visual shell would not have accepted the name Vi. Remember, you cannot have two menu options that begin with the same letter. This rule would hold true even if you had attempted to enter *vi* with a lowercase *v* as opposed to the View command's uppercase *V.* In this situation, upper- and lowercase are treated as equivalent.

259

ADDING NEW COMMANDS

Whether or not you rename the Edit command, you always have access to *vi.* There's also the possibility that you might want to use *ed* as well. Although it's not as flexible as *vi, ed* can be faster to use if you're just making a few changes to an existing document.

To add access to *ed,* press @ again to bring up the Modify menu and then press I for *Insert.*

Here, for *menu item:,* enter the word *Ed* and press the Tab key. (Note that *Ed* is acceptable now that you've renamed Edit to Vi). After *for command:,* enter the name of the editor itself, *ed.* Press the Tab key once more, and you see that *vsh* suggests inserting your new command just before Help in the menu. That location places Ed in the correct alphabetic order, so press Enter.

One final note: The next time you log in, look at the list of files in the window. You'll see a new one. It's **menu.def,* the executable menu-definition file. This file contains all the modifications you've made to your Visual shell environment, including insertions and deletions. If you delete this file, *vsh* will reset itself to its default menu options the next time you enter the shell.

This general command-insertion procedure can help you display directory listings as well. There is no inherent implementation of the *ls* command in the Visual shell. The normal listing of files in the window looks like the result of an *lc* (list in columns) command. If you wanted to look at a long directory listing (*ls -l*) —for example, if you wanted to determine existing file permissions—you'd need to use the Run command and specify *ls* as the file and *-l* as the parameter to run the command. At least that's what you would need to do if you didn't know how to create new menu options.

Bring up the Modify menu, press I to insert a new option, and enter *List* as the menu item, followed by *ls* as the command. Press Enter to complete your newly created List command. Now that it's part of the command menu, you can press L to request a directory listing. When you do, you'll see the command line:

```
LIST parameters: ▓           output:

Enter options
```

After *parameters:,* you can enter any of the available *ls* options. You might, for example, enter -*l* for a *long* listing (the dash must be included, or the shell will interpret what you typed as a directory name). The parameters can also include a particular directory path if you want to list the contents of a directory other than the current one. Likewise, if you want to send the results to a file instead of to the screen, also include the name of the output file after *output:*.

MODIFYING SUBMENUS

If nothing else, using an operating system should be as quick and easy as possible. Yet you may have noticed a small amount of redundancy in the preceding examples. Both the *Ed* and *Vi* command options perform the same basic function: They let you edit a file. It would be nice to include both of them under a single menu item, perhaps a reworked version of the original Edit command. Let's do it.

First delete the *Vi* and *Ed* options you added. Then use @ again to bring up the Modify menu and select *Insert.* Fill in the options as shown here:

```
INSERT menu item: Edit        for command: menu
        before item: Help
Enter name of menu item or select from list
```

Press Enter to submit your entries.

The name of the menu item (Edit) is not new, but the *for command:* response may be. When XENIX sees *menu* in the *for command:* slot, it accesses a shell routine that adds a submenu to the new command you entered.

Now you must add the submenu, and the procedure is just a little different from those you've seen so far. First, select your new command, Edit, from the menu. It will appear as *EDIT:,* with no apparent command line or submenu. That's to be expected: None exists—yet.

On the status line, you'll see the prompt *Select option or type command letter,* but you haven't told *vsh* what Edit is supposed to do, so almost any response you make at this point will be rejected. The only valid keystroke is the @ key (Modify command). Use it and you'll see the standard Modify menu. Press I to insert the new submenu and fill in the parameters as shown here:

```
INSERT menu item: Ed          for command: ed
        before item: <END>
Enter name of menu item or select from list
```

Ed will be an inserted submenu option that, when it's selected, executes the command *ed* to start up the text editor. The ⟨*END*⟩ parameter is supplied by the system and indicates no other submenu options are currently available. Press Enter, and the main command menu will reappear.

Now, you still want to add *vi* to the submenu. Select the Edit command again. This time, it appears as:

```
EDIT: Ed

Select option or type command letter
```

because one submenu option is now available. With this showing on your screen, press @ once again, to modify the submenu, and select the *Insert* option. Fill in the following parameters:

```
INSERT menu item: Vi          for command: vi
        before item: <END>
Enter name of menu item or select from list
```

261

(⟨*END*⟩ will again be supplied after you enter the menu-item name, because *vi* follows *ed* in alphabetic order.) Press Enter again to get the main command menu.

Now, whenever you select the Edit command, you'll see the submenu:

```
EDIT: Ed Vi

Select option or type command letter
```

You can press E or V to select one and display the additional command line:

```
EDIT ED parameters: █            output:

Enter options
```

or

```
EDIT VI parameters: █            output:

Enter options
```

where you can supply the name of the file you want to edit.

(Even though XENIX is generally fussy about whether you type upper- or lowercase characters, the menu and submenu creation functions are among the very few places where you can type entries in either upper- or lowercase with no ill effects. For example, if you had entered the main command as *EDIT,* it would automatically have been changed to *Edit.*)

2

For the System Administrator

265

INSTALLING XENIX If you are the system administrator for your XENIX system, your first task is to set up a viable XENIX environment. Installing XENIX is not difficult. You need only know what type of computer system you have, how large the hard disk is, the time zone in which you live, and if you want to install another operating system on your hard disk along with XENIX.

None of that information requires that you know anything about XENIX. But some background information will make the task easier, especially since you will need to make some decisions about your particular system.

INSIDE YOUR HARD DISK

You will be installing XENIX on a hard disk. In the process, you may encounter terms that are new to you, so let's take a quick and very much simplified look at the way your hard disk is constructed.

Unlike a floppy diskette, which you can see, hold, and even take apart, a hard disk is tucked away from view (and dust and smoke and wayward air currents) inside a rigid case. The disk itself consists of two or more polished metal platters mounted on a spindle. Information is read from and written to each platter by a read-write head that moves horizontally over the surface in much the same way the arm on a turntable moves across the surface of a record.

This record-player analogy is limited, however. The read-write head never actually touches the surface of a platter. Furthermore, it reads from and writes to both sides of the platter, and, since there is more than one platter in a hard disk, there is a corresponding number of read-write heads, arranged one above the other on a vertical assembly. When the hard disk is in operation, the read-write heads move in unison, each reading from or writing to the same relative location on its own platter.

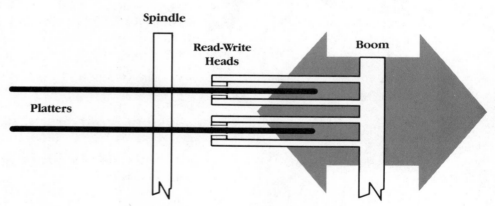

Figure 3-1. Typical hard-disk construction

Information on a hard disk is stored magnetically, as it is on a floppy diskette. Likewise, the data on each platter are recorded in concentric rings, or tracks, that are "drawn" on the disk by the operating system and are numbered consecutively, beginning with 0 on the outer rim.

Unlike a floppy diskette, however, a hard disk has depth, in the form of several platters. Since the platters are stacked one above the other, a track on one platter is matched by corresponding tracks on each of the other platters. These matching sets of tracks are called cylinders, after the geometric shape they would form if you were to peer downward at them through the different platters in the disk. Cylinders are numbered according to the track location they represent. Thus, cylinder 51 refers to track location 51 on all disk platters. Sequential data are recorded vertically, in cylinders, rather than horizontally (filling one platter before moving to the next and the next).

Even though a hard disk actually consists of several platters and a series of separate disk surfaces, operating systems and people alike treat these surfaces as if they were all together, on a single large platter. Thus, we refer to the hard disk's surface, not surfaces, and storage space on this surface is considered to be contiguous (uninterrupted) whether or not it is physically located on a single platter.

267

DEALING WITH PARTITIONS

Early in the XENIX installation procedure, you will encounter the concept of a partition. On your hard disk, a partition is a portion of available disk space that is set aside for a specific purpose. An analogy would be the rooms in your house: The kitchen is a partition used for cooking; the bedroom is a partition used for sleeping. If you intend to install XENIX on a computer that currently runs the single-user, MS-DOS operating system, then at least one partition on your hard disk has already been dedicated to MS-DOS and the files and programs you've used with it.

In order to run, XENIX requires three partitions:

■ One partition is almost negligible in size, but it contains important information about the disk itself. In this partition, XENIX stores a list of all physically unusable sections of the disk. It keeps this information as a reference to avoid using any of these *bad tracks* in later operations. This partition is so important that it's actually created before the XENIX installation begins.

■ The second, or active, partition is used to store the XENIX operating system itself, along with all of its ancillary programs, such as *vi.*

■ The third partition is a general operations area that becomes the work and storage partition for any users who are on the system.

Altogether, XENIX requires at least 15 contiguous megabytes of space on your hard disk. It's the latter two partitions that actually need the room. The first, which is called the root partition, requires 9 megabytes. The other, called the user partition, needs a minimum of 6 megabytes.

KNOWING YOUR OPTIONS

When you install XENIX, you will be given a choice of three options, two of which create partitions on your hard disk, and one (option 3) which upgrades XENIX System III (IBM Version 1.0) to System V (IBM Version 2.0). XENIX steps you through the upgrade procedure, so we'll concentrate here on installing a new XENIX system.

You can choose to partition your hard disk for the root and user partitions in either of two ways when you install XENIX. Let's look briefly at these options.

USING THE ENTIRE DISK

The first, and most automatic, of these procedures is option 1 of the installation. It uses the entire disk surface, no matter what else may already exist on it. XENIX will calculate the size of the user partition by subtracting the root and bad-track partition sizes from the total disk space.

The easier of the installation procedures, this is the option to choose if you are installing a new XENIX system and have no need to leave room for another operating system, such as MS-DOS. This option leaves the actual work of installing partitions to XENIX alone. In the process, any existing contents of the hard disk are erased. XENIX installs the three partitions it needs within that space, transfers all of the files it needs, and then exits the installation procedure after requesting information about your time zone.

RESERVING DISK SPACE

In this procedure, option 2 of the installation, the root and user partitions are installed on the majority of the disk surface—again, no matter what may already exist on it—but you tell XENIX to reserve a specified area of the disk for some non-XENIX use (if you want to, this is where you'll put MS-DOS). XENIX calculates the size of the user partition by subtracting the sizes of the root, bad-track, and reserved partitions from the total disk space you make available.

This procedure is semi-automatic in the sense that XENIX asks you how much space you want to reserve on the hard disk for other uses. During installation, XENIX will ignore this reserved space and use only the remaining portion of the disk for the root and user partitions.

A LOOK AT YOUR SYSTEM

Before moving on to the actual installation procedures you must follow, we'll look at the two possible directions from which you might be approaching XENIX.

First, you might be planning to devote your entire system to XENIX and XENIX-based application programs, such as Microsoft Word and Microsoft Multiplan. If this is the case, you can skip to the section "The Installation Diskette."

Alternatively, you may be planning to replace an existing MS-DOS system with XENIX, or you may be planning to install both MS-DOS and XENIX on the same hard disk. If this is so, your hard disk may already contain DOS-based data files and directories. Before you install XENIX, you will need to back up all of the MS-DOS files you intend to keep. This step is mandatory for any files you don't want to lose, because your existing MS-DOS partition—along with all of your programs and files—will be deleted during the installation procedure.

PLANNING AHEAD

MS-DOS was installed on your system with a program called Fdisk, which lets you create, modify, and delete MS-DOS partitions and view information about partitions that have already been created. With Fdisk, your hard disk may have been divided into one full-disk or several partial-disk MS-DOS partitions. In either case, before you install XENIX, you must plan for 15 uninterrupted megabytes of disk space and no more than four partitions on your hard disk—three of which are needed by XENIX itself. If you also decide to install MS-DOS on your hard disk, you'll need to use the Fdisk program again to create a functional MS-DOS partition out of the space XENIX has reserved for another operating system. This will be explained in detail later in the chapter. For now, however, simply save any files on your current system you might need later.

BACKING UP YOUR FILES

There are several methods you can use to transfer files you want to save from the hard disk. The slowest is MS-DOS' Copy command. Copy transfers files one by one, and you must determine whether there is enough room on the destination medium to hold each file before you attempt to copy it.

Most hard-disk-based computers also have backup software available or an archival storage command, such as Store or Backup. Your system's documentation will be your best reference, but basically these backup programs work in either of two ways.

Some perform a rapid file-by-file transfer of information to either floppy diskettes or tape cartridges. The program will determine when new diskettes or cartridges are needed during the procedure and prompt you to insert them at the appropriate times. Essentially, this method duplicates the features of the Copy command, but at a much faster rate, and requires a minimum of participation from you. This file-by-file method is the one you should use if you plan to create partitions or alter the sizes of existing partitions.

Other backup programs transfer files from your hard disk by using a streaming system that creates a mirror image of the hard disk on diskettes or tape cartridges. Streaming is one of the faster transfer methods, but it is not advisable if you're planning to restore files to new or modified partitions on the hard disk. A streaming system recreates the disk contents exactly, so any changes you make to the disk after backup are ignored and overwritten.

REMOVING MS-DOS PARTITIONS

Once you've backed up all necessary MS-DOS files, you may wonder what to do with all the system, program, and other files remaining on the hard disk. The answer, depending on your own preference, is either to leave them alone or remove your MS-DOS partition(s).

Since XENIX must be installed before you can install or reinstall MS-DOS, you can elect to leave your hard disk as is, and XENIX will clear it for you. If you take this course, during the installation XENIX will, after removing the MS-DOS partition(s), request that you reboot by pressing the Enter key. Do this, and continue with the installation.

If you prefer, you can use the MS-DOS Fdisk command to remove the MS-DOS partition(s) before starting the installation.

MANAGING PARTITIONS

If you're backing up files and changing partition sizes, it's quite possible that the quantity of material you take off the hard disk will not fit when you try to return it to a new and smaller partition.

For example, suppose that you have a 20-megabyte hard disk, all of which is currently dedicated to MS-DOS. After installing XENIX, you'll have five or six megabytes available for MS-DOS. Simple arithmetic is enough to show that you will have to allocate and manage those five megabytes much more carefully than you did twenty—perhaps archiving onto storage media more often or trimming extraneous program and data files that are seldom, if ever, used.

USING MS-DOS AND XENIX

If you are thinking of installing both XENIX and MS-DOS on the same computer, bear in mind that you will be working with two distinct operating systems.

270

They cannot be run simultaneously. Nor can MS-DOS be run from any attached terminals. MS-DOS must be accessed from the XENIX computer, so while the MS-DOS system is being used, your XENIX system is effectively shut off to anyone who might want to use it.

As you'll see later, you can easily move back and forth between the XENIX and MS-DOS partitions, but the point here is simply to remind you of the importance of planning ahead and, if possible, scheduling convenient hours of operation for both operating systems. Also, if the hard disk in your system is relatively small (in the 20-megabyte range), you might want to consider using XENIX alone, rather than both XENIX and MS-DOS.

DISK COMPATIBILITY

Finally, if you run both XENIX and MS-DOS you'll have to remember that they use different diskette formats. XENIX provides eight commands for reading and working with DOS disks, but you cannot, for example, use the MS-DOS Dir command to view the contents of the XENIX installation or program diskettes. If you try, you'll see a partially scrambled list.

If you are already familiar with MS-DOS, you may know that some disk problems can be handled with MS-DOS' Chkdsk (Checkdisk) command. Chkdsk works, of course, but not with XENIX disks. A XENIX disk is not and should not be readable under MS-DOS. In fact, using Chkdsk, especially with its /F option, can destroy the information on a XENIX disk.

THE INSTALLATION DISKETTE

Now that we've covered the most likely approaches to a new XENIX system, let's move on to the installation itself. Your first step is to make certain your hard disk has been formatted. Most likely, this was done for you already. If it was not, check your hardware manual. If you cannot tell whether the hard disk is formatted, the easiest way to find out is to try and use it. XENIX will generate error messages telling you that it isn't able to use the hard disk.

Once you've checked your hard disk, locate the XENIX diskette labeled *XENIX OPERATING SYSTEM INSTALLATION*. With the exception of a few program names and one or two multiple-choice questions, the XENIX installation is just about automatic. Even if you make a mistake answering the questions, the programs XENIX uses to accomplish the installation know that the operating system is to be installed on a hard disk. They will not damage your installation diskette. At most, all you'll need do is correct your answer.

BEGINNING THE INSTALLATION

Whether your system is currently turned off or on, begin by inserting the installation diskette in the 1.2MB floppy disk drive. If your system has only one floppy drive, place the diskette in it. If your system has more than one floppy drive, place the diskette in the "boot" drive (if you are not certain which it is, the boot drive is usually on the left or on the top). For IBM PC XENIX (Version 2.0) you must have a 1.2MB (high-density) diskette drive to accept the 1.2MB XENIX installation diskette. If you are installing the Santa Cruz Operation's version of XENIX System V for the IBM PC AT (Release 2.1), you may also use a 360K (low-density) diskette drive to read the four low-density SCO XENIX installation diskettes.

Now, if your system is off, turn it on (if you made a mistake in selecting the boot drive, note which drive light comes on first, wait until the system settles down, place the installation diskette in the appropriate drive, and reboot the system by pressing the Ctrl-Alt-Del key combination). If the computer is already on, reboot the system by pressing Ctrl-Alt-Del.

The computer will check the installation diskette, check the hard disk, and then come back to the diskette and begin reading it. After some introductory memory statistics, a message like the following will appear on your screen:

```
IBM PC XENIX Boot

Enter:     hd program
           fd program
           dos
           cf [-c conf_file][device program]

Press Enter for default:    fd /xenix.fd
    :
```

There may be some variation in what you see at this point. This illustration, like the rest in this book, shows what you see with IBM PC XENIX Version 2.0 (sometimes called XENIX System V/286). If you're installing another version of XENIX, the messages may be slightly different. Such differences are acceptable.

On the other hand, if you see an error message, such as *Unable to load operating system from disk,* you may have a faulty installation diskette. Likewise, if your system ignores the floppy diskette and boots directly from the hard disk, you may have an inoperative or incompatible disk drive. For example, as already mentioned, IBM's XENIX for the IBM PC AT and its compatibles is supplied on 1.2-megabyte floppy diskettes. If you have a PC AT or compatible equipped with low-density 360K drives, you cannot install XENIX unless you purchase and install a 1.2-megabyte, PC AT–compatible floppy drive.

Assuming that your system is ready for the installation procedure, note that XENIX is now waiting for your input at the colon (sometimes called the program prompt because it appears on a line by itself whenever XENIX expects you to enter the name of a program).

As you can see on the second-to-last line of the display, XENIX suggests that you use its default device, *fd* (the floppy drive), and the program */xenix.fd*. Since you're booting from the floppy disk drive, the installation program assumes you want to run XENIX from the floppy diskette. (Above the default choice are some other responses XENIX suggests, among them: running a program from the hard disk (*hd program*) and accessing MS-DOS (*dos*). Press Enter to select the default.)

USING */xenix.fd*

Now, you'll see the message *Loading* during the several seconds it takes to call in */xenix.fd*. When the program is successfully loaded, you see the message *Loaded, press Enter to start.*

```
fd /xenix.fd
Loading
Loaded, press Enter to start
```

Press Enter. The next display gives you some copyright information and some facts about your version of XENIX and the computer on which you're installing it. For our installation, the screen looked like this:

```
                    The IBM Personal Computer XENIX
                              Version 2.00
                    (c) Copyright IBM Corp. 1984, 1985
                (c) Copyright Microsoft Corp. 1983, 1984, 1985

           XENIX is a registered trademark of the Microsoft Corporation


Reserved memory = 2k
Kernel memory = 176k
Buffers =  100k
User memory = 2282k

No single-user login present
Entering System Maintenance Mode
Terminal type is ansi
#
```

Toward the bottom of the display, XENIX tells you it has entered system maintenance mode. XENIX did this because it found nothing on the floppy diskette that it could use to start up the system. Happily, the system maintenance mode is just where you want to be.

Note also that XENIX has assumed you have an ANSI-compatible terminal— one that uses screen-control codes defined by the American National Standards Institute. This is a safe assumption, since the IBM PC AT and most compatibles are ANSI-compatible.

INITIALIZING THE HARD DISK

274

At the system-maintence shell prompt type:

hdinit

and press Enter. (The somewhat cryptic word you just typed is the name of a program and stands for hard-disk initialization.) Almost immediately you'll see:

```
During the next part of the installation procedure, the
hdinit program installs IBM PC XENIX on your fixed disk.
As the program proceeds, information messages print on the
screen.

Do not press any keys unless you are asked to reply to
a question from the hdinit installation script.


Press ENTER to continue:
```

The installation script XENIX refers to here is a special file (script) of instructions that *hdinit* accesses to determine what it should do. Among those instructions are the initialization and file-transfer commands that are needed to complete this procedure. As they are called into play, these commands are echoed (printed) to the screen just as if you had typed them in at the keyboard. While most of these commands won't require any action on your part, don't ignore them completely and do pay attention to any message that contains the word *error.*

Right now, XENIX has more to tell you. Press the Enter key, and additional information will be displayed, as shown on the next page.

```
Choose one of the following options for setting up the partition table
on your fixed disk:

1.   Dedicate the entire disk to IBM PC XENIX.

2.   Dedicate the disk to IBM PC XENIX but leave a gap at
     the end for the installation of another operating system.

3.   Upgrade an existing IBM PC XENIX version 1 system to
     IBM PC XENIX Version 2.00.

***   Warning - Options 1 and 2 remove all existing partitions.  ***
***             If you have another operating system installed   ***
***             on your fixed disk, you must back up your user   ***
***             files before continuing.  You may press DEL to   ***
***             abort this installation now.                     ***

Enter option number:
```

You were introduced to these three options early in this chapter. If you haven't already done so, decide which option you want. In addition, as XENIX' warning makes clear, if you have MS-DOS installed on your hard disk and have not yet removed valuable files, you must back them up now (you can press the Delete key to exit *hdinit*). Both option 1 and option 2 will destroy any existing files on your hard disk.

If, at this point, you still have any existing partitions on your hard disk, *hdinit* will halt the installation, delete all partitions, and display the following message:

```
A valid partition was detected during fixed disk initialization.
The partition was cleared, and the machine halted.  PC XENIX must
restart the installation to check for bad tracks on the cleared
partitions.

1. Wait for the shutdown message, then press ENTER to reboot.
2. When the boot prompt appears, type "fd /etc/badtrack".


**  Normal System Shutdown  **

Press Enter to reboot:
```

If this happens, don't worry. XENIX has saved you the trouble of deleting the partitions yourself, and is directing you to check your hard disk for bad tracks. Press Enter to reboot. After a few moments you'll see the XENIX boot prompt again, but don't take the default this time. Rather, type:

fd /etc/badtrack

When you press Enter, XENIX will begin scanning all of the cylinders on your hard disk. After it's looked at every track, you'll see the results on-screen, referenced by cylinder and track. The bad-track information for our system appeared in about a minute and looked like this:

```
Map for drive 0 is:

cyl 507 track 2 cyl 603 track 0

Enter additional bad tracks for drive 0,

Enter cylinder [1-613] and press ENTER,
or
Press ENTER if there are no more badtracks:
```

276

■ NOTE: *If you're coming to XENIX from MS-DOS and are accustomed to thinking of tracks only as concentric circles on the disk surface itself, you're going to have to rearrange your definition a little bit here. Remember that a cylinder number refers to a particular disk (track) location extending vertically through a stack of platters. Thus, cylinder 500 refers to disk (track) location 500 on all platters. The track that XENIX refers to here pinpoints the read-write head that located a bad track—in other words, cylinder 500, track 2, can also be read as "disk track 500, head 2."*

We installed XENIX on a 20-megabyte hard disk, which contains 614 cylinders numbered 0 through 613. Cylinder 0 (the first available cylinder XENIX found) is reserved for the bad-track information. In our case, XENIX found that track 2 of cylinder 507 and track 0 of cylinder 603 were not suitable for use, so the message above informed us that those cylinders and tracks were to be noted in the bad-track table and locked out of use.

Your list of bad tracks may be larger or smaller. A hard disk can have several bad tracks—or none. Since, typically, a 20-megabyte hard disk actually has 21 megabytes of storage or more available before formatting, any hard disk has a generous allowance for bad tracks, usually more than XENIX will ever find.

If, for whatever reason, XENIX finds an unacceptably large number of bad tracks, it will tell you and terminate the installation. If that happens, consult your service technician.

Returning to the previous illustration, notice the third and fourth lines, in which XENIX asks for additional bad-track information. The source of that information may not be immediately apparent to you, but this request provides you with an additional safeguard.

Some hard-disk manufacturers provide a paper copy of the bad-track table that their own diagnostic equipment has discovered for their add-on or built-in hard disks. These diagnostics are usually more intensive than */etc/badtrack*. If you have such a list, and if your list contains references to bad tracks that */etc/badtrack* did not find, take this opportunity to enter the additional information.

If you have no additions to the bad-track table, press Enter to continue. The resulting screen display will look something like this:

```
Map for drive 0 is:

cyl 507 track 2 cyl 603 track 0

IBM PC XENIX Boot

Enter:    hd program
          fd program
          dos
          cf [-c conf_file][device program]

Press Enter for default:   fd /xenix.fd
  :
```

Press Enter to boot again from the installation floppy and press Enter again to load XENIX. Now you're ready to continue with the installation. Once again, type *hdinit* and move to the partition setup menu.

SELECTING AN OPTION

Options 1 and 2 share certain common procedures, so to some degree they can be discussed together. Of the two, option 1 is the more automatic and requires less interaction from you during the initial phase of the installation. Since it poses no immediate need for information, we'll start with option 2, then bring in option 1 when the procedures coincide.

OPTION 2—RESERVING SPACE AT THE END OF THE DISK

When you select option 2, XENIX asks you for the size of the gap you want to leave at the end of the hard disk before it proceeds with the installation. On our 20-megabyte system, it prompted like this:

```
Type the size of the gap that will
remain at the end of the disk (in KB blocks):
```

You can respond with any number, as long as that number, plus the 15 megabytes XENIX requires, does not exceed the capacity of your hard disk. Note, however, that XENIX requests the size of the gap in *kilobyte-sized*, not *megabyte-sized*, blocks. If, for instance, you wanted to reserve 4 megabytes of a 20-megabyte hard disk, you would respond with 4000. XENIX would then set aside 4000 kilobytes (4,000,000 bytes, or 4 megabytes) at the end of the disk, while preserving the 15 megabytes it needs for itself.

With an actual capacity of about 21 megabytes on a typical 20-megabyte hard disk, you can probably set aside a 5500K gap and still leave 15 of the "20" megabytes open for XENIX.

◼ NOTE: *Take a little time to think about how much space you will need for XENIX before you give too much away to another operating system. Remember, each user will have his or her own storage needs, too.*

Once you've entered an acceptable value, XENIX will reserve the appropriate amount of disk space for you and clear any existing partitions. Then, it continues at the same place option 1 begins, so we will now cover both options in a description of the remaining installation procedures.

278

COMPLETING THE XENIX INSTALLATION

After your bad-track table and partitions have been created with either option 1 or option 2, XENIX requests your time zone with this display:

```
Enter the name of your local time zone.  Choose one of the
following time zones or create a custom time zone by choosing
Option 7 (Other):

 1. Greenwich
 2. Atlantic
 3. Eastern
 4. Central
 5. Mountain
 6. Pacific
 7. Other

Enter option number:
```

If you need to choose *Other,* XENIX will prompt you for some additional information:

```
The following information is necessary to set the system time zone:

1) A three-letter abbreviation for your current
   time zone (For example: EST for standard time).

2) The difference in hours from Greenwich, England (GMT).
   (The difference is negative if the position is east of
   Greenwich.)

3) A three-letter abbreviation for the daylight time zone
   if applicable. (For example: EDT for daylight time)

Enter time zone abbreviation:
```

For example, if you live in Fairbanks, Alaska, or Honolulu, Hawaii, you are in the Alaska-Hawaii time zone. Since none of the options on XENIX' list apply to you, you would choose the *Other* option. In response to the *Enter timezone abbreviation:* prompt, you might type:

AHT

Then, you'd tell XENIX that Fairbanks (or Honolulu) is 10 hours from Greenwich, England (the number is positive because you are west of Greenwich). Finally, you might indicate that, during daylight savings time, the zone label for Fairbanks should be ADT (for Alaskan Daylight Time)…or, in Honolulu, you might specify NST (for No Savings Time), since Honolulu does not observe daylight savings time.

Whether you've accepted one of the existing time zones or created one for your own time zone, after this step XENIX goes to work. This is also the point at which Option 3 begins.

For about the next two and a half minutes XENIX will be busy creating the user and root file systems on your hard disk and transferring the appropriate programs into each system. You'll see all of this action on your screen as the contents of the XENIX script are printed on the display. As mentioned earlier, you needn't pay close attention to any of these messages unless you see one that contains the word *error.* When XENIX has finished, you'll see the following:

279

```
IBM PC XENIX VERSION 2.00 INITIAL SYSTEM INSTALLATION COMPLETED

When the prompt appears, do the following:

1. Type "haltsys" and press ENTER.
2. Wait for the "Normal System Shutdown" message.
3. Remove the installation diskette.
   (disregard the red light in the disk drive)
4. Return to the installation section of "Starting PC XENIX".

#
```

XENIX is now officially installed on your hard disk. But it isn't quite ready for use yet. At the least, there's still the matter of loading the remaining XENIX programs onto the disk. You also need to select a master password to control access to the system.

To begin, follow the directions on the screen in the order they're presented (you can ignore number 4, since you've completed the installation). First, type:

haltsys

and press the Enter key. You'll soon see the *Normal System Shutdown* message, followed by an instruction to press Enter to reboot the system. When you see this, remove the installation diskette and store it away in a safe place.

On certain systems, the floppy drive light will not go out when the messages appear. In fact, the floppy drive mechanism may continue spinning. If that happens, don't be concerned. As long as the two messages appear on the screen, you can open the drive door and remove the installation diskette for safe storage. Then press the Enter key.

INSTALLING THE XENIX SOFTWARE PACKAGES

When the system reboots, it proposes *hd /xenix* as the default:

```
IBM PC XENIX Boot

Enter:    hd program
          fd program
          dos
          cf [-c conf_file][device program]

Press Enter for default:   hd /xenix
:
```

Since the *hd /xenix* device and program now exist, you can accept the default, so press Enter. XENIX replies with:

```
            The IBM Personal Computer XENIX
                     Version 2.00
            (c) Copyright IBM Corp.  1984,1985
        (c) Copyright Microsoft Corp.  1983,1984,1985

    XENIX is a registered trademark of the Microsoft Corporation


Reserved memory = 2k
Kernel memory = 176k
Buffers = 100k
User memory = 2282k

No single-user login present
Entering System Maintenance Mode
Terminal type is ansi
#
```

Note that XENIX has once again entered system maintenance mode. Even though you've installed XENIX correctly and can boot the system from your hard disk, you still haven't given XENIX anything to do. It's time to add substance to the framework you've sketched onto your hard disk.

The XENIX operating system came with several diskettes. Aside from the installation diskette, there are three diskettes labeled Base Package (non-IBM versions of XENIX may have more). If you also got the Software Development system, you'll have three labeled Software Development. If you purchased the Text Processing system, you'll have one diskette labeled Text Formatting. At the minimum, you must install the Base Package (sometimes called the "runtime system"). Without it, you have no XENIX—no file-handling structure, no mail, no text editor, and no user-oriented command-interpreter shells. The Software Development and Text Formatting diskettes, on the other hand, are more or less optional. You can run XENIX without them, though at a level beneath its full capability.

All three packages are installed in pretty much the same manner. For the Base Package, type:

xinstall base

and press Enter. XENIX will perform a few system checks on the hard disk. At the end, you'll see:

```
Choose one of the following options:

1. New IBM PC XENIX BASE package installation.

2. Installing PC XENIX 2.00 BASE package on a PC XENIX Version 1 system.


Enter option number:
```

Choose the number appropriate to your system. If it is a new installation, your choice will be option 1. If you are upgrading to Version 2.00, the choice will be option 2.

XENIX will print some messages on your screen as it checks the available space on your disk and finally will display the message:

```
Install the IBM PC XENIX Version 2.00 distribution diskettes in order
starting with number 1.  If you are installing more than one XENIX
option, you must install the base package first.

Follow the instructions on your screen as the installation
proceeds.  After installing the last diskette, answer "n" to
the prompt and press ENTER.


Press ENTER to continue:
```

Press Enter, and you'll see the message:

```
Insert the next diskette after the drive light goes out.
Answer "y" to the prompt and press ENTER.

After installing the last diskette, answer "n" to the prompt
and press ENTER

First Diskette?  [y,n]
```

Place the first Base Package diskette in the floppy drive, type *y,* and then press Enter. (If, at any time, you make a mistake and XENIX informs you of a "tape" error, check the diskette; "tape" is a throwback to the days of *UNIX* and tape storage.)

When the contents of all three diskettes have been successfully transferred to the hard disk, IBM PC XENIX will reply:

```
Installation program setting file permissions; please stand by:

IBM PC XENIX VERSION 2.00 BASE PACKAGE INSTALLATION COMPLETED

Now return to the installation section of "Starting PC XENIX".
```

as it sets access permissions and completes installation of the Base Package.

Installing the Software Development Package follows the same pattern, except that you begin by typing:

xinstall soft

Likewise, you begin installation o the Text Formatting Package with:

xinstall text

When all packages have been installed, the only remaining task you must take care of immediately is to create the superuser password. You should do this now, since it's the key to keeping your system safe from unauthorized tampering.

CREATING THE SUPERUSER PASSWORD

As the name implies, the superuser password is an "Open, sesame" to the entire XENIX system. As the system administrator, you need access to all of XENIX' maintenance and account-creation utilities. The superuser password is your key, but like any key it must be used wisely and protected adequately. Without the password, you cannot use XENIX' utilities. If you've forgotten it, the only way to assign a new superuser password is to reinstall XENIX (you can change the password once you're logged into the system, but without it you can't even log in). Conversely, if your password is common knowledge or available to everyone, the door to the XENIX system, like an unlocked door to your house, is wide open to whoever wishes to enter.

The basic rule of thumb is to keep the superuser password simple enough to remember easily, yet not so simple that just anyone might guess it. Since XENIX differentiates between upper- and lowercase characters, one easy method of rendering your superuser password both easy to remember and difficult to guess is to use a combination of upper- and lowercase letters. For example, JONes or jonES would be much more secure than jones or JONES. Likewise, adding a few random letters to a simple password makes it significantly more difficult to guess—gjonesxl or REJONESN—while keeping it easy to commit to memory.

To assign the superuser password, type at the shell prompt:

passwd root

XENIX answers with *New password:*, and that's where you type the password—up to eight characters long—that you've selected.

As a security precaution, XENIX will not echo the letters to the screen as you type them. That will be true whenever you enter your password, and will keep anyone who might be walking by from seeing the password as you type it.

When you press Enter after you type your password, XENIX will prompt you to retype the password, just to ensure that you both understood what was originally entered. If, for some reason, the password you type the second time is not identical to the one you originally entered, XENIX will respond with:

    They don't match; try again.

and place you back at the *New Password:* prompt. If that happens, re-enter your password and, as XENIX suggests, try again.

Once XENIX has accepted your superuser password, the shell prompt will reappear. If there is still a diskette in the floppy drive, remove it and type:

haltsys

When the shutdown messages appear, press Enter to reboot the system and again accept *hd /xenix,* XENIX' default device and program, but don't do anything else right now. There are subtle differences in the ways a superuser can log in, and what you can do depends upon the way that login is initiated. Let's look at the two ways a superuser can log in.

283

DIFFERENCES IN SUPERUSER LOGINS

With the superuser password created, XENIX has login information available and does not automatically slip into system maintenance mode. Rather, when the machine settles down after rebooting, the screen displays:

```
               The IBM Personal Computer XENIX
                       Version 2.00
              (c) Copyright IBM Corp. 1984,1985
            (c) Copyright Microsoft Corp. 1983,1984,1985

         XENIX is a registered trademark of the Microsoft Corporation


    Reserved memory = 2k
    Kernel memory = 176k
    Buffers = 100k
    User memory = 2282k

    Type Ctrl-d to proceed with normal startup,
    (or give root password for system maintenance):
```

As the preceding screen display indicates, simply entering the superuser (root) password places you in system maintenance mode. While there, you can re-configure XENIX, install any system packages you had not already installed and, generally, do whatever is needed to maintain the system.

You cannot, however, install accounts for other users—a vital part of your responsibilities as system administrator on a multiuser system (we'll cover this in the next chapter). To perform other tasks besides system maintenance, you need to initiate a normal startup by pressing Ctrl-D. In this case, XENIX returns the current system time and date, followed by a *login:* request that looks something like this:

```
Current System Time is: Mon Apr 7 23:00:00 PDT 1986

AT Console Login:
```

When this happens, type:

root

as the login name, then enter the superuser password you just created. (Although any valid login name and password would work, if you've followed our sample installation, you only have the superuser password right now.)

SWITCHING BETWEEN XENIX AND MS-DOS

If you include MS-DOS on your hard disk with XENIX, you will want to switch back and forth between the two and be able to boot either MS-DOS or XENIX from the hard disk. The procedure to make this happen is simple.

◩ NOTE: *We'll assume that there are no other users on your system. Remember, XENIX and MS-DOS do not run simultaneously, so if other XENIX users are on your system, protect their work by making certain everyone has logged out before you begin installing MS-DOS.*

After you've installed XENIX, place an MS-DOS system diskette (Version 3.00 or above) in the boot floppy drive and reboot the system from the diskette. An *A:* prompt will appear. When it does, invoke the MS-DOS fixed disk setup program by typing the command:

fdisk c:

Select option 1 to create an MS-DOS partition and accept the values *fdisk* suggests for the partition size (the default will be the remaining unclaimed portion of the hard disk). Exit the *fdisk* program. Next, make the new MS-DOS partition bootable by typing the command:

format c: /s

This will format the MS-DOS partition and copy all necessary MS-DOS system files to the hard disk.

You can now load or reload any MS-DOS files onto the hard disk (bear in mind the possible space constraints we discussed earlier). From this point on, you can keep your MS-DOS system diskette in storage. Both XENIX and MS-DOS are bootable from the hard disk. To select the MS-DOS partition, type:

dos

from the initial XENIX boot prompt.

XENIX will always be the boot system and will always prompt for a XENIX hard-disk boot, but it will also give you the option of booting *dos* if you choose.

If you want to return to XENIX from MS-DOS, make sure there's no diskette in the floppy drive, then press Ctrl-Alt-Del to reboot your computer. Soon after, you'll see the XENIX boot message.

MANAGING THE SYSTEM
Now that XENIX is installed on your hard disk, you are ready to open up the system—install user accounts and tell XENIX the types and locations of the terminals you'll connect to it. Since the XENIX computer is at the heart of your system, we'll work outward from there, beginning with a fundamental rule of sound system management: As system administrator, you must control access to the XENIX computer and, if possible, limit use of this machine to yourself alone.

USING THE XENIX COMPUTER

In XENIX' multiuser environment, you and all other users on the system must bear in mind that the XENIX computer and the terminals attached to it differ in one obvious and very important respect. The computer is independent of every terminal on the system, but no terminal can provide access to XENIX without the host computer. This difference means that the computer cannot be turned off when someone has finished using it.

While XENIX is in operation, a great deal of behind-the-scenes activity goes on. You've been introduced to some of this activity in the form of foreground and background processing, the *mail* system, and so on. But there is much more that you never see or directly influence. One such process is XENIX' automatic generation of temporary files, in which it maintains current work in progress while the system is running. When the system is shut down properly, these temporary files are neatly closed and put away. All current activities are systematically terminated and any needed files are appropriately saved or updated.

But if you or anyone else turns off the XENIX computer without going through the shutdown procedure, XENIX abandons its temporary files, and they become inaccessible for the next session. At the very least, the next time you start up, XENIX will request permission to do housekeeping, at which time it will close and delete the temporary files that were left open when the system was improperly shut down. In some instances, you may be able to recover the contents of these abandoned files, but generally speaking the housekeeping functions exist to correct the shutdown error and restore the system's integrity, rather than to retrieve the contents of abandoned files.

More seriously, if the system is shut down incorrectly while other users are online at their terminals, any of the work they have not yet saved to disk will be irretrievably lost.

Given these possible consequences, the easiest and safest means of protecting your XENIX system and all work being done on it is simply to restrict access to the XENIX computer. Keep in mind that the most capable of people can fall victim to habit. Someone who has become accustomed to shutting off the terminal after logging out may reflexively reach for the on/off switch on the XENIX computer.

INSTALLING TERMINALS

When you attach a terminal to the XENIX computer, you must provide the two with a means of communicating. In local-access situations, the most visible link between the computer and a terminal is the cable that connects them. The cable may run across the floor or through the walls, but in every instance it is the physical connection between the two machines. In remote-access situations, the connection is somewhat more elaborate, since both the terminal and the computer require modems that act as intermediaries, translating information into a form that can be sent and received via the telephone system. Again, though, just as in local-access setups, the machines are joined by hardware of some sort.

In addition to modems and cables, both the terminal and the computer need outlets through which information can be transmitted. For each, that outlet is a serial port—a type of "channel" that sends and receives a well-defined stream of data bits in the form of higher and lower electrical voltages representing the two binary numerals 1 and 0 respectively.

The serial port itself is another piece of hardware. On the outside of each machine, the port simply looks somewhat like an electrical outlet into which you plug the end of a cable. If you look inside the machine, however, you will notice that a serial port is part of a printed circuit board which, itself, is plugged into a network of processing hardware. In a computer such as the IBM PC AT, the board fits into one of eight expansion slots inside the computer case.

For a ready-made terminal, there is no need to concern yourself with serial ports. The port you need should be built in and properly set up to receive a cable.

In the case of the XENIX computer, however, you may find that your machine does not have enough serial ports to handle the number of terminals and other devices you wish to attach to the system. Each terminal requires a different port, so if you have six terminals, you obviously need six serial ports (the IBM PC series is designed to support up to seven serial ports). You have a number of choices here, but all boil down to adding more ports to the system. Where and how you add the ports will depend on your own preferences and the advice of your hardware dealer. Serial ports can be purchased with or without extra memory and built-in parallel ports and clocks. Others are multiplexers that expand one serial port into many. The alternatives are varied, and the choice is yours.

HOW MANY TERMINALS?

As you review the following procedures, you may wonder whether to install all possible terminals at one time, rather than return later to install future additions. Efficient though this course may sound, it actually may not be your best choice.

As a multiuser operating system, one of XENIX' many tasks is to keep track of what is happening on each of the terminals attached to the system. It must know when commands are issued, and at which terminals. In order to monitor such activity, XENIX polls (checks) each of the serial ports to which it has been told that a terminal is connected. That polling process requires a portion of the system's overall response time.

On machines, such as the COMPAQ 286 and the IBM PC AT, which run at a relatively high speed, the serial-port polling interruptions for several terminals are hardly noticeable. On slower systems, such as the IBM PC XT, those same interruptions can slow the system's response time and become annoying to users.

Furthermore, once a port is activated, XENIX will poll it whether or not a terminal is turned on or even physically connected to it. Polling is part of what XENIX has been designed to do, but it is quite literally a waste of time if XENIX is polling ports that are not or never will be in use.

Now, with these preliminaries out of the way, let's get to work.

LOGGING IN AS SUPERUSER

As mentioned in Chapter 13, there are two ways that you, as superuser, can log in after booting XENIX. One way is to type the superuser (root) password when XENIX prompts:

```
Type Ctrl-d to proceed with normal startup,
(or give root password for system maintenance):_
```

The other is to press Ctrl-D and then log into XENIX as the superuser at the normal *AT Login:* prompt.

If XENIX is not currently running on the host computer, turn the computer on or reboot it and, when prompted, press Enter to run the XENIX boot program from the hard disk.

While you can activate serial ports from system maintenance mode, you can do both this and add user accounts only when you're logged into the system as the superuser. Thus, when XENIX prompts, press Ctrl-D and, at the *AT Login:* prompt, type the login name *root,* followed by the system password you chose.

If you're already logged in, you may be in system maintenance mode. Visually, there's no simple way to tell whether you are or not—the system prompt for either situation is the pound symbol (#). If there is a terminal close by, you can easily check by trying to log in on it. In system maintenance mode, XENIX turns the host computer into a single-user system, so any attached terminal will not respond to your login attempt.

If you are, or think you are, in system maintenance mode, you can also press Ctrl-D to log off the system and log back in again as described earlier.

DETERMINING CURRENT SERIAL-PORT CONFIGURATION

Before you attach new terminals to the system, you must know how XENIX currently "sees" your serial ports and any terminals attached to them. The information in two data files governs whether or not XENIX considers a serial port to be active and whether it recognizes the specific terminal type that might be attached to that port. These files are called *ttys* and *ttytype,* and they can be located in the */etc* directory.

Let's first look at *ttys.* Enter the command:

cat /etc/ttys

to display its contents. XENIX will show you that it contains:

```
# cat /etc/ttys
1Cconsole
03tty00
07tty01
#_
```

XENIX displays three parameters for each of the ports in *ttys*. The first is the port status:

0	if the port is inactive
1	if the port is active

In the preceding illustration the first port, which is the computer's console or display device, is active; the other two are inactive.

The second parameter is the communication speed (baud rate) at which information passes through that port:

3	for speeds at or below 1200 baud
4	for 2400 baud
5	for 4800 baud
6	for 9600 baud
7	for 9600 baud on an IBM 3101 terminal
C	for communication through the computer's own video display

The third parameter is the name of the device that represents that port. In the illustration, you see three such device names:

console	the computer's own video display
tty00	the primary serial port, equivalent to MS-DOS' COM1:
tty01	the secondary serial port, equivalent to MS-DOS' COM2:

The configuration for your own system will depend on what you are connecting to it. *Console,* as the XENIX computer's own display, must remain. For purposes of example, we'll configure the remaining two ports as if you were connecting a terminal to tty00 and a modem to tty01. Unless you want to use the values exactly as they are shown here, you may prefer to either read through the following instructions or, if you are comfortable with editing files, try out the commands without saving the modified file to disk.

SETTING THE SERIAL PORTS

To set up these ports to work correctly, you must change their descriptions in the *ttys* file. To do so, you can use XENIX' visual editor, *vi,* which you met in Chapters 5 and 6 (the commands we'll use here should look familiar). Begin by loading the contents of *ttys* into *vi* with the command:

vi /etc/ttys

Vi responds by displaying the three-line text file it has loaded from disk and includes relevant information on the status line at the bottom of the screen.

Now, let's assume you want to activate tty00 and tell XENIX that the attached terminal will communicate at 9600 baud. Although this is a standard speed, it might not be correct for the particular terminal you're installing. If you don't know a terminal's operating speed, check its operations manual.

291

In our example, tty00 is on the second line of text. To change its value, move the cursor (currently in the upper lefthand corner) down one line by pressing a downward direction key or by pressing Enter.

Now press the *x* key twice to delete the characters *03*. Next, press *i* to enter insert mode, type *16,* and then press the Escape key to tell *vi* to change the line that currently reads *03tty00* to *16tty00*. (Recall that the *1* indicates the port is now active and the *6* indicates a 9600-baud communication speed.)

You can change the parameters of tty01 in the same way. This time, as we described earlier, we are assuming that the port is to be used for remote access, via a modem. Even so, the only difference in the parameters will be in the transmission speed. XENIX does not care whether a port has been set up for local or remote access. To XENIX, a terminal is a terminal. As long as it can communicate properly with the terminal, the hardware itself can be located anywhere. In fact, there is nothing to stop you from attaching a terminal, instead of a modem, to your "remote-access" port—as long as the terminal operates at the speed for which the port is configured.

Currently, 1200 baud is considered by some the optimum communications speed over voice-grade telephone lines, so if we assume a transmission speed of 1200 baud, you would change *07tty01* to read *13tty01*.

Of course, technology marches on: 2400-baud modems that can handle the inconsistencies of standard voice-grade telephone lines are becoming more popular, just as 1200-baud devices replaced their 300-baud predecessors a few years ago. If your system uses a 2400-baud modem, the new *ttys* line would be *14ttys01*.

As well, your system may have a private (or dedicated) telephone line. These lines are more expensive than normal telephone lines, but much less prone to random static and line noises. Communication speed through a dedicated line can be higher than 1200 or 2400 baud, depending upon the operating speed of the modem you're using, so you would set up the port accordingly.

If you've followed our example, your file should now look like this:

```
1Cconsole
16tty00
13tty01
~
~
```

Once you've changed the contents of *ttys* to match your system, you must save the modified file back to the file */etc/ttys*. You can do so with *vi*'s *exit* command, which saves the current buffer contents to disk and, at the same time, exits *vi*. From command mode, type:

    :x

Your updating process will now be complete.

FINDING TERMINAL TYPES

Once the ports that you'll be using are activated, your next step is to tell XENIX what types of terminals will be accessing those ports. These definitions are contained in the file called *ttytype*. Again, you can use *vi* to work with the contents of the file. As before, look at the contents of the file to see what it contains and decide what choices must be made. At the system prompt (#), enter:

cat /etc/ttytype

XENIX will display something like the following:

```
# cat /etc/ttytype
ansi console
3101 tty00
3101 tty01
#_
```

The first part of each line describes the terminal type, and the second part names the port to which the terminal is attached. If your file differs from what you see here, don't be concerned. More likely than not, you'll be changing it.

DISTINGUISHING AMONG TERMINALS

In our example, the console device is defined as an ANSI terminal. As we've mentioned before, the ANSI designation means that character placement and removal on the screen follow a standard set of rules described by the American National Standards Institute. ANSI is widely known and accepted, so this designation almost certainly applies to your host computer. If, for some reason, it does not, check with your dealer or manufacturer for details.

The default values for tty00 and tty01, however, as shown in our example, use screen-control codes established by the IBM Corporation for its 3101 series of terminals. But there are many different types of terminals. Yours may or may not match these descriptions.

The distinguishing feature between two different brands of terminal may very well be the way in which special control characters and commands are used to control their screens. Some terminals follow the ANSI rules, but there is, at present, no overriding standard in this area of hardware manufacture.

Because XENIX must know what type of terminal is attached to a particular port, it contains a special data file, called *termcap,* in the */etc* subdirectory. This file contains the information XENIX needs to work with any of a wide selection of terminal makes and models. The file is quite long, but you can quickly determine whether your particular terminal type is included by using a single XENIX command, *grep.*

FINDING A TERMINAL TYPE

The *grep* utility was explained earlier, in Chapter 9. It's use here is to provide pattern matching. Given the manufacturer's name (ADDS, Zenith, Hazeltine, DEC, IBM, TeleVideo, and so on), you can use *grep* to search the file */etc/termcap* to find out if that word is contained in the file. For example, suppose you used DEC as the search criterion. Your command line would read:

grep -y DEC /etc/termcap

(Notice we included the *y* option to search for both upper- and lowercase occurrences of DEC.) XENIX would respond with the following list of DEC terminal types contained in *termcap*:

294

```
$ grep -y DEC /etc/termcap
d1|vt100|vt-100|pt100|pt-100|dec vt100:\
d2|gt42|dec gt42:\
d4|gt40|dec gt40:\
d5|vt50|dec vt50:\
dl|dw1|decwriter I:\
dh|vt50h|dec vt50h:\
ds|vt100s|vt-100s|pt100s|pt-100s|dec vt100 132 cols 14 lines:\
dt|vt100w|vt-100w|pt100w|pt-100w|dec vt100 132 cols:\
dv|vt52|dec vt52:\
dw|dw2|dw3|dw4|decwriter II:\
$ _
```

Each line of text *grep* reported does, indeed, contain the pattern *dec*. The first two characters of each line represent the terminal-definition code that XENIX understands. The remainder of each line is a description of the terminal to which the code refers.

◼ NOTE: *If you were to look at the contents of* termcap *itself, you would see that there is actually much more to each DEC entry than* grep *has reported. Each terminal code and description is followed by a list of parameters that XENIX requires to operate the particular terminal. Right now, however, in terms of the* /etc/ttytype *file, all XENIX needs is the two-character terminal code itself.*

If you were using a DEC terminal, you would scan the list of *termcap* entries, looking for your terminal model. A standard DEC VT-100 terminal, for instance, would have the code d1. (Note that you cannot simply use the first code that matches your terminal type. Codes *ds* and *dt* also refer to the VT-100, but with different parameters. The former is for a VT-100 in 132-column, 14-line mode, while the latter is for one used in 132-column mode.)

CHANGING A TERMINAL TYPE

Let's assume that the terminal you want to attach to tty00 is a DEC VT-100 with the code d1. To change the definition in */etc/ttytype,* you could invoke *vi* and specify the file by entering:

vi /etc/ttytype

Since the tty00 definition is in the second line of text, you would move down one line by pressing Enter and press *dw* to delete the "word" *3101.* Next, you would press *i* to enter insert mode and type:

d1

followed by a blank space. Press the Escape key to leave insert mode, and save the new version to disk by typing:

:x

(Remember, the description *3101 tty00* is from our example. If different information is displayed for tty00 in the *ttytype* file contained on your XENIX system, use that information instead.)

IF *grep* DOES NOT FIND YOUR TERMINAL

If the terminal manufacturer for which you tell *grep* to search is not represented in *termcap, grep* will not be able to return any lines from the file. Instead, the system prompt will reappear. But that outcome doesn't necessarily mean that *termcap* does not contain a definition of your terminal.

It could be that your terminal or its manufacturer is too new to be listed in the XENIX file. If you suspect that this is so, check the terminal's manual to see whether the terminal is compatible with one that is listed in *termcap.*

Then, too, remember that *grep* is not intelligent—it matches patterns of characters. You may not have entered the name of your terminal as it exists in the *termcap* file. For example, the Radio Shack model 100 can be found if you use either *radio* or *shack* as the search pattern, but you won't find it under *tandy.* Conversely, the definition for a TRS-80 model 16, a XENIX-compatible computer, can be located by using *trs,* the abbreviation for Tandy/Radio Shack.

In any case, you may simply want to print the contents of */etc/termcap* with the command *lp /etc/termcap* and scan the listing for yourself.

ADDING AN UNDEFINED TERMINAL

Of course, you may find that no definition for your terminal, either actual or compatible, exists in *termcap.* In that case, you can use a generic terminal definition called *dumb* (the code is *su* if the terminal is unlisted in *termcap,* but *y1* if it is a Teleray terminal, model 3700).

295

Dumb, however, is not the best of choices in terms of using XENIX to its fullest capacity. The control codes used by *dumb* are based on the codes used to describe teletype equipment—terminals that print on paper, rather than on a screen. For most of the operations you want to perform in the Bourne and C shells, these codes are fine. But they do offer few alternatives in those instances in which XENIX needs a considerable amount of control over the screen.

For example, *vi,* the XENIX visual editor, controls the screen more than most other XENIX programs do, and users may thus experience display problems when trying to use *vi* with a terminal defined to XENIX as dumb or tty (teletype).

Likewise, the Visual shell exercises a great deal of control over the screen. Again, dumb and tty terminals don't offer this functionality. XENIX will return an error message if a user attempts to enter the Visual shell from either a dumb terminal or a tty terminal.

ADDING DIAL-UP TERMINAL TYPES

Once a terminal has been hardwired to the system, overseeing its use or replacement is relatively straightforward. In a dial-up situation, however, you encounter a set of "what if" situations with any number of answers. Given the system's telephone number, a login name, and a password, a XENIX user can plug any handy terminal into a modem and try to access the system. In addition, a number of dial-up users, each with a different type of terminal, can also require access through the same port or ports. Your solution to this situation will depend on how your system is used, and by whom.

If your dial-up users access XENIX from the Bourne or C shell and use it primarily for mail messages and other such straightforward tasks, the simplest recourse is to define the device attached to the dial-up port as *dumb.* This definition should permit any dial-up terminal to converse with XENIX. There will, however, be no screen control at all, and that involves the restrictions to *vi* and the Visual shell that we've already mentioned.

A more effective alternative, especially if you want to offer the full range of XENIX' capabilities to your dial-up users, is to modify the information in each user's *.profile* file. XENIX keeps a separate *.profile* file (or equivalent) for each user account on the system. These *.profile* files maintain information about each person. Additional information about a user's terminal type can be placed in it as well, as you'll see later in the chapter, after you've installed one or two user accounts.

Finally, if your situation is one in which you cannot predict what type of terminal will be used to access XENIX—for example, if you have an outside sales force who access the system from whatever terminals are available—you can have each user set the terminal type after logging in. Unless some or all of these users are assigned to the Visual shell, this procedure will work well, because XENIX makes no screen-control demands immediately following login. (If your users are assigned to the Visual shell, it's best to reassign them or have them use a particular type of terminal defined in their *.profile* files.)

Assuming, however, that your dial-up users can set the terminal type, you'll need to provide them with a list of valid terminal types for the system (as listed in */etc/termcap*) and instruct them to enter their terminal information in the following format after logging in:

TERM = [terminal code]; export TERM

where they substitute the correct terminal code in place of *[terminal code]*. The word *TERM* in this command is a XENIX variable that holds the terminal-definition code; it must be typed in uppercase. Once this line has been entered, XENIX will be able to deal with the terminal by using the related parameters that it finds in */etc/termcap*. The result for the user (although it only lasts until logout) is no different from having the terminal defined in */etc/ttytype* or the *.profile* file.

297

USING COMPUTERS AS TERMINALS

As we mentioned early in this book, a computer, as well as a terminal, can be used to access XENIX. In this case, the computer must be equipped with a telecommunications program that enables it to emulate a terminal that XENIX will recognize. Although XENIX itself will make no distinction between a computer that attempts to communicate with it and a terminal that does the same thing, you will need to exercise some special care when you tell XENIX what type of terminal the telecommunications software is attempting to have the computer emulate.

Almost every telecommunications software package has an option that will make your computer ANSI-compatible as part of its terminal-emulation function. In terms of emulating a terminal for use with either the Bourne or the C shell, this level of ANSI-compatibility is usually sufficient. Neither shell makes many demands on total compatibility with the terminal type you've assigned, and most telecommunications terminal-emulation software works well under these conditions.

But for a real terminal, ANSI-compatibility is usually a subset of all the control instructions the manufacturer has built into the device. If you install a user in the Visual shell, total compatibility with the terminal that the computer is emulating becomes much more critical. The telecommunications software you select should not only be ANSI-compatible, but should also conform to the enhancements a manufacturer has made.

Because it takes absolute control of the screen to position its menus, its options, and the peripheral details surrounding them, the Visual shell demands a high degree of compatibility with the parameters it uses from your terminal-code assignment. It is not unusual to find that a terminal-emulation package has some trouble at this point, resulting in missing lines and wayward characters scattered across the Visual shell display.

If you do experience problems, you can supply */etc/ttytype* with the definition *dumb,* and have the computer treated as if it were a teletype machine with no screen-control mechanism. Bear in mind, however, that you will not be able to assign the person using the computer to the Visual shell and that the definition *dumb* may cause problems if that person wants to use *vi.*

Also, although there are exceptions for computers that both run XENIX and are used as terminals on XENIX systems, it's important to remind users that present versions of XENIX cannot normally interact with the file system of the computer. For example, an IBM PC XT, when used as a terminal (perhaps running the DOS-based Microsoft Access communications program), is simply a keyboard and video display as far as XENIX is concerned.

You'll find that it's easy to hook up terminals and provide people with access to XENIX. This operating system has been designed to be both flexible and powerful, so you not only have a variety of options from which to choose, you also have effective commands, such as *grep,* with which to probe the information. You'll find additional information about manipulating terminal-communication characteristics in the System Administration section of your XENIX documentation.

ADDING A PRINTER

While you could, in theory, run a XENIX system efficiently and well without ever printing a document on paper, you almost certainly want to add one or more printers for system users to share. The process is not difficult, and printer installation can be accomplished with either of two commands: *lpinit* or *lpadmin.* Of the two, however, *lpinit* is better suited to installing printers, while *lpadmin* is better for reconfiguring existing printer installations. We'll begin with a few definitions, and then use *lpinit* to install an IBM Proprinter on a sample system.

Printers are always installed individually, with names of their own. You assign each printer a name of up to 14 characters (any combination of letters, numbers, and underlines). Each printer can also be installed either as a "freestanding" printer or as part of a class, or group, of printers. In operation, the main difference between the two is that a printer you have defined as one of a class will be used by XENIX to print any document sent to that class of printers. For example, if you install two laser printers named *laser1* and *laser2,* and both belong to the class you've defined as *hplaser,* any print request sent to *hplaser* will be printed on either *laser1* or *laser2,* depending on which is available at the time the request is received by the system.

298

The actual printing request is managed by a program called *lpsched*. This program starts up automatically whenever you start or restart the system and, as it receives requests, routes them through an intermediary called a printer interface program and then to the appropriate printer.

PRINTER INTERFACE PROGRAMS

Printer interface programs handle a number of important tasks that ensure correct print operation and safeguard the print requests that are routed through them. Among these tasks are:

■ Providing appropriate communication and parameters for the printer.

299

■ Examining a system file named */etc/default/lpd* to determine whether one or more "banner" pages should be printed at the beginning of each job.

■ Sending a numeric exit code to *lpsched* that indicates whether or not a printing job was successfully completed.

■ Disabling printers when necessary (as when a paper jam occurs) and maintaining a record of print requests not yet completed.

An appropriate printer interface program must exist for each printer on your system. One general interface program already exists in XENIX, in a script file named */usr/spool/lp/model/dumb*. It assumes a very basic form-feed printer with no special codes or requirements. You can, if need be, use *vi* to modify a copy of this file whenever you need to add specific codes for print enhancements, top-of-page commands, automatic linefeeds, and the like. (See your printer manual for this kind of printer-specific information.)

As it has been written, */usr/spool/lp/model/dumb* performs the tasks outlined earlier and also manages the following items of information:

■ The name of the printer and the identification number XENIX automatically assigns to the file forwarded to the printer.

■ The comment field of the user who is making the print request.

■ The current day, date, and time.

■ The number of copies that are to be printed.

■ Any suitable print options, such as small (12-pitch) or condensed (132 characters per line) type, that are requested and the printer can handle.

■ The path name of the file that is to be printed.

MAKING THE CONNECTIONS

Physically connecting your printer to the system is easy, but you'll want to remember a few things as you do it. (As always, check your printer documentation for specific instructions.) XENIX can handle both serial and parallel printers. You need to determine which type your printer is and plan accordingly. If you have a choice, you'll want to use parallel connections, as the serial lines (which are often in short supply) can be used for adding more terminals. The IBM PC series of computers come equipped with one parallel port, but can support two. If you have two and are connecting a parallel printer, decide which port to use, make note of it, and then make the hardware connections.

You'll be asked during the installation whether you've attached the printer to the primary or the alternate parallel port (or serial/parallel adapter). If you have an IBM monochrome display and printer adapter board, you must select option 3.

◼ NOTE: *If you are running IBM PC XENIX on a non-IBM machine, you might have some trouble using the parallel ports or other parts of the hardware, as IBM PC XENIX is not specifically designed for that machine. Many versions of XENIX are available. If possible, get the one specifically designed for your machine.*

Finally, you need to set the appropriate DIP switches for your printer. IBM PC XENIX includes printer interface programs in the */usr/spool/lp/model* directory for the IBM PC Proprinter, the IBM PC Color printer, and the IBM PC Graphics printer. To set the DIP switches for one of these machines, look in the appropriate printer interface program and read the DIP-switch information found near the beginning. For example, to see the IBM PC Proprinter information, type:

```
more /usr/spool/lp/model/proprinter
```

Note that switches 3 and 7 should be set to 0 (off), switch 6 should be set to 1 (on), and the settings for switches 1, 2, 4, and 5 don't matter. Facing the IBM Proprinter, open the cover in the upper left corner and set the switches with an appropriate tool (a sturdy ballpoint pen will do). Your printer is now ready to go. Setting up printers not included in */usr/spool/lp/model* will take a little work if you want to use every special feature your printer has to offer. If you don't, use the printer interface program */usr/spool/lp/model/dumb*.

USING *lpinit*

As we mentioned earlier, to install a new printer on a XENIX system, use the *lpinit* command. To do this, log in as the superuser and enter the command:

```
lpinit
```

300

You will see the first of a series of prompts:

```
# lpinit

The printer is attached to a

1. Serial/Parallel Adapter, Parallel Port.

2. Alternate Serial/Parallel Adapter, Parallel Port.

3. Monochrome & Printer Adapter.

Enter one of the options above
(default = 1)                         :
```

301

Enter the number of the option that matches the port to which the printer is connected. Press Enter.

Next, you will be prompted for a printer name with the message *Enter a name for the printer.* Here, you can type whatever printer name you like, using up to 14 letters, numbers, and underscore characters (you may not use hyphens). If you press Enter without typing a printer name, XENIX will assign the default, *linepr,* to the printer. In our example we'll name the printer *ibm_proprinter.*

After you name the printer, XENIX requests the name of the printer interface program to use, with the message *Enter an interface program.* Type the complete path name of the printer interface program, or press Enter to accept the default, */usr/spool/lp/model/dumb.* If you are using the IBM Proprinter, you should enter */usr/spool/lp/model/proprinter* (additional printer information file scripts appear in the */usr/spool/lp/model* directory).

Your installation at this point is complete, so XENIX displays the message:

```
scheduler stopped
destination printer "ibm_proprinter" now accepting requests
printer "ibm_proprinter" now enabled

Is this the default printer ? [y|n]
(default = y)                         :
```

telling you that it has temporarily stopped *lpsched* so that the printer can be added to the system. The line *printer "ibm_proprinter" now enabled* indicates that the printer is online and able to begin working.

At the bottom of the display, XENIX also asks one more question: *Is this the default printer? [y|n].* Answer *y* or press Enter if you wish this printer to receive all print requests sent with the command *lp [file name].*

MANAGING PRINTERS

Once you've installed the printer or printers you want, XENIX offers some additional commands to help you manage this aspect of your system. Using these commands, you can stop and start print activities, create classes of printers, enable and disable particular printers, and transfer print requests from one destination to another.

STOPPING AND STARTING THE SCHEDULER

All print requests for your system are handled by *lpsched,* which, as we mentioned, runs automatically whenever you start XENIX. The *lpinit* command automatically stops and restarts *lpsched* when you add a printer, but in administering printer operations you will also need to be able to stop and start the scheduler on your own. To begin with, you can find out whether the scheduler is currently running by typing the command:

lpstat -r

If it is running and you wish to stop it, you type the command:

/usr/lib/lpshut

This command stops both the scheduler and all current printing operations. To restart the scheduler, type:

/usr/lib/lpsched

At this point, you can verify that *lpsched* is running by typing the *lpstat -r* command. If, for some reason, it is not running, type the command:

rm -f /usr/spool/SCHEDLOCK

followed by the *lpsched* startup command.

THE *lpadmin* COMMAND

You can use the *lpadmin* command to define or redefine printer information. When you use it in this way, the general format of the command is:

/usr/lib/lpadmin -p[printer] [options]

Among the options you can use with -p are:

Option:	Description:	Example:
-c	Creates a class of printers or adds a printer to a class	*/usr/lib/lpadmin -plaser1 -chplaser*
-i	Sets a new printer interface program for [printer]	*/usr/lib/lpadmin -plaser1 -i/usr/spool/lp/model/lasers*
-r	Eliminates a printer from a class	*/usr/lib/lpadmin -plaser1 -rhplaser*

303

The *lpadmin* command also includes two options other than -p. They are -x and -d. The -x option removes printers or classes of printers from the system and is used in the form:

/usr/lib/lpadmin -x[printer]

When you use this option, the printer or class you specify is permanently removed from the system. If you simply need to remove a printer temporarily, you can use the *disable* command discussed shortly.

The -d option specifies a default printer and is used in the form:

/usr/lib/lpadmin -d[destination]

HANDLING PRINT REQUESTS

On occasion, you will want to be able to shuffle print requests and printers. Perhaps a printer will need to be taken off the system for repair. Or, perhaps, you'll need to move a print request from a busy printer to one that can do the job immediately. For this type of administration, you can use the following commands:

■ The *lpmove* command moves a print request from one installed printer to another. Example: */usr/lib/lpmove laser1-123 laser2* moves print request *laser1-123* from *laser1* to *laser2*.

■ The *accept* command enables a printer or printer class to accept print requests submitted with the *lp* command. Example: */usr/lib/accept hplaser* enables the class *hplaser* to accept print requests.

■ The *reject* command, the converse of *accept*, tells the system that the specified printer or printer class cannot receive print requests. If you include the command's -r option and an explanatory comment enclosed in double quotation marks, a user requesting the printer will receive a message stating that the printer cannot be used, along with your comment as to the reason why. Example: */usr/lib/reject -r "malfunctioning printer" laser2* will take *laser2* out of circulation and inform users of the malfunction.

■ The *enable* command enables the specified printer to actually print the files routed to it. Example: *enable laser2* causes *laser2* not only to accept print requests (via the *accept* command), but to print the documents, as well. This must be done each time you start up the XENIX system.

■ The *disable* command is the opposite of the *enable* command. Like the *reject* command, it can be used with an *-r* option and an explanatory comment. Example: *disable -r "uneven printing" laser1* will disable *laser1* whether or not it is set up to accept print requests.

As jobs are submitted to the printer, they are stored in a print queue. To see the jobs waiting in the order they arrived, type *lpstat*.

You can cancel a job by using the command *cancel [request-id]*. For example, to cancel the printing of the job *proprinter-18* you would type:

```
cancel proprinter-18
```

ADDING USER ACCOUNTS

Now that we've covered the main features of activating ports, assigning access devices, and installing printers, we can move on to adding user accounts.

☒ NOTE: *If you are the system administrator on a new XENIX system with no current users other than yourself, you can try an endless variety of commands and sample situations in learning to add and modify user accounts. If one or more of your experiments go wrong, you can start over again by deleting the accounts and, as a last resort, by reinstalling XENIX. If you are a new administrator on an established XENIX system, you may want to create a few "dummy" accounts on which to try out modifications.*

To add a new user to the system, you begin by typing the command:

```
mkuser
```

Recall, from the beginning of this chapter, that you must be logged into XENIX as the superuser, rather than being in system maintenance mode when you do this. If XENIX responds to the command by terminating the procedure and telling you that one or more file systems must be mounted before it can proceed, you're probably in system maintenance mode. If this happens, press Ctrl-D, then log into the system as the superuser.

After you enter the *mkuser* command, XENIX will respond:

```
# mkuser
                            Newuser

                    Add a user to the system


Do you require detailed instructions? (y|n|q): _
```

Press *y* and then Enter to continue (the *q* prompt allows you to quit, if necessary). You'll see the following instructions:

305

```
        -------- Add a new user to this system -------

This program will guide you through the steps required to add a new XENIX
user to the system.  It will ask for the following information.  If you
don't know any of these items, press DELETE and come back later.

        login name,  comment,  group,  shell,  password

Generally the program will tell you what it wants (such as the login name),
describe the acceptable responses, and prompt you for an answer.

Nothing is updated on the system until you confirm that everything is
correct.  You will be asked to do this after you have entered all the
information.

At any time until then, you can press DELETE to exit without adding the
user.  In addition, some questions accept a 'q' response to quit this
program.

Press RETURN to start:  _
```

ASSIGNING THE LOGIN NAME

As you can see from the instructions, there are few surprises in the account-creation routine. Press the Enter key to begin:

```
Please give the new user's login name. This must be at
least 3 characters long, begin with a lower case letter,
and contain only lower case letters and digits. It must
also not already exist in this system

Enter new user's login name:  _
```

(If you had not requested instructions, XENIX would not display the descriptive text that you see accompanying each prompt. The routine, however, is otherwise the same.)

Assigning the login name is simple, and you should try to keep the name itself simple, too, as it also becomes the name of the user's home directory. The login name can consist of any combination of lowercase letters and numbers and can be from three to eight characters long. Typically, system administrators use some form of the person's own name. For example, a user named Susan Gray might have a login name of *susang* or *susangr*. In general, you should try to use elements of both the user's first and last names. Login names formed from only the person's first name or from a word that might be a first name can cause problems when you attempt to install another user account for someone else with the same first name. Throughout this book we've used user names comprised of a first name and a last initial. You'll find this adequate most of the time. Some administrators create task- or department-oriented login names, too. An example would be a login name like *finance*, which could be used by one or more people working in the Finance department. (This is not the same as assigning a user to a group, as will be discussed next—to XENIX, the login name *finance* is still as individual as the login name *susang*.)

ASSIGNING THE GROUP

Once you've entered the new user's login name, XENIX will prompt:

```
Enter new user's login name:  susang

Users are usually assigned to the default user group.
This is group name "group", number 50. If you want to
assign the new user to some other group, you can either
specify an existing group, or a new group to be created.

Do you want to use the default group? <y|n|q>: _
```

Assigning a user to a group is just as straightforward as creating his or her login name. A XENIX group is simply a group of people who have some aspect of work in common. For example, all the people in the word-processing department might be in a group called *words*; all accountants could be in one called *accounts*.

The primary reason for including someone in a specific group is to give that person access to files created by others in that group (and vice versa). This access can range from the ability to read, write, or execute files up to the ability to do all three on files shared by the group's members. (Read/write/execute access is discussed in Chapter 4; modifications to these privileges are controlled by the *chmod* command discussed in Chapter 9.)

If there are no specific-interest groups on your system, you can choose to place everyone in the same group, either accepting the XENIX default group, *group*, or specifying a different group name. As you can see from the instructions, the group name need not even exist when you specify it. Nor is the group assignment permanent. As you'll soon see, you can create the group name at a later time or you can change the group to which you've assigned a user.

ASSIGNING THE PASSWORD

Passwords are both the strongest and weakest link in your XENIX system security. You assign the new user's password when XENIX prompts:

```
Please give the initial password for this user.

For maximum security a minimum number of characters is required
Up to eight characters are significant.
You may use any characters except RETURN and LINE FEED.

Note that the password entry will NOT echo on the screen.
This is just to provide an extra degree of security.

Please enter at least 5 characters for the password
Enter  password: _
```

Passwords can be from five to eight characters in length (if they are longer than eight characters, XENIX recognizes only the first eight), and they can be any combination of characters other than Enter and Linefeed. Just as when you created the superuser password, you should make a user's password individual enough so it's not easily guessed by others, but not so complex that its owner must write it down to remember it.

Before assigning a password, it's advisable to talk to the user and decide on one that is mutually agreeable. If you take the task upon yourself, there's always the chance that you might decide on a password that ends up written down somewhere near the terminal—hardly the security for which password protection was originally intended.

Whatever approach you take, enter the password here. As with the superuser password, you'll be required to enter it twice (once for verification). XENIX will not display the word either time.

ASSIGNING THE WORKING SHELL

There are four possible shell choices:

```
Please specify the type of shell (command interpreter)
this user requires. You can type 1, 2, 3 or 4 as follows:

        1         Standard (Bourne) Shell.
        2         Visual Shell.
        3         C Shell.
        4         /usr/lib/uucp/uucico.

ENTER Shell type (1,2,3 or 4) and press ENTER: _
```

(The Bourne, C, and Visual shells are described in detail in Chapters 10 through 12, so we'll just mention them here.)

The Bourne shell is, perhaps, the most frequently assigned. It closely resembles the one from which you are currently operating, although you are given a different environment when you are in system maintenance mode or logged in as the superuser. To use the Bourne shell comfortably, a user should have an adequate grasp of XENIX commands or a reference guide such as the one in Appendix A.

The C shell was originally designed for C programmers but is well suited to anyone who is reasonably proficient with XENIX. In the C shell, users have a wide range of opportunities to customize their working environment.

The Visual shell is ideal for new or transient XENIX users. The structured arrangement of information and command menus provided by the Visual shell enables such users to work efficiently within the XENIX environment while becoming more familiar with the system.

The fourth shell-assignment option is to create a remote *uucp* account. Don't do this unless you have previously installed a *uucp* communications system for using dial-in lines to transfer files and commands between XENIX computers. For more information on the installation and operation of such a system, see the section "File Transfer Using a uucp System" in the System Administration section of your XENIX documentation. (This is not the same as the micnet network software discussed in Chapter 16.)

As with the password, the decision about which shell you assign should be based on discussions with the user. Although users can change shells at any time, it's important to remember that first impressions are significant, and a new user's introduction to XENIX (or any operating system) will set the tone for the rest of that person's work with it.

FINISHING THE ACCOUNT INSTALLATION

For the last entry in creating a user account, XENIX prompts for a comment:

```
There is an optional field in the password file
where you can put a comment, such as the user's
full name, phone #, room #, etc. If you wish to
leave this blank, just type RETURN. The comment
should be short (up to 20 characters).


Please Enter Comment:   >--------------------
                        >_
```

This is an optional portion of the installation in which you can enter up to 20 characters' worth of information about the user. Whether or not you actually enter a comment, press the Enter key when you've finished. XENIX responds with a display like this:

```
User name is "susang", user id is 210.
Group name is "group", group number is 50.
Comment Field is: Susan G. ext. 8374
Shell is "/bin/sh"

Do you want to change anything? (y|n|q): _
```

The user name and I.D. number that you see will depend upon what you've assigned for the former and what XENIX generates for the latter. As for the other details in our example, we've selected the default group, added a comment listing the user's telephone extension, and assigned this user to the Bourne shell (*/bin/sh*). (The C shell would be indicated by */bin/csh,* the Visual shell by */bin/vsh,* and a *uucp* account by */usr/lib/uucp/uucico.*) For security reasons, the password is not shown on the screen.

If you have any changes to make, you can make them now by responding *y* to the prompt. Once you have finished, XENIX will create the user account and, as it does, display the following:

```
Password file updated
Group file updated
Home directory /usr/susang created
/usr/susang/.profile created
Test mail sent to user: susang
User susang added to this system

Do you want to add another user? (y|n|q): _
```

Note that XENIX tells you certain files have been modified or added to accommodate the new user account. The file containing the relevant passwords is one of them; another is the group file. Furthermore, a home directory and a *.profile* file have been created for the new user.

THE *.profile* FILE

Even though they may not be aware that such files exist, all Bourne shell users have a personal *.profile* file in their home directory. The dot (.) in front of the name keeps the file hidden whenever an *ls* command is used. (C-shell users have two files that form the equivalent of the *.profile* file — *.login* and *.cshrc,* which are discussed in Chapter 11. Visual shell and UUCP users have no personal startup files.)

309

Hidden files can be listed with the command *ls -a.* To see what type of information a *.profile* file contains, let's take a quick look inside the *.profile* file for the user whose account was created for our preceding examples. Enter the command:

cat /usr/susang/.profile

and XENIX reveals:

```
# cat /usr/susang/.profile
# Copyright Microsoft Corporation, 1983
# User $HOME/.profile - commands executed at login time
#
TERMCAP=/etc/termcap; export TERMCAP    # terminal database
tset -r                                 # do terminal initializations
PS1='$ '                                # set prompt
PATH=/bin:/usr/bin:$HOME/bin:.          # set command search path
MAIL=/usr/spool/mail/$LOGNAME           # mailbox location
umask 022                               # set file creation mask
export PATH MAIL
# _
```

The lines and line fragments that begin with the pound sign (#) are comment lines that XENIX does not evaluate. The remaining lines are instructions that contain startup information—mailbox locations, command search paths, and so on.

To see the difference between a Bourne shell user and a superuser, compare the preceding *.profile* file with the one for the superuser account:

```
# cat /.profile
:
# Copyright Microsoft Corporation, 1983
# /.profile - login commands for super user
#
PATH=/etc:/bin:/usr/bin
HOME=/
PS1="# "
MAIL=/usr/spool/mail/root
TERMCAP=/etc/termcap
TERM=`tset - -r`
HZ=50
export PATH HOME MAIL TERM TERMCAP HZ
stty echoe erase "^h" kill "^u"
umask 022
# _
```

The two files contain essentially the same variables, but with different values. For example, in the superuser's *.profile* file, the variable MAIL is set to */usr/spool/mail/root*. When XENIX directs *mail* messages to *root* (as it does occasionally to report on system details), those messages are placed in this file. In *susang*'s *.profile* file, however, the MAIL variable is set to */usr/spool/mail/$LOGNAME,* which corresponds to */usr/spool/mail/susang* when XENIX adds the value of the $LOGNAME variable. The prompt variable PS1 is another example: same variable, different value (the system "shell" for the superuser, but the Bourne shell for *susang*). Notice also that the superuser's *.profile* includes some setup commands not included in other users' *.profile* files. These commands are primarily for administrative purposes.

311

CHANGING THE *.profile* FILE

Since we're looking at the *.profile* file, let's use it to make some changes mentioned earlier.

■ NOTE: *The work described in the remainder of this chapter shows you how to modify several important files that supply information about the user accounts and about XENIX in general. If you want to try entering the commands we'll describe, use the* cp *command to create a backup copy of the file you intend to modify. For example:*

cp /usr/susang/.profile /usr/susang/.oldprofile

will create a duplicate .profile *file called* .oldprofile. *By creating this duplicate, if you do find that you've corrupted the file's information, you can restore the system parameters by changing the* .oldprofile *file back to its original name (while overwriting the current problematic* .profile*) with the* move *command:*

mv /usr/susang/.oldprofile /usr/susang/.profile

CHANGING THE TERMINAL TYPE

As mentioned earlier, you can modify the *.profile* file for people who consistently use the same type of terminal for calling in to XENIX through remote access. Let's assume you want to change this file for user *susang,* who accesses the system from a VT-100 terminal.

First, call the *.profile* file into *vi*:

vi /usr/susang/.profile

For our example the *vi* screen looked like this:

```
# Copyright Microsoft Corporation, 1983
# User $HOME/.profile - commands executed at login time
#
TERMCAP=/etc/termcap; export TERMCAP    # terminal database
tset -r                                  # do terminal initializations
PS1='$ '                                 # set prompt
PATH=/bin:/usr/bin:$HOME/bin:.           # set command search path
MAIL=/usr/spool/mail/$LOGNAME            # mailbox location
umask 022                                # set file creation mask
export PATH MAIL
~
~
~
~
~
~
~
~
~
~
~
~
"/usr/susang/.profile" 10 lines, 385 characters
```

You want to add the information for this user's terminal so that XENIX will modify the screen-control commands whenever *susang* logs into the system. To do this, press Enter twice to move down two lines, and press the letter *o* to enter insert mode on a fresh line. Type:

TERM = d1; export TERM

and press the Escape key to leave insert mode.

Recall that d1 is the code for a VT-100 terminal. The *TERM = d1* part of the command stores the terminal code in the XENIX variable TERM; the *export* command tells XENIX to accept the code as a valid terminal definition. Embedded in the *.profile* file, this command relieves the user from the necessity of typing the same terminal-definition line each time he or she logs in from a VT-100 terminal.

To write the modified file to disk and exit *vi,* enter:

:x

CHANGING A PASSWORD

As system administrator, you may find yourself called upon now and then to change a user's password. To make the change, log in as superuser and enter the command:

passwd [login name]

Essentially, this is the same command you used to create the root password. XENIX will take you through the same double-entry procedure that it did then.

REPLACING PASSWORDS PERIODICALLY

Ideally, XENIX users should change their passwords periodically to protect them from accidental discovery. If a password has been discovered by someone who is not authorized to use the account, it should be changed immediately to reduce the amount of time the account is accessible. As one feature of system security, you can have XENIX regularly remind users to change their passwords.

XENIX includes a file called */etc/default/passwd*. The contents of that file look like this:

```
# cat /etc/default/passwd
MINWEEKS=0
MAXWEEKS=999
PASSLENGTH=0
# _
```

This display shows three variables that affect how and when a user changes an account password:

■ MINWEEKS, the first variable, defines the minimum number of weeks a user must wait before a password can be changed. The default value is 0, which indicates that a password can be changed at any time, regardless of how recently it was last changed.

■ MAXWEEKS, the second variable, defines the maximum number of weeks, up to 63, that can have elapsed since a password was last changed. If the specified time limit is reached without the password's being changed, XENIX will prompt the user for a password change at the next login. Because password aging has not yet started, the default value for MAXWEEKS is 999, meaning "infinity." When password aging does start, MAXWEEKS will automatically be reset to 4 if it has a value of greater than 63 weeks.

■ PASSLENGTH, the third variable, indicates the minimum number of characters XENIX will accept in a new password. (That number is displayed on the screen when the user attempts to change a password.) Left at the default value of 0, the minimum length of a new password is XENIX' default length of five characters. If the new password is shorter than the minimum length, XENIX will reject it.

You can change the value of any of these three variables by modifying it with *vi* as we've done with other files in this chapter. You cannot set both MINWEEKS and MAXWEEKS to 0. In addition, the minimum must always be lower than the maximum, and both must be within the range of 0 to 63 weeks.

Once you've either set these variables or accepted XENIX' default values, they will affect how and when a user changes a password. However, XENIX will not consider or act upon */etc/default/passwd* for any user unless you tell it to do so with a XENIX utility program called *pwadmin* (short for password administration). This command has several possible options. For example, the form:

    pwadmin -a [user name]

activates the password *aging* routine for the user you've specified, using the variables in */etc/default/passwd*.

    pwadmin -n [user name]

deactivates the password aging feature. Then, again, if a password needs to be changed immediately (at the next login), you would use:

    pwadmin -f [user name]

to force the change the next time the user logs in.

Or there may be some account passwords you want to prohibit users from changing (perhaps if more than one user uses the same account). To use *pwadmin* in this way, type:

    pwadmin -c [user name]

In addition, some users, such as those in the Accounting department, may have higher security requirements than standard users and may need their passwords changed more often than the variables in */etc/default/passwd* provide for. You can accommodate the needs of these people without disturbing others who are governed by the existing values. The command format is:

    pwadmin -min [number] -max [number] [user name]

Finally, if you should forget the password-aging criteria you've applied to any account, you can check on them with the command:

    pwadmin -d [user name]

to display that information.

CREATING A GROUP

One of the steps in adding a user account caused XENIX to prompt you to assign that user to a group. XENIX suggests that you use the default, *group,* or specify another group name that either exists or that you intend to create. XENIX groups have three elements in common:

■ Each has a unique name, such as *group.*

■ Each has a unique group I.D. number, such as 50 for the default group, *group.*

■ The list of all groups, their I.D. numbers, and the persons assigned to them is in a XENIX file named */etc/group.*

Using the *cat* command to list the contents of the */etc/group* file, you'd see something like this:

```
# cat /etc/group
root:x:0:root
cron:x:1:cron
bin:x:3:bin
uucp:x:4:uucp
asg:x:6:asg
sysinfo:x:10:uucp
network:x:12:network
group::50:juddk,robertp,mikes,kates,susang
# _
```

315

Each line of the file consists of several fields of information separated by colons. The information found in the first seven lines of the file lists portions of the operating system (called system accounts) to which all of the users, including *root*, have access.

The last line in the file is the entry *group,* which contains the group I.D. number (50), and the login names of the users who are assigned to the group (the names are in the order that the users' accounts are installed on the system). Each user name is separated from the others by a comma.

To add a group name to this file, you simply load */etc/group* into *vi* as you've seen several times already. Then, you append a line of text with the required information, using the format:

[group name]:[comment]:[group I.D.]:[user 1],[user 2],...[user n]

The ellipses (...) are not part of the text you enter—they simply indicate that a variable number of items have not been shown here.

Suppose, for example, you wanted to add a group named *accounts,* which will include three users: *jimtu, barbda,* and *terrym.* After reading in the */etc/group* file, you would move to the bottom of the file, press *o* to open a new line, and then enter the line:

accounts:financial concerns:51:jimtu,barbda,terrym

You can choose any I.D. number you wish, as long as it has not already been assigned to an existing group. The group name and I.D. number are followed by the names of the users who are assigned to it.

After you've written the file back to disk, you can run a XENIX utility called *grpcheck,* which will scan */etc/group* and verify that each line has the correct number of fields and that each field has the appropriate information stored in it.

You can assign users to more than one group by including their user names in the appropriate group definitions. Whenever people belonging to more than one group log into the system, they will be placed in the group to which you assigned them when you created their accounts, but they will also be able to change their primary group identification to any one to which they have access, by using XENIX' *newgrp* command. To use the *newgrp* command, users simply type *newgrp* and the name of the group to which they are changing their primary group identification. For example, to change to the group *accounts,* a qualified user would type:

newgrp accounts

316

Using *newgrp* without an argument changes the primary group to the one specified in the */etc/passwd* file. As a system administrator, you should notify system users about their group options and the *newgrp* command available for their use.

CHANGING A USER'S LOGIN GROUP

Although it's easy enough to give users access to more than one group, there will also be times when you want to transplant a user from one group to another. For example, if a clerical employee transfers from the Accounting department to the Personnel department, you will want to change this person's login group from, say, *accounts* to *people.* To do so, you alter information in a file named */etc/passwd.* (This is not the same as the */etc/default/passwd* file you saw earlier.)

◼ NOTE: *If you attempt to modify this file, you'll notice that XENIX has removed the write access from the file and you'll have to restore it before you can make any changes. Take this precaution of XENIX' as a warning: While it's acceptable to make some modifications to this file, manipulating other parts can be disastrous. Be careful.*

To restore the write access, type:

chmod u+w /etc/passwd

When you're finished, remove write access from the file by typing:

chmod a−w /etc/passwd

If you display the contents of */etc/passwd,* you see information about the system accounts at the top of the file, and the information for each user in separate lines at the bottom (the following illustration shows the display for the five users on our sample system).

```
# cat /etc/passwd
root:w7gfx.o/lbn16:0:0:The Super User:/:/bin/sh
cron:NOLOGIN:1:1:Cron Daemon for periodic tasks:/:
bin:NOLOGIN:3:3:The owner of system files:/:
uucp::4:4:Account for uucp program:/usr/spool/uucppublic:/usr/lib/uucp/uucico
asg:NOLOGIN:6:6:The Owner of Assignable Devices:/:
sysinfo:NOLOGIN:10:10:Access to System Information:/:
network:NOLOGIN:12:12:Account for mail program:/usr/spool/lp:
juddk:j9/XUJGHp8euU:201:50:Judd "f(x)" Keim:/usr/juddk:/bin/sh
robertp:j93lqcXDGUNpy:202:50:Robert Perman:/usr/robertp:bin/csh
mikes:j9dm.AykhpeUY:203:51:Mike Steen:/usr/mikes:bin/sh
kates:Ue8JkKoji1S41,2.JB:204:51:Kate S. ext. 8125:/usr/kates:bin/sh
susang:j9.2/Rso4w5.6:205:50:Susan G. ext. 8374:/usr/susang:bin/sh
# _
```

Each line of user information consists of seven fields separated by colons. From left to right, these are: the user account name, the account password in encrypted format, the user I.D. number, the group I.D. number, the comment (if you added one when you created the account), the home directory name, and the shell to which that user is assigned.

To change the user's login group, just load the *etc/passwd* file into *vi* and substitute the new group I.D. for the one currently listed in the file.

◪ NOTE: *Do not attempt to make any changes to the system-account information. You can identify these accounts by their user I.D.'s, which are always less than 200.*

After you've changed a user's login group, you can save the file to disk, add the write protection, and then use a XENIX utility called *pwcheck* to verify the accuracy of the file (as you did for *etc/group*). This utility examines *etc/passwd* to determine whether each line contains the correct number of fields and the appropriate information is in each field.

On occasion, you may also wish to change the comment or shell-type fields in the *etc/passwd* file. Do this in the same way you changed the group I.D. Beyond this, you're best advised to leave the other fields alone. If at some time you need to change them, refer to the section titled "Preparing XENIX for Users" in the System Administration portion of your XENIX documentation.

REMOVING A USER

No system ever remains static, so at one time or another you will not only need to add new user accounts, you will need to remove old ones. To do so, log in as the superuser and type:

rmuser

You'll soon see the following:

```
# rmuser
                RMUSER - remove a user from the system.

This program allows you to remove users from the system.  It will ask
you for the username, and then delete the corresponding password file
entry, the user's mail box and home directory.  The following files,
if they exist in the user's home directory, will be removed:

      .cshrc            .logout         .newsrc        .profile
      .exrc             .mailrc         .plan          .project
      .login

Before removing a user you should check that the corresponding mail
box is empty, and that all the files owned by the user have either
been deleted or transfered to some other user. The program will check
this for you, and refuse to remove the user if the check fails.

Press ENTER when you are ready: _
```

The information XENIX provides is very clear: Before a user can be removed, all associated mail and files must be deleted. XENIX is reminding you that users have the right to keep or transfer their information. If you or the user have not checked and deleted all existing files, press the Delete key to exit *rmuser* and make accommodations for the appropriate files. If all the files have been checked and deleted, press Enter as *rmuser* suggests and enter the user name of the account you want to remove from the system. After you press *y* to confirm your request, *rmuser* will delete the account from the system and display a message regarding the departed user.

DISK MANAGEMENT In the preceding fourteen chapters we have taken a tour through many features that contribute to the power and functionality of XENIX. Now we come to the place where, in a sense, everything begins and ends: the disks and disk drives through which you gain access to XENIX and all your files. We'll cover the main points of managing your disks and drives effectively, and to do that we'll begin by looking at the way XENIX treats the drives, both hard and floppy, that you may have connected to your computer. This information will be especially valuable if you're moving to XENIX from MS-DOS. In terms of disks and disk drives, you'll find that there's a considerable amount of difference between the two operating systems.

TYPES OF DEVICES

XENIX "knows" about the types of devices it may encounter on your system because it comes to you with a built-in directory, called *dev,* that contains a number of files describing various types of devices. The devices themselves have been categorized for XENIX in several ways, the broadest being by type.

320

To see a list showing device types, log in as the superuser and, when your prompt appears, enter the following command (the resulting list will begin to scroll off your screen, but you can press Ctrl-S once to stop scrolling and once again to restart it). Type:

ls -l /dev

If you press Ctrl-S after the first 22 files scroll by, the response will look like this:

```
# ls -l /dev
total 0
crw-rw-rw-   3 bin      bin       0,   2 Jan 30 11:30 cga
crw-r--r--   1 sysinfo  sysinfo   8,   0 Jan 30 11:30 clock
crw-r--r--   1 sysinfo  sysinfo   7,   0 Jan 30 11:30 cmos
crw-rw-rw-   3 bin      bin       0,   2 Jan 30 11:30 color
crw-rw-rw-   3 bin      bin       0,   2 Jan 30 11:30 colour
crw--w--w-   1 root     root      0,   0 May 14 10:32 console
crw-rw-rw-   3 root     root      5,   0 May  9 09:39 cua0
crw-rw-rw-   3 root     root      5,   0 May  9 09:39 cul0
crw-rw-rw-   1 bin      bin       0,   4 Jan 30 11:30 ega
brw-rw-rw-   3 bin      bin       2,   7 May  4 21:55 fd0
br--r--r--   2 bin      bin       2,   3 May  5 09:46 fd048
br--r--r--   1 bin      bin       2,   2 Jan 30 11:30 fd048ds8
br--r--r--   2 bin      bin       2,   3 May  5 09:46 fd048ds9
br--r--r--   1 bin      bin       2,   0 Jan 30 11:30 fd048ss8
br--r--r--   1 bin      bin       2,   1 Jan 30 11:30 fd048ss9
brw-rw-rw-   3 bin      bin       2,   7 May  4 21:55 fd096
brw-rw-rw-   3 bin      bin       2,   7 May  4 21:55 fd096ds15
br--r--r--   2 bin      bin       2,  11 Jan 30 11:30 fd148
br--r--r--   1 bin      bin       2,  10 Jan 30 11:30 fd148ds8
br--r--r--   2 bin      bin       2,  11 Jan 30 11:30 fd148ds9
br--r--r--   1 bin      bin       2,   8 Jan 30 11:30 fd148ss8
br--r--r--   1 bin      bin       2,   9 Jan 30 11:30 fd148ss9
```

We'll cover the names you see in a short while. Right now, it's the file types that concern us, and you can see them indicated at the leftmost edge of the display.

The first ten characters of each line represent the file-permissions block, and the first of these ten characters represents the file type. Until now we've only seen two file types, directory files (denoted by a *d*) and ordinary files (denoted by a hyphen). As you can see, there are two new types of files in the *dev* directory: *c* and *b*.

As device file types, both *c* and *b* refer to physical devices, such as hard disks, floppy disks, printers, and terminals, that are attached to the system. Type *c* files refer to *character* devices, while type *b* files refer to *block* devices. Character devices are generally terminals, printers, or other such devices that are read from or written to, one character at a time. Block devices, on the other hand, are generally disk drives, in which data are read and written in chunks, or blocks. Typical block sizes are 512 or 1024 bytes (or characters).

UNDERSTANDING DEVICE FILES

Bearing in mind that devices can manage data either by character or by block, let's move on to another way XENIX differentiates one device from the other. This time, we'll concentrate on disk drives, and again start with a directory listing. Here, however, use the *lc* command to produce the listing in columnar format:

lc /dev

XENIX responds with:

```
# lc /dev
cga         fd048ss9      hd04      mem          rfd148ds9      rhd13
clock       fd096         hd0a      monochrome   rfd148ss8      rhd14
cmos        fd096ds15     hd0d      null         rfd148ss9      rhd1a
color       fd148         hd10      pga          rfd196         root
colour      fd148ds8      hd11      rfd0         rfd196ds15     rroot
console     fd148ds9      hd12      rfd048       rhd00          rswap
cua0        fd148ss8      hd13      rfd048ds8    rhd01          rusr
cul0        fd148ss9      hd14      rfd048ds9    rhd02          swap
ega         fd196         hd1a      rfd048ss8    rhd03          tty
fd0         fd196ds15     hd1d      rfd048ss9    rhd04          tty00
fd048       hd00          kmem      rfd096       rhd0a          tty01
fd048ds8    hd01          lp0       rfd096ds15   rhd10          usr
fd048ds9    hd02          lp1       rfd148       rhd11
fd048ss8    hd03          lp2       rfd148ds8    rhd12
#
```

Among the file names that appear on your screen, you can see that the majority begin with the letters *fd, rfd, hd,* or *rhd.* These are the names of the disk-drive files: *fd* and *rfd* refer to floppy disk drives; *hd* and *rhd* refer to hard disk drives.

HARD DISKS

In terms of your system's primary hard disk, there are three types of device files you should note: *hd, root,* and *usr.*

Hd refers to the whole of the hard disk installed on your system. If it is the primary hard disk, the third character in the file name is 0; if the hard disk is a secondary disk, the third character is 1. As with the floppy device files we'll discuss next, the *hd* files have been tailored to the requirements of the hard disk most

321

commonly associated with the computer you are using. The function of the fourth character in the file name varies from one version of XENIX to another. In IBM PC XENIX, it refers to the hard disk's partitions.

Note that the *hd* file names appear twice in the listing, once in the form *hdxx,* and once in the form *rhdxx.* The *r* prefixing the second group of hard-disk file names indicates that these files manage data on a character-by-character basis.

The *root* and *usr* files are device files that refer to the partitions of the hard disk that, when mounted at system boot time, become the root (/) and /*usr* directories. In most hard-disk operations, you should use *root* and *usr,* rather than *hd0,* to guide XENIX to the appropriate part of the disk surface. (These names are not, by the way, the same as the directory names *root* and *usr*; they are data files in the *dev* directory, and refer to the disk itself—not the data on it.)

FLOPPY DISK DRIVES

If you look at the *fd* and *rfd* file names, you can see that they, like the names for the hard disks, fall into four groups: *fd0, fd1, rfd0,* and *rfd1.* Here, the 0 indicates the boot floppy drive; the 1 indicates the secondary floppy drive, if one is attached to the system.

The remaining characters of these file names specify the format of the floppy diskette with which the drive is used. Again, you need not try to remember which file name refers to the floppy drive or drives on your system, but to help you feel more at home with these names, the following two tables show the diskette format (in tracks per inch) each refers to:

48	48-track drives
48ss8	48-track drives, single sided, 8 sectors per track
48ds8	48-track drives, double sided, 8 sectors per track
48ss9	48-track drives, single sided, 9 sectors per track
48ds9	48-track drives, double sided, 9 sectors per track
96	96-track drives
96ds15	96-track drives, double sided, 15 sectors per track

In chronological order of appearance, these are the IBM PC and the IBM PC-compatible computers and floppy drives for which these files were created:

48ss8	IBM PC with 170K drives
48ds8	IBM PC with double-sided, 340K drives
48ds9	IBM PC and PC XT with 360K drives, running MS-DOS 2.0 and above
96ds15	IBM PC AT series with 1.2-megabyte floppy drives

Finally, just as in the hard-disk file names, an *r* at the beginning indicates that the device file works on a character, rather than a block, basis. If, for example, you were to look at a long listing for *fd0* and *rfd0,* you would see:

```
# ls -l fd0 rfd0
brw-rw-rw-   3 bin      bin       2,  7 May  4 21:55 fd0
crw-rw-rw-   3 bin      bin       2,  7 May  5 09:45 rfd0
# _
```

Note that *fd0* is a block device file, whereas *rfd0* is a character device file. The reason for this difference is that some XENIX commands require use of the "raw" or character device name while others require the use of the "buffered" or block device name.

323

FORMATTING A DISKETTE

Even though XENIX and all your system's working files may be stored on the hard disk, you shouldn't place all your "eggs" in this single electronic "basket." Especially in a multiuser system, there's always the chance that valuable files may inadvertently be deleted or overwritten. Then, too, you cannot overlook the possibility of a system failure, sudden power loss…even accidental damage or destruction occurring to the hard disk itself. Among XENIX' many other features is a set of utilities that back up and restore files to and from floppy disks. These utilities, used regularly, can help you archive important data and thus safeguard the information on your system.

The first step in managing your files is to format blank diskettes. To do this, place an appropriate floppy diskette in your system's boot drive (for example, a high-capacity diskette for the IBM PC AT and compatibles, or a double-sided, 360K diskette for the PC XT and compatibles).

◼ NOTE: *High-capacity drives have the capability of* reading *diskettes formatted on the older systems, but they cannot, reliably,* write *information for drives of the lower densities. Formatting is the most critical write operation of all. (You can write data files to a diskette that has been formatted with a lower-capacity device file. But be warned: There's no guarantee that the operation will be successful 100 percent of the time. Reading from any of the lower-capacity diskettes should prove no problem so long as you use the correct device file name.)*

Enter the command:

format /dev/rfd0

(You must include the *dev* portion of the path name. If it is possible with your disk drive, you may specify a different device file in place of */dev/fd0.*)

To abort the format, press the Delete key. Depending on which device file you specified, the formatting itself may take from 30 seconds to about two minutes.

◼ NOTE: *It's possible for anyone to use this command and begin the formatting process at the console computer. If you do not want this to happen, change the executable permission for the format command so that it is usable only by the root. Type:*

```
chmod  u = rwx  /bin/format
```

You can do the same for any other XENIX commands found in the /bin directory and thus control and protect your operating environment.

324

The single, short format command you just typed is all you need to format a diskette, but bear in mind that there is a vast difference between the amount of data even a high-capacity diskette can hold and the amount that your hard disk can store. As you'll see, one of the programs you'll use automatically copies your files onto as many disks as are required. This program, *sysadmin,* prompts you to insert new, formatted diskettes as it needs them. If you do not have enough diskettes on hand, you'll have to stop, format some more, and then start all over again. To avoid delays, always have a supply of formatted disks handy.

Regardless of how you decide on the number of diskettes to format, you can use XENIX to help streamline the task.

PLANNING BACKUP STRATEGIES

As the system administrator, you are responsible for ensuring the integrity of your own XENIX system. It's important that you develop a backup strategy early. If it helps, keep notes about the growth of the file system during the first few weeks. If disk usage doesn't level off after everyone has had a chance to settle in, start checking each user directory to determine where the logjams will form and try, as well as you can, to anticipate problems.

There are two ways in which you can provide adequate file protection. One is to back up files on a system-wide basis, keeping copies of every file on the hard disk. The other is a file-specific method in which you use your own criteria, perhaps based on the needs of a special user account or activity, to determine which files should be backed up, and when.

Let's look at the system-wide backup method first, as it is the simpler of the two procedures.

CLEARING USERS FROM THE SYSTEM

It's best to do system-wide backups when there are no users on the system, so that you don't catch users in the middle of modifying their files. Before starting your backup, you can use the *who* command to determine whether any users are logged in. Then you can send a message with the *wall* command, requesting them to log out for the time you plan to be using the system for backups.

The *wall* command is a variation on the *write* command (but available only to superusers). It has no parameters. When you use *wall,* XENIX saves everything you type, including carriage returns, until you press Ctrl-D. Then it sends the message to all users on the system. To exit *wall,* you press the Delete key.

Once you've informed all users that the system needs to be cleared, you can program a timed shutdown of the entire XENIX system from the console with the command:

shutdown

XENIX will respond with the question:

```
Minutes till shutdown? (0-15):  _
```

If 10 minutes is sufficient, you can enter that number in response, and all the users on the system will see the message:

```
$ Broadcast Message from root
XENIX Shutdown in 10 minutes.
Clean up and log off.
_
```

In a few moments, information about any users still on the system will be displayed on the console. You can send a message to each user telling him or her how much time is left by pressing the Delete key, but you won't be able to stop the shutdown process or do anything else from the XENIX console until the system has halted. *Shutdown* needs to run in the foreground on the console itself. Starting at the five-minute mark, however, XENIX will broadcast *Clean up and log off* messages until the system has halted.

When you log back in, enter maintenance mode so no other users can access the system while you're doing backups.

USING *sysadmin*

The preliminaries over, you can begin your system-wide backup by typing the command:

sysadmin

A menu will appear on the screen:

```
# sysadmin
                 File System Maintenance
                 -----------------------

         Type    1  to do daily backup (root file system)
                 2  to do daily backup (usr  file system)
                 3  to do a periodic backup (root file system)
                 4  to do a periodic backup (usr  file system)
                 5  to get a backup listing
                 6  to restore file(s)
                 q  to quit



Enter Number: _
```

Notice that *sysadmin* treats the *usr* and *root* areas on your hard disk individually. Although your choice of options will depend on your activities on the system, you'll probably find that most of your backup work is done to the *usr* area.

CHOOSING BETWEEN PERIODIC AND DAILY BACKUPS

Although the *sysadmin* menu asks you to choose either a daily or a periodic backup from either of the two disk areas, the first time that you use the program, *sysadmin* will perform a periodic backup no matter what you select.

For subsequent backups, however, there is a difference. If you choose a periodic backup, *sysadmin* will back up all files in the selected area, no matter when or how they were last backed up. If you choose a daily backup, *sysadmin* will back up only the files that were created or modified since the last periodic backup. (*Sysadmin* can tell which files have been created or changed because it keeps its own record of periodic backups. It records the date of backup and the name of the file system involved in a data file called *etc/ddate*.)

PERIODIC BACKUPS

Let's assume this is either your first backup or a subsequent periodic backup of the *usr* file system. (The technique would be the same if you performed a periodic backup of the *root* file system.) Select option 4 from the *sysadmin* menu, and the program responds with the display:

```
PERIODIC BACKUP - /dev/usr filesystem
Insert first disk in drive zero, then press ENTER: _
```

If, for some reason, you find that you are not ready to continue, press the Delete key to terminate the program. Otherwise, insert a blank, formatted diskette in the boot drive and press the Enter key.

Soon you'll see a display like this one:

```
    date = Wed May 21 02:59:16 1986
backup date = the epoch
backing up /dev/usr to /dev/rfd096ds15
I
II
estimated 5240K on 5 volumes(s)
III
IV
```

The actual date you'll see in your listing will be the current date as your system knows it. This is the date that *sysadmin* will record in */etc/ddate* when the backup is complete. For your first backup and all periodic backups, the *backup date* will be shown as it is here: *the epoch,* meaning "the beginning." On daily backups, this date will be the date extracted from */etc/ddate*.

The next line of the report indicates the source and the destination for the backup. Farther down, you see the amount of data to be backed up (in kilobytes) and the number of diskettes (volumes) you'll need in order to complete the operation successfully. The Roman numerals are the screen result of checks being made to the source file system. Barring any error messages, they can be ignored.

During the backup procedure itself, *sysadmin* will prompt you to insert new disks as they are needed. When you remove the diskettes, number them sequentially, starting with 1 for the first. This numbering is important, because the XENIX *restore* and *backup* options refer to the diskettes by number.

When the backup is complete, you'll see the message:

```
level 0 backup on Wed May 21 02:59:16 1986
DONE
5542K on 5 volume(s)
# _
```

and you'll be returned to the shell prompt.

(*Sysadmin* is actually a built-in XENIX shell script that accesses a program called *backup,* which performs your actual backup. As with many programs, *backup* includes several options that focus its operation, some of which ensure that the appropriate device is used as the destination. One of *sysadmin*'s contributions to the process is supplying the options that specify the particular floppy disk drive in your system.

Another *backup* option specifies the level of the operation relative to the date in */etc/ddate.* This level is a number between 0 and 9. A periodic backup uses the 0 option, indicating that it should proceed from the epoch. Daily backups are level 9.

If you wish to use *backup* directly, refer to the XENIX Commands Reference portion of your documentation for instructions.

328

CREATING A LIST OF BACKUP FILES

Even though information has been transferred to backup disks, you, yourself, cannot physically read that information. You cannot tell, by looking, which files have been backed up, so part of your system procedure should include generating a list of the names of the files you've copied. You can do that with option 5 of the *sysadmin* program.

After you choose option 5, *sysadmin* prompts you to insert the first disk from the backup series you created. On this disk is a list of all the files you copied. *Sysadmin* reads the contents of the disk and, when the names of all the copied files have been read, writes the list to a file called */tmp/backup.list,* which it maintains on the hard disk. (If, during the backup procedure, *sysadmin* wrote the list of files on more than one disk, it will prompt you to insert the additional disk or disks, as they are needed.)

Once *sysadmin* writes the list (or related error messages) to */tmp/backup.list,* you can use *vi* or the *more* command to view the file, or you can send the file to the printer so you will produce a hard copy. The latter course is preferable, because */tmp/backup.list* is the default file name *sysadmin* uses each time you produce a backup list. Thus, each time the list is generated, the new version overwrites any prior version, and the old list is lost to you. In addition, all files in the */tmp* directory are deleted each time the system is rebooted.

Alternatively, since you are placed back into the shell when the *sysadmin* command has ended, you can save the list permanently on disk by employing the *mv* command to change its name from */tmp/backup.list* to a unique name that describes its contents. For example, if your list includes the files resulting from a monthly *usr* backup performed in September 1986, you might call the list *mo9-86.* Like a hardcopy printout, this disk file will provide a handy reference list that shows what files you backed up on a particular series of diskettes.

When you choose *sysadmin*'s option 5, the program accesses another program, named *dumpdir,* which actually performs the task. When *dumpdir* extracts the list, it records each file's name and inode number. It does not include a reference to the actual disk which contains a specific file, but if and when you need to know the disk on which a file is located, the procedure is simple, if somewhat roundabout, as you'll see shortly.

RESTORING FILES

The whole point in backing up files is to be able to restore them if information on your system's hard disk is lost. To do this, you once again use *sysadmin,* this time selecting option 6, *to restore file(s).* When you choose this option, you see:

```
RESTORE FILE(S)

Type full pathname of file/directory to restore
or press ENTER if there are no more: _
```

Actually, *sysadmin*'s prompt to *Type full pathname of file/directory to restore* is somewhat ambiguous. The reference here is to the full destination path name— not, as you might at first think, to the name of the file as it currently appears in your */tmp/backup.list* file. For example, suppose you had backed up all of the user files on the system, then found you needed to restore those for a user named *kates.* The files would be listed in */tmp/backup.list* as *kates,* but to restore the files to their rightful directory you would need to enter the full path name:

/usr/kates

To restore the single file *budget,* belonging to *kates,* you would enter:

/usr/kates/budget

Note that a slash is the first character in the path names in the preceding examples. You cannot omit that opening slash when you enter the destination path name. If you do, *sysadmin* assumes you want to restore the files to the root directory. Thus, the path name:

usr/kates/budget

would cause *sysadmin* to attempt to restore a file named *usr/kates/budget* to the *root* directory. The attempt would fail, however, because *sysadmin* would not be able to locate that file name—the file would be listed on the backup diskettes as *kates/budget.* On the other hand, if you were to use the path name:

kates/budget

because that is the way the file is listed in */tmp/backup.list, sysadmin* would restore that file to the root directory, not the */usr/kates* directory.

Once you've entered the complete path name, the next message you see is:

```
Restoring file(s) to /usr

Insert first disk in drive zero, then press ENTER:
```

Insert the first diskette of the backup series and press Enter. *Sysadmin* now invokes a program called *restore,* which handles the actual restoration.

As mentioned earlier, the first diskette will be scanned to determine if the file you've specified exists on any diskette in the series. If the name is found, you'll see something like this:

330

```
kates/budget:   inode 523
Mount desired dump volume:   Specify volume #:
```

(The inode number, which XENIX uses to keep track of files, will be the one it assigned specifically to your file. Thus, the actual response you see will depend on the file name you supplied and the inode number it was assigned.)

The *dump volume* in the second line of this display refers to the backup diskette containing the file you specified. Recall, however, that */tmp/backup.list* tells you the names, but not the locations, of the files that were backed up. Now, you need to find the specific disk in the backup series that contains the actual file. As we mentioned, there is a method.

For a small number of diskettes (let's say six or less), start with the first diskette in the series. Since it is the disk from which the file name is read, it should already be in the drive, so enter 1 as the volume number. The *restore* program will search the diskette and, if it doesn't find the file, it will find information that tells it the file is further on in the series of diskettes. You'll see the prompt:

```
Mount volume 2:
```

Place diskette number 2 in the drive, press Enter, and the search will continue, with *restore* prompting for each diskette in sequence until it finds the file that you named. When this happens, you will see the message:

```
Extract file kates/budget
```

After the file has been copied to the hard disk, you will be returned to the shell.

This search method is not especially time-consuming with a small number of diskettes, but as the number increases, so does your search time. Once you verify, through the contents of */tmp/backup.list,* that the file you're trying to restore does exist in the series of diskettes you intend to search, you can shorten the time it takes to find the correct diskette by starting the search with a diskette near the end of the series, rather than right at the beginning. For example, if there are 20 backup diskettes, you might insert diskette number 17 and enter that number as the first volume to search.

This way, if *restore* happens to find the file on that diskette, you will see the extract message and the program will end. If *restore* discovers that the file is on a later diskette, you'll be prompted to mount the next volume in the series, and the program will continue to request new volumes sequentially until it finds the file.

If, on the other hand, the file is not on that diskette and *restore* finds no indication that the file exists later in the series, you'll see a repetition of the prompt:

```
Mount desired dump volume:  Specify volume #:
```

Moving backward through the series of diskettes, this time insert number 13 and enter 13 as the volume number. If you keep repeating this procedure until the file is found, *restore* will not have to search forward through more than four diskettes from the point at which you insert either the diskette that contains the file or one that precedes the diskette on which the file can actually be found.

CREATING A BACKUP SYSTEM

Once you've established a comfortable method for making backups, the next step is to fit the process into a systematic backup procedure. The system we will describe here is for system-wide periodic backups, in which you rotate three sets of diskettes for each file system. This description is based on two-week intervals between backups, but you should lengthen or shorten the period to suit your own system. (We'll cover daily backups of specific files shortly.)

You begin by making a periodic backup of both *usr* and *root.* This becomes your *archive copy.*

Two weeks later, at the beginning of week three, you make another periodic backup of both systems on another set of diskettes. This will be your *backup copy.*

At the beginning of the fifth week, again with a new set of diskettes, you back up both systems for the third time. This becomes your *working copy,* from which you can restore any needed files.

Now, at the beginning of the seventh week, you rotate back to your archive copy and back up both file systems on that set of diskettes. (You need not reformat them, as the program will overwrite existing information.) This new backup now becomes your working copy, and each of the others moves back one class.

Actually, under more stringent backup systems, the archive copy is stored away and a new set of diskettes is used to make the new working copy. Depending on your system and the value of the work being done on it, you may find this approach preferable.

331

Whether you decide to place your archive copies into storage or reuse them for the newest backup, the object of this system is to continue the rotation, so that every two weeks you create a new backup, with the remaining two dropping back to fill the gaps. This way, even if the worst were to happen and both your working and backup copies were destroyed, you would still have your archive copy to fall back on with, at most, no more than about a month's work lost.

DAILY BACKUPS

You can reduce the potential loss of information still further by performing daily backups to fill the gap between periodic backups.

Again using a rotation system, create a daily backup at the end of each day. Use new diskettes for each day of the first two weeks. Then, on the first day of the third week, reuse the diskettes from the first day of the first week and continue cycling through them for each two-week period.

DETERMINING YOUR OWN SCHEDULE

As mentioned earlier, the time periods in these backup schedules should be adjusted to match the activity on your system. A schedule of periodic backups every two weeks, supplemented by a daily backup procedure, is designed primarily for a system that is heavily used. For a lightly used system on which critical work is limited to a few areas, such as accounting, you may be able to schedule periodic backups every third or fourth week (still certainly not less often than once a month). You may also be able to drop daily backups to every second or third day. Your schedule will really depend on your feel for the system.

If you decide that your backups need not be as closely spaced as those we've described here, try to err on the side of caution in working out your own schedule. If you start out on the lenient side, you may find you have nothing to fall back on. It's better to begin strong and use the daily backups as a gauge. If you find that you back up only a small amount of data each day, start to stretch time between backups, but try not to go beyond three days. At that point, you probably stand to lose more than you gain in terms of time saved versus work lost.

USING THE *tar* COMMAND

Even if you extend the time between backups, there are always special cases to consider. For example, if your accounting system is online, its files may need daily backup even though no other work does. To handle such a situation, you can use XENIX' *tar* (tape archiver) utility.

INCLUDING *tar* OPTIONS

⊠ NOTE: *Before we discuss the* tar *command itself, note that all of the file-name specifications you will see represent the superuser's point of reference. If you allow system users to access* tar, *be sure to instruct them to adjust their path name usage accordingly.*

Tar was originally designed to work with tape storage, but several of its options are used to make diskette activity easier. We'll discuss these here; for a complete list of *tar* options, you can refer to the XENIX Commands Reference portion of your documentation.

The general format of the *tar* command line is:

tar [primary option][secondary option(s)] [secondary option argument(s)] [path]

333

Note that, in contrast to most XENIX commands, the list of *tar* options is not preceded by a hyphen (-). This is because the hyphen has its own meaning in the *tar* command—it is used as a redirection symbol.

There are two types of *tar* options: primary, which tell *tar* what needs to be done, and secondary, which refine the command. The first (and possibly the only) option in a *tar* command must be a primary option.

The command line can include as many arguments as are required by the *tar* options you include. If including several options and arguments, be sure to enter the arguments in the same order you enter the options that make them necessary.

The *tar* options you need in using diskettes as archive devices are described in the following table:

Primary *tar* options

c   Creates a new file system on the archive device; any existing files are overwritten.

t   Displays a list of the files on the archive device; depending on the arguments specified, displays either all files or specified file names, if they are on that device.

u   Adds specified files to the archive device, if they are not already on the device, or if they've been modified since they were last written.

x   Extracts the named files from the archive device and writes them to the current working directory.

r   Writes the named files to the end of an archive; any existing files in the archive are preserved.

Secondary options

f   Uses the argument corresponding to its position in the list of options as the archive device. If used with a diskette, the *n* option must also be included, or *tar* will believe that the archive device is a tape.

k   Uses the argument corresponding to its position in the list of options as the size of the archive device in kilobytes (250K minimum). This option and its argument must be included if the archive device is a diskette and the total size of all files being transferred exceeds the capacity of the diskette. With this option, *tar* will prompt for new diskettes as required and continue the transfer. Without this option, *tar* will continue transferring files even when the diskette is full, behaving as if the capacity of the diskette were endless.

b   Specifies the blocking factor, a value originally intended for use with magnetic tape storage devices, but also required with diskettes when transferred files will require more than the storage capacity of a single diskette. The argument of *b* is specified in number of blocks (one block equals approximately $^1/_2$ K). The value of *b* should always be 20, unless you have an unusual requirement for a different blocking factor. If this option is not included, and files extend to more than one diskette, XENIX displays the message *Can't open device [device name],* and the backup operation stops, even though the *tar* command prompts for a new diskette.

n   Indicates that the archive device is not a tape device and, therefore, *tar* need not read sequentially through the files to arrive at those you've specified (it would do so if the files were stored on magnetic tape). Use of the *n* option speeds up the *t* option considerably. If it is included, this option must be accompanied by the *f* option. The *k* option can be added, but is not essential unless the size of the files being transferred exceeds the capacity of the archive diskette.

v   Places *tar* into verbose mode. The names of all transferred files are printed to the screen (normally, error messages only are displayed). If this is used with the *t* option, file names are displayed in verbose form, including the file size, modification date, permissions, and owner and group identifications, as well as the name.

e   Instructs *tar* not to split files across separate volumes. If only a portion of the file will fit on the diskette, *tar* will refrain from using the remaining space and begin the file on the next volume in the series. (You cannot use this option with a file that is larger than the capacity of a single diskette.)

COPYING FILES

Now that you've been introduced to some of the *tar* options, let's see how they might be used. We'll assume a user account called *Accounting.* In keeping with our previous discussion of daily backups for selected files, we'll also assume that *Accounting* contains the only information on your system that requires a daily backup procedure.

To back up the files in *Accounting* with *sysadmin,* you would also have to copy all other user files. With *tar* and a formatted diskette, however, your backup procedure becomes a matter of entering a command like this:

tar cvfkb /dev/rfd0 1200 20 /usr/Accounting

Here is a breakdown of options of the command options and their corresponding arguments:

■ The *tar* option list must begin with one (and only one) of the primary options. Here, we used *c* to have *tar* create a new file system on the archive device.

■ The *v* option places *tar* in verbose mode and prints the name of each file (and any additional information necessary) as it is copied.

335

■ The *f* option and its argument (*/dev/rfd0*) name the archive device—here, a diskette in the boot floppy drive. *Tar* will accept either *rfd0* or *fd0,* but using *rfd0* is usually faster.

■ The *k* option and its argument (*1200*) give the size of the archive device in kilobytes (1200). This is a standard high-density 1.2 MB drive.

■ The *b* option and its argument of 20 specify a blocking factor of 10K.

■ The path name, */usr/Accounting,* defines the source of the files to be transferred. When no more arguments are required by the options you listed, *tar* assumes that the next entry in the command line is the source path name.

Note the order of the *f, k,* and *b* options and the corresponding order of the arguments in our command line. The option list could as easily have been entered as:

cvkfb

But in that case, the order of the arguments */dev/rfd0* and *1200* would have had to be reversed.

COPYING FILES TO MORE THAN ONE DISKETTE

After the system has been running for awhile, it's quite possible that the cumulative size of the files in a directory you archive with the *tar* command will exceed the capacity of a single floppy diskette.

If *tar* comes to the end of the available space on a diskette, it will prompt you to insert the next diskette, and the operation will continue. Without the *b* option and its corresponding value, *tar* would try to access the new diskette and, failing, would display its error message and halt the operation. It's always a good idea to add this option with an argument of 20.

LISTING THE CONTENTS OF *tar* DISKETTES

You cannot use any of the normal directory-listing commands on either *tar* or *backup* diskettes but, as with any other backup diskettes, you should keep a list of the names of the files contained on your *tar* diskettes. The simplest way to generate such a list is with a command like this:

    tar tnf /dev/rfd0

which tells *tar* to display the names of the files on the archive device (*/dev/rfd0*) you've specified. If you modify that command line to read:

    tar tvnf /dev/rfd0

the effect is the same as producing a long listing with XENIX' *ls -l* command, so you see a list of all the copied files, with their permission levels and associated dates of creation or modification.

To save this listing, you can redirect the output of the *tar* command to a disk file—for example, *tar1*—or to the printer. To write the listing to a disk file named *tar1,* the command would be:

    tar tvnf /dev/rfd0 > tar1

RESTORING *tar* FILES

To transfer *tar* files back to the hard disk, you use the *x* option.

Tar restores files in one of two ways, depending on how you used it to save the files to floppy disk (or tape) in the first place. If you specified an absolute path name when you first used *tar,* as we did in the previous example, you can only restore the files to the same place they were copied from. To do this, simply type:

    tar xvfn /dev/rfd0

to extract the files from the archive and store them in their initial directory spot (*/usr/Accounting* in our example).

If you copied the files from the current directory with *tar,* and just specified the file or directory name rather than an absolute path name, you may use *tar* to restore the archived material to the directory you are currently in. For example, if you would like to restore material you archived in such a way to the */usr/mikeh* directory, first change directories to */usr/mikeh* by typing:

    cd /usr/mikeh

and then restore the archived files with *tar* by typing:

    tar xvfn /dev/rfd0

▇ NOTE: *The* n *option can speed matters by telling* tar *to use "random" rather than "sequential" access. Files in a* tar *archive are stored with a header that tells how big the file is. For example, assume that* tar *just read the header for a file, determined the file size was 1000 bytes, and understood that it was a file you did not want to extract from disk. This means* tar *should skip forward and look at the next file header, and continue in such a manner until it has found the file you want to restore to the hard disk. Because magnetic tapes are sequential-access devices, the only way the tape drive can skip ahead 1000 bytes is to read and count 1000 bytes of tape and then begin looking again at byte 1001. Modern disk drives, however, can read data stored on the disk simply by moving the read/write heads to the spot on the disk where the next header is located (the 1001st byte in our example). This is generally a lot faster than sequential access. If you don't tell* tar *you are using a disk drive by specifying the* n *option, it assumes you are using a tape and reads each byte instead of skipping ahead.*

337

MAINTAINING ADEQUATE OPERATING ROOM

While *tar* and *sysadmin* ensure the integrity of your system's files, you also need help in maintaining operating integrity of the system's hard disk itself. XENIX requires at least 15 percent of the disk area to be available at all times. When available disk space drops below 15 percent, the system's responses begin to slow. If no space is available, many commands won't function. No work can be done.

DETERMINING FREE DISK SPACE

It's important to impress on your users that a multiuser environment like XENIX relies on a cooperative effort. Every time you need to shut the system down to do housekeeping is also a time when other users are denied access. Users can limit those periods of forced inactivity by keeping their own directories clean. And that's as simple as removing unneeded files or relegating seldom used files to diskette. (As you'll see later, you can always give users access to diskettes when they need their files again.)

Several commands help you monitor system activity and the availability of disk space. One is the *df* (device free-space) command. Its syntax is:

df −[option] [device file]

and it reports the number of blocks that are free on the named device. (Since a block is 512 bytes, divide the reported number of blocks by 2 for a rough estimate of the available space in kilobytes.)

The command gives additional information if it is invoked with the *v* option. To use this option to take a closer look at the hard disk itself, type:

df -v

On our system, XENIX responded:

```
# df -v
Filesystem  Mounted on    blocks    used      free  %used
/           /dev/root     12000     8110      3890  68%
/usr        /dev/usr      41002     10224     30778 25%
# _
```

To check the free space remaining on a disk in the boot drive, type *df -v /dev/fd0* (note the use of *fd0* rather than *rfd0*).

If your report indicates the amount of free space is at or near the 15 percent level, you'll need to look at how your disk is being used, and for what purposes. The most obvious places to look are the mail spool file and the printer spool file, and the *dead.letter,* core, and *mbox* files in each user account. All can become collections of unneeded or canceled files. In addition, if you've created a Micnet network (as described in Chapter 16), don't forget to check the Micnet *LOG* files.

DETERMINING DIRECTORY USAGE

In ferreting out the files that clutter your system, you'll need assistance on the directory and data-file levels. The *du* (directory use) command can help here. Used by itself on the command line, *du* generates a list of directories and subdirectories in the current directory, along with the number of blocks each occupies (linked files are only reported once). The *du* command also includes several options:

s   Displays only the total number of blocks being used in the specified directory.

a   Displays information for all files, as well as all directories.

r   Displays error messages if it encounters files or directories that cannot be read.

u   Ignores files with more than one link. Normally files with more than one link are reported once. With this option they are not reported at all.

f   Reports only on the current directory entries.

When you use the *du* command, look for large block counts. Data or directory files that occupy a large amount of space are among the first places you should look for unneeded files.

338

FINDING UNUSED FILES

Faced with a long list of files and directories belonging to other users, you may feel you have no basis for determining which are needed and which are not. In actuality, that's true; only a file's owner can ever tell you whether it can be removed. But on a system-wide basis, one criterion you can use to narrow the selection is file aging—how long a file has remained in storage without being used.

You can put XENIX' *find* utility, with the *atime* (access time) option, to work here. The command line:

find /usr -atime +15 -print

will search the directory named */usr* for all files that have not been accessed in more than 15 days. It's reasonable to assume that a file not accessed for that length of time is no longer active. (Even so, of course, file aging remains a criterion, not a cause, for removal. You must still consult a file's owner before removing it.)

When you include the *print* parameter, *find* displays the results on your screen. (Without *print*, it doesn't record the results anywhere.) If you wish to send the results to a file, perhaps one called *oldfiles*, you can append an instruction that includes output redirection:

find /usr -atime +15 -print > oldfiles

(Note that you leave the *print* option intact.)

REMOVING OLD FILES

Once you've determined which non-system files haven't been used for a certain length of time, you can mail the owners and ask them to remove the files or notify you of those (within reason) they wish to keep. An easier approach, however, is to create a message that each user will see when he or she logs in.

MODIFYING THE DAILY MESSAGE

When you first installed XENIX, you were probably greeted with a line that read something like *The IBM Personal Computer XENIX*. This message is stored in a text file called */etc/motd* (message of the day). Since it is a text file, you can use *vi* to load a copy and add your own message. You might, for example, add something like this about a week before your scheduled cleanup date:

All files not accessed since 8/15/86
will be removed on 9/15/86. Please mail root
if there are any exceptions.

When your message is complete, just write the file back to disk and quit *vi*. From that point on, until you change the message, all users who log into the system will see your note each time they log in.

SAVING DELETED FILES

Of course, people are charmingly fallible and prone to temporary, if sometimes frustrating, lapses of memory or intent. So, even though you may want to sweep the house clean, don't just delete files from user accounts. First *tar* them over to a diskette and hold them for a few days—just in case. Even if you have received approval from the users, follow this procedure whenever you delete files other than your own. (In emergencies, bear in mind that, even if you've disposed of the temporary copies you made, additional copies of the files should still reside for about a month on your archive diskettes.)

ALTERNATIVE FILE SYSTEMS

There's a possibility that your file system can benefit from having some users work from diskettes, rather than from the hard disk.

Providing diskette access is very effective if you have someone who is on the system infrequently. In fact, you can provide a whole series of users with one user account and a staggered login schedule, while having them use no more than the minimum disk space necessary for that account.

In addition, if someone on the system is engaged in very private or sensitive work, the safest way to protect a file is to make it totally unavailable to other users by keeping it on diskette, waiting there until the user who owns the file is ready to work with it.

CREATING A FILE SYSTEM

In setting up diskette access for users, you begin with a formatted floppy diskette, but you also need to create a file system on that diskette. *Backup* and *tar* procedures do not require this step, because the commands manage files in their own way (that's the reason normal *ls* and *cp* commands won't work with *backup* and *tar* diskettes).

To create a file system, you need four pieces of information about the diskette: the device file that controls it, its block size, its gap, and its block number. The device file is one you've already used: */dev/fd0*. The other values, on IBM and compatible machines, are:

Equipment	Block Size	Gap	Block number
PC AT and compatibles	1200	3	30
PC XT and compatibles	360	3	18

Thus, for example, if you're working from an IBM PC AT, place a formatted diskette in the boot drive and enter the command:

mkfs /dev/fd0 1200 3 30

Mkfs, the make file-system command, examines the diskette. If the diskette is not freshly formatted, *mkfs* may find a file system already on the diskette, and you'll see the message:

```
mkfs: /dev/fd0 contains data. Overwrite? (y/n): _
```

This message may or may not mean that the diskette contains data files. It could be that it contains a directory structure, a previously created file system, or some blank files, but no actual data. If you respond *y* to this question, however, any files that do exist on the diskette will be overwritten and thus become inaccessible to you. XENIX offers you a way to check the diskette later on, so if you're uncertain of the diskette's contents, it's best to answer *n* to the prompt, remove the diskette, and use a newly formatted one.

341

MOUNTING A DISKETTE

Once you've created a file system on a floppy diskette, your next step is to make XENIX aware of the diskette. At present, you cannot address the diskette by its device file name. For example, if you used the command:

ls /dev/fd0

XENIX would respond with a listing of the hard-disk directory named */dev/fd0,* not with information on the diskette in that disk drive.

To tell XENIX to use the diskette, you mount it, via software, in the system. The place you mount it is a directory. Once it has been mounted as a directory, you can make the diskette your working directory, create more directories on it, or run executable shell scripts from it. Whatever you can normally do within XENIX to a file and a file system can be done, through the "diskette directory," to the contents of the diskette itself.

It isn't essential to create a directory specifically for your diskette. If the directory name you specify happens to be an existing XENIX directory, the contents of the directory remain unchanged and, while the diskette is in use, inaccessible.

Mounting file systems this way, however, is not advisable. It's best to create an extra subdirectory in your home directory, giving it a descriptive name like *Floppy.* To mount the diskette onto that directory, you use the command format:

/etc/mount [device] [directory]

Thus, the command to mount the diskette to the *Floppy* directory for user *mikeh* would be:

/etc/mount /dev/fd0 /usr/mikeh/Floppy

(Note that you must use the leading slash with the directory name.) You may also use the directory */mnt,* which XENIX provides in the root directory for mounted file system use. However you do it, you must specify an existing directory when you use the *mount* command.

Once you mount the diskette, any work related to the *Floppy* directory will be performed with the diskette in */dev/fd0.* XENIX uses the directory name as a gateway to that device.

The *mount* command cannot be used with *tar, sysadmin,* or *backup* diskettes. The file structures are dissimilar. For example, you could pick any group of files in your *Floppy* directory and use the ordinary XENIX copy command *cp [filenames] Floppy,* then use either *lc Floppy* or *ls Floppy* to list the contents of the directory. The names of the files you just copied would appear. (Recall that, to list copied files, you would use either option 5 of the *sysadmin* command or the *tf* or *tvf* option of the *tar* command.)

UNMOUNTING A DISKETTE

The complement of mounting a diskette is, predictably enough, the *umount* command, which takes the form:

umount [device name]

Before a file system can be unmounted, all open files in the mount directory must be closed and all users must be out of the directory and any of its related files. To unmount the diskette in the preceding example, the command would be:

umount /dev/fd0

After unmounting, if you were to try the directory listing again when the shell prompt reappeared, you would no longer receive a listing of the file system on the floppy in the disk drive. However, unmounting a diskette does not cause any work and files to disappear. If you remount the diskette, you again have access to all the files contained on it.

Keeping XENIX' treatment of mounted diskettes in mind, you can evaluate your system and available disk space in terms of your users. If a user needs absolute privacy for one or more tasks, you can mount a diskette to take care of his or her needs—as long as that person understands that access to XENIX will be limited to the diskette alone at those times. Conversely, you can juggle a number of occasional XENIX users, providing access to them on a staggered schedule, and maintaining each person's work on a diskette. If you were to give each user two hours on the system per day, you could provide access to three additional people, each with a 1-megabyte file system area on a diskette you can mount at the appointed time— and all using only a few extra bytes of storage space on your hard disk.

342

In addition, to back up data for people working from diskettes, you need only copy the information to a temporary directory on the hard disk and then copy it back to a diskette. As long as such users' work never exceeds the capacity of one diskette, neither you nor they need be concerned about what means they use to access XENIX.

RECOVERING DISK ERRORS

Whether you're using the hard disk alone or in combination with diskettes, you may at some point be informed of a disk error. The error can result from something as simple as an improperly closed file, or from aging or corrupt media (neither diskettes nor hard disks last forever).

No matter what the cause, a disk error doesn't correct itself. And it can get worse if you leave it alone or try to ignore it. Hardware difficulties aside, if either you or your users are having difficulty reading or writing files, or if a diskette won't mount properly, run the XENIX *fsck* (file system check) utility. (It's roughly equivalent to MS-DOS' Chkdsk program.)

Since *fsck* checks on the file systems on the hard disk, the argument to the command can take any of several forms. For example, the correct *fsck* command for the diskette in the boot drive is:

fsck /dev/fd0

For the *usr* segment of the hard disk, it's:

fsck /dev/usr

And for the *root* file system of the hard disk, it's:

fsck /dev/root

Fsck requires that you unmount a file system (with the exception of */dev/root*) before you attempt to clean it. The easiest way to deal with this requirement is to do all file cleaning and checking from system maintenance mode, before any file systems have been mounted. Using the *-n* option, you may also run *fsck* "read only" on mounted file systems.

In all cases, as the program is running, you'll see this series of reports:

```
** Phase 1 - Check Blocks and Sizes
** Phase 2 - Check Pathnames
** Phase 3 - Check Connectivity
** Phase 4 - Check Reference Counts
** Phase 5 - Check Free List
```

If *fsck* encounters any problems, it will print appropriate messages to the screen and clean the system.

343

If *fsck* finds no problems, it will display a one-line report when it is finished. The report will show you the number of files in the system, the number of blocks used, and the number of free blocks remaining.

■ NOTE: *As mentioned before,* tar *and* sysadmin *use a different file format. Because of this,* fsck *will always report problems with diskettes generated by one of those utilities, and any corrections you tell it to make to* tar *and* sysadmin *diskettes will destroy the file structure on those diskettes.*

MICNET Micnet is networking software that is included with XENIX and is designed for connecting your XENIX system with other independent XENIX systems. Although the benefits of networking a system that is already open to multiple users may not be immediately apparent, Micnet actually expands the work you can do by bringing together the resources of other XENIX users and machines. For example, networking is a logical choice if users of independent computing systems need access to each other and to work stored on separate computers. They might, per-haps, need to transfer program or data files, access large databases, or communicate through an electronic mail system.

If the users of your XENIX system fit this category, you probably should con-sider a network solution. If you want to connect your system with other XENIX machines, use Micnet. The setup procedure is straightforward and, since Micnet is a part of XENIX, you begin with the assurance that the program will work with your operating system. Another alternative you may want or need to consider is Microsoft Networks, a comprehensive networking package that must be purchased separately, but which allows XENIX and MS-DOS users to communicate.

NETWORKS IN GENERAL

346

In a multiuser environment like XENIX, a single processor or computer ser-vices the terminals, printers, and other devices connected to the system. Of neces-sity, the number of people who can access that system simultaneously is limited, because the computer's time must be divided among the users. As more people make requests of the system at the same time, the computer's reaction to those requests slows down.

In a network, on the other hand, two or more computers are linked together. No single computer bears the burden of providing service to all users, although some networks are designed so that one computer in the system does do more work than the others.

NETWORK TOPOLOGIES

Any network exists in one of three basic configurations, or topologies. These topologies are known as star, bus, and ring networks, and describe the manner in which the elements of the network are physically connected. Individually, these topologies can be described as follows:

Star
One computer is used as the communication node of the network and the others are connected to it. All communications between net-work components pass through this central machine. The topology is called a star system because the other computers radiate out from the one at the center of the group.

Bus
The computers are connected in a line. There is a definite starting point and ending point to the network, but no computer is actually

defined as first or last—they're just physically at the ends of the network. Communications between network components are passed back and forth along the line, with each machine capturing those transmissions that are intended for it.

Ring   In a ring network, the computers are connected together in a circle. The machines communicate by passing information from computer to computer, around the circle. As with the other topologies, special internal rules govern the manner in which network communications occur. Micnet does not support a ring topology.

Your multiuser XENIX system, with terminals clustered around a central computer, most closely resembles the star topology. With Micnet, you can use either a star or a bus topology, or a mixture of the two. Your resulting XENIX network will consist of a series of starlike multiuser clusters strung together in a single network system, as you can see in Figure 16-1.

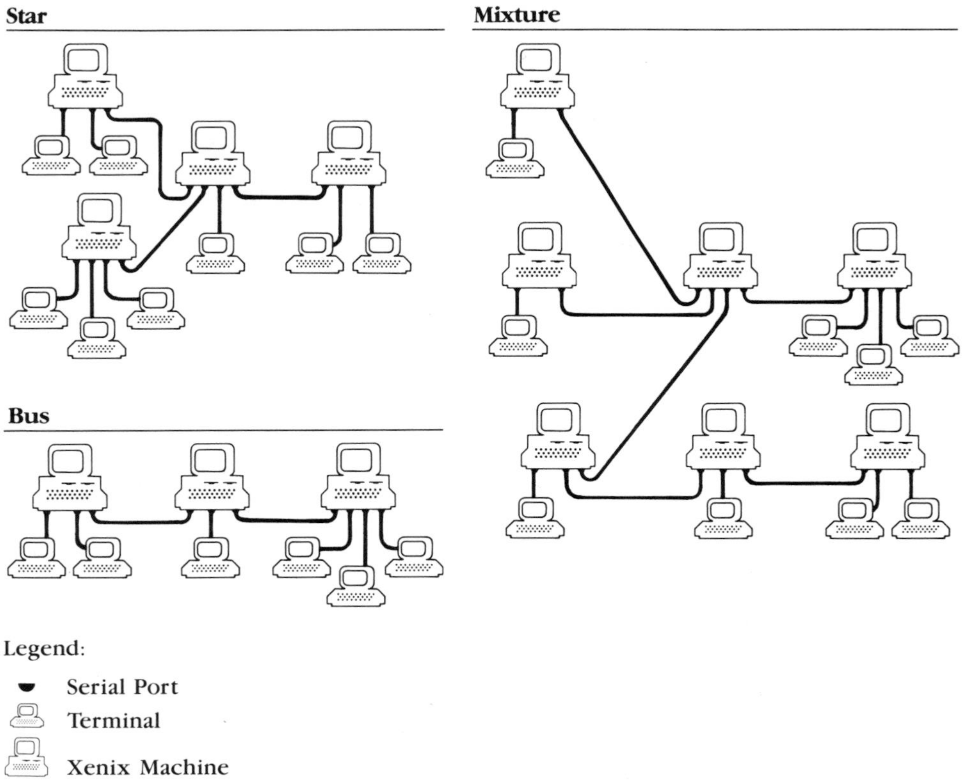

347

Star

Mixture

Bus

Legend:

- Serial Port
- Terminal
- Xenix Machine

Figure 16-1. Sample XENIX networks.

348

Before you go about networking XENIX computers, you should decide which network scheme best suits your needs. You may wish to create a starlike network in which some of the individual XENIX systems are connected to more than two other XENIX computers. This approach is fine, as long as you don't inadvertently create a ring within the network, but star systems are not always the most practical approach to networking.

The star topology provides fast communication between computers but, since all transmissions pass through the central computer, it also requires a considerable amount of this machine's processing time. In addition, the star configuration will require a serial port for each connected machine—sometimes a problem if ports on the central computer are in short supply.

A bus topology, on the other hand, requires no more than two serial ports per computer—one to connect the machine with the computer preceding it on the bus and the other to connect it with the computer next in line. The disadvantage of using a bus topology is that it is rather slow if transmissions must travel along the bus through many XENIX computers.

Given the advantages and disadvantages of each topology, it often happens that a combination of the two methods works best. Select your own Micnet topology by grouping the XENIX systems you think will communicate most heavily. Beyond that, a good rule of thumb to follow is to limit the number of attached XENIX systems to two, as the bus topology does. This approach will strike a good balance between the processing delays within Micnet and within each independent XENIX system.

CONNECTING THE SYSTEMS

To connect your XENIX systems, you need one available serial port on each of the systems at the "ends" of the network, and two or more (depending on the number of network connections) on each XENIX computer within the star or bus topology. You may need to install additional serial ports or reconfigure the system to accommodate both the network and your normal group of attached terminals and devices. As you do so, don't forget the IBM PC family's limit of seven serial lines.

In a bus topography, the connections are made from the first computer into the second, from the second into the third, from the third into the fourth, and so on down the line. No computer has more than one connection to the one before it. If it did, your network would become a ring system and Micnet would not function or, worse, might function erratically.

In a star topology, the connections are made from the central computer (there can be more than one) outward to the second, third, and so on. Aside from the central computer, no computer can have more than one connection to any other computers attached to the central computers. Again, such multiple connections would form a ring and interfere with operations within your Micnet network.

Once you decide on the topology that best suits your network, your next step is to determine the physical means by which you will join the computers. The simplest method is to hardwire them together, just as terminals are hardwired to the XENIX computer.

Hardwiring, of course, requires that you install connecting cables from one machine to the other, so before your cables are installed, you should check on regulations and required permits for installation. In some areas, cables that run through walls or ceilings must have Teflon jackets, rather than plastic or pvc casing. Likewise, cables may need to be installed by union labor or by maintenance personnel employed by the building in which your office is located. Also, if the cables are being installed by people unfamiliar with computers, networks, and data cables, you shouldn't overlook the importance of providing a competent supervisor to oversee the installation from start to finish.

349

BRIDGING THE DISTANCE BETWEEN COMPUTERS

In networking computers, just as in installing terminals, you must consider the distance the computer signals have to travel between devices. Computer signals are, simply, patterns of electrical signals representing the two binary digits, 0 and 1. A specific voltage (with a small plus or minus factor) is assigned to signify 1, and another is assigned to signify 0.

Under ideal conditions—if they encountered no resistance of any sort—the electrons in the signals transmitted through the computer cable would remain in motion and travel any distance between devices. In the real world, however, the signals encounter resistance from the cable itself. As a result, as the signals travel along the cable between two devices, the resistance in the wires begins to lower their strength. The farther the signals must travel, the lower their strength becomes until, finally exceeding the variance allowed, the signals become unrecognizable.

While there is some margin for error, and the quality of your cables will add to or detract from their overall effectiveness, the maximum distance typically recommended between devices that communicate serially over unenhanced cable is 100 feet. Beyond that, reliability becomes unpredictable.

However, XENIX networks can and do extend well beyond the 100-foot range, so solutions to the distance problem do exist. The following sections provide a list of possible alternatives. Evaluate them in terms of your needs, but contact your hardware supplier before making any final decision as to what means of connection you want to use.

SHIELDED CABLES

The Federal Communications Commission requires that, under certain conditions or with specified computer equipment, you must use shielded data cables. The shielding encases the wires in the cable and acts as a barrier that prevents the cable from "transmitting" interference—electrical noise. If shielding is mandatory for your computer to prevent it from generating such interference, the equipment's manufacturer is required to say so in the manual.

Aside from FCC regulations, however, shielded cables may actually be essential for cable runs greater than 15 to 20 feet. In fact, the longer the cable, the more important shielding becomes, because the data traveling between two computers may well be affected by other interference sources. As well as keeping noise in, shielded cables tend to prevent outside noise from entering your data line.

BOOSTING COMPUTER SIGNALS

Even though 100 feet is about the maximum distance a cable can carry serial data, this is not always a practical distance between XENIX computers. Over longer distances, you can safeguard your data transmissions by using signal enhancers or short-haul modems.

If the cable will run as far as 300 feet, you should consider installing signal enhancers (also known as line drivers) at 75-foot intervals in it. Signal enhancers are electronic devices, into one end of which you plug an incoming data cable. The driver analyzes the arriving signals, cleans them of any noise, and restores the original voltage levels. The signals are then sent out the other end, to which you have connected the next segment of the cable.

Effective as they are, signal enhancers have two disadvantages in situations that require exceptionally long cables. They require power, so you must have an electrical outlet handy for the power supply at every signal enhancer. In addition, signal enhancers are expensive. At current prices, three signal enhancers cost about as much as the next available alternative, short-haul modems.

Convenient for boosting signals over distances in excess of 300 feet or so, short-haul modems convert standard serial transmissions to a format that can be carried either by simple twisted-pair cabling or by existing telephone lines. To use these modems, you attach one at each end of the connection. During transmission, the short-haul modem attached to the sending computer translates the signals into a format known as current loop. These modified signals can travel up to two miles or so and, when received by the short-haul modem at the other end of the connection, can be retranslated to the format readable by the serial port on the receiving XENIX computer.

Within or between nearby office buildings, short-haul modems can enable you to use existing telephone lines to make the connection between XENIX computers. (You'll need the permission of the telephone company to make use of their lines and, probably, be asked to pay a fee.)

DETERMINING TRANSMISSION SPEED

Once your cables have been installed and the XENIX computers are connected, you can determine the speed at which they will communicate. Your first thought may be to set all devices for the highest possible communication speed, but that is not necessarily the best choice. High transmission speeds do enable devices to communicate quickly, but when interaction occurs between two computers, rather than between a computer and a terminal, high-speed communications place a great burden on the systems and may interfere with the computers' normal workloads.

Rather than begin at the top speed (typically 9600 baud) and work down, start intersystem communications at 1200 baud (the speed recommended in the XENIX manual). It's quite likely that 1200 baud will be perfectly acceptable. If not, or if you wish to experiment with higher speeds, work your way up to the maximum transmission rates your systems can handle and still accommodate the needs of their assigned users.

DRAWING A NETWORK MAP

One final detail you should include is a topological map of your Micnet, showing the systems you are connecting, where they are, and what you intend to call them. As with any other aspect of computer use, documenting the system is the safest way to ensure that potential questions or problems can be managed, whether or not you are available to take care of them.

DOCUMENTING THE NETWORK

Begin your network map by selecting names for the various computers that will be included. Like XENIX users and XENIX terminals, the computers in your network need identifying names. These will be used when you install the network software, and they will be needed for future reference, if any problems occur.

The clearest means of documenting your network is to draw an actual map of the system, labeling the various parts with their correct identifcations: machine names, names of the serial ports (tty00, tty01, and so on) used for the network, and the names of the computers to which those serial ports are connected. On the map and on the computers themselves, mark the serial ports that are used in the network, noting where they arrive from or go to. On paper, you should also specify the physical route taken by each cable used to connect the devices.

Finally, list the users in each XENIX system on the network, as well as any network aliases to which they are to be assigned. Micnet primarily uses the XENIX *mail* system to perform network communications, so it is important to create and list well-conceived aliases. Micnet will prompt for these during installation.

When you've created a complete map for all the computers in the network, you'll have a visible, interlocking documentation scheme that anyone can use to install, modify, or troubleshoot the system. Such a map is shown in Figure 16-2 (we'll use this for the sample installation).

352

Machine ID:	IBM PC AT	IBM PC AT	COMPAQ Deskpro 286	COMPAQ Portable 286
Serial no:	1460565553	1466416670	1529641P2812	1529033B1234
Machine name:	kirk	bones	scotty	spock
Users:	pata pamj deand rogers deant	finance robink jeffh chrisk barryp daver	admin humanres kenh lindaz	juddk robertp mikes
Standard aliases:				
optics:	deand	robink	kenh	
techgrp:		jeffh chrisk barryp daver		
supply:				juddk
Serial ports:	tty00 Micnet tty01 terminal tty02 terminal tty03 terminal	Micnet Micnet terminal terminal	Micnet Micnet terminal terminal	Micnet terminal
Network topology map:				

Figure 16-2. Sample Micnet topology map

INSTALLING THE NETWORK SOFTWARE

The preparations complete, you're now ready to install Micnet itself. If your network will include some computers with only low-density (360K) floppy drives and others with only high-density (1.2MB) floppy drives (a combination of IBM PC XTs and IBM PC ATs, for example), install Micnet on a machine with low-density drives. Even though you install the network on the hard disk, you will later need to copy the network files to a diskette and transfer them to the other machines in the network (we'll cover this later in the chapter). High-density drives can usually read low-density diskettes, but the converse is not true, so it is much better to begin the installation on a machine whose diskettes can be read by all computers in the network. Alternatively, install Micnet twice—once on a machine with low-density drives and once on a machine with high-density drives—and use separate sets of diskettes for each type of floppy drive.

To install Micnet, log in as the superuser and, from the pound sign (#) system prompt, type Micnet's network-utility installation command:

netutil

Press Enter, and a menu appears:

```
# netutil
Micnet network utility

        1       install new network configuration
        2       save the current network configuration to disk
        3       restore the network configuration from disk
        4       start the network
        5       stop the network

enter desired option number or name: _
```

If, at this point, you need to stop the installation, press the Delete key and you will be returned to the system prompt. To continue, choose option 1 and press Enter. You'll soon see:

```
Compiling new network topology

Enter the name of each machine (or press RETURN to continue installation)
  Machine name: _
```

(If a network configuration already exists on your hard disk, you'll also see a message saying *Overwrite existing network files? (yes/no)?* To install a new Micnet network, press *y* ; to stop the procedure, press *n.*)

ENTERING COMPUTER NAMES

Now, enter the names you've decided upon for each of the XENIX computers in the network. You can either type the names one at a time, pressing Enter after each (*netutil* will keep repeating the *Machine name:* prompt) or you can enter all the names on the same line by separating each with a space or a comma.

No matter which method you use, after you've entered all of the names for the computers in your network, press Enter in response to *Machine name:* to exit this entry procedure. *Netutil* will repeat the names you've entered—in alphabetic order, not the order in which you entered them—and ask if you want to make any changes:

354

```
Enter the name of each machine (or press RETURN to continue installation)
  Machine name: kirk bones scotty spock
  Machine name:

Machine names are:  bones  kirk  scotty  spock
Do you wish to make any changes? (yes/no)? _
```

If you respond *y*, you'll need to re-enter all of the names, not only the one(s) you want to change. Make the appropriate response and press Enter.

Once you have entered the machine names and indicated that no changes are necessary, the next message you see is:

```
For each machine, enter the names of machines to be connected with it
Machine bones:
  Connect to: _
```

It's now time to tell Micnet how the machines are connected to one another. If you refer to the drawing in Figure 16-2, you can see that the computers in our example are connected in this manner:

kirk	to	bones
bones	to	scotty
scotty	to	spock

The computers labeled *kirk* and *spock* are at the ends of the bus network we've mapped. The other two are in the middle. (In a star network or a mixture of star and bus topologies, the connections from the central computer to others on the network will differ—for example, *kirk to bones, kirk to scotty,* and *kirk to spock.*)

⊠ NOTE: *In our example,* kirk *is the name of the machine on which the network installation software is running. This will become obvious when the installation concludes. Also, note that* netutil *need not know the names you enter— you'll see how to give them to each machine later in the chapter.*

Right now, however, *netutil* has asked you to specify the machine to which *bones* is connected. According to our map, it's connected to two other computers, *kirk* and *scotty.* In our example, you would enter both these names, again typing them on the same line if you wished, separating them with a comma or a space.

When you've typed the appropriate names, press Enter again to tell *netutil* that you've entered all the XENIX computers that are attached to the machine whose name is currently displayed.

Continue to supply the machine names *netutil* prompts for, until all the connections are accounted for. As you work, you'll notice that *netutil* completes some of the information for you, because it keeps track of the connections you've already entered. When you're finished, you'll see some summary information like this:

355

```
Machine names are:  bones  kirk  scotty  spock
Do you wish to make any changes? (yes/no)? n

For each machine, enter the names of machines to be connected with it
Machine bones:
  Connect to: kirk scotty
  Connect to:
Machine kirk:   (already connected to: bones)
  Connect to:
Machine scotty:  (already connected to: bones)
  Connect to: spock

network connections completed.

Machine pairs are:
  bones          kirk
  bones          scotty
  scotty         spock
Do you wish to make any changes? (yes/no)? _
```

If you need to correct any of the connection names you entered, respond *y* when *netutil* prompts for changes. If all the connections are correct, respond *n* to the prompt and press Enter.

ASSIGNING SERIAL-PORT NAMES AND SPEEDS

Netutil's next prompts refine the connections you've established. Each prompt begins by specifying *For the [machine 1]* ⟨==⟩ *[machine 2] pair:* and requests the serial port on each and the speed of transmission. You can see the screen questions and replies for our example in the following illustration:

```
For each machine pair, enter the tty names and tty speeds
For the bones <==> kirk machine pair:
  Tty on bones: tty00
  Tty on kirk: tty00
  Speed: 1200
For the bones <==> scotty machine pair:
  Tty on bones: tty01
  Tty on scotty: tty00
  Speed: 1200
For the scotty <==> spock machine pair:
  Tty on scotty: tty01
  Tty on spock: tty00
  Speed: 1200

Machine pairs are:
  bones        tty00      kirk       tty00    1200
  bones        tty01      scotty     tty00    1200
  scotty       tty01      spock      tty00    1200
Do you wish to make any changes? (yes/no)? _
```

356

Your network topological map is an invaluable guide here. Using it, you can be certain you assign the correct serial ports without duplicating any of the *tty* assignments. (*Netutil* would warn you of a duplication, but knowing and assigning the ports correctly will still save time and possible frustration.)

Be careful not to assign ports that are currently attached to terminals, unless you plan to remove those terminals in order to accommodate the network. As you'll see later, *netutil* checks the */etc/ttys* file and deactivates any serial ports used in the network when you have completed installing the network parameters.

ADDING USERS TO THE NETWORK

Once you've defined the connections and communication speeds between the computers, *netutil* prompts for the users who will be accessing the network. Using your network map as a reference, enter user names for each machine, as shown in the following illustration. (It doesn't matter whether the users you list already have XENIX accounts. *Netutil* will accept the user names without attempting to verify that they are real. This can be helpful if you plan to add some user accounts but have not done so yet.)

```
For machine bones:
  Users on bones: finance robink jeffh chrisk barryp daver
  Users on bones:

Users on bones are:
  barryp  chrisk  daver  finance  jeffh  robink
Do you wish to make any changes? (yes/no)? n
For machine kirk:
  Users on kirk: pata pamj deand rogers deant
  Users on kirk:

Users on kirk are:
  deand  deant  pamj  pata  rogers
Do you wish to make any changes? (yes/no)? n
For machine scotty:
  Users on scotty: admin humanres kenh lindaz
  Users on scotty:

Users on scotty are:
  admin  humanres  kenh  lindaz
Do you wish to make any changes? (yes/no)? n
For machine spock:
  Users on spock: juddk robertp mikes
  Users on spock: _
```

Note that it isn't necessary to include *root* in your list. *Root* is a reserved name, and the network software assumes it is on each of the XENIX computers. Also, even though the prompt reads *Users on [machine name],* you should list only the network participants—not every user currently assigned to that particular machine. Remember, each of these computers is a XENIX system in its own right. The people who are not included as network users will still be able to log into their respective systems, but only within the local XENIX environment, rather than as network participants.

CREATING ALIASES

In the final installation phase, *netutil* asks if you wish to create any network aliases. As you saw in Chapter 8, an alias is, basically, a descriptive title you can create to refer to one or more XENIX system users. Using an alias, you can send a message to everyone on the alias list without having to type each user's name.

Within Micnet, you can create aliases that refer to users, network machines, a combination of the two...even aliases referring to other aliases. As you will see later, you can also create temporary aliases for network users. These are called forward aliases and cause mail sent to network users' home systems to be forwarded to the XENIX computer on which they are temporarily working.

Micnet itself includes two types of standard aliases: *all* refers to every user you've included from every XENIX computer in the network; additional aliases for each of the machine names that you've defined refer to the users you've included from any single XENIX computer in the network.

Although aliases are not essential to creating a smoothly functioning network, let's look briefly at the procedure you follow to create them.

To enter one or more aliases, repond *y* to *netutil*'s prompt asking if you wish to enter any. You'll see the following message on your display:

358

```
Do you wish to enter any aliases? (yes/no)? y

Each alias consists of two parts, the first is the alias name,
the second is a list of one or more of the following:
        valid user names
        previously defined aliases
        machine names

   Alias: _
```

The instructions are clear and self-explanatory, so you can simply enter the aliases you've outlined on your network map. As with *mail* aliases, be certain you begin all aliases with a letter, rather than a number or symbol. Otherwise, they can be any combination of eight letters or numbers. A network alias cannot be the same as an existing user name or alias but, as we mentioned, you can include previously defined aliases or machines in the alias list. For the aliases in our example, the prompts and responses look like this:

```
   Alias: optics
   Users/aliases: deand robink kenh
   Alias: techgrp
   Users/aliases: jeffh chrisk barryp daver
   Alias: supply
   Users/aliases: juddk
   Alias:

Aliases are:
   optics: deand, kenh, robink
   supply: juddk
   techgrp: barryp, chrisk, daver, jeffh
Do you wish to make any changes? (yes/no)? _
```

When Micnet displays *Do you wish to make any changes?*, respond *y* to make additions or corrections, *n* to complete the procedure.

ENDING THE INSTALLATION

Once you've responded to *netutil*'s request for any aliases, you'll see the following messages on your screen:

```
/usr/lib/mail/top updated
/usr/lib/mail/top.next updated
/usr/lib/mail/aliases updated
/usr/lib/mail/aliases.hash updated
This machine is named "IBM PC AT"
 It is NOT in the network machine list
 Enter this machine's name: _
```

Note that *netutil* has updated four XENIX *mail* files with the network information you entered and has prepared the communication system for network use.

In the fifth line of this display, *netutil* informs you that the name by which it identifies the machine you are currently using does not match the Micnet information you entered. Do not be concerned; as we mentioned earlier, neither the machine names nor the user names you entered need to have been defined before the installation procedure. Micnet is now simply telling you that it does not recognize the network name for the machine you are using. All you need do is enter the correct machine name from your network map (in our example, the machine name would be *kirk*).

■ NOTE: *If you are making modifications to the network on a machine that* netutil *recognizes, and the machine name has not changed, this prompt will not appear.*

After you have entered the machine name, two additional lines appear on your display:

```
/etc/systemid updated
Disabling tty lines: tty00
```

The first of these lines tells you that the machine name you entered has been written into XENIX' system identification file, */etc/systemid* (again, you will see this only if you changed the current machine's name).

The second line—in our example, not necessarily on your system—reports that serial port tty00 has been disabled. If you refer to the sample network map in Figure 16-2, you can see that serial port tty00 on *kirk* represents the machine's connection to the network. Serial ports used for the network are deactivated in terms of the local XENIX system, so when you see this type of report, it is an indication to move any non-network devices currently attached to the port.

It is also possible that you will receive other messages at this time. If so, read and respond to them now.

When you have taken care of these final details, your Micnet software installation is complete. You will now have one working node in the XENIX network, and your next task will be to notify the other machines on your network that they are now part of a larger family.

TRANSFERRING MICNET INFORMATION

The first step in "awakening" the other machines in your network is to distribute the network files you've just created among them. To do this, you'll need a formatted diskette for each XENIX machine and a technique for copying the information. (Recall from Chapter 15 that the command to format a diskette in the boot floppy drive (0) is *format /dev/rfd0*).

SAVING NETWORK FILES TO A DISKETTE

As the superuser, enter the command *netutil* once again. This time, when the opening menu appears, select option 2, *save the current network configuration to disk*. The opening menu and *netutil*'s response look like this:

```
# netutil
Micnet network utility

        1         install new network configuration
        2         save the current network configuration to disk
        3         restore the network configuration from disk
        4         start the network
        5         stop the network

enter desired option number or name: 2
  Save to /dev/fd0 (yes/no)? _
```

(*Fd0* is the boot floppy drive on which you originally installed XENIX itself.)

If all of the Micnet machines have the same type of floppy drive, or if you will be transferring the network files from a low-density drive to a high-density drive, simply place a formatted diskette into your computer's boot floppy drive and enter *y* at the *netutil* prompt *Save to /dev/fd0 (yes/no)?* The network information will be copied from the hard disk to the diskette. When the process is complete, remove the diskette and label it appropriately. Repeat this process to create a Micnet diskette for each XENIX system in the network.

360

RESTORING NETWORK FILES FROM A DISKETTE

Using the diskette or diskettes to which you just copied the network files, you can now copy those files to the hard disk on each of the other computers in the network. Again, the procedure is straightforward. Log in as the superuser on each machine, then type *netutil* to call up the opening menu. Insert the diskette in the boot floppy drive and this time select option 3, *restore the network configuration from disk*. You'll see the response:

```
# netutil
Micnet network utility

        1        install new network configuration
        2        save the current network configuration to disk
        3        restore the network configuration from disk
        4        start the network
        5        stop the network

enter desired option number or name: 3
  Restore from /dev/fd0 (yes/no)? _
```

You can accept *netutil*'s default, */dev/fd0*, if the floppy drive containing the diskette is either the same as, or compatible with, the drive in which you copied the network files (for example, if both the source and destination floppy drives use 360K diskettes or both use 1.2MB diskettes).

If, however, you are reading a low-density diskette in a high-density drive, you can't use */dev/fd0*. In this case, answer *n* to *netutil*'s prompt and specify the drive as:

/dev/rfd048ds9

This is the designation that enables a high-density drive to adapt to a low-density diskette format. Most high-density drives will have no trouble with this adaptation. If you encounter problems with any aspect of the installation, install Micnet individually on each machine in the network. We especially recommend this course if the machines are using different versions of XENIX.

When *netutil* finishes the copying, it checks the system's */etc/systemid* file for the machine name of the computer to which you've just copied the Micnet files. It will then prompt you to enter the correct name for this system and will rewrite */etc/systemid* with that information.

Once the copying and machine identification have been performed for all computers in the network, you're ready to start your Micnet. If you haven't already done so, make the appropriate hardware connections for all network machines.

STARTING MICNET

There are three ways to start up the Micnet network. One way is to log into each computer as the superuser, type *netutil,* press Enter and, when the main menu appears, select option 4, *start the network.* Alternatively, you can type the compound command:

netutil start

at the # prompt on each XENIX machine in the network. *Netutil* will assume you want option 4 and will thus start the network.

You'll see the following:

```
# netutil start
Do you wish to log errors? (yes/no)? n
Do you wish to log every transmission? (yes/no)? n
daemon started
# _
```

(The line *daemon started* tells you that Micnet is up and running.)

Although answering *y* to the questions Micnet is asking will let you track problems and activity on the network, you might want to answer *n* instead the first time you start up Micnet. Doing so will keep system overhead to a minimum while you are trying out the network.

BOOTING MICNET AUTOMATICALLY

If you want Micnet to start up automatically when the XENIX machines are booted, you can modify a file called */etc/rc* on all computers in the network. This file contains the startup information XENIX needs each time the system is booted.

◼ NOTE: *As always, before you modify any of the XENIX system files, use* cp *to make a copy of that file with a different name. In this way, if you damage the file, you can always replace the modified version with a copy of the unmodified original. To replace this file if something goes wrong, you'll first have to enter system maintenance mode.*

You can edit a copy of */etc/rc* with *vi* by typing:

vi /etc/rc

(You'll see quite a few lines in the file that begin with a pound symbol, #. These are comments explaining portions of the file. The pound symbol tells XENIX to ignore these lines when it executes the startup commands.)

At the end of the */etc/rc* file, add a line of the form:

netutil [-option] start

You must include an option. If you fail to, the system will hang when you boot (XENIX waits for a reply to the prompts you normally see when you start *netutil* from the command line). The valid options are:

-	Suppresses prompts and does not create a log.
-e	Suppresses prompts and logs all network error messages.
-x	Suppresses prompts and logs all network transmissions.

Don't use this autoboot feature until you know your network is up and running without error. The simplest way to detect low-level errors is to send some network mail to every network user.

TESTING THE NETWORK

Once all of the XENIX systems on the network have been started up, enter the *mail* command:

mail all

The *all* alias routes your trial letter to every user you assigned to each network computer. Enter *Micnet* as the subject, so you can distinguish this letter from any others, and type any text you want.

(Although it might now occur to you to include the line:

R root

to request a return receipt that confirms the delivery of all letters, don't do this. A receipt would be sent to you, at the originating computer, only for letters successfully delivered to network users on that machine. Each root account on each of the other XENIX systems in the network would receive its own confirmation.)

Soon after you press Ctrl-D to send your letter, you may receive one or more messages that look like this:

```
No local user named "deand"
Letter saved in "/dead.letter" [Appended] 7/98
```

(You may see different wording, but the meaning will be the same.)

We mentioned earlier, in describing the installation procedure, that you can create network users who do not yet have accounts on the system for which you've defined them. Now that the network is in operation, XENIX won't be able to find any network users you've forgotten to add and will report that fact to you for each applicable user name.

Other than such "phantom" users, the only other immediate problem you may encounter is that some of the persons on the network do not receive their mail. Assuming that you do not receive error messages, allow about 15 minutes for your message to be delivered, and then check the user mail accounts on each system. As the superuser, you can read files in any user account, even those on another computer in the network, by changing to the *\/usr\/spool\/mail* directory and listing each network user's mail with the *cat* command. Do this on each XENIX machine to verify that your message was delivered to all who should have received it.

This is the point at which you can see whether you have any network communication problems and, if so, whether they are related to the Micnet software or to your hardware. Generally speaking, the software installation is simple and straightforward enough that it's unlikely your Micnet software would cause a problem. Hardware, on the other hand, and especially the cables and their connecting points, can be another matter.

364

SOLVING NETWORK PROBLEMS

If one or more network users are known to Micnet but did not receive your test message, it could be that:

■ The affected computer has not been turned on.

■ The Micnet software was not installed on that computer.

■ The tty assignments are incorrect.

■ The cable connecting that computer to the network is defective.

All of these potential trouble spots are relatively easy to check.

The first is simple—either check the computer yourself or have someone check it for you. If you find that it hasn't been turned on and is running XENIX, start it up and try the *mail* test again.

The second is also straightforward. First, log in as the superuser on the computer in question, then check to see if the network has been started by typing:

ps

(for process status) at the shell prompt.

If the machine is currently running the Micnet software, you'll see a display something like this:

```
# ps
  PID TTY TIME COMMAND
 1196 01  0:04 sh
 1510 01  0:03 daemon.m
 1597 01  0:02 ps
# _
```

The presence of *daemon.m* tells you the network is now running.

If *daemon.m* does not appear, try again to start the network by typing:

netutil start

at the shell prompt. If you still see no evidence of *daemon.m* or of Micnet, check a file called */usr/lib/mail/aliases.hash* (described in detail later in this chapter) to get information about the current network configuration. If the information you find is incomplete or does not match the information on your network map, use *netutil* to reinstall Micnet on that computer.

The third possible cause of network problems, incorrect tty assignments, will require more work from you than the other possibilities. You will need to inspect the */etc/ttys* file on each computer and make certain the port you assigned via the Micnet software is actually the one to which you've connected the hardware.

(Pay particular attention to this area if you're installing Santa Cruz Operations' version of XENIX System V. The tty devices in this system start at tty11, not tty00. The devices from console to tty10 are for the XENIX system's use only and are not available for Micnet or terminal use.)

TROUBLESHOOTING THE HARDWARE CONNECTIONS

Once you've determined that Micnet has been correctly installed and is currently running, and that the tty ports have been assigned properly, you must turn to the cable to see if it is at fault. Complicated though it may seem, checking the cable connections can be simple. In a star-type network, for example, the cable is a likely culprit if some XENIX machines connected to the central machine receive a test message when others don't, but none of the problems we've described so far are the cause.

On a bus-type network, checking the cables is a little less direct, but still not particularly difficult. For example, the four-computer Micnet system that we have described is set up as a bus network. In its basic form, the topological map looks like this:

kirk—bones—scotty—spock

If you send your test letter from *kirk*, the messages destined for users on each of the systems following it in line must pass through the computer immediately preceding that system. Letters destined for *scotty* pass through *bones,* and letters for *spock* pass through both *bones* and *scotty.*

If the cabling is suspect, note which computer(s) didn't receive the mail. For example, if you send your message to *all* from *kirk* and the cabling between *scotty* and *spock* is defective, the message will only be received by *bones* and *scotty.*

Before you test or replace the cable, however, run two double-checks. First, send mail to all network users from the machine you suspect is afflicted with a hardware ailment. If you find that the mail is received by all network users, you

365

may have a machine alias problem, rather than a cable problem. Check the machine name you have listed for the computer in the file */etc/systemid.*

Second, check the serial ports connected to the cable you think might be bad. The simplest test here is to attach to the port a device and cable that you know are operational—a terminal you're using, perhaps. To begin the attachment, stop the network and disconnect the network cable. Then, attach the device and cable to the same serial port and enable the serial line with the XENIX *enable* command. You may also need to set various communications parameters, as described in Chapter 14.

At this point, if the test device works as it should, you can test or replace the cable. If it does not work, you may have a problem with your serial port. If problems still persist, you'll need to call on an experienced troubleshooter to help you.

366

IF THE CABLE IS NOT THE PROBLEM

Although this is less likely, it's also possible to encounter a communication problem with one machine when those beyond it on a bus network function perfectly well. The cable and serial port will not be at fault, because the machine will transfer information to and from the others on the network without itself responding to communications.

In a situation like this, your best approach is simply to begin all over with that particular computer. Reinstall XENIX, and then install Micnet. If the problem goes away, the cause was probably corrupt software or bad sectors on the hard disk. If the problem persists, try substituting another computer (with different serial ports and hard disk) in its place.

No matter what network problems you may encounter, only rarely will a logical approach fail to solve them. In each case, try to develop a series of logical steps that focus on the cause of the problem. You may feel unsure at first, but as you work with XENIX and Micnet, you'll find your way becoming easier.

READING THE ALIASES FILE

Before you add any type of alias to the network, you should first check an existing network alias file. Your best source of information will be the file named */usr/lib/mail/aliases.hash.* The file may be longer than one screenful of information, so use the *more* command to display it. Type:

```
more  /usr/lib/mail/aliases.hash
```

At the top of the screen, you'll see some numbers and letters that XENIX uses to convey network information. Next, you'll see some lines like these:

```
# network aliases file

network: "$n network mail recipient", root

# the `all' alias:
all: bones, kirk, scotty, spock

# machine to user mapping
bones: "$n users on bones", barryp, chrisk, daver, finance, jeffh, robink
kirk: "$n users on kirk", deand, deant, pamj, pata, rogers
scotty: "$n users on scotty", admin, humanres, kenh, lindaz
spock: "$n users on spock", juddk, mikes, robertp
```

367

(The lines beginning with a # symbol are explanatory remarks; recall that XENIX ignores both these and any blank lines.)

Notice the line referencing the *all* alias. It emphasizes a point we made earlier: An alias can be a list of other aliases. In this case, Micnet defined *all* as the list composed of the aliases *bones, kirk, scotty,* and *spock.* These aliases are the machine names in our example.

Next, note the machine-to-user mapping information. This is where XENIX looks for the names of the network users associated with each machine alias.

If you used the *more* command, press the Spacebar to see the remainder of the *aliases.hash* file. You'll see two more groups of Micnet data:

```
# additional aliases
optics: deand, kenh, robink
supply: juddk
techgrp: barryp, chrisk, daver, jeffh

# user to machine mapping
admin: scotty:admin
barryp: bones:barryp
chrisk: bones:chrisk
daver: bones:daver
deand: kirk:deand
deant: kirk:deant
finance: bones:finance
humanres: scotty:humanres
jeffh: bones:jeffh
juddk: spock:juddk
kenh: scotty:kenh
lindaz: scotty:lindaz
mikes: spock:mikes
pamj: kirk:pamj
pata: kirk:pata
robertp: spock:robertp
robink: bones:robink
rogers: kirk:rogers
```

The first section, labeled *additional aliases,* shows the standard alias information you entered when you installed the network. The second section shows the actual mapping that XENIX uses when information is sent through the *mail* system to network users. Notice that it uses the form:

[user name]: [machine name]:[user name]

This redefines user names to represent the users in terms of their locations in the network. The network identification for *deand,* for example, is *kirk:deand,* indicating that *deand* can be found on the machine named *kirk.*

ALTERING THE *faliases* FILE

368

Now that you've seen how XENIX keeps track of network users and network aliases, we can look at a situation that is likely to occur on your network. Suppose a network user temporarily moves to another network machine to do some work. How can you ensure that this user will receive messages and mail?

The answer is simple: You create a temporary *forward alias* for this person by altering the contents of a file named *usr/lib/mail/faliases.*

Before you make any changes to any network files, make sure Micnet isn't running. To halt the network, enter the command:

netutil stop

(If others are counting on network services, be sure to alert them in advance.)

Now, to create a forward alias, load the contents of */usr/lib/mail/faliases* into *vi* with the command:

vi /usr/lib/mail/faliases

You will find that *faliases* is a blank file, existing in name alone. But you will soon remedy that.

Let's assume that you're working at the machine named *kirk.* One of its users, *rogers,* will temporarily be working on *bones.* While there, he'll be logged in on *daver's* account. (You could, if you wished, create a new user account on *bones* to accommodate the temporary transfer. If you prefer this method, substitute the appropriate name for *daver* in the example that follows.)

You want to forward any mail that's sent to *rogers* on *kirk* to *daver* on *bones.* To do that, use *vi* to enter these three lines in the *faliases* file:

#Forwarding Addresses [Enter]
[Enter]
rogers: bones:daver [Enter]

The first line is a comment that explains the function of this file. The second line is a blank line. Neither one is necessary, but the third line is.

Here you've specified the user and then defined his forwarding address. All that remains to be done is to write the file back to disk and quit *vi* using the command *:x*. Then restart the network. You need not change any other *faliases* file on any other system.

As long as the network is active, Micnet always checks the alias files (*aliases, faliases,* and *maliases*) before it routes mail. (*Maliases,* a machine alias, is currently empty.) So now, when anyone from his home system sends a message to *rogers,* Micnet will find his name in the *faliases* file and forward the message to his temporary address.

If the mail arrives from another system in the network, Micnet again checks the *faliases* file before allowing the message to be placed in the specified mailbox. Again, it would find the forwarding address and send *rogers'* mail to the correct location. Furthermore, even though *rogers'* mail arrives in *daver's* mailbox, it is addressed to *rogers.*

369

MAINTAINING THE *faliases* FILE

Forwarding addresses remain in effect as long as they remain in the *faliases* file. Thus, even if *rogers* returns to *kirk,* his mail will continue to be forwarded to the *bones:daver* address until you remove that instruction from *faliases.* On a busy network, such housekeeping chores could easily be overlooked or performed too early or too late. What you need is a reminder and, as you saw in Chapter 8, XENIX offers one in the form of its *calendar* file. Each day, XENIX checks this file and, if you've used it as a personal reminder, posts mail to you with a copy of the entries that are dated for that day and the following day.

Using *calendar,* you can insert start and end dates for forwarding services into the *calendar* file and have XENIX remind you when you should add or remove names from *faliases.*

CLEANING THE LOG FILE

Each time you start Micnet, a record of that startup is appended to a file named */usr/spool/micnet/remote/[machine name]/LOG*. The machine name included here is the name you gave a computer when you first installed Micnet. However, its use here does not indicate the machine on which you're operating, but the names of the machine(s) to which it's connected within the network. For instance, in our sample Micnet system, the machine named *bones,* which is connected to *kirk* and *scotty,* will have two *LOG* files:

/usr/spool/micnet/remote/kirk/LOG

/usr/spool/micnet/remote/scotty/LOG

If your network is functioning correctly, the contents of the *LOG* files are not really necessary, but if you're having problems with a machine on the network, you may find the reason for the difficulty contained in the *LOG* file of one of the network computers. For example, if *netutil* cannot initially access the serial port you assigned to it, you'll find that report in *LOG*.

Each time you start up the network, the new *LOG* data are appended to the *LOG* file, making data from prior startups obsolete, although they remain available for historical use if needed. Whether you use that information or not, you will find that *LOG* can become enormous after about a month—especially if you start and stop the network a few times during the day.

Given a healthy, working network, there's no reason to save the contents of a *LOG* file forever. You can empty the *LOG* file for any machine connected to your computer with the command format:

370

    cat 〉/usr/spool/micnet/remote/[machine name]/LOG

Immediately after entering the command, press Ctrl-D to close the file. Doing this will overwrite the existing *LOG* file with a blank *LOG* file. Micnet will thus be able to record subsequent startup information, but using the *cat* command periodically for all machines in the network will clear the old *LOG* files on every machine.

If you are starting a new Micnet network, you can, of course, back up the *LOG* files to diskette until you are certain you no longer need old records. At any point, you can also schedule reminders to yourself through the *calendar* file and *mail* or automate the process with a script.

SENDING UNDELIVERABLE MAIL

There are two times when mail sent to another computer in a network cannot be delivered: when the destination computer is turned off, and when the computer hasn't been included in the network with the *netutil start* command. As long as a computer has been defined within the network, however, you can send mail to it—even if Micnet cannot find the computer at the time you send the message.

If Micnet cannot deliver network mail, it stores the mail in the subdirectory */usr/spool/micnet/remote/[machine name],* giving each letter its own file name. When the destination machine once again becomes available, the letters are automatically distributed to their appropriate destinations.

This temporary mail storage is a valuable aid to you and network users because it means messages can be sent without regard to network schedules and machine availability. For example, if you need a 24-hour mail service for your network, you need not leave all computers in the network turned on all of the time.

Rather, you can keep just one computer (or one for on-site users and another for dial-in users) working to collect the mail. When the other systems are turned on, that mail will be distributed throughout the network.

USING MICNET

Once you've established your Micnet, its operation will be transparent to the network users. As with intrasystem mail, there's no limit to what can be sent among users—data files included. From your point of view, one of the best features of *mail* under Micnet is that, with the exception of the *LOG* files, it's completely maintenance free.

You've already used *mail* to send messages to other network users. There are two other network commands you can use, too. As the system administrator, you should, if the situation requires it, share information about the following commands with the users on your system.

371

THE *remote* COMMAND

The *remote* command enables you to use the network *mail* system to run commands on other XENIX machines in the network. This command is very useful if special programs or utilities are installed on another computer, but not on yours, or if that machine is running a different version of XENIX. The form of the *remote* command is:

```
remote [machine name] [command] [arguments]
```

The arguments here are optional, and represent any arguments appropriate to the command you issue.

One good use for *remote* is to request information about another XENIX system—perhaps a listing of the users currently logged in (in this respect, *remote* acts as the network intermediary for the *who* command). For example, you could use *remote* from a terminal in the *bones* system in this chapter's sample and request a *who* listing for the XENIX system named *kirk* with the command:

```
remote kirk who
```

Don't be surprised, however, if you use the *remote* command and receive no immediate response other than a shell prompt. Since XENIX replies to *remote* commands through the *mail* system, the processing of these commands, like others in network operations, usually takes a few minutes. You can, during this time, continue with whatever work you were doing, and soon you will receive a *You have mail* message indicating (in this case) that your *remote* requests have been completed. At that time, enter *mail* and look at the message. For our example, the message reads:

```
Message 8:
From kirk:network Tue May  6 11:45:11 1986
To: bones:jeffh
Subject: network (who)

kirk who
        completed (Ok)
root        console      May  6 08:33
pata        tty02        May  6 08:51
deand       tty03        May  6 09:24

_
```

372

Note that XENIX filled in the *From:, To:,* and *Subject:* portions of the *mail* header, indicating the machine name we specified and the command we issued.

In this example, *remote* was initiated by the user *jeffh.*

THE *rcp* COMMAND

XENIX also provides a remote file-copying command called *rcp,* which you can use after your network has been successfully installed. *Rcp* works much like *cp,* except that you include a valid network machine name in addition to the file's source and destination. The form for *rcp* is as follows:

    rcp [source machine]:[source file] [destination machine]:[destination file]

(It is not necessary for the user who *initiates rcp* to include his or her machine name in the command.)

For example, suppose that the user *deand,* on the machine named *kirk,* wants to send the file */usr/deand/document* to user *jeffh,* on the machine named *bones,* and wants to name the file */usr/jeffh/document. Deand* could type:

rcp kirk:/usr/deand/document bones:/usr/jeffh/document

Or, since he is initiating the command, *deand* could omit the name of the source machine and type:

rcp /usr/deand/document bones:/usr/jeffh/document

Likewise, *jeffh* could have initiated the *rcp* command to acquire the same file by typing:

rcp kirk:/usr/deand/document /usr/jeffh/document

(Notice that in this case *jeffh,* as the originator of the command, did not specify *his* machine name.)

Before *rcp* can be used, however, read protection must be removed from the source file and write protection must be removed from the directory the file will be placed in. Use the *chmod* command to do this (see Chapter 9 or Appendix A).

Also, note that there are two important differences between the *rcp* command and the *cp* command: First, no wild cards can be used in *rcp* commands; second, with *rcp,* source and destination files must be specified by complete path names. In using *rcp* it is not possible to specify only a destination directory for the incoming file. If you do this, Micnet will mail an error message.

THE MANUALS—YOUR FINAL AUTHORITY

In this chapter, and in this book, there are many aspects of XENIX we have not been able to discuss. In terms of Micnet, for example, we have not covered remote system access via modem by *mail* or through the UNIX-to-UNIX series of programs known as *uucp, uux, cu,* and so on.

373

There are two reasons why certain XENIX features have not been included. One is space—this book was not, and is not, intended to be a XENIX encyclopedia. For that, you have a more than adequate set of reference manuals. Second, and perhaps more important, is that our intent was to provide XENIX users and system administrators alike with the foundation for using and appreciating this multifaceted operating system called XENIX.

As we mentioned in the Introduction, the XENIX operating system offers its users a wealth of multiuser, multitasking capabilities. Use them to your advantage. They are yours, and they are XENIX.

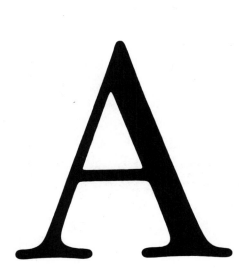

XENIX COMMAND REFERENCE

The following command summaries provide a quick reference to XENIX commands discussed in this book. This guide is by no means complete: the XENIX operating system offers a multitude of commands and command options. But this listing should be useful as a memory aid in showing the form in which to enter a command, options you can include, or arguments that can be used.

Where appropriate, command syntax is shown on a separate line, with options and arguments enclosed in square brackets, [ ]. Commands are listed alphabetically, with reference(s) to the chapters in which they are discussed, unless they are commands you invoke through a XENIX utility, such as *vi* or *mail*. These are discussed under the utility headings.

⊠ NOTE: *Many XENIX commands offer more options than have been discussed in this book. Only those we feel are most useful on a day-to-day basis are described here. Also, the commands used by the system administrator are, necessarily, described very briefly. In terms of system management, the XENIX manuals themselves are the ultimate reference.*

alias

Creates a collective name that can be used to send mail to several users without entering each user name separately; see the entry on *mail. For aliases used within the Micnet network, see Chapter 16.*

bc

Invokes the XENIX calculator, BC, which is useful for calculations ranging from addition and subtraction to the evaluation of complex mathematical expressions. Operators include: + (addition), − (subtraction), * (multiplication), / (division), % (modulo, or remainder), and ^ (exponentiation). Entries to be evaluated separately can be grouped within parentheses. The order of evaluation is as follows:

first level:	parentheses
second level:	exponentiation
third level:	multiplication, division, modulo
fourth level:	addition, subtraction

In the event of a "tie," the expressions are evaluated from left to right. *Discussed in Chapter 2.*

cal

Displays a calendar for the specified year and, if requested, for the specified month. Syntax:

    cal [month] [year]

where *[month]* is a number between 1 and 12 or an unambiguous set of letters identifying the month—for example, *Jul,* rather than *Ju.* The *[year],* if specified, must be a four-digit number for the years 1000 and above—the year entered as 86 would be the year 86, not 1986. If no year is specified, the current year is assumed. If no month is specified, the current, prior, and coming months are displayed. *Discussed in Chapter 8.*

377

calendar

Represents a special XENIX file that can be used to store appointments and other reminders that will then be sent automatically through the *mail* system on the day before and the day of the date specified. Entries can be appended to the *calendar* file with the command *cat ⟫ calendar.* Entries need not be in chronological order, nor in a particular date format. *Discussed in Chapter 8.*

cat

Displays files on the screen. Syntax:

    cat [file name]

If no file name is specified, the command displays keyboard input.

When used with the redirection symbol(s) ⟩ or ⟫, *cat* creates or joins files under the file name specified. Syntax:

    cat ⟩ [file name]

to create a file, or:

    cat [file name(s)] ⟩ *or* ⟫ cat [file name]

to join (⟩) or append (⟫) files. *Warning:* Using a single redirection symbol (⟩) will overwrite the destination file. *Discussed in Chapter 4.*

cd

Changes the current (working) directory. Syntax:

    cd [directory name]

If no directory is specified, the user's home directory becomes the current directory. If the directory is specified as .., the current directory moves up one level in the directory structure. *Discussed in Chapter 3.*

chmod

Changes access permissions for files or directories. Syntax:

chmod [who][permission level] [file or directory]

Who can be specified as:

a	All users.
g	The group.
o	Others.
u	The user.

Do not include blank spaces between items in the *who* and *permission* lists.

Permissions are set with + (to add permission), − (to remove permission), or = (to add permission and remove any others currently in effect). *Permission levels* can be:

x	Execute.
r	Read.
w	Write.

Discussed in Chapter 9.

copy

Copies files or groups of files from one directory to another. Syntax:

copy [-(options)] [source] [destination]

The *[source]* can be any existing file or a directory. If the *[destination]* file or directory does not exist, it is created. Useful options include:

a	Requests confirmation before making the copy.
r	Copies recursively, including all subdirectories within the specified directory.
v	Displays reports on-screen as the copy procedure is carried out.

Discussed in Chapter 3.

cp

Copies the contents of an existing file to another file or directory. Syntax:

cp [source] [destination]

If a file is copied to another file, the *[source]* and *[destination]* file names cannot be the same. *Discussed in Chapter 4.*

csh

Invokes the C shell. *Shell options and variables are discussed in Chapter 11.*

date

Entered by itself, displays the current day, date, time, and year. Entered in conjunction with the following argument, sets the current date. (You must be a superuser to do this.) Syntax:

date [mmddhhmm[yy]]

where *mm* is the month (01 to 12); *dd* is the day of the month (01 to 31); *hh* is the hour (00 to 23); *mm* is the minute (00 to 59); and, optionally, *yy* is the last two digits of the current year (00 to 99). *Discussed in Chapter 2.*

diction

If the Text Processing System has been installed, this command invokes the *diction* program, which checks word usage in a document. Syntax:

diction [-(options)] [-f phrase file] [file name]

If *[-f phrase file]* is included, the program checks a user-created list of words and phrases. If the *n* option is included, the default list of phrases is not used. *Discussed in Chapter 7.*

DOS COMMANDS

Seven XENIX commands are available to handle MS-DOS text files. All commands require mounting a DOS diskette (or accessing the DOS partition on the hard disk) and must be coordinated through the system administrator to avoid unpredictable effects on the system. The drive names A and B can be used for any 48 track-per-inch (low-density) DOS diskettes placed in drives 0 and 1, respectively. You may

also use the drive names X and Y for any 96 track-per-inch (high-density) DOS diskettes placed in drives 0 and 1, respectively. In addition, you can use the drive
name C to access the DOS partition on your hard disk (if one has been installed).
The DOS commands and syntax for each are as follows (the -r option available with
some of them displays the DOS file without newline conversions):

doscat [-r] [drive name]:[file name]	Prints a DOS file to the screen.
doscp [-r] [drive name]:[file name] [XENIX file name]	Copies a DOS file onto a XENIX disk, giving it the specified XENIX file name.
doscp [-r] [drive name]:[file name] [XENIX directory]	Copies the specified file into the specified directory on a XENIX disk.
dosdir [drive name]:[DOS directory]	Lists contents of a DOS disk's directory in standard DOS format.
dosls [drive name]:[DOS directory]	Lists contents of a DOS disk's directory in XENIX format.
dosmkdir [drive name]:[DOS directory]	Creates a DOS directory on the specified DOS disk.
dosrmdir [drive name]:[DOS directory]	Removes the specified DOS directory from a DOS disk.
dosrm [drive name]:[file name]	Removes the specified DOS file from a DOS disk.

Discussed in Chapter 9.

echo

Prints results of a command to the screen without actually carrying it out. Syntax:

echo [command]

In a script file, *echo* can also be used to print text to the screen when used in the
format:

echo "text"

or:

echo 'text'

Discussed in Chapters 4, 10, and 11.

ed

Invokes the XENIX line editor, *ed.* Syntax:

ed [file name]

If a file name is specified, the editor reads the file's contents into its buffer. Useful commands include:

a   Appends text. If a line number is specified, appends after that
                line. To stop entering text, enter a period at the beginning of
                a new line.

w   Writes the contents of the buffer to disk, using the currently
                remembered file name, unless another is specified.

s   Substitutes one text string for another; used in the format
                [line number]s/[existing text]/[replacement text]/. If no line num-
                ber is specified, the command affects only the first occurrence of
                [existing text] on the current line. To substitute throughout a line,
                use the command form *s/[existing text]/[replacement text]/g.* To
                substitute throughout a document, use the command form
                1,$s/[existing text]/[replacement text]/g.

r   Reads in a specified file; used in the format *r [file name].*

p   Prints specified lines to the screen; used in the format
                [number],[number]p.

Discussed in Chapter 4.

grep

Searches a file for a specified pattern of characters. Syntax:

    grep [-(options)] [pattern] [file name(s)]

When the pattern is found, the entire line is printed to the screen. Exact matches can be found by enclosing the search pattern in single quotation marks and, if appropriate, blank spaces. Actually, there are three XENIX commands that can search for patterns of characters:

■ *Grep* can search for patterns specified by pattern-matching characters; for example, *grep ' [a-z]at '* searches for any three-letter word that begins with the lower-case letters *a* through *z* and has a blank space in front of and behind it.

■ *Egrep* can search for multiple patterns; *egrep ' bat | cat ',* for example, searches for all occurrences of *bat* or *cat,* or both, that exist with both leading and trailing blank spaces.

■ *Fgrep* can search for multiple strings of characters separated by newline characters, but does not recognize pattern-matching characters; *fgrep ' [a-z]at ',* for example, searches for an exact match for *[a-z]at* and not for the range of words that are specified.

381

Useful options include:

v	Prints all *except* matching lines.
x	With *fgrep* only, prints lines that, in their entirety, exactly match the specified pattern.
c	Displays only the number of matching lines that were found.
l	Gives only the file names containing matching lines.
n	Gives the relative line number of each matching line in the file.
y	With *grep* and *fgrep,* ignores case in searching for matches.

Discussed in Chapters 9 and 10.

head

Displays the first few lines of files. Syntax:

    head [-number] [file names]

where *[-number]* specifies the number of lines to be displayed. If no number is entered, the first 10 lines are shown. *Discussed in Chapter 4.*

lc

Lists the contents of directories in column format. If entered without a directory name, lists the contents of the current directory. Syntax:

    lc [-(options)] [directory name(s)]

When used without any options, the command lists entries alphabetically. Useful options include:

C	Maintains column format even when output is redirected to a file.
F	Places a slash (/) after each directory name and an asterisk (*) after the name of each executable file.
R	Lists the contents of subdirectories within the specified directory.
a	Lists all files, including hidden files.
c	Lists files by time of creation.
d	Lists only the name of a specified directory, not its contents.
l	Lists entries in long format, showing file type and permissions, links, owner, group, file size, time of last change, and file name.
r	Lists entries in reverse order.
t	Lists entries according to the time they were last modified.
x	Lists entries sorted across the screen, rather than down columns.

Discussed in Chapter 4.

lp (or lpr)

Prints a document on a line printer attached to the system. Syntax:

    lp [-(options)] [file name(s)]

Files are printed in the order in which they are entered. Useful options include:

d[destination]	Sends a file to the printer or class of printers specified; *see Chapter 14 for a discussion of printers and printer names.*
m	Sends notification through the *mail* system when a file has been printed.
n[number]	Prints the specified number of copies.
w	Writes to the user's terminal announcing completion of printing.

Discussed in Chapters 7 and 14.

ls

Lists the contents of a directory. Syntax:

    ls [-(options)] [directory name(s)]

If entered without a directory name, lists the contents of the current directory, alphabetically and in a single vertical column. If directory names are specified, the command lists the files in each directory alphabetically. Useful options include:

a	Lists all entries, including hidden files.
d	Lists only the name of a directory, not including its contents.
x	Lists entries in multiple-column format, sorted across the screen.
l	Lists entries in long format, showing file type and permissions, links, owner, group, file size, time of last change, and file name.
r	Lists entries in reverse order.
t	Lists entries by time of last modification (latest first).
p	Places a slash (/) after the name of each directory.

Discussed in Chapter 3.

mail

Invokes the electronic mail utility used to send and receive messages between system users. The following commands are used within *mail.*

To send a message:

m [user name(s)]	Sends a message to the named recipients. After composing the message, press Ctrl-D on a new line to send it.

383

To send messages to more than one user:

alias [alias name] [user name(s)]	Groups the specified users under a single alias name so that messages or copies of messages can be sent to all users within the group without typing each user name. Temporary unless added to the *.mailrc* file.

To display messages:

h [message number(s)]	Typed by itself (*h*), produces a numbered list of message headers, with the most recent listed first. Typed with message numbers, produces a list of the headers for the specified messages.
h [start]-[end]	Produces a list of the headers for the messages specified in the range [start]-[end]. Pressing Enter or + displays the first message in the current header list. Each subsequent press of Enter or + displays the next message.
rest	Displays headers for newly arrived mail.

To display specified messages or groups of messages:

+[number]	Jumps forward [number] messages toward the newest message and displays the message at the location specified.
−[number]	Jumps backward [number] messages toward the oldest message and displays the message at the location specified.
^	Displays the oldest message in the list.
$	Displays the newest message in the list.
p [message number(s)]	Displays a non-sequential series of messages.
p [start]-[end] [user name]	Displays a range of messages. If [user name] is included, displays messages from the specified user.
t [message number(s)]	Displays the first five lines of each specified message. The number of lines displayed can be changed with the *toplines = [number]* command.
t [start]-[end]	Displays the first five lines of each message in the specified range. Again, the *toplines* command can be used to change the five-line default setting.

To reply to a message from within *mail*:

r [message number] Typed by itself after a message is displayed, *r* incorporates the lines you type until Ctrl-D is entered at the beginning of a new line. Typed with a message number, *r* specifies a reply to a message other than the one currently displayed.

To forward messages:

f [message number(s)] [user name(s)] Forwards the specified message, list of messages, or range of messages to the user or users specified. If no message number is included, the current message is forwarded. Messages are indented one Tab stop on the recipient's screen.

F [message number(s)] [user name(s)] Forwards messages in the same way, but without the indentation.

To delete messages:

d [message number(s)] Typed by itself, *d* deletes the current message. Typed with a list of message numbers, it deletes the messages specified.

d [start]-[end] Deletes the range of messages specified. The complementary command, *u* (for undelete), used in the same format, recovers messages deleted during the current session. The *undelete* command does not work after you exit *mail*.

To save mail:

mb [message number(s)] Transfers the specified mail to a mail-storage file named *mbox* which is found in the home directory.

s [message number(s)] [file name] Saves the specified message (or messages if a list or range is entered) in the file specified. Header lines are also saved.

w [message number(s)] [file name] Saves the specified message (or list or range of messages) in the file specified, but does not include the header lines.

ho [message number(s)] Holds a specified message (or list or range of messages) that have been marked for transfer during the current session, keeping them in the mailbox.

To quit the *mail* system:

q   Quits and returns you to the shell, as does
                                          pressing Ctrl-D.

x   Quits, but represents an abort command
                                          that leaves the contents of the mailbox un-
                                          changed. All transfers, deletions, and so on
                                          that were requested during the current ses-
                                          sion are ignored.

To print mail:

l [message number(s)] [user name]   Prints the specified range or list of messages
                                          on the line printer attached to the system. If
                                          [user name] is included, the command prints
                                          only the letters sent by the specified user,
                                          within the list or range specified.

To change *mail* options:

set   Typed alone on a line, displays the current
                                          options settings in the *.mailrc* file. To change
                                          a setting, the command is *set [option]*. To re-
                                          store the default options, the command is
                                          unset [option].

In addition, the *mail* facility includes the following useful message compose-
escape sequences.

To include messages in the current (unsent) message:

~m [message number(s)]   Typed on its own line within a message,
                                          causes the specified message, list of messages,
                                          or range of messages to be included in the
                                          body of the message, indented one Tab stop.

~M [message number(s)]   Includes one or more messages, as described,
                                          but without the indentation.

~r [file name]   Typed on its own line within the body of a
                                          message, causes the specified text file (for
                                          example, one created in *vi* or *ed*) to be read
                                          into the message at that point.

To preview the current (unsent) message:

~p   Displays the current message, including
                                          header lines.

To edit the current (unsent) message:

~h	Typed on its own line in a message, displays each header line in turn. You can edit each line or you can accept what is displayed by pressing Enter.
~s [subject]	Typed on its own line in the body of a message, substitutes the new [subject] for the current subject.
~t [user name(s)]	Typed on its own line in the body of a message, appends names of the specified users to the *To:* header.
~v	Invokes the *vi* editor, which assigns a temporary file name to existing text and can then be used to edit the body of the letter. When finished, exit the editor and write the letter to disk with the *:x* command, and you'll be returned to the *mail* system with a message requesting that you *(continue)*.

To send copies to other users:

~c [user name(s)]	Typed on its own line at the end of a message, includes the specified users in a *Cc:* (carbon-copy) line and sends a copy of the message to them.
~b [user name(s)]	Typed on its own line at the end of a message, includes the specified users in a *Bcc:* (blind-carbon-copy) line and sends a copy of the message to them without informing other recipients.

To confirm receipt of mail:

~R [user name]	Typed on its own line, acknowledges receipt of mail by adding a *Return-receipt-to:* field to the header of a message.

The mail *system is discussed in Chapter 8.*

mesg

Sets the message permission status on your terminal. Syntax:

    mesg [y/n]

Typed without an argument, displays the current message permission status. The arguments *y* and *n* set status to *yes* or *no.* If set to *no,* users attempting to write to your terminal receive the message *Permission denied. Discussed in Chapter 8.*

mkdir

Creates a new directory. Syntax:

    mkdir [directory name(s)]

Directory names are limited to 14 characters. Unless specified with an absolute path name, [directory name] is created as a subdirectory of the current directory. To create more than one directory, separate the directory names with a space. *Discussed in Chapter 3.*

more

Displays one screenful of information at a time, pausing between displays until Enter is pressed to request the next line, the Spacebar is pressed to request the next screen, or the Delete key is pressed to quit. *Discussed in Chapter 4.*

mv

Moves (renames) a file or directory. Syntax:

    mv [source] [destination]

If a file is moved to another directory containing a file with the same name, the existing file is overwritten. If the destination is a directory, the source files are moved to that directory. *Discussed in Chapter 3.*

newgrp

Changes the primary group identification for a user who has been assigned to more than one group by the system administrator. Syntax:

    newgrp [group name]

Discussed in Chapter 14.

nohup

Ensures completion of a command being processed in the background, even if the user logs out before execution is complete. Syntax:

    nohup [command] [arguments]

Discussed in Chapter 7.

388

nroff

If the Text Processing System has been installed, invokes the XENIX text-formatting program. Formatting can be accomplished by using dot commands and the memo-randum macros (called into play with the *mm* command). Useful *nroff* and *mm* formatting commands include:

nroff commands:

.ce	Centers a line of text.
.sp[number]	Inserts [number] blank lines in a document.
.ad b	Aligns text on both left and right edges.
.ad r	Aligns text on the right edge, leaving the left edge ragged.
.ad l	Aligns text on the left edge, leaving the right edge ragged.
.ad c	Centers each line of text, leaving both right and left edges ragged.
.fi	Signals a change in text alignment within a document.
.nf	Turns off text alignment.
.po [number]i	Sets page offset in [number] of inches (*i*); if *i* is omitted, offset is in [number] of characters.
.pl [number]i	Sets page length; see *.po.*
.ll [number]i	Sets line length; see *.po.*
.ls [number]	Sets line spacing.

389

memorandum macros (*mm*)

.VM [top] [bottom]	Sets vertical (top and bottom) page margins.
.PH	Prints a header at the top of each page.
.EH	Prints a header at the top of even-numbered pages.
.OH	Prints a header at the top of odd-numbered pages.
.PF	Prints a footer at the bottom of each page.
.EF	Prints a footer at the bottom of even-numbered pages.
.OF	Prints a footer at the bottom of odd-numbered pages.
\fB	Begins boldfacing.
\fI	Begins underlining.
\fR	Ends boldfacing or underlining.

Discussed in Chapter 7.

passwd

Changes the current password. The command takes no arguments; XENIX prompts for all required information. *Discussed in Chapters 2 and 13.*

pr

Invokes the XENIX *print* utility which, with its numerous options, can be used to emulate paper printing on the screen. Syntax:

pr [-(options)] [file name(s)]

Useful options include the following.

For page setup:

w[number]	Sets line width to [number] characters; default is 72.
o[number]	Indents each line [number] characters; default is 0.

For formatting output:

+[number]	Starts printing at page [number]; default is 1.
d	Double-spaces printing.
p	Pauses and rings a bell before displaying the next page; waits for a carriage return before continuing.
f	Pauses for a form-feed to advance to next page.
h	Uses the next string of text (enclosed in quotation marks) as the page header; default is date, file name, and page number.
n	Prints each line with a line number.

For printing multiple columns:

[number]	Formats printing in [number] columns.
a	Prints multiple-column output across the page; lines are alternated between the left and right.
m	Merges and prints all files, one per column; negates the effects of *[number]* and *a*.
t	Suppresses the default five-line header and footer at the top and bottom of each page.

Discussed in Chapters 9 and 11.

pwd

Prints the path name of the current (working) directory. Syntax:

pwd

Discussed in Chapter 2.

rm

Removes one or more specified files. Syntax:

rm [-(options)] [file name(s)]

If wild cards are used to specify file names, the *i* (interactive) option provides a safeguard against inadvertently removing wanted files by causing XENIX to prompt for confirmation before each file is deleted. *Discussed in Chapter 4.*

rmdir

Removes one or more specified directories. Syntax:

rmdir [directory name(s)]

This command removes empty directories only. Files within the directory must be deleted or transferred to another directory before the *rmdir* command can be carried out. *Discussed in Chapter 3.*

sed

Invokes the XENIX non-interactive stream editing utility. Syntax:

sed [-(options)] [file name(s)]

Options are:

n	Suppresses output; can be used to test an editing script without sending the results to the screen or to a file.
e	Precedes script instructions that are written into the command line, instead of read from a separate file.
f	Precedes the name of the file from which *sed* should read its editing commands.

Discussed in Chapter 9.

sb

Invokes the Bourne shell. *Shell options and variables are discussed in Chapter 10.*

sort

Sorts the lines of one or more files. Syntax:

sort [-(options)] [+number] [−number] [file name(s)]

Sorting can be performed on more than one field by including [+number] and [−number]; [+number] begins the sort at the specified field (counting from 0 at the leftmost edge) and [−number], if included, restricts examination to only the field specified. *Sort* options include:

b	Ignores leading blanks.
d	Sorts in dictionary order, ignoring punctuation and special symbols.
f	Interprets lowercase letters as uppercase, so case is not considered in sorting.
i	Considers only the ASCII characters in the decimal range 32 to 126 in non-numeric comparisons.
n	Sorts numbers according to their arithmetic value, not the ASCII value of each of their components.
o	Precedes the name of the output file in which the sorted data are to be stored.
r	Sorts in reverse (high to low) order.
t[character]	Recognizes [character] as the new field delimiter.
c	Checks to determine whether the file is already sorted according to any other options included in the command. If it is, another sort is not performed.

Discussed in Chapter 9.

spell

If the Text Processing System has been installed, this command invokes the XENIX spelling checker. Syntax:

spell [-(options)] [+word list] [file name(s)]

Unless redirected to another file, output is printed to the screen. If [+ word list] is included, the document is checked against a user-created file of correctly spelled words. Useful *spell* options include:

v   Displays assumptions in combining root words with prefixes
              and suffixes.

b   Checks British spelling.

Discussed in Chapter 7.

split

393

Breaks one file into smaller segments. Syntax:

    split [-lines per file] [file name] [new name]

Breaks [file name] into the number of lines specified and gives the resulting files the new name, appending a two-letter suffix, beginning with *aa*, to the new file names. *Discussed in Chapter 6.*

style

If the Text Processing System has been installed, invokes the *style* program, which analyzes the writing style in a document. Syntax:

    style [-(options)] [file name]

Discussed in Chapter 7.

SYSTEM ADMINISTRATION

The following list gives some commands available to the system administrator in managing a XENIX system:

■ accept.
Causes an installed printer or class of printers to accept print requests; printer must be activated with the *enable* command.

■ cancel.
Causes an installed printer to reject print requests.

■ df [-(option)] [device file].
Reports available space, in blocks, on the specified device. Options include: v, to report percentage of blocks used; t, to report both free blocks and the total number allocated; b, to report both free bytes and the total bytes allocated; and i, to report a complete summary. Can also be used by users to check */usr* and /.

■ disable.

Deactivates a terminal; also removes a printer from service even if it is set to accept print requests.

■ du [-(option)] [directory].

Reports on disk usage by displaying a list of directories and subdirectories, along with the number of blocks occupied. Options include: *s*, to display the total number of blocks for the specified directory; *a*, to display information for all files, as well as all directories; *r*, to display error messages if files or directories cannot be read; *u*, to ignore files with more than one link; *f*, to report on current directory entries only. Can also be used by users to check */usr* and /.

■ enable.

Activates a terminal; also used to cause a printer to print documents.

■ find [directory] [-atime] +[number] [-print].

Finds and displays the names of all files in the specified directory that have not been accessed in +[number] days. Can also be used by users to check */usr* and /.

■ format [device name].

Formats a diskette.

■ fsck [file system(s)].

Checks on and cleans the file system specified; used in clearing up disk errors.

■ haltsys.

Shuts down the system immediately; offers users no opportunity to clean up and save current work. Under normal circumstances, *shutdown* is preferable.

■ lpinit.

Adds a printer or class of printers.

■ lpstat [-(options)].

Reports line printer status information. Options include: *r*, to display data about the request scheduler; *d*, to display the default printer; and *t*, to display all status information.

■ mkuser.

Creates a new user account.

■ mount [device] [directory].

Mounts a diskette onto the specified directory.

■ netutil.

Activates the Micnet Network-installation utility.

■ ps.

Reports the status of processes currently running.

■ pwadmin [-option] [login name].

Allows password administration for specified users. An option must be used; options include: *a*, to activate password aging; *n*, to deactivate password aging; *f*, to force a password change at the next login; *c*, to prevent a password from being changed; − *min [number of weeks]* − *max [number of weeks]*, to allow for more frequent password changes for specified users; *d*, to display password-aging criteria.

■ rmuser.

Removes a user from the system.

■ shutdown.

Shuts down the system after a specified period of time (the default is five minutes); prompts users to clean up and log out. The command cannot be terminated once it has been invoked.

■ sysadmin.

Activates the file-system backup facility.

■ tar [primary option] [secondary option(s)] [secondary option argument(s)] [file].

Activates the tape archiver facility (used for backing up specified files).

Primary options are: *c*, to create a new file system on the archive device; *t*, to display a list of files on the archive device; *u*, to add specified files to the archive device; *x*, to extract specified files from the archive device; *r*, to write specified files to the end of an archive.

Secondary options include: *f*, to use the corresponding argument to name the archive device; *k*, to use the corresponding argument to specify the device's size; *b*, to specify a blocking factor (normally, 20); *n*, to indicate that the archive device is not a tape device; *v*, to display the names of all transferred files; *e*, to avoid splitting files across separate volumes (tapes or diskettes).

■ umount [device name].

Unmounts the specified diskette.

■ wall.

Writes a message to the screens of all users logged in.

XENIX system-administration commands and techniques are discussed in Chapters 13 through 15; Micnet is discussed in Chapter 16.

tail

Displays the last few lines of a file. Syntax:

> tail [+ *or* − number] [file name]

where *[+ number]* starts the display [number] of lines from the top of the file, and *[− number]* starts the display [number] of lines from the end of the file. If no number is specified, the last 10 lines are shown. *Discussed in Chapter 4.*

test

Evaluates conditions and returns a value of true or false. Syntax:

> test [expression]

Useful expressions include:

-r [file name]	Evaluates as true if [file name] is found and has read access.
-w [file name]	Evaluates as true if [file name] is found and has write access.
-x [file name]	Evaluates as true if [file name] is found and has executable access.
-f [file name]	Evaluates as true if [file name] is found and is a regular file.
-d [file name]	Evaluates as true if [file name] is found and is a directory.
-c [file name]	Evaluates as true if [file name] is found and is a character-device type of file.
-b [file name]	Evaluates as true if [file name] is found and is a block-device type of file.
-s [file name]	Evaluates as true if [file name] is found and has a size greater than zero.
-z [string]	Evaluates as true if [string] has a length of zero.
-n [string]	Evaluates as true if [string] has a length other than zero.
[string 1] = [string 2]	Evaluates as true if [string 1] is identical to [string 2].
[string 1] != [string 2]	Evaluates as true if [string 1] is not identical to [string 2].

[string]   Evaluates as true if [string] is not the null string.

[integer 1] -eq [integer 2]   Evaluates as true if [integer 1] is algebraically equal
                                  to [integer 2]. Other comparison operators that can
                                  be used are: -*ne,* not equal; -*gt,* greater than; -*ge,*
                                  greater than or equal to; -*lt,* less than; -*le,* less than
                                  or equal to.

Discussed in Chapter 10.

uniq

Finds lines that are repeated in a file. Syntax: 397

uniq -[option] [+number] [−number] [input file] [output file]

Only one option can be included. Options are:

u   Prints only non-duplicated lines in the output.

d   Includes only one copy of each duplicated line in the output.

c   Includes one copy of each line in the source file, preceding
           the line with a number showing how many times the line is
           repeated in the file.

If [+number] is included, the command skips the first [number] characters of each
line or, if a field is specified, the first [number] characters of the field. If [−number]
is included, the command skips the first [number] fields of each line and begins the
comparison at field [number]+ 1. *Discussed in Chapter 9.*

vi

Invokes the visual text editor. When typed by itself, the command *vi* starts the editor without loading a file.

To start *vi* in other ways:

vi [file name]   Starts the editor and loads the specified file.

vi +[line number] [file name]   Starts the editor with the cursor on the speci-
                                        fied line of the specified file.

vi +/[word] [file name]   Starts the editor at the first occurrence of
                                        [word] in the specified file.

vi [file name(s)]   Starts the editor and queues the specified files.

vedit   Starts the editor and displays *INPUT MODE* on
                                        the status line during insert mode.

To enter text:

a	Inserts text after the current cursor location; used with a new file, has the same effect as *i*.
A	Inserts text after the last characters on the current line.
i	Inserts text, beginning at the space before the current cursor location.
I	Inserts text before the first character on the current line.
o	Opens a new, blank line immediately below the one containing the cursor.
O	Opens a new, blank line immediately above the one containing the cursor.

To move the cursor:

0 (zero)	Moves to the beginning of the line.
$	Moves to the end of the line.
[number]h	Moves left [number] characters.
F[character]	Moves left, stopping at the first occurrence (moving right to left) of [character].
T[character]	Moves left, stopping at the character immediately to the right of the first occurrence (moving right to left) of [character].
[number]l	Moves right [number] characters.
f[character]	Moves right, stopping at the first occurrence of [character].
t[character]	Moves right, stopping at the character immediately to the left of the first occurrence of [character].
[number]j	Moves down.
[number]+	Moves down and to the first character in a line.
[number]k	Moves up.
[number]−	Moves up and to the first character in a line.
H	Moves to the top left corner of the screen.
L	Moves to the bottom left corner of the screen or to the bottom left corner of the document, if less than a full screen.

To move the cursor to a word:

[number]w	Moves [number] words to the right; counts punctuation marks as words.
[number]W	Moves [number] words to the right; does not count punctuation marks as words.
[number]b	Moves [number] words to the left; counts punctuation marks as words.
[number]B	Moves [number] words to the left; does not count punctuation marks as words.

To move to a line:

G	Moves to the last line in a document.
[line number]G	Moves to the first character of the line specified.

To move screen by screen:

Ctrl-U	Scrolls up half a screen.
Ctrl-D	Scrolls down half a screen.
Ctrl-F	Scrolls one screen toward the end of the document.
Ctrl-B	Scrolls one screen toward the beginning of the document.

To number lines:

:set number	Turns on line numbering.
:set nonumber	Turns off line numbering.
:[number],[number]nu	Temporarily displays the numbers of the lines specified by [number],[number]; entered by itself (*:nu*), displays the current line and its number.

To rearrange line lengths:

r[Enter]	Breaks a line just to the left of the cursor location after you press Enter.
J	Joins the line below to the end of the current line.

To specify a file:

:r [file name]	Reads in the specified file. If no file is specified, the current one is read in.

To edit a list of files:

:args	Displays the names of queued files.
:n	Reads in the next file in the queue.
:rew	Reads in the first file in the queue.
:e [file name]	Reads in the specified file (not restricted to files in a queue).
:e#	Reads in the previously edited file.

To delete text:

[number]x	Deletes [number] characters to the right, beginning at, and including, the current cursor location.
[number]X	Deletes [number] characters to the left, beginning at, but not including, the current cursor location.
[number]dw	Deletes [number] words to the right of the word containing the cursor.
[number]dd	Deletes [number] lines below, beginning at and including the line containing the cursor.
:[start],[end]d	Deletes the range of lines specified by the actual line numbers [start],[end].

To undo an editing command:

u	Undoes the last command issued.

To copy and move text:

"[buffer][number of lines]yy	Yanks the specified number of lines to the insert buffer named by [buffer].
"[BUFFER][number of lines]yy	Yanks the specified number of lines and appends them to the current contents of the insert buffer named by [BUFFER].
m[letter]	Marks the first line of text that is to be yanked with [letter].
"[buffer name]y'k	Yanks lines from the line containing the cursor through the line marked with *m[letter]*.
"[buffer]p	Puts the contents of the specified buffer on the line(s) immediately below the current line.

"[buffer]P	Puts the contents of the specified buffer either above the current line or just before the current cursor location.
:[first,last] co [destination]	Duplicates the lines specified by [first,last] immediately below the [destination] line that is specified.
:[start,end]m[destination]	Moves the lines specified by [first,last] to immediately below the [destination] line specified.

To search for text strings:

/[search text]	Searches forward (toward the end of the document) for the first occurrence of [search text].
?[search text]	Searches backward (toward the beginning of the document) for the first occurrence of [search text].
n	Continues a search for the next occurrence of the text that is specified by /*[search text]* or *?[search text]*.
:set nowrapscan	Stops a search at the end of the file, rather than wrapping back to the top of the file, even if the search text has not been found.
:set wrapscan	Wraps a search back to the top of the file if the search text has not been found when the end of the file is encountered.
:set ignorecase	Ignores case variations in a search.
:set noignorecase	Makes a search case-sensitive.
:set nomagic	Disables the editor's ability to recognize special characters (* \ [ ] ~ $ ^).
:set magic	Enables recognition of special characters.

To replace text:

:g[search for]/s//[replace with] /[options]	Searches every line of the file and substitutes the specified replacement text for the search text. [Options] include *g,* to replace search text whenever and wherever it occurs in the file; *p,* to print on-screen a copy of each line change; and *c,* to prompt for confirmation before the replacement.

To save a file:

:w [file name]	Writes the file to disk under the file name specified. If the command includes no file name, the file is written to disk under the currently remembered file name.

401

| :x [file name] | Writes the file to disk under the specified or currently remembered file name and quits the editor. |
| :q | Quits the editor. If unsaved changes exist, the command prompts with the message *No write since last change....* To abandon the document, type the absolute form of the command, *:q!.* |

The vi *editor is discussed in Chapters 5 and 6.*

vsh

Invokes the Visual shell. *Shell commands and their uses are discussed in Chapter 12.*

who

Lists the login names of users currently on the system. In addition, shows the terminal identifier and the date and time of login for each user. Syntax:

who [-(options)]

Options include:

| q | Shows only user names and the number of users currently logged in. |

Typed as *who am i,* the command displays *who* information about the requesting user. *Discussed in Chapters 2, 8, and 10.*

write

Sends a message directly to the terminal of another user. Syntax:

write [user name] [terminal name] [<(file name)]

Once issued, the *write* command sends all subsequent keyboard input to the recipient until transmission is ended by pressing Ctrl-D at the beginning of a new line.

The [terminal name] argument can be included to write to only one of a number of users sharing a common user name.

The [file name] argument can be included to send the contents of a text file to the recipient if the redirection symbol (<) is used.

B

FREQUENTLY USED XENIX FILES

The following files and directories are often used in the day-to-day tasks of XENIX system administration and file handling. Feel free to look in them if you wish, but consult the appropriate pages in this book or your XENIX documentation before you make any changes to them.

THE *root* (/) DIRECTORY

404

/bin	A XENIX command directory; contains most of the commonly used commands.
/dev	The special device directory; contains device files for the floppy and hard disk drives, attached terminals and printers, system boards, and a clock.
/etc	An additional program and data directory; contains many of the system-level commands.
/lib	A C program library directory.
/mnt	The mount directory; an empty directory reserved for mounted file systems.
/usr	The directory containing all users' home directories and additional user information.
/tmp	A temporary directory; reserved for temporary files created by programs; entire contents of this directory are deleted each time the system is shut down.

COMMUNICATION

/usr/lib/mail	The system *mail* directory; contains *mail* help messages, alias information, and system identification files.
/usr/spool/mail	The system mailbox directory; contains *mail* files for each user.
/usr/spool/lp	The system printer directory; contains printer programs and information.
/usr/spool/lp/model	The printer interface program directory.
/usr/spool/micnet/remote	The Micnet remote system directory; contains information about other machines in the network.
/etc/systemid	The system identification file used in the Micnet network.

/etc/ttys	The status file for the Console and attached terminals.
/etc/ttytype	The terminal-type file for the Console and attached terminals.
/etc/gettydefs	The default communication-parameter and login-prompt lists for the Console and attached terminals.
/etc/termcap	The communication-parameter database for attached terminals; contains information for most terminals currently available.

XENIX STARTUP FILES

/etc/rc	Command file containing shell scripts used to boot the system.
/.profile	Startup file for the superuser; contains custom shell instructions.
/usr/*/.profile	Startup file for Bourne shell users; found in the home directory. (Replace * with your user name.)
/usr/*/.login	Startup file for the C shell; found in the home directory. (Replace * with your user name.)
/usr/*/.cshrc	Additional startup file for the C shell, also found in the home directory. May be used by any user to set the environment upon entering the C shell. (Replace * with your user name.)
/usr/adm/messages	Message file; contains various system messages, including errors generated by the system upon startup.
/etc/motd	Message-of-the-day text file; contents are displayed on each user's monitor at each time of login.
/etc/ddate	Text file; contains the date of each system backup.
/etc/group	System file; contains information about defined groups.
/etc/default/passwd	Text file; contains password aging variables.
/etc/passwd	System file; contains seven fields of information for each user and system account.

Index

410

411

P

415

417

418

Colophon

The manuscript for this book was prepared and submitted to Microsoft Press in electronic form. Text files were processed and formatted using Microsoft Word.

Cover design by Ted Mader and Associates

Interior text design by The NBBJ Group

Principal typographer: Bonnie Dunham

Principal production artist: Becky Johnson

The high-resolution screen displays were created using the Apple Macintosh and the Compaq DeskPro 286, and were printed on the Apple LaserWriter.

Text composition by Microsoft Press in ITC Garamond, using MagnaType composition software on a Compaq DeskPro 286 and the Mergenthaler Linotron 202 digital phototypesetter.